CHILD'S PLAY

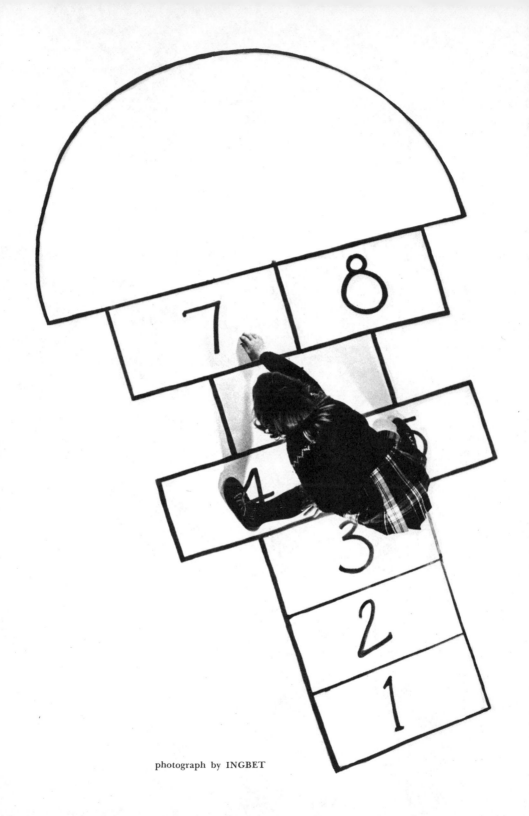

photograph by INGBET

CHILD'S PLAY

R. E. Herron

Baylor College of Medicine

Brian Sutton-Smith

Teachers College
Columbia University

John Wiley & Sons, Inc.

New York · London · Sydney · Toronto

Library of Congress Catalogue Card Number: 73-136714

ISBN   0-471-37330-3

Printed in the United States of America

10   9   8   7   6   5

Dedicated to those who maintain that there is more than one way to play hopscotch.

Preface

The study of children's play has attracted the attention of individual researchers and professionals from many fields, including anthropology, biology, child development, education, psychology, psychiatry, recreation, and sociology, but it has never been an organized focus of attention in science. Margaret Lowenfeld's observation "There is hardly any feature of human life to which so little serious consideration has been given as that of children's play" is as true today as when she stated it in the introduction to her book *Play in Childhood,* written over 30 years ago. Yet some progress has been made and scientific interest in the phenomenon of "child's play" has picked up noticeably in the last five years.

Our major aim in compiling this collection was to meet the needs existing among those who desire or require a broad introduction to the scholarly literature on children's play. Perhaps the outstanding virtue of a book of readings (if the selections have been well chosen) is the opportunity that it provides for a student to obtain first-hand exposure to the viewpoints and styles of numerous thinkers on the subject in question. The present volume consists of an eclectic selection that illustrates research in this field over the past 70 years. It would be highly pretentious for us to suggest that the articles included here constitute an "ideal" sampling of the field; at best, perhaps they constitute a fairly representative choice, sufficient to whet the appetite for further reading and investigation. Many excellent articles had to be omitted because of overlapping with other articles, expensive publishing costs, problems of abridgement, and restrictions imposed by the limited size of the book. Hopefully, the omissions will lose us fewer friends than we shall gain through trying to foster an area of common interest.

The emphasis throughout this book is on *play*. Games and the sources for the study of games are dealt with in a companion volume by Eliot Avedon and Brian Sutton-Smith entitled *The Study of Games,* also published by Wiley.

The interstitial material was the responsibility of Dr. Brian Sutton-Smith.

R. E. Herron
Brian Sutton-Smith

Acknowledgments

The present work was written in two phases, the first at the University of Illinois, the second at Teachers College, Columbia University. The book's initiation owes much to the late Professor C. K. Brightbill, who as a scholar, teacher, and administrator greatly expanded the play opportunities of children everywhere. At Illinois we are especially indebted to Mrs. Sharyn Haines, who worked diligently at obtaining reprints and requesting preliminary approval from authors and publishers. Drs. W. P. Hurder and A. V. Sapora gave most generously of their time and energy to simplify administrative and financial aspects of the operations. We would also like to thank the staff members of the Motor Performance Laboratory, Children's Research Center; in particular, Mrs. Barbara Haines, Mrs. Lois Lanto, Mrs. Jo Wolff, Mrs. Gwen Zylyagi and Miss Jean Hughes.

At Columbia we are indebted to Jerry Chiappa and Shirley Sutton-Smith for aid with the typing, and to Dr. Milly Almy for her comments on the interstitial materials. These latter materials bear the stamp of some of our earlier mentors and collaborators who have helped to sustain and direct our interest in play over the past two decades. In New Zealand we remember, in particular, Professors Philip Smithells of the University of Otago and H. C. D. Somerset of Victoria University, Wellington; in Ireland, Alistair McDonald and Cyril White at Queen's University, Belfast; in the United States, Harold Jones at the University of California, Nelson Foote and David Riesman at the University of Chicago, Howard Hoyman at the University of Illinois, Fritz Redl and Paul Gump at Wayne State, John M. Roberts at Cornell University and Bernard Kaplan at Clark University. All of these have shared and encouraged interests that underlie the present materials.

R. E. H.
B. S.-S.

Contents

CHILD'S PLAY

Chapter I

Introduction

The present work is an outcome of current attempts to reformulate the nature of the boundaries between work and play, as well as of the quite urgent practical need to find ways of stimulating children who suffer from play deficits. It is clear from anthropological and historical studies that the fairly arbitrary dualism between work and play that has characterized the treatment of these activities in the Western world during the past several hundred years, has not been typical of mankind in general as is illustrated in the enclosed article on the history of play by Gregory Stone.

Those contemporary theorists who have stressed this fact, such as Huizinga (1949), Caillois (1961), and Goffman (1961) have at the same time been pioneers in exploring what the new boundaries might be. While the matter is complex and at this time not entirely clear (these days we "play" at hunting, fishing and boating; while we "work" at group creativity, synectics, and divergent thinking), what we appear to be witnessing is a very basic shift in the treatment of play and other expressive activities. This book reveals some of the tension growing from this change.

The older point of view that play is a segregated and not very important activity still finds its expression in psychological theories that seek to reduce play's significance to some other "more important" psychological function. In these theories play is described as a polarity of thought or affect or conation. Its significance is found in the way in which it assists cognition, leads to the mastery of anxiety, or helps the player test his courage. Most of the articles that are included in this work are expressions of one or another of these points of view. For the paradox arises, that play does not exist in isolation. The player brings with him his thoughts, anxieties and determinations—all of which are mirrored and transformed in his play. Hence, even if play is not "explained" in terms of the contents brought to it, it can still be used practically this way for understanding other matters in the player's life. Currently, for example, one of the most important practical needs is to understand why children in Head Start programs do not always play the same sorts of imaginative games that are found in typical middle-class nursery schools. These children do not always show the same sort of make-believe capacity, nor are they as interested in story make-believe, nor as capable of thinking about matters remote in time and place. Their paucity of representative play and their paucity of abstract thought seem to be of one piece. Does it then follow that the middle-class parent, by playing with his children, laughing and joking with them, reading to them, and giving them play equipment and time for social and solitary play, actually encourages the development of representative capacity? Is the play critical to thinking? The importance of answers to practical questions of this character, forces us to continue to act as if play may be the servant of some other usefulness. Yet, while this potential discovery of play's usefulness perhaps redeems it from its traditional "triviality," it need not be taken as tantamount to an explanation. (Sutton-Smith, 1970).

Though play along with other expressive phenomena has been treated characteristically as an "epiphemonena" and justified, if at all, in terms of some tangential payoff; there has been an increasing inclination recently to put primary stress on play's more intrinsic functions. It has been said, for example, that although play may well be, in many respects, a reassemblage of thoughts and feelings from everyday life, it still has unique properties. It is a polarization with its own character. This point of view, underpinned by the philosophical writings of Ernst Cassirer, Susan K. Langer, and the historical presentation of Huizinga (*Homo Ludens: The Play Element in Culture*), would suggest that play is a uniquely adaptive act, not subordinate to some other adaptive act, but with a special function of its own in human experience. What this function might be, however, is not so explicit. We are accustomed to viewing adaptive behavior within a utilitarian "survival-" or "achievement-" oriented context. Whereas it may be that the intrinsic function of play is only very indirectly related to any of these things, it would appear to have more to do with whatever satisfaction comes from making one's own unique expressive response to one's own experience. Unfortunately, while it is possible to make general assertions (such as "the player is less alienated from his own experience" or "gives more meaning to his existence" than the non-player), these notions are, as yet, not operational in psychological research and they beg the question of equal rights for animals! Yet they do respond to the cultural shift in values spoken of earlier. Whether or not play has always required this intrinsic type of explanation, a new generation of young people is certainly insisting that adaptation of this type must now be given primary rather than fugitive acceptance. Unfortunately, this book on the psychology of play is mainly a record of older attitudes, though the reader will note throughout that much of the critical tension arises from the attempts of the authors to take such an emerging point of view into account.

The organization of the book proceeds along two lines, one in terms of an historical approach and the other in terms of various theoretical and subject-matter approaches. The work begins with the earlier normative and correlational studies (which still continue), and proceeds to the early ecological and quasi-experimental studies and to a chapter on the psycho-analytic tradition, that is the largest in terms of derivative studies of play therapy and doll-play diagnosis. The rest of the chapters deal with other major modern approaches to this subject-matter, including animal play, cognition and play, development through play, and theoretical approaches to play.

The introductory historical article by sociologist Gregory Stone sets the stage for the relativity of both the subject matter and our treatment. Although Stone has an ear for the diversifications of history and play, his major intent here is with the determinism rather than waywardness of play in personal and cultural history.

The Play of Little Children

Gregory P. Stone[1]

Physical educators too often have a restricted view of play, exercise, and sport, asking only how such activities contribute to the motor efficiency and longevity of the organism. Yet, the symbolic significance of recreation is enormous, providing a fundamental bond that ties the individual to his society. Indeed, many of society's forms—its myths and legends—endure only in play. Play is recreation, then, because it continually re-creates the society in which it is carried on. Social psychology, concerned as it is with the meaningful aspects of human life, is well suited to the analysis of play as a symbolic process.

Social psychologists have long recognized the significance of play for preparing young children to participate later on in adult society. But social psychology, when viewed against the backdrop of history, is very young. Furthermore, there is a disquieting tendency for many social science disciplines to lose their sense of history and develop what they conceive to be universal propositions based on observations made in quite

SOURCE. Reproduced here with the permission of the author and the publishers of *Quest*, 1965, **4**, 23–31, an organ of the National Association for Physical Education of College Women.

[1] Dr. Gregory P. Stone, Professor of Sociology at the University of Minnesota, is primarily a student of social psychology, urban sociology and social stratification. He is the only American representative in the International Committee for the Sociology of Sport, established under the auspices of the International Council of Sport and Physical Education. He is presently engaged in the preparation of a book on the sociology of sport which is expected to appear this year.

spatially and temporally delimited milieux. This article is primarily designed to place the play of children in historical perspective and, then, to set forth some functions of contemporary child's play, reserving judgment about the universality of such functions. It is hoped that the very tentativeness with which such assertions are set forth will inspire the curiosity of others and encourage them to extend the spatial and temporal focus of their studies of childhood. Play, like other collective enterprises, is a collective representation: it *re*presents the arrangements of the society and historical era in which it is carried on.

Historical Emergence of Children and Child's Play

In an extraordinary work (1), Philippe Ariès asks the seemingly naive question: where do children come from? He is not, of course, concerned with the biological origins of infants, but with the historical origins of the social *identity,* "child." Although the classical Greek civilization (and those it influenced directly) had distinguished children socially from babes and adults if only as objects of aesthetic appreciation, children did not emerge as social entities in the subsequent history of Western civilization until the early seventeenth century.

FRANCE AS AN EARLY SOURCE OF CHILDREN

Prior to the seventeenth century there were babes and adults in Western civilization, but no in-betweens. Babes were swaddled; adults attired; children were, in fact, *homunculi.* There was no distinctive dress to differentiate them, and expectations directed toward them were not age-specific. The elaborate record of the life of Louis XIII kept by his doctor, Heroard (1:62–67, 100), amazes us today. The Dauphin was betrothed by his first birthday. At seventeen months, he was singing and playing the violin. By the age of two years, he was dancing various kinds of dances. At three and a half, he was reading, and he was writing at four. It must be emphasized here that the child, Louis, was not thought of as particularly brilliant. Such activities were merely expected of the little people we call children today. Nor was this seemingly precocious activity necessarily confined to children of royalty and aristocracy, although such intricate play forms were undoubtedly concentrated in that estate. Paintings of the period, as well as earlier paintings, show the children of commoners and peasants freely participating in what we think of today as adult settings, e.g., taverns and wine shops.

It is not as though there were no play at that time. Louis had his hobby horse, tops, and balls. Rather, play permeated all segments of the society.

Ariès chides the contemporary historian Van Marle for his amazement upon discovering that the games played by grown-ups were no less childish than those played by children, retorting, "Of course not: they were the same" (1:72). Festivals were another matrix of community-wide play in medieval Europe. Despite the fact, however, that play was general in the society, its unanticipated consequences were probably different for children and adults as they are today. Certainly some child's play provided young people with a vehicle for anticipatory socialization, permitting them to rehearse roles they would enact or encounter in later life, as in military play. Then as now, the play of children pulled them into the larger society. Adult play, on the other hand, undoubtedly released the players at times from everyday social demands and obligations. That adult and children played the same games makes such differences difficult to verify.

If play was general in the society of medieval Europe, attitudes toward play were not. In fifteenth and sixteenth century France, the Catholic clergy took a dim view of play, unless it followed the performance of work, and this view was subsequently adopted by police and other authorities. Yet, play could not be suppressed by such moralizers in a society where play was general in the population and work did not have the significance it was to acquire with industrialization. The only enforceable suppression of play was accomplished in universities where clergy were recruited and trained, and there is evidence to suggest that this was not very effective. Possibly for this very reason, the Jesuits assimilated the play of the larger society in the seventeenth century. Play was redefined as educational and incorporated in college curricula (1:88–89). At the end of the eighteenth century, emerging nationalism provided a further legitimation of play. Play was conceived as a way of preparing young people for military service. The inclusion of play forms in military training programs is a frequent mode of legitimation. Thus, boxing or "prize-fighting" became legal in the United States in 1917 when it became an integral part of the U.S. Army's physical training program (13:258).

As play acquired the approval of the moral custodians of seventeenth and eighteenth century French society, childhood also became established as a separate social identity in the human biography, and play became rather more of a childish thing. Ariès interprets this emergence of the child in the social morphology as one consequence of the rise of an entrepreneurial stratum in European society. As work moved to the center of social arrangements, play became increasingly relegated to childhood, and *pari passu,* children were established as identifiable social beings. This may have been the case with France, but play and children were to have a more painful birth in the Protestant nations.

PLAY IN THE HISTORY OF ENGLAND AND AMERICA

Protestantism provided a religious justification for the tremendous expansion of work in the emerging industrial societies. Work was the key to the gates of the Protestant heaven: by your works are ye known. In contrast to the relegation of play to childhood in seventeenth and eighteenth century France, play had been generally suppressed in England by the end of the eighteenth century. In particular, the legislated inclosures of open areas deprived much of the population of play space. Play was further suppressed by legislation in English towns which, for example, forbade children from playing with tops in the streets or running races on the roads (7). When Wesley drew up the rules for his school at Kingswood, no time was set aside for play, because, in his view, "he who plays as a boy will play as a man" (7:123).

In America, the status of play in the seventeenth and eighteenth century is less clear. We do know, of course, that child labor persisted in the United States into the twentieth century. Tocqueville thought that the Americans of his time were so wrapped up in work that they could not enjoy play: "Instead of these frivolous delights, they prefer those more serious and silent amusements which are like business and which do not drive business wholly out of their minds" (15:221). On the other hand, Green has observed that play was smuggled into many areas of earlier American life in the guise of work, as in quilting parties and barn-raisings (5:480), and, by the end of the nineteenth century, Bryce was impressed by the "brighter" life afforded the factory workers in New England through their "amusements than that of the clerks and shopkeepers of England" (2:223). The picture is, at best, a confused one. Moreover, what seemed "serious and silent" to a Frenchman may well have seemed "bright" to an Englishman.

Probably, however, there was no overall moral consensus on the value of work and play. In a very careful study, Miyakawa has shown that there were sharp regional differences and, within regions, denominational differences (11). In nineteenth century Ohio, Presbyterians led a gayer life than Methodists, and, in Connecticut, the Congregationalists did not hesitate to dance and enjoy musical entertainment (11:143). Even on the frontier, "at least some German, Swedish, and other continental settlers had occasional songfests, plays, dances, and music" (11:143). Miyakawa's observations, given the relatively high social status of Presbyterian and Congregational denominations, permit the inference that play was looked upon with favor in the higher socio-economic strata of nineteenth century America. At this status level, as Veblen has shown (16), we find a leisure class straining to shed the trappings of work, and I would offer the general hypothesis that play is introduced into the bleak ages of any society by high status circles and spread throughout the society as a consequence of the emulation carried on in lower status circles and aggregates. Once this is accomplished, the moral "character" of the society is transformed. Yet, the mere emulation of play styles is not a sufficient explanation for the spread of play in society. It is a necessary condition.

Ariès may well be correct in his assertion that the emergence of an entrepreneurial stratum in France established the identity of child and cloaked that identity with distinctive play forms, but in England and America it is a very different matter. It required a social movement *against the excesses of capitalism,* in the Protestant countries, to release children from the bonds of work and confer the privileges of play. The movement had its inception in the reformist and revolutionary thought of the mid-nineteenth century and persisted until the twentieth. Indeed, Ritchie and Kollar maintain that, for the United States, the "institutionalization of children's play and games is largely a twentieth century phenomenon" (12:205). It is even possible that this institutionalization was not formally secured until the formulation of the Children's Charter of the 1930 White House Conference on Child Health and Protection which proclaimed: "With the young child, his work is his play and his play is his work" (12:206).

IMPLICATIONS FOR THE SOCIAL PSYCHOLOGY OF PLAY

Children and child's play, then, emerged much later on the social scene in the Protestant than in the Catholic countries. As I have pointed out elsewhere, this difference persists today in contrasting Protestant and Catholic attitudes toward gaming or gambling (13:257). Nevertheless, the fact remains that children and child's play have not always been with us, particularly as we know them today. Thus, when we speculate upon the social significance of child's play, we may well be developing hypotheses that have relevance only for a particular and relatively recent era of Western civilization. I have often wondered whether or not this is the best any social scientist can do—to dramatize effectively his own socio-historical era. As Marx, Veblen, and Freud effectively dramatized the industrial era, so have Mills, Riesman, and Harry S. Sullivan effectively dramatized the era that Walter Rostow calls high mass consumption. This may well be the case because of the interaction between the social scientist and his subject matter. The very publication of social science theory and research alters the behavior it attempts to explain. For example, the incorporation of Keynesian economics into national fiscal policy introduced a political variable into business cycle theory, and nothing has altered sexual attitudes more than the dissemination of Freudian theory, with the result that contemporary psychoanalysts, such as Allen Wheelis, are confounded by the presence of disorders which defy explanation in classical Freudian terms.

Differentiation and Integration of the Child's Self Through Play

It is the task of society to make the lives of its members meaningful. This is accomplished by bringing little children into a meaningful communication with adults and one another, and, at the same time, by establishing their selves as objects so they can refer the other objects of their worlds to such established selves, thereby imbuing these worlds with significance (9). Play has a major part in the accomplishment of these tasks.

THE PLAY OF MOTHER AND CHILD

Meaning only exists in communication, and it is established when one's own symbols call out in the other about the same symbolic responses as they call out in himself. (Thus, this article can only be meaningful if readers respond to these words about the way that I have responded. Failing this, the article is nonsense!) This seems to be accomplished very early by the infant when it takes over the response patterns of the mothering one as its own. It may be that babbling is a kind of playing with noise, but we shall never know, for we cannot ask the babbler. Nevertheless, in the course of babbling, the infant may hit upon a word-like sound which is then re-presented by the mothering one as a word, together with an appropriate response pattern. "Baa," for example, may be re-presented as "ball" as the round object is grasped and held up before the babbling baby. In time, the infant takes over the response pattern: "ball" *means* grasping the round object.

Too, in this early stage of the development of meaning, the infant is often a plaything, while the mothering one is the player. In time, both the child and the mothering one are mutually players and playthings:

As actions become possible for him and as words take on meanings, the child is increasingly able to respond to the play actions of his mother with play actions of his own. Thus, for example, he uses his hands to play "peek-a-boo" and "patty cake." (12:202)

Such commonalty of responses establishes a rudimentary domestic universe of discourse which can serve as a base from which a vast social symbolism can be elaborated.

CHILD'S PLAY AS DRAMA

"Play" has several meanings, among which *drama* must be included, and drama is fundamental for the child's development of a conception of self as an object different from but related to other objects—the development of an *identity*. To establish a separate identity (many identities depend for their establishment and maintenance on counter-identities, e.g., man-woman, parent-child, teacher-student), the child must literally get outside himself and apprehend himself from some other perspective. Drama provides a prime vehicle for this. By taking the role of another, the child gains a reflected view of himself as different from but related to that other.[1] Thus, we find little children playing house, store, or school in which they perform the roles of parent, merchant, or teacher, gaining a reflected view of their own identities from the perspective of those identities whose roles they perform. Indeed, in playing house, it is difficult to recruit a child to play the role of child or baby. Such a role has no implication for the building of his own identity. A doll, therefore, is better suited to the role.

We may note an additional consequence of such drama. In the examples cited, the child prepares himself for the subsequent enactment of such roles in later life or for communication with those who will be performing such roles. Merton speaks of such drama as anticipatory socialization (10:384–386). However, not all childhood drama is of this anticipatory character. Many of the roles the child performs are fantastic, in the sense that the child can not reasonably be expected to enact or encounter such role performances in later life. I have in mind such identities as cowboy and Indian, creatures from outer space, or pirate. In much fantastic drama, incidentally, we can detect an additional function of child's play. Fantastic drama often serves to maintain and keep viable the past of the society—its myths, legends, villains, and heroes. This is also true of toys and other items of the technology of child's play. As one example, the jousting tournament disappeared in the sixteenth century and was replaced by the quintain and the unhooking of a ring by a galloping horseman. The latter persists today in the merry-go-round. This function of child's play has inspired Ariès to remark that "children form the most conservative of human societies" (1:68).

Fantastic drama seems more to characterize the play of male children in our society than that of female children (14:110–112). Thus, the dramatic play of children in our society may function more to prepare little girls for adulthood than little boys (3:333). This observation, however, may not necessarily be confined to contemporary American society and its recent past. In discussing the dress of children in eighteenth century France, Ariès points out: "the attempt to distinguish children was gen-

---

[1] George H. Mead, from whom many of these ideas have been taken, refers to this phase as "play," but, as we have already shown, there are many varieties of play. Drama is the more precise term. (See 5:149–151 and 14:108–113)

erally confined to boys . . . *as if childhood separated girls from adult life less than it did boys"* (1:58). It may well be that the drama of childhood makes it difficult for boys to establish an early well-founded conception of adult life and, consequently, hinders their assumption of an adult identity. In contrast, such drama may facilitate the transition of female children to adulthood. However, once boys do become men (in the social psychological sense), given the sexual arrangements of our society, they have a relatively easy time of it, while the problems of females begin when girls become women!

Children differ, too, according to their *knowledge* of the roles they perform in childhood drama. Although he was not always consistent, Mead presumed an "open awareness" of the roles performed in drama (4:673–674). There are at least two reasons why such an assumption can not be maintained. First, the details of the role performance may not be objectively accessible to the young actor. For example, a colleague, Duane Gibson of Michigan State University, noticed a boy and girl playing house in a front yard. The little girl was very busy sweeping up the play area, rearranging furniture, moving dishes about, and caring for baby dolls. The boy, on the other hand, would leave the play area on his tricycle, disappear to the back of the (real) house, remain for a brief while, reappear in the play area, and lie down in a feigned sleep. The little girl had a rather extensive knowledge of the mother role, but, for the boy, a father was one who disappeared, reappeared, and slept, *ad infinitum!* Second, nuances of the role performance may be deliberately concealed from children. We tend to conceal domestic difficulties from children, e.g., financial troubles. Should a child overhear such a discussion, we play it down, encouraging the child not to worry about it (12:215).

Finally, in this discussion of childhood drama, we ought to acknowledge that one child's fantasy is another child's reality. The probability that the roles children enact in their dramas will be assumed or encountered in adult life is very much restricted by their position in the various orders of stratification—income, prestige, and accessibility to political office—, their rural or urban residence, their "race" or ethnicity, or their sex. It is, in short, anticipatory for the boy to play the role of baseball player, but not for the girl.

We have very few empirical studies of childhood play and, particularly, drama. When we do conduct them, then, we ought to realize the complex nature of drama. Is it anticipatory or fantastic? Is knowledge of the dramatized role accessible to the young performer? Is it probable that the actor will, in later life, enact or encounter the role performance that he is dramatizing? Above all, how is recruitment into the adult roles that the drama of childhood represents organized by larger social arrangements. When such questions are answered, we will have far better knowledge of precisely how childhood drama provides children with identities, casting them in the character of meaningful objects.

Obviously, as Mead insisted (9:151–164), drama is not a sufficient source of identity, for it provides the young actor with many parts and scripts, and these are often unrelated. The development of an integrated self requires the playing of team games in which one can generalize the related team positions and adapt his own behavior to the generalized expectations of the entire team. Such games occur later in childhood and are beyond the scope of this article. However, one final form of play found in early childhood will be considered here, namely, tests of poise.

CHILDISH TESTS OF POISE

It is not enough only to establish an identity for one's self; it must be established for others at the same time. Identities are *announced* by those who appropriate them and *placed* by others. Identities must always be validated in this manner to have reality in social interaction. Usually such announcements are silent, accomplished by clothing, the posturing of the body, painting of the face, sculpting of the hair, the manipulation of props, or the physical location of the self on the scene of action. For these reasons, child's play demands costume and body control, and it is facilitated by props and equipment (toys) appropriate to the drama. Moreover, as Huizinga has remarked, play spaces are usually clearly marked off (8), and one's location within them communicates to other players and on-lookers the part he is playing. Thus, child's play demands the assembly, arrangement, and control of spaces, props, equipment, clothing, and bodies, as well as other elements. If crucial elements are missing, if they become disarranged, or if control over them is lost, the play is spoiled, and the drama can not be carried off. Loss of control over these elements is literally embarrassing and may be equated to loss of poise (6).

We know that much of the drama of childhood replicates the interaction of the larger society in which it occurs. Indeed, it is almost trite to observe that society *is* drama. In everyday interaction, we must always announce to others who we are and be poised or prepared for the upcoming communication. This requires the assembly, arrangement, and control of a host of objects and demands considerable skill, for the staging of social interaction is an intricate affair, a highly complex juggling and balancing act.

Much childhood play takes the form of deliberately perpetrating loss of poise with the unintended but highly important consequence of preparing the child for the maintenance of self-control in later life. Thus, everywhere we find little children spinning about inducing dizziness, pushing and tripping one another, disarranging clothing, teasing, playing pranks, or bringing play to a sudden halt by depriving the players of some crucial item ("I'm going to take my ball and go home"). Indeed, a technology has developed to facilitate such play and is found in playgrounds, amusement parks, and carnivals.

All this is well known, but I have the distinct impression that such play is viewed almost exclusively as contributing to body control or motor efficiency. Playful tests of poise reach out beyond the body to include clothing and grooming. Pranks can be perpetrated by disturbing any element essential to the staging process—furniture, equipment, locations, and a host of other objects and arrangements.[1] The analysis of such play, then, ought to take into account the development of body control and coordination, but the emphasis ought to be on its symbolic significance in relation to the other elements of staging essential to the silent definition of situations in everyday life.

Conclusions

This article has placed the play of little children in the context of social symbolism. It has shown how playing with children, childhood drama, and childish pranks function to prepare little children for their meaningful participation in adult society. Such play, however, is not always functional. Some childhood drama may militate against later social participation because of its relative inappropriateness, and I suppose some pranks may be so severe as to have unforeseen traumatic effects. In any case, the play of little children demands extensive scientific investigation. However, any propositions formulated as a consequence of such research may not have universal validity. Both children and child's play, like all other social beings, are creatures of history.

References

1. Ariés, Phillippe. *Centuries of Childhood*. Translated by Robert Baldick, New York: Alfred A. Knopf, Inc., 1962.
2. Bryce, James. *Social Institutions of the United States*. New York: Grosset and Dunlap, 1891.
3. Erikson, Erik H., "Sex Differences in the Play Configurations of American Pre-Adolescents," in Margaret Mead and Martha Folfenstein (eds.). *Child-*

---

[1] My colleague, Edward Gross, and I have isolated about fifty of these "elements" as we pursue the study of staging prompted by our earlier study of embarrassment (6).

hood in Contemporary Cultures. Chicago: The University of Chicago Press, Phoenix Edition, 1963, pp. 324–341.

4. Glaser, Barney G. and Anselm L. Strauss, "Awareness Contexts and Social Interaction," *American Sociological Review,* XXIX (October, 1964), pp. 669–679.

5. Green, Arnold, *Sociology.* New York: McGraw-Hill Book Co., Inc., 1956.

6. Gross, Edward and Gregory P. Stone, "Embarrassment and the Analysis of Role Requirements," *American Journal of Sociology,* LXX (July, 1964), pp. 1–15.

7. Hammond, J. L. and Barbara Hammond. *The Bleak Age.* Middlesex, England: Penguin Books, 1947.

8. Huizinga, Jan. *Homo Ludens: A Study of the Play Element in Culture.* London: Routledge and Kegan Paul, Ltd., 1949.

9. Mead, George Herbert. *Mind, Self, and Society,* Chicago: University of Chicago Press, 1934.

10. Merton, Robert K. *Social Theory and Social Structure.* Glencoe, Illinois: The Free Press, 1957.

11. Miyakawa, T. Scott, *Protestants and Pioneers.* Chicago: University of Chicago Press, 1964.

12. Ritchie, Oscar W. and Marvin R. Koller. *Sociology of Childhood.* New York: Appleton-Century-Crofts, 1964.

13. Stone, Gregory P., "American Sports: Play and Display," in Eric Larrabee and Rolf Meyersohn (eds.), *Mass Leisure.* Glencoe, Illinois: The Free Press, 1958, pp. 253–264.

14. ———. "Appearance and the Self," in Arnold M. Rose (ed.), *Human Behavior and Social Processes.* Boston: Houghton-Mifflin Co., 1962, pp. 86–118.

15. Tocqueville, Alexis de. *Democracy in America,* II, translated by Henry Reeves. New York: Alfred A. Knopf, Inc., 1946.

16. Veblen, Thorstein. *The Theory of the Leisure Class.* New York: Modern Library, Inc., 1934.

Chapter II

Normative Studies

The anthropological, folkloristic, and psychological studies of play and games that emerged as significant scholarly endeavors at the end of the nineteenth century had in common an underlying and sustaining evolutionism. In anthropology this manifested itself in the notion that the games of the world had diffused from Asiatic centers of civilization, or that they had had their origins in various primitive dramatic, sacred, or economic activities. Analogously in folklore, the position was taken that children's games were surviving vestiges of earlier customs, while in psychology, the play of children was seen as a ludic recapitulation of the general history of mankind. In all cases, though with these different emphases, the development of children was regarded as a part of a universal scheme of events. There was a plan and system to the child's development, and the study of play could be used to learn both about the child and about the larger scheme of things. Much effort was devoted in early folklorist and anthropological writings to demonstrations of such universality. Many books were written in order to show that games all over the world were similar.

In anthropology these "universalist" views of games faded from prominence when "evolutionist" and "diffusionist" theories were replaced by the functionalist and cultural relativistic viewpoints. In psychology, universalism continued for some time under the guise of "stages of play." Students of the subject attempted to discover whether in fact, as Stanley Hall had said, "The child's play recapitulated the phylogenetic transition from animal to human play, and the cultural transformations through

15

savage, nomadic, agricultural and tribal stages" (1916). By the 1920s, empirical studies began to show that continuity rather than stage-based discontinuity was the rule in children's play. Children did not necessarily reproduce these stages as they might have been expected to if they were tracing the phylogenetic steps of human evolution. More importantly, these first empirical studies showed that play was affected by a host of contingent variables such as sex, play materials, the urban or rural setting, economic differences, racial differences, language, and intelligence. The studies of Lewis Terman (1925) and Lehmann and Witty's *Psychology of Play Activities* (1927), which emphasized the psychological "relativism" of play, symbolized the end of the normative era. Although some child psychologists continued to base their work on biological and universalist metaphors in subsequent years, this was not the sustaining note in most later studies. Other excellent partly normative accounts were those of Buhler (1930), Isaacs (1933), and Lowenfeld (1935). The observations of Susan Isaacs, in particular, remain an excellent source for ideas on the meaning and diversity of nursery-school play.

Still, even if evolutionist premises are no longer accepted, this early pursuit of universality had the value that many investigators of those days sought to give adequate descriptions to the characteristics of play and games. The distinctions offered by Groos in the *Play of Man* (1899) between, for example, the playful activity of sensory operators, the playful use of the motor apparatus, and the playful use of the higher mental powers (including experimenting with memory, imagination, attention, reasons, etc.) are still useful to the modern investigator. One limitation of the causal approach of more recent years has been that this "descriptive" task undertaken by Groos and others has not been continued with the complexity that more modern forms of analysis require. As a result, much of the current confusion concerning the antecedents and character of children's play probably results from a lack of sufficiently well controlled descriptive data, against which initial hypotheses can be checked. The most detailed observations of young children's play, those of Piaget (*Play, Dreams and Imitation in Childhood,* 1962) are still of a rudimentary descriptive character. At the middle-childhood level, however, the earlier normative accounts of Lehmann and Witty have recently been extended by the massive investigations of Rivka Eifermann of the psychology department of Hebrew University of Jerusalem. She has accumulated over one hundred thousand units of observation on some ten thousand children in a sample of Israeli schools (1968).

In the Readings of this section we deal with some of the attempts that have been made to describe children's normative development through play. The earliest large scale applications of quantitative methods to play were those of Monroe, 1899; Croswell, 1899; and McGhee, 1900. Each of these investigators submitted questionnaires or inventories to many thousands of children. They add point to the Sutton-Smith and Rosenberg article on historical changes in children's play, which uses the same method with a large group of children in Ohio—thus permitting contrasts across the 60 years. Hurlock's review (1934) of the Experimental Investigation of Childhood Play is useful as a source of references for the play studies up to that time, and is somewhat more comprehensive than Helen Marshall's review of several years earlier (1931). It also contains useful information on developmental changes in play. It is important to this work because it makes reference to the many other contemporary sources of information on play, including baby biographies, the study of gangs, etc., no examples of which are provided here. The fact that there has been no comparable review of "experimental" studies since 1934, except perhaps the 1941 review of Britt and Janus, indicates that Hurlock's review was also in part, an obituary for this earlier evolutionary-oriented period of normative studies.

In Chase's paper we are confronted with the contention that observational methods yield different results from those afforded when children make pencil-and-paper responses to play inventories. Again, in the brief study by Sutton-Smith (not completed because of the untimely death of the coinvestigator, Vaughn Crandall) we also find that what children say they play is not always the same as what they are observed to play. Eifermann's work in Israel also reports complex relationships between play as observed and play as reported. While play methodology of this sort is not a well-developed area, there are a number of papers that should be mentioned for their largely methodological concern; for example, Levin and Wardwell, 1962, which is reproduced in Chapter IV, and also Despert, 1940; Erikson, 1951 (reproduced here); Friedlander, 1966; Guerney, 1965; Hutt, 1966 (reproduced here); Levenstein and Sunley, 1967, and Herron and Frobish (in press). The last paper describes the use of computer-plotter combinations for automatic analysis and display of interorganism and organism-environment interaction patterns in children's play. It may be anticipated that such automatic procedures will play an increasing part in recording and perhaps unraveling the complexities of group play.

Sixty Years of Historical Change in the Game Preferences of American Children

B. Sutton-Smith and B. G. Rosenberg

The changes which have occurred in children's games during the past fifty years have not been studied extensively. These changes merit investigation because games are a genuine folk phenomenon, and they may reveal subtle changes in culture and in child nature. For a long time it has been taken for granted that traditional games are central to peer group activities. It has been assumed that certain games belong to girls, and that others belong to boys, and that the differences between them are clear-cut and unchangeable. This paper investigates both of these assumptions.

Previous attempts to gather material on historical change have involved, in the main, the use of reminiscence, as when Yoffie contrasted the singing games of her own childhood in St. Louis, Missouri, 1895, with collections which she made subsequently in the same place in 1914 and 1944.[1] Sutton-Smith used interviews involving reminiscence together with extensive documentary materials to date the changes in the games of New Zealand children from 1870 through 1950.[2] In the present investigation it is proposed to approach the same problem by comparing the results of four large-scale studies of children's games which were made in the years

SOURCE. Reprinted from *The Journal of American Folklore*, 1961, **74**, 17–46, with the permission of the authors and The American Folklore Society.

1896, 1898, 1921 and 1959. This method has the virtue that each of these studies is reasonably representative of the time and place at which it was taken. The four studies are: (A) in 1896 Crosswell presented a questionnaire to 1,929 children between the ages of six and eighteen years in Worcester, Massachusetts. The children were asked to write down their preferences for games, plays, toys, and amusements. This technique yielded a list of approximately 500 items.[3] (B) in 1898, McGhee furnished 8,718 children in South Carolina between the ages of six and eighteen years, with a 129 item check-list of games from which they were to choose the five games that they liked the most.[4] (C) in 1921, Terman presented a check-list of 90 games and activities to 474 children between the ages of six and seventeen years in the metropolitan area of San Francisco. The children were asked to check the things they had played, the things they could do well, the things they liked to do or play, and the things they liked very well.[5] (D) in 1959 Rosenberg and Sutton-Smith presented a check-list of 181 items to 2,689 children between the ages of 9 and 15, in seventeen townships in northwestern Ohio. The list was composed of games and activities and was derived from a preliminary survey of the written lists of 450 children throughout the same area. The children were asked to mark their preferences (like or dislike) for those games they recognized.[6]

In Tables 1 and 2 the results of these four investigations are presented for boys and girls separately. The items are ranked in order of preference with each item being followed by the number of children checking it in the particular study. The differences between these rankings are the major basis for drawing conclusions about the changes in children's games during the period 1896 through 1959. In addition, further comparisons are made among the thirty-five items which the three check-lists (1898, 1921, 1959) have in common.

It would be naive to assume that all differences between these lists are due to historical change. In interpreting results a number of precautions need to be kept in mind: (a) each of the studies was carried out in a different geographical locale. Differences between the lists, therefore, may be the results of sampling in different places, rather than due to historical change. Some check on this is possible. The 1896 and 1898 lists can be checked against each other for consistencies and inconsistencies. The 1921 collection can be checked against the large scale Kansas collection of games and activities by Lehmann and Witty also taken during the twenties.[7] Unfortunately, this latter collection cannot be used *in toto*, as the authors did not publish their data in full. There are, in addition, other small collections from that period.[8] The contemporary collection is derived from seventeen towns and cities in northwestern Ohio. It is not

Table 1

Boys

No.	N. W. Ohio, 1959 N=1370	f	Bay Area, Cal., 1921 N=225	f	South Carolina, 1898 N=3958	f	Worcester, Mass., 1896 N=1000	f
1	Football	1221	Baseball	312	Baseball	2697	Ball	679
2	Throw Snowballs	1213	Ride Bicycle	297	Football	2216	Marbles	608
3	Bicycle Riding	1211	Fly Kites	195	Swimming	953	Sled	555
4	Hide and Seek	1181	Play Tag	190	Marbles	603	Skates	538
5	Basketball	1180	Do Garden Work	189	Fox and Geese	562	Football	455
6	Marbles	1140	Use Tools	187	Crokinole	437	Relievo	356
7	Tag	1137	Marbles	172	Checkers	398	Tag	356
8	Swimming	1136	Hide and Seek	172	Battle	387	Hockey, Shinny, Polo	313
9	Baseball	1117	Football	161	Leapfrog	370	Checkers	277
10	Cowboys	1116	Walk on Stilts	158	Spinning Tops	344	Hide and Seek	241
11	Checkers	1108	Racing or Jumping	157	Buffalo Bill	343	Dominoes	185
12	Cops and Robbers	1091	Basketball	156	Foot and a Half	300	Top	176
13	Cards	1090	Shoot	154	Policeman	278	Play Horse	166
14	Bows and Arrows	1089	Skate	143	Fox and Hounds	275	Cards	163
15	Shooting	1086	Spin Tops	143	Cards	260	Bicycle	160
16	Racing	1080	Volleyball	142	Croquet	250	Snowballing	123
17	Fly Kites	1070	Ride Horseback	139	Hide and Seek	233	Swimming	119
18	Climbing	1063	Boxing	139	Flying Kite	232	Kite, Parachute	107
19	Darts	1055	Wrestling	138	Mumble Peg	226	Black Tom, Black Jack	102
20	Soldiers	1050	Hunt	138	Punch and Judy	218	Horse Chestnuts, Horse Cobbles	85
21	Tic Tac Toe	1041	Cards	135	Parchesi	208	Books, Reading	83
22	Fish	1038	Tug-O-War	132	Tennis	191	Fishing	80
23	Tug-O-War	1028	Fish	125	Tag	190	Boats, Canoes, Rafts	78
24	Boating	1028	Snap the Whip	122	Drop the Handkerchief	187	Leaves	75
25	Horseshoes	1026	Checkers	121	Lotto	179	Hoop	71
26	Horseriding	1022	Swim	120	Basketball	179	Stilts	70
27	Camping	1017	Jump the Rope	118	Goosie Goosie Gander	178	Play School	69
28	Skating	1002	Hike	112	Jail	170	Hare and Hound	65
29	Make Model Aeroplanes	992	Bow and Arrows	111	Base	170	Snow Shovel	65

Table 1 (*Continued*)

No.	N. W. Ohio, 1959 N=1370	f	Bay Area, Cal., 1921 N=225	f	South Carolina, 1898 N=3958	f	Worcester, Mass., 1896 N=1000	f
30	Dodgeball	983	Follow the Leader	109	I Spy	167	Guns, Rifles Hunting	64
31	Wrestling	974	Work with Machinery	102	Circus	166	Croquet	62
32	Building forts	971	Roll Hoops	99	Dancing	163	Shovel, Hoe	61
33	Bingo	969	Leapfrog	98	Bull in the Pen	163	Play House	59
34	Bandits	968	Fox and Geese	96	Authors	163	Run Sheep Run	58
35	Hunt	966	Handball	89	Clap in Clap Out	148	Snow Shoes, Skiis	58
36	Ping Pong	965	Row a Boat	88	Steamboat	147	Pick Knife	57
37	Seven Up	958	Drop the Handkerchief	87	Wrestling	146	Play War	55
38	Roller Skating	944	Anty Over	86	Stealing Chips	145	Tenpins	53
39	Hunting	940	Hopscotch	83	Shinny	138	Tennis	51
40	Use Tools	950	Farmer in the Dell	81	Swinging	136	Racing	51
41	Boxing	928	Puss in the Corner	79	Open the Gates as High as the Sky	134	Leapfrog Foot and Half	48
42	King on the Mountain	928	Dominoes	78	Dominoes	133	Nutting	48
43	Stoop Tag	899	Tennis	75	Dog on Wood	128	Hill Dill	45
44	Red Rover	892	Cat and Mouse	73	Up Jinks	127	Jumping	44
45	Bowling	887	Dare Base	69	Book	125	Blindman's Buff	42
46	Monopoly	878	Post Office	69	Hide the Switch	122	Bull in the Ring	42
47	Building Snowmen	859	Ring Around the Rosy	64	Jackstones	120	Bar Up	42
48	Crack the Whip	856	London Bridge	63	Ten Pins	116	Snap the Whip	41
49	Frozen Tag	847	Cook	62	Roly Poly	112	Play Fire	41
50	Pool	843	Pom Pom Pull Away	61	Pig in the Pen	110	Carpentry, Tools	41
51	Volleyball	838	Soccer	61	Keeping Store	109	Dolls	39
52	Puzzles	825	Pool	60	Blindman's Buff	109	Old Maids	38
53	Raise Pets	821	Play School	59	Black Maria	105	Duck on Rock	37
54	Tennis	792	Shinny	59	Jump Rope	102	Snowman	36
55	Follow the Leader	791	Guessing Games	57	Bull Pen	100	Dog	36
56	Work With Machines	784	Blindfold	57	One Hole Cat	95	Puss in Corner	35
57	Dice	776	Simon Says	57	Working Puzzles	94	Stealing Eggs	35
58	Toy R. Trains	766	Solve Puzzles	57	Jackstraws	92	Tip Cat	33
59	Shuffleboard	765	Tiddleywinks	54	Kitty Wants a Corner My Father	90	Tents	33

Table 1 (*Continued*)

No.	N. W. Ohio, 1959 (N = 1370)	f	Bay Area, Cal., 1921 (N = 225)	f	South Carolina, 1898 (N = 3958)	f	Worcester, Mass., 1896 (N = 1000)	f
60	Fox and Geese	760	Play Store	54	Had a Rooster Chick a My Chick a My	89	Flowers	32
61	Dominoes	759	Blackman	50	Granny Crow	86	Messenger Boy Errand Boy	31
62	Ghosts	758	Play House	49	Little Sallie Walker	84	Grass	31
63	Stunts in Gym	757	In and Out Window	47	Picking Eggs	82	Jackstones	28
64	Tail on the Donkey	755	Red Rover	46	Devil and Angel	82	Snow House	28
65	Cars	753	Duck on Rock	45	Having Show	81	Authors	28
66	Musical Chairs	742	Dance	44	Tiddley Winks	79	Chess	25
67	Wall Dodge Ball	740	Fox and Hounds	44	Hull Gull	67	Climbing Trees	25
68	I Spy	737	Anagrams	44	Pig in the Parlour	63	Drop the Handkerchief	22
69	Leap Frog	731	Jackstraws	42	Jack in the Bush	62	Tiddleywinks	22
70	Horses	730	Snap	41	Pillow Dex	61	Gymnasium	22
71	Drop the Handkerchief	723	Parchesi	36	Guessing Riddles	61	Drawing, Painting	22
72	Pick up Sticks	717	Croquet	35	Golf	59	Puzzles	21
73	Clay Modeling	714	Billiards	33	Anty Over	59	Lotto	21
74	Blind Man's Buff	703	History Cards	32	William My Tremble Toe	59	Sand, Dirt	21
75	Dance	702	Geography Cards	32	Walk to Jerusalem	58	Snow Fort	20
76	Spin the Bottle	698	Roly Poly	32	Spin the Plate	58	Playing in Hay	20
77	Wood Tag	696	Bowling	31	I See a Ghost	58	Musical Instruments	20
78	Spacemen	693	Sewing	29	Goodnight	58	Horseshoes, Quoits	19
79	Kick the Can	689	Jackstones	29	Knucks	57	Apples	18
80	Hide the Thimble	675	Coast or Toboggan	28	Cross Questions and Crooked Answers	55	Sticks	18
81	Hiking	668	Church	27	Mother May I Pick a Rose	54	Wheelbarrow	18
82	Make Collections	662	Dolls	24	Tit Tat Taw	53	Parchesi	17
83	Ball Tag	661	Dress-Up	23	Keeping House	47	A Trip Around the World	17
84	Doctors	657	Authors	23	Club Fists	47	Cat	17
85	Walk on Stilts	650	Chess	22	Catcher	47	Hop Scotch	16
86	Simon Says	645	Knit	18	Old Dame Wiggins is Dead	44	Pillow Dex	16
87	Kissing	614	Crokinole	17	Dolls	44	Carriage, Sleigh Buckboard Tallyho	16

Table 1 (*Continued*)

No.	N. W. Ohio, 1959 N=1370	f	Bay Area, Cal., 1921 N=225	f	South Carolina, 1898 N=3958	f	Worcester, Mass., 1896 N=1000	f
88	Chess	610	Ski	15	Here we go Round the Rosy Bush	42	Berrying	16
89	Scrabble	600	Backgammon	14	Stagecoach	40	Hide the Thimble	15
90	Tiddleywinks	588	Charades	11	Snap	40	Policeman	15
91	Poison Tag	586			Five Hundred	40	Hide the Buttons	14
92	Statues	579			Chess	35	Walks	14
93	Soccer	578			Hop Scotch	33	Pinch Me, Oh!	13
94	Make Scrapbook	576			Thimble	31	Billiards, Pool	13
95	Dog and Bone	574			Having Parade	31	Swinging	13
96	Kick Dodge	567			Jake Grin at Me	30	Bear "When Younger"	13
97	I've Got a Secret	566			Green	30	Backgammon	12
98	Jacks	566			Smiling Angel	29	Fish Pond	12
99	Draw or Paint	551			Sheepie	29	Stones	12
100	School	548			Quaker Meeting	28	Jack-knife	12
101	Hoops	548			Introducing to K & Q	28	Rake	12
102	Cooking	541			Ring (on a String)	27	Go Bang	11
103	Post Office	538			Teacher	25	Tic-Tac-Toe	11
104	Jump Rope	536			Sting-a-Miree	25	Singing	11
105	Make Radio	533			Table Rapping	22	Indians	10
106	Mother and I	523			Bean Bags	22	Guessing Games	10
107	Hopscotch	506			Simon Says Wig Wag	19	Steps	9
108	Handball	501			Parlor Croquet	17	Birds	9
109	Skiing	492			Geography	17	Tin Cans	9
110	Redlight	482			Pretty Maids Country	15	Farmer in the Dell	8
111	Cat and Mouse	479			Borrowed Property	15	Tea Set	8
112	Inventors	477			Making Play-House	14	Water	8
113	Name That Tune	460			Key	14	Robinson Crusoe	8
114	Store	460			Charades	14	Anagrams, Letters Spelling	8
115	Chicken	437			Rachel and Jacob	13	Horseback Riding	7
116	Clue	435			Stooping Catcher	11	Camera	7
117	Garden	427			Consequences	11	Talking	7
118	Church	424			Proverbs	10	Lost Heir	7

Table 1 (*Continued*)

No.	N. W. Ohio, 1959 N=1370	f	Bay Area, Cal., 1921 N=225	f	South Carolina, 1898 N=3958	f	Worcester, Mass., 1896 N=1000	f
119	Toboggan	419			Night Dodge	10	Chicopee	7
120	Farmer in the Dell	409			King-a-Mount	10	On the Green Carpet	6
121	London Bridge	404			Selling Forfeits	9	Colors	6
122	Matching Coins	381			Philopoena	8	Trades	6
123	See-Saw	379			Twenty Questions	7	Old Witch	6
124	Actors	367			Hat Stack	7	Bonney	6
125	Steal the Bacon	330			Backgammon	6	Rachel and Jacob	6
126	Dressing-Up	330			Clumps (yes and no)	5	Chase the Squirrel	6
127	Handsprings	327			Object Guessing	4	Slate	6
128	Colors	320			Gossip	3	Piano	6
129	Black Magic	317			Dumb Scrambo	2	Gardening	6
130	Huckle Buckle Beanstalk	316					Snap	6
131	Cartwheels	316					Napoleon	6
132	Crochet	312					Yacht Race	5
133	Spin Tops	307					Quaker Meeting	5
134	Ring Around the Rosy	306					Grandmother Grey	5
135	In and Out the Windows	305					Ring Around the Rosy	5
136	Capture the Flag	297					Billy, Billy Button	5
137	Houses	296					Doll Carriage	5
138	Charades	294					Pig Tail	5
139	Fox and Hounds	272					Fire	5
140	Pom Pom Pull Away	270					Violin	5
141	Squirrel in the Tree	265					Fox and Geese	4
142	Here I Come, Where From?	261					Cuckoo	4
143	Flashlight	261					Go In and Out the Window	4
144	Prisoner's Base	256					Horse	4
145	Snap	255					Lion in the Den	4
146	Black Tom	248					Pig, including Pig Pen	4
147	Poor Pussy	236					Salvation Army	4
148	Crows and Cranes	202					Santa Claus	4

Table 1 (*Continued*)

No.	N. W. Ohio, 1959 N = 1370	f	Bay Area, Cal., 1921 N = 225	f	South Carolina, 1898 N = 3958	f	Worcester, Mass., 1896 N = 1000	f
							Play Sunday School	4
149	Find the Ring	202						
150	What Time is It?	200					Play Church	4
151	Blackman	199					Rush	4
152	Punt Back	199					Bean Bag	4
153	Twenty Questions	196					Jackstraws	4
154	Sewing	191					Trunk	4
155	Bull in the Ring	190					Golf	4
156	Two Deep	189					Cricket	4
157	Letters	183					Matches	4
158	Hoki Toki	179					Dance	4
159	Beast, Bird or Fish	176					Paper, Paper Cutting, Colored Paper	4
160	Mulberry Bush	175					Tell Stories	4
161	Initials	171					Riddles	4
162	Buzz	155					Parties, Social	4
163	Muffin Man	145					Dr. Busby	3
164	Roly Poly	142					Cinderella	3
165	Noughts and Crosses	141					House that Jack Built	3
166	Quoits	140					Jack the Giant Killer	3
167	Four Square	138					U. S. Puzzle	3
168	Beater Goes Round	129					Old Mother Goose	3
169	Knit	126					Cash	3
170	Puss in Corner	126					Innocents Abroad	3
171	Dolls	125					Post Office	3
172	Billiards	120					Doll Furniture	3
173	Kingsland	119					Toll Gate	3
174	Forfeits	112					Farmer	3
175	Actresses	109					Dress Up	3
176	Cobbler Cobbler	108					Acorns	3
177	Oranges and Lemons	96					Skip	3
178	Perdiddle	93					Bells	3
179	Draw a Bucket of Water	85					Buttons	3
180	Nuts in May	70					Pail	3

Table 2
Girls

No.	N. W. Ohio, 1959 N=1319	f	Bay Area, Cal., 1921 N=249	f	South Carolina, 1898 N=4760	f	Worcester, Mass., 1896 N=1000	f
1	Jump Rope	1210	Tag	223	Dolls	1365	Dolls	621
2	Hide and Seek	1189	Do Plain Sewing	214	Jump Rope	1029	Sled	498
3	Tag	1170	Ride Bicycle	208	Croquet	923	Tag	442
4	Bicycle Riding	1162	Baseball	207	Clap In Clap Out	907	Hide and Seek	427
5	Hopscotch	1138	Hide and Seek	204	Drop the Handkerchief	778	Skates	412
6	Checkers	1116	Basketball	200	Dancing	732	Ball	409
7	Roller Skating	1115	Hopscotch	197	Crokinole	696	Play House	365
8	Dolls	1111	Play With Dolls	194	Parchesi	664	Jackstones	341
9	Bingo	1101	Skate	193	Keeping House	595	Play School	257
10	Cooking	1098	Cook a Meal	189	Open the Gates as High as the Sky	517	Teaset	242
11	Swimming	1096	Dance	189	Authors	516	Doll Carriage	233
12	Cards	1089	Jump the Rope	187	Hide and Seek	492	Relievo	194
13	Stoop Tag	1088	Play House	180	Little Sallie Walker	449	Checkers	189
14	Jacks	1082	Play School	172	Jackstones	406	Hopscotch	154
15	Red Rover	1077	Play "Dress-Up"	172	Checkers	384	Cards	151
16	Dressing-Up	1066	Farmer in the Dell	140	Cross Questions and Crooked Answers	378	Croquet	148
17	Tic Tac Toe	1065	Do Garden Work	138	Goosie Goosie Gander	378	Dominoes	133
18	Dance	1062	Volleyball	138	Tennis	370	Doll Cradle	131
19	Skating	1058	Drop the Handkerchief	136	Blind Man's Buff	366	Marbles	130
20	School	1054	Play Store	132	Fox and Geese	357	Leaves	112
21	Musical Chairs	1025	Racing or Jumping	131	Lotto	353	Hoop	110
22	Mother May I	1024	Cat and Mouse	130	Up Jinks	335	Books, Reading	108
23	Building Snowmen	1020	Cards	129	Mother May I Pick a Rose	326	Flowers	102
24	Drop the Handkerchief	987	London Bridge	124	Kitty Wants a Corner	318	Drop the Handkerchief	101
25	Seven Up	980	Ring Around Rosy	121	Stealing Chips	318	Snowballing	98
26	Houses	963	Guessing Games	115	Devil and Angel	313	Black Tom and Black Jack	97
27	Follow the Leader	958	Ride Horseback	121	Smiling Angel	303	Bicycle, Tricycle and Velocipede	91
28	Sewing	951	Follow the Leader	115	Cards	265	Lion in the Den	80

Table 2 (*Continued*)

N. W. Ohio, 1959 No. N=1319	f	Bay Area, Cal., 1921 N=249	f	South Carolina, 1898 N=4760	f	Worcester, Mass., 1896 N=1000	f
				Chick-a-My Chick-a-My			
29 Horse Riding	939	Knit	114	Cranny Crow	256	Doll Furniture	79
30 Monopoly	938	Puss in the Corner	111	Baseball	245	Old Maids	73
31 Simon Says	937	Checkers	105	Dominoes	240	Puss in the Corner	73
32 Throw Snowballs	925	Walk on Stilts	103	Spin the Plate	239	Bean Bag	72
33 Frozen Tag	924	In and Out the Windows	103	Pretty Maids Country	232	Steps	65
34 Puzzles	922	Dare Base or Prisoner's Base	99	Jackstraws	223	Blindman's Buff	64
35 Store	912	Blindfold	99	Introducing the King and Queen	216	On the Green Carpet	62
36 Raise Pets	912	Fox and Geese	94	Hide the Switch	216	Musical Instruments	60
37 Racing	907	Hike	92	I Spy	212	Hide the Buttons	55
38 Pick Up Sticks	904	Simon Says Thumbs Up	89	Guessing Riddles	211	Grandmother Grey	53
39 Basketball	902	Post Office	86	Good Night	209	Piano	51
40 Ping Pong	901	Solve Puzzles	86	Walk to Jerusalem	208	Authors	50
41 Dodgeball	890	Snap the Whip	83	Here We Go Round the Rosy Bush	204	Snap the Whip	50
42 Fly Kites	881	Swim	81	Teacher	199	Hill Dill	47
43 Actresses	874	Fly Kites	81	Swinging	194	Lotto	47
44 Marbles	871	Anty Over	80	Dog on Wood	182	Play Horse	47
45 Boating	869	Tennis	80	Hopscotch	166	Colors	40
46 Crack the Whip	858	Jackstones	79	Base	157	In and Out the Windows	40
47 Statues	856	Dominoes	78	Making Play House	154	Parchesi	40
48 Hoops	854	Leapfrog	72	Old Dame Wiggins is Dead	148	Duck on the Rock	36
49 I Spy	852	Handball	71	Thimble	147	Run, Sheep Run	36
50 Blind Man's Buff	848	Play Church	68	Mumble Peg	145	Lazy Maid, Lazy Mary, Lazy Bessie	33
51 Clay Modeling	840	Tug-O-War	65	Keeping Store	141	Water, Water Wild Flowers	33
52 Fox and Geese	839	Roll Hoops	62	I See a Ghost	137	Tennis	31
53 Camping	839	Pom Pom Pull Away	60	Consequences	134	Tiddleywinks	31
54 Climbing	834	Tiddleywinks	58	Football	132	Ring Around a Rosy	31

Table 2 (*Continued*)

No.	N.W. Ohio, 1959 (N=1319)	f	Bay Area, Cal., 1921 (N=249)	f	South Carolina, 1898 (N=4760)	f	Worcester, Mass., 1896 (N=1000)	f
55	London Bridge	825	Blackman	54	Working Puzzles	127	Nutting	28
56	Spin the Bottle	815	Marbles	52	Punch and Judy	122	Boats, Canoes	27
57	Baseball	814	Fish	51	Quaker Meeting	121	Farmer in the Dell	26
58	Draw or Paint	812	Play Jackstraws	47	Book	120	Hide the Thimble	26
59	Leapfrog	809	Spin Tops	45	Tiddleywinks	120	Snowman	26
60	Farmer in the Dell	809	Row a Boat	45	Pillow Dex	114	Birds	25
61	Tug-O-War	808	Bow and Arrow	44	Pig in the Parlor	106	Walks	25
62	Volleyball	808	Fox and Hounds	44	Ring on a String	101	Snowhouse	23
63	I've Got a Secret	791	Anagrams or Word-Building	41	Basketball	95	London Bridge	23
64	Wood Tag	784	Football	40	William My Tremble Toe	94	Trades	23
65	Doctors	783	Snap	40	Pig in Pen	90	Carriage, Sleigh Buckboard, Tallyho	22
66	Tennis	779	Red Rover	35	Bean Bags	90	Singing	22
67	Name That Tune	767	Duck on Rock	34	Proverbs	86	Swinging	22
68	Stunts in Gym	735	History Cards	34	Parlor Croquet	84	Pillow Dex	21
69	Fish	727	Shoot	33	Tit Tat Taw	83	Bar Up	20
70	Horseshoes	723	Wrestling	31	My Father Had a Rooster	82	Snow Shovel	19
71	Horses	722	Geography Cards	31	Swimming	80	Old Witch	19
72	Dog and Bone	720	Authors	31	Geography	79	Acorns	19
73	Tail on the Donkey	719	Croquet	29	Borrowed Property	79	Sand, Dirt	18
74	Make Collections	713	Parchesi	28	Sheepie	78	Playing in Hay	18
75	Shuffleboard	712	Roly Poly	27	Jake Grin at Me	69	Pig Tail	18
76	Tiddleywinks	711	Hunt	26	Charades	69	Messenger Boys, Errand Boy	16
77	Redlight	708	Use Tools	25	Snap	66	Poison	16
78	Darts	707	Shinny	22	Table Rapping	62	Swimming	15
79	Make Scrapbook	706	Boxing	20	Selling Forfeits	59	Backgammon	15
80	Scrabble	700	Coast or Toboggan	19	Having Show / Battle	59	Fish Pond	15
81	Ghosts	696	Work With Machinery	17	Key	59	Slate	15
82	In and Out the Windows	694	Bowling	15	Hull Gull	57	Dance	15
83	Bowling	691	Chess	15	Simon Says	57	Peter Coddles	15

Table 2 (*Continued*)

No.	N. W. Ohio, 1959 N=1319	f	Bay Area, Cal., 1921 N=249	f	South Carolina, 1898 N=4760	f	Worcester, Mass., 1896 N=1000	f
84	See-Saw	668	Charades	15	Wigwag	56	Stove	15
85	Hide the Thimble	667	Pool	14	Marbles	56	Doll Table	15
86	Church	666	Crokinole	13	Tag	53	Tents	14
87	Garden	647	Ski	13	Circus	53	Show Fort	14
88	Cowboys	635	Soccer	11	Stage Coach	52	Fox and Geese	14
89	Ring Around the Rosy	632	Billiards	11	Ten Pins	51	Old Mother Goose	14
90	Cat and Mouse	627	Backgammon	9	One Hole Cat	51	Round the Mulberry Bush	14
91	Post Office	624			Picking Eggs	49	Bull in the Ring	13
92	Walk on Stilts	619			Rachel and Jacob	47	Puzzles	13
93	Mulberry Bush	616			Jack in the Bush	45	Bear "When Younger"	13
94	Dominoes	612			Club Fists	42	Stones	13
95	Kick Dodge Wall	581			Green	41	Blackboard	13
96	Dodge Ball	577			Policeman	40	William Tell	13
97	Poison Tag	572			Anty Over	38	Kite, Parachute	12
98	Bows and Arrows	571			Leap Frog	37	Stilts	12
99	Cops and Robbers	570			Catcher	36	Shovel, Hoe	12
100	Clue	570			Buffalo Bill	36	Sticks	12
101	Kick the Can	563			Flying Kite	35	Tell Stories	12
102	Football	561			Gossip	34	Gypsy	12
103	Hiking	554			Shinny	33	Lead, Leadman	12
104	Building Forts	553			Spinning Tops	31	Last Couple Out	12
105	Ball Tag	542			Chess	30	Top	11
106	Actors	529			Golf	29	Dog	11
107	Kissing	528			Jail	26	Trees, Climbing Trees	11
108	Knit	521			Bull in the Pen	25	Gymnasium	11
109	Here I Come Where From	521			Roly Poly	23	Go Bang	11
110	Bandits	517			Philopoena	23	Jackstraws	11
111	Charades	493			Backgammon	22	Snow Shoes, Skiis	10
112	Crochet	485			Black Maria	17	Tip Cat	10
113	King on the Mountain	454			Foot and a Half	16	Tic Tac Toe	10
114	Poor Pussy	451			Fox and Hounds	15	Quaker Meeting	10
115	Colors	451			Object Guessing	14	Play Sunday School	10
116	Dice	424			Twenty Questions	13	Stealing Eggs	9
117	Chess	410			Stooping Catcher	13	Cat	9

Table 2 (*Continued*)

	N. W. Ohio, 1959		Bay Area, Cal., 1921		South Carolina, 1898		Worcester, Mass., 1896	
No.	N = 1319	f	N = 249	f	N = 4760	f	N = 1000	f
118	Squirrel in the Tree	405			Steamboat	13	Play Church	9
119	Huckle Buckle Beanstalk	402			Having Parade	11	Drawing, Painting etc.	9
120	Hunting	399			Five Hundred	11	Hockey, Shinny, Polo	8
121	Pool	395			Clumps	11	Play War	8
122	Handball	390			Sting-a-Miree	10	Racing, Running	8
123	Hunt	386			King-a-Mount	8	Jumping	8
124	Shooting	376			Bull Pen	8	Grass	8
125	Use Tools	375			Dumb Scrambo	6	Apples	8
126	Soccer	369			Night Dodge	4	Snap	8
127	Snap	362			Knucks	3	Horse Chestnuts	7
128	What Time Is It?	347			Hat Stack	3	Fishing	7
129	Spin Tops	342			Wrestling	2	A Trip Around the World	7
130	Cars	341					Tin Cans	7
131	Black Magic	331					Robinson Crusoe	7
132	Skiing	312					Talking	7
133	Wrestling	311					Show, Circus, etc.	7
134	Inventors	299					Riddles	7
135	Handsprings	290					Hare and Hound, etc.	6
136	Flashlight	286					Tenpins	6
137	Soldiers	273					Berries, Berrying	6
138	Toy Trains	270					Gardening	6
139	Hoki Toki	268					Cuckoo	6
140	Initials	255					Salvation Army	6
141	Twenty Questions	248					Parties, Social	6
142	Letters	247					Post Office	6
143	Find the Ring						Dress Up	6
144	Pom Pom Pull Away	240					Pound the Back	6
145	Steal the Bacon	240					Anagrams, Letters Spelling Game	5
146	Matching Coins	238					Halma	5
147	Two Deep	236					Bible Game	5
148	Buzz	233					Christmas Goose	5
149	Chicken	219					Horseback Riding	4
150	Black Tom	210					Paper, Paper Cutting, Colored Paper	4
151	Fox and Hounds	198					Steeple Chase	4

Table 2 (*Continued*)

No.	N. W. Ohio, 1959 N = 1319	f	Bay Area, Cal., 1921 N = 249	f	South Carolina, 1898 N = 4760	f	Worcester, Mass., 1896 N = 1000	f
152	Crows and Cranes	191					Three Kings	4
153	Boxing	191					Jack and Jill	4
154	Work with Machines	187					Tin Tin a Poppy Show, Pin Pin, etc.	4
155	Puss in the Corner	186					Guns, Rifles, Hunting	3
156	Beast, Bird or Fish	184					Pick Knife	3
157	Toboggan	184					Play Fire	3
158	Spacemen	182					Carpentry, Tools, Toolbox, etc.	3
159	Prisoner's Base	178					Rake	3
160	Muffin Man	176					Water	3
161	Make Model Aeroplanes	175					Bonney	3
162	Oranges and Lemons	167					Rachel and Jacob	3
163	Blackman	144					Horse	3
164	Roly Poly	126					Pig, including "Pig Pen," etc.	3
165	Noughts and Crosses	125					Santa Claus	3
166	Bull in the Ring	121					Trunk	3
167	Four Square	116					Matches	3
168	Beater Goes Round	114					Dr. Busby	3
169	Draw a Bucket of Water	101					Cinderella	3
170	Make Radio	100					Bells	3
171	Kingsland	100					Pails	3
172	Forfeits	98					Baby	3
173	Cobbler Cobbler	94					Bagatelle	3
174	Capture the Flag	91					Studying	3
175	Cartwheels	91					Pencil	3
176	Billiards	75					Pussel	3
177	Perdiddle	60					Shopping Game	3
178	Quoits	69					Little Miss Muffit	3
179	Nuts in May	58					Shouting Proverbs	3
180	Punt Back	53					Milkman	3

Bowling Green State University
Bowling Green, Ohio

at present known how representative this current list is of the country as a whole. If games are as universally played and as similar from place to place, as has often been averred, these various sampling differences may well be unimportant.

(b) Each of the lists of games required the children to record their responses in a different way. The 1896 study had the children write down their own games. All the other investigations (1898, 1921 and 1959) had the children mark games on a prepared check list. This makes the latter lists more directly comparable in method, so they alone are used in making the comparison of the thirty-five common items. The 1921 and 1959 lists are most directly comparable, since in each instance the children were asked to mark all the games that they wished; whereas in the 1898 list, they were asked to mark only five games. The different techniques are reflected in the different frequencies of response in these studies (see tables). The 1896 study required children to differentiate between the games played (frequency) and the games most preferred (popularity). The frequency responses were the larger of the two and were used for the rankings of the 1896 collection which is found in Tables 1 and 2. The 1898 study was based on the five most popular games. The 1921 authors combined both frequency and popularity counts into a combined index. The 1959 list was based on recognition and popularity. Terman claims that the method of response, frequency or popularity, makes little difference to over-all ranking, so this reported variety of techniques may not be too important.

(c) The composition of the different lists may have an effect upon the order of ranking. The 1896 list composed by the children themselves contained a wide assortment of games, plays, and pastimes. The 1898 list, however, contained only games. The 1921 and 1959 lists contain a mixture of games and pastimes. This means that the rank position of a game in the list may depend partly upon the nature of the other items which can be elected. In this respect the 1896, 1921, and 1959 lists are more alike than the 1898 list which is restricted to games alone. As the 1921 and 1959 lists are comparable, and the 1896 and 1898 can be checked against each other, it is possible to exercise some control over differences arising from this source. In addition, all the lists are of different length. It was decided therefore to include all the items from the three check lists [1898 (129 items), 1921 (90 items), 1959 (180 items)], but only the first 180 from the 1896 list (of approximately 500 items) as beyond that level of preference there were only one or two responses to each item on this list.

(d) There are some differences in the age of the respondents. The 1896, 1898 and 1921 investigations involve a wider age range than the 1959 investigation. However, in all these investigations the largest number of respondents is in the same age group, 9 through 15 years. The effect of the responses of those in the higher age levels presumably balanced the responses of those at the younger age levels in the averaging procedure which is used in the present comparisons. This procedure, rather than an age-by-age comparison, had to be followed as it was the method adopted in both the studies of the 1890's.

In sum, it will be seen that these many differences in the nature of the lists imply that the generalizations made about historical changes in this article must be accepted as tentative in nature.

Results

In the results that follow, the matter of historical changes in sex preference for games is dealt with first. There follows a treatment of a variety of different types of plays and games. The games are arranged in groups according to certain obvious unitary characteristics which they have. The order of treatment is approximately "developmental," that is, games which tend to be played by younger children are dealt with first. The reasons for this classification and ordering of games have been dealt with elsewhere.[9]

CHANGES IN BOY-GIRL GAME PREFERENCES

A number of recent studies have demonstrated that differences between the sexes, as measured by check-list preferences, have been considerably reduced during the past 30 years. Jones reported that ninth grade boys and girls of today are more like each other in their attitudes towards heterosexual activities, religion, and sports.[10] Rosenberg and Sutton-Smith reported that fourth, fifth, and sixth grade girls of today are substantially more like boys in their game choices than was the case in 1921.[11] These and other studies have served to indicate that not only has there been a definite shift in attitudes and preferences of children over the last 25 years, but in particular, the studies show the increasing incorporation of masculine preferences by females.[12] It seems reasonable to assume that this trend toward increasing similarity of the sexes has been occurring over a period greater than 30 years.

The thirty-five items which were common to the 1898, 1921 and 1959 lists are as follows: Baseball, Football, Basketball, Swimming, Hide and seek, Tag, Marbles, Checkers, Cards, Kites, Wrestling, Puzzles, Blindman's buff, Tennis, Dancing, Dominoes, Drop the handkerchief, Leapfrog, Simon says, Tiddleywinks, Store, Fox and geese, Chess, Jacks, Jumprope, Hopscotch, Parchesi, Fox and hounds, Houses, Spin tops, Charades,

Prisoner's base, Snap, Puss in corner, Dolls. If these items are arranged by rank order of preference for boys and girls separately in each of the years 1898, 1921 and 1959, and rank-order correlations are run between the lists, there is evidence of increasing similarity between the sexes in game preferences. There is little relationship between the sexes in game preferences in 1898 (rho = −.023), which means that the sexes prefer quite different games. There is a slight relationship in 1921 (rho = +.328), and a moderate relationship in 1959 (rho = +.451) which means that the sexes have become increasingly similar in their sex preferences.

When the rankings of each sex are treated separately, and rank order correlations run between each period, the following results obtain. Between 1898 and 1921 the rho correlation for boys is: = +.672. Between 1898 and 1959 the rho = +.595. Between 1921 and 1959 the rho = +.707. These results suggest a high similarity in game preferences among boys during this period. The same rank correlations for the girls are: 1898 to 1921, rho = +.490; 1898 to 1959, rho = +.397; 1921 to 1959, rho = +.680. These rank order correlations for the girls are smaller, suggesting that the increasing similarity between the sexes from 1898 to 1959 has been brought about more by changes in girls' play preferences than by changes in those of the boys. This finding is consistent with the other investigations of changes in boy-girl differences.

If we choose, arbitrarily, a change in ten rank points between these three separate studies as indicative of an historical change, then those game choices which show a tendency towards increasing similarity between the sexes between 1898 and 1959 are:

> Puss in the corner
> Swimming
> Tag
> Leap frog
> Fox and hounds
> Drop the handkerchief
> Dancing
> Marbles
> Kites
> Tops

The games which remain fairly constant retaining their rank difference of less than ten points between the sexes from 1898 and 1959 are:

> Parchesi
> Charades
> Hide and seek
> Checkers

Tennis
Blindman's buff
Fox and geese
Cards
Dominoes
Prisoner's base
Puzzles
Tiddleywinks
Snap
Simon says
Chess

The games which remain constant by continuing to hold more than ten rank point differences between the sexes throughout this period are:

Jackstones
House
Hopscotch
Football
Wrestling

Closer examination of the items showing increasing similarity between the sexes with time reveals that there are a variety of reasons for these changes. In some cases, the increased similarity is due to the fact that the girls now favor these games less than they used to and have thus become more like the boys (e.g., Puss in the corner, Drop the handkerchief). Other games have gained in favor with the girls and made their choices more like those of the boys (e.g., Swimming, Tag and Kites). There are games that have lost favor with boys and now make their choices more like those of the girls (e.g., Fox and hounds, Tops); games that have lost favor with the boys and gained favor with the girls (e.g., Leapfrog and Marbles); and games that have lost favor with both sexes (e.g., Parchesi, Fox and geese, Prisoner's base). It should be noted, however, that although the sexes have become more similar in these respects, there are still statistically significant differences between them in their responses to some of these items. In particular, Football, Marbles, and Wrestling which are more preferred by the boys, and Dance, Dolls, Drop the handkerchief, Fox and geese, Hopscotch, Houses, Jacks, Jumprope, Leapfrog, Puzzles, Simon says and Store which are more preferred by the girls.[13]

CHANGES IN TYPES OF GAMES

It has seemed worthwhile to analyze the changes that have taken place in the children's preferences for games in terms of a variety of *types* of games. The types of games that are dealt with are as follows:

imitative or make-believe games
singing games
dialogue games
leader games
chasing games
central person parlor games
undifferentiated team guessing and chasing games
central person games of low power
games of individual skill
skilled pastimes
undifferentiated team games of skill
indoor or backyard games of skill
board and card games
major sports
co-operative parlor games
couple and kissing games

IMITATIVE OR MAKE-BELIEVE GAMES

It is noticeable that boys' make-believe games where two groups participate in dramatized conflict have remained remarkably stable over this period of time. Ranking high in choice within the first twenty in all periods are Play horse (1896), Buffalo Bill and Policeman (1898), Cowboys (Kansas, 1924, Lehmann and Witty's investigation reported in *The Psychology of Play Activities*), and Cops and robbers, Bow and arrows, and Soldiers (1959). Within the first forty ranked are War (1896) and Bandits (1959). The preferences of girls for these games has not changed appreciably from 1898 until present, their rank position ranging from the low second fifty downwards. Apparently, in becoming more masculine, girls have not been concerned to identify themselves with these fantasy roles which are so important to boys. This raises an important question: Why should girls show an increasing preference for the minor and major sports of boys (e.g., Marbles and Swimming), but not for these dramatized male games? The simplest interpretation is that girls are following the lead of women, that while women have shown increased interest and participation in men's sports, they have not so extensively taken over the warrior-like activities of men (Soldiers, Cops, Cowboys). It would be of interest to know whether girls' play is similar in those cultures where the women have, in recent years, been assuming warriorlike functions (Israel and China). It has often been observed that boys follow fantasy models in their imitative play (Cowboys and Indians) and that girls follow realistic models in theirs (Mothers, Nurses, etc.); and it has been suggested that for boys this is due to their lack of clear-cut father models to imitate, their fathers being absent most of the time and involved in abstract and complex white collar functions.[14] If these imitative games do reflect such basic issues of sex-role identification, this would be an additional reason for the girls' avoidance of them.

The imitative games which are usually associated more with girls than with boys, seem to have decreased in importance for boys over the years. In the 1896 and 1898 lists, playing at School, House, and Store are in the first fifty ranked items for both boys and girls. They remain in the first fifty for girls through 1959. For the boys, they drop to the second fifty in preference in 1921 and to the third fifty (ranking lower than 100), in 1959. The marked change in the rank order of these games for boys is not a result of changes in the lists, or this would have been reflected in the girls' preferences also. It suggests rather the hypothesis that boys have lowered their liking for games of this sort because they are strongly preferred by girls. Further, it suggests that because girls have encroached upon the play preferences of boys, and appear therefore less separate from boys than they once were, boys have attempted to clarify their own distinctness, by lowering their preference for any games that are not obviously masculine. In an attempt to remain as separate in their games from girls as they once were, boys have had to surrender interest in pursuits that were not completely and exclusively masculine. If this generalization is veridical, then it follows that in these respects at least the play of boys today is more circumscribed than it was at the end of the nineteenth century. This generalization is a refinement of the customary view which suggests that differences between the sexes has decreased over the years. Nominally differences may have decreased but apparently at the expense of variety in boys' role behaviors. We will note, as we proceed, other types of female-associated games in which the same tendency can be seen to operate. [For example, boys rank play at Dolls as 51st (1896), 87th (1898), 82nd (1921) but 171st (1959).] This indicates, we believe, that we are recording a genuine historical change, and not merely a change resulting from geographic locale or sample selection. Other changes in boys' imitative play refer more to obvious historical content than to fundamental changes in child behavior. In the 1890 collections we have mention of Steamboat, Buffalo Bill, Black Maria, and Robinson Crusoe, which are less familiar to children today. In their place are games like Spacemen and Inventors. It is not surprising, in view of the population shift from rural to urban areas, that playing at Horses has dropped some fifty rank positions.

The major girls' imitative games, Dolls, Houses, and Schools, may have lost rank to some extent but the change is relatively small. Dolls rank first in both 1896 and 1898, but in 1921 and 1959 it is 8th. More active games have taken Dolls' position of priority (Jump rope, Bicycle-riding, Roller-skating, etc.). Apparently modern girls play the more active games at an earlier age than used to be the case. These games have slipped down the age levels making today's children appear more sophisticated. Playing at Houses moves from 7th (1896) and 9th (1898) to 13th (1921) and 26th (1959). Playing at School goes from 9th (1896) to 14th (1921) and 20th (1959). It would be interesting to know whether the increasing masculinity of girls' choices has led to a decrease in their interest in more central feminine concerns as these shifts in game preferences seem to indicate. Perhaps the relatively greater interest in play at Dressing-up which is not found in the earlier lists but ranks as 15th (1921) and 16th (1959) reflects a shift in interest from the feminine domestic to the feminine glamor role. Some writers have suggested that one price women have paid for their emancipation has been increasing confusion about their own distinctive role behavior. The new situation has made it simpler for younger girls to identify with the more obvious "glamor" role than with the domestic sex roles once thought appropriate for women.[15]

SINGING GAMES

Yoffie found in her study of "Three Generations of Children's Singing Games in St. Louis" that children at the end of the last century played more traditional singing games than do children today.[16] This finding seems to be confirmed by the present investigation. The 1896 Worcester list in which the children wrote down their own responses contains some twenty-five games.[17] Very few of these games were written by children on the lists from which the 1959 check-list was originally derived. The games mentioned in the 1896 list, most of them with only one or two frequencies, were in order of popularity: Drop the handkerchief, On the green carpet, Grandmother Grey, Go in and out the windows, Lazy maid, lazy Mary, lazy Bessie, Water, water, wildflowers, Ring a round the rosy, Farmer in the dell, London bridge, Round the mulberry bush, Round the barley bush, Billy Billy button, Three kings, Bushel of wheat, bushel of rye, Fly Kitty through peals, Jenny a Jones, Jemima Jones, Joor Tommy is dead, Little Sally Water, Forty girls go round the ring, Merry girls, Draw a pail of water, Here comes an old woman from Farmerland (Cumberland), Here comes one king, Here's the way we wash our clothes, Have you bread and wine. No description is given of these games in the 1896 report.

Although not as many basic game items are listed in the 1921 investigation, the games that are listed seem as high in popularity as those listed in the 1896 and 1898 reports. This is also true in the 1924 report from Kansas,[18] which makes it appear as if the large change that has come about in the playing of girls' traditional singing games has, in the main, occurred after the 1920's. There may, however, have been fewer games known by the twenties, even though those played were very popular. Yoffie found this in St. Louis, and Sutton-Smith obtained similar results in New Zealand. It is further confirmed by the fact that a collection of approximately 600 games from 10,000 children in 1931 in the states of Massachusetts, Ohio, Michigan, Texas and Florida appears to have yielded no more singing games than the list above from Worcester alone.[19] (Only game names are listed so it is difficult to be definite about this point.) Contemporary girls have many rhyming interests, but these find their expression mainly in Jump rope, ranked number one in the 1959 list and ball bouncing, also ranked high (25th). Individual games reflect the above general picture. Drop the handkerchief has probably maintained its position of high rank in the first thirty because it is as much a chasing as a singing game. It ranked 24th (1896), 5th (1898), 19th (1921), 24th (1959). In and out the windows was 46th (1896), 33rd (1921), 82nd (1959). Ring a round the rosy was 54th (1896), 41st (1898), 25th (1921), 89th (1959). Farmer in the Dell was 57th (1896), 16th (1921), 60th (1959). London Bridge dropped from 24th (1921) to 55th (1959). The Mulberry bush changes little from 90th (1896) to 93rd (1959). Several games popular in the Nineties are not on subsequent lists, namely, Little Sallie Water, 13th (1898); On the green carpet, 35th (1896); Lazy maid, 50th (1896) and Water wild flowers, 51st (1896). The boys' rankings of these games, although lower than the girls, reflect similar trends, except that they have dropped proportionately much lower than the girls in the 1959 period. This is further evidence apparently of their increasing withdrawal from feminine pursuits.

DIALOGUE GAMES

These are chasing games played by young girls which involve a traditional dialogue and a dramatization of conflict between an old witch or mother and her children. Several rank highly with girls in the earlier studies: Goosie, goosie, 17th, Mother may I pick a rose, 23rd, and Chick-a my chick-a-my crany crow, 29th (all of 1898); Grandmother Grey, 38th, Old witch, 71st, Old Mother Goose, 89th (all of 1896). There is no mention, let alone high ranking of any of these games in the 1921 and 1959 studies. The Kansas 1924 study, however, lists Old witch. And the Schwendener 1931 study in five states lists Old Mother witch with high frequency, but lists with only one frequency in ten thousand children, Grandmother Grey and Mother may I go out to play. We would assume that these dialogue games, like the singing games, have fallen into desuetude largely because of their inappropriate symbolism. On the other hand it seems hardly likely that dual-mother play is no longer important to young girls. Perhaps they get that sort of play representation while playing schools and at leader games.

LEADER GAMES

These games are usually played by young girls of seven to nine years and involve one girl taking a commanding position over others. She is part of the game but is also its arbiter. As far as can be judged games of this sort have increased in number. All earlier lists contain only one or two of these games, whereas the 1959 list has Mother may I (22nd), Follow the leader (27th), Simon says (31st), Statues (47th), I spy (49th), Initials (140th), Letters (142nd). The 1896 list has Steps (33rd) and this is similar to Mother may I. Simon says improves rank position from 84th (1898) to 38th (1921). Follow the leader and I spy maintain rank position from 1921 to 1959. Statuary is mentioned in the Kansas list, 1924. Schwendener mentions Follow the leader, Redlight and Initials as played in 1931. We can generalize, though the evidence is meager, that playing at this type of leader role-taking is more important to young girls than it used to be. Once again, we find that the boys' response to these girls' games is less favorable than it was. Whereas Follow the leader and Simon says retain rank position for girls, both descend in importance for boys. Follow the leader from 30th (1921) to 55th (1959), and Simon says from 57th (1921) to 86th (1959).

CHASING GAMES

Chasing games have played an important part in the play of both boys and girls throughout the sixty years involved in this study. The physical activity of running and the themes of pursuit and capture are apparently very basic motifs in this culture. With few exceptions girls show higher rankings in more of these games in all historical periods. The games which have remained most constant over this period are Tag and Hide and seek. Girls rank Tag, 3rd (1896), 1st (1921) and 3rd (1959). Boys rank Tag, 7th (1896), 4th (1921) and 7th (1959). Girls rank Hide and seek 4th (1896), 5th (1921), 2nd (1959). Boys rank Hide and seek 10th (1896), 8th (1921), 4th (1959). Rather unexpectedly both of these games had much lower rankings in the 1898 list from South Carolina. Girls ranked Tag and Hide and seek respectively as 86th and 12th and boys ranked them respectively as 23rd and 17th. For girls the highest ranking chasing game in South Carolina was Drop the handkerchief (4th) and for boys Fox and geese (5th). Both of these are more formal chasing games than Tag or Hide and seek. In addition Tag is more popular with boys than girls in Carolina, which is not the case elsewhere. These differences, together with the higher ranking given to other formal chasing games in South Carolina to singing games, to parlor games and to dancing, suggest that play in that state at that time was more decorous and formal than it was at the other places sampled in this study.

Although chasing games are generally more popular with girls, exceptions occur for the following games which are more popular with boys: Relievo, Black Tom, Run sheep run (1896), Tag, Fox and geese (1898), Fox and geese, Pom pom pull away (1921), Ghosts, Kick the can, Poison tag, Pom pom pull away, Black Tom, Blackman (1959). The fact that there are still these distinctive and vigorous boys' chasing games probably accounts for the fact that boys' preferences for these games have not yet decreased. If the circumscription of the masculine role continues however, it might be predicted that boys would show decreasing favor for girl associated chasing games in the years ahead. The tagging games which are preferred by girls today are Hide and seek, Tag, Stoop tag, Red Rover, Frozen tag, Fox and geese, Blindman's buff, Wood tag, Cat and mouse, Squirrel in tree, What time is it? and Two deep.

CENTRAL PERSON PARLOR GAMES

As in other central person games (chasing and leader games), these games contain one or two persons occupying central roles and steering the course of the game. These games can be played by the under tens because of their simple organization. They are games played at parties and on indoor social occasions and are preferred more by girls than by boys. Games of the Nineties which are not played today are Stagecoach, William my tremble toe, Guessing riddles, Geography, Jake grin at me, Proverbs, and Object Questions. Games played in 1898 which are still played today but preferred to a slightly lesser extent are, Find the ring or Ring on a string, Hide the thimble (also 1896), Twenty questions, and Forfeits. The only comparable game of today with a higher ranking is Musical chairs which is the same game as Walk to Jerusalem of 1898. The new but similar games of today are Tail on the donkey, I've got a secret, Name that tune, Black magic, and Poor pussy. These games seem still to be important, but perhaps not quite as important as they once were.

UNDIFFERENTIATED TEAM GUESSING AND ACTING

In these games there are two teams or groups of loose formation. Characteristically, one group performs and the other must guess the nature of the performance. The games involve mainly dramatization and guessing. They are universally girls' games played by children nine years and over and often take place on formal indoor occasions such as parties. While all the lists contain one or two of these games, the largest number are in the South Carolina list, presumably further evidence of more formal social play in that state at that time, 1898. The games itemized in that list were Devil and angel, Clumps, Charades, Up jinks, Pretty maids country, Dumb scrambo, and Open the gates. Four of these were ranked in the first forty by the girls. None of the similar games in other lists, Trades (1896), Here I come, where from? (1924, Kansas and 1959), Charades (1959) have this rank importance.

CENTRAL PERSON GAMES OF LOW POWER

In the leader, dialogue, central person parlor and chasing games, the person at the center of the action, the central person, has been given relatively high power by the nature of the game. He can choose whom to chase, when to run, and so on. At the ages of 9 to 10 years, children especially boys, begin to play central person games in which the central person is not given great power by the game and must use his own skill to fight off the challenge of the other players. The most popular games of this sort today are Dodgeball, King on the mountain, and Wall dodge ball. In earlier lists, positions of similar importance were held by Snap the whip (1921), Duck on rock (1921 and 1896), Pig in the pen, and Bull in the pen (1898).

There seems to have been little historical change in the position of these games. Indeed the fact that there is so little change in chasing games which are games of high central person power, and so little change in these games of low central person power, suggests that these two types of game are the major stepping stones in game development. First, the child experiences games of high central person power, where the game provides support and protection for his own inadequacy; then there are these games at the later age where the child must face the other players without such protection. The transition from protected to unprotected game status is perhaps the major one that a child must be able to accomplish in his game development if he is to be a successful gamesman! This argument has been developed more fully elsewhere.[20] If and when games ever decrease in children's own spontaneous play it is reasonable to assume that recreationists will continue to use a game series of this sort for educational purposes.

GAMES OF INDIVIDUAL SKILL

Increasingly from 9 or 10 years of age onwards, boys and girls play games where all players are on equal terms, and they compete with each other to see who can win. Games of this sort were more varied in earlier years than they are today. For example, Mumble peg, Foot and a half, Five hundred, Philopoena, Green, Bean bags, Book, Roly poly, Hide the switch (1898), Jacknife, Pick knife and Horse chestnut (1896). A few of these games, however, have remained remarkably constant. For boys these are Marbles: 2nd (1896), 4th (1898), 7th (1921) and 8th (1959). For girls: Jump rope, 3rd (1896) [Omitted from Table 2. Frequency of 480.], 2nd (1898), 12th (1921), 1st (1959) and Jacks 10th (1896), 12th (1898), 46th (1921), 14th (1959). Some have lost popularity with boys, such as Spin tops 12th (1896), 10th (1898), 15th (1921) and 133rd (1959), and Leapfrog which was 41st (1896), 9th (1898), 33rd (1921) and 69th (1959). Hopscotch has gained in popularity with girls from 14th (1896), 45th (1898), 7th (1921) to 5th (1959). Racing has gained popularity with both sexes. For the three girls' games of Hopscotch, Jacks, and Jump rope, boys' preferences have drawn further away from those of girls, especially since 1921. For the three boys' games of Marbles, Leapfrog, and Spin tops, however, the girls' preferences have drawn closer to those of the boys over these years. This may be due, in part, to the fact that boys' preferences for these games have decreased.

It is interesting to note that the older skill games with a penalty written into their laws find few counterparts in modern play; games such as Quaker meeting, Hat stack, Hide the switch, Foot and a half, Club fists, Forfeits, Book Knucks, Jake grin at me (1898) and Duck on rock (1896). Modern children are apparently less rough in their play, a finding which is consistent with the general view that the play of children has been increasingly supervised and controlled throughout this period of sixty years.[21]

SKILLED PASTIMES

These are activities which are usually carried on by individuals alone or among others. These activities may give rise to competitive, gamelike activities, but are not in themselves formally organized games. Bicycle riding, Horse riding, and Climbing are activities which have increased in importance for both sexes over this period of time. The girls have narrowed the difference between themselves and the boys in Climbing, and have erased the difference in Horse and Bicycle riding. Swimming, Kites, and Fishing are activities which have remained fairly constant in rank for boys, but girls have shown increased preference for these items, so that they now show equal preference with the boys for Swimming and much greater preference than formerly for the other two. The only item in which the boys show a much greater preference than formerly and the girls do not, is Throwing snowballs. Boating remains fairly constant for both sexes. Markedly decreased interest is shown over the years in winter time activities such as Skating, Skiing, and Tobogganing, and in the antique pastimes of Hoops, Stilts and Hiking. Roller-skating seems to have taken the place of some of the earlier winter pastimes, particularly with girls. This is partly a reflection of urbanization. Roller-skating ranked 10th with Brooklyn girls of the 1890's according to Croswell. One must have open spaces to ski and toboggan.

Children's hobbies permit few comparisons with the earlier period except in terms of item content. Play with leaves and flowers, nuts, grass, etc., ranks high in the Nineties, but is unmentioned today. However, comparison with the 1921 list shows less interest for both sexes today in Model aeroplanes, Using tools, Machinery, Gardening, Sewing, and Knitting. The girls have held their rank position on Cooking, but the boys have decreased theirs greatly, apparently being once again less willing to be associated with a feminine type activity than in earlier times. It seems that hobby-type activities are less important than they were, their place perhaps being taken by the greater availability of movies, radio, TV, etc. The number of skilled activities in the first forty rank positions for boys does not change greatly in the 1896, 1921 and 1959 lists. The girls' list of 1896 contains fewer of these activities in the first forty than do the girls list of 1921 and 1959, another respect apparently in which the girls have become more like the boys. (The 1898 list was restricted to formal games, and as such cannot be used in this comparison.) As almost half of boys' preferences in the first forty are for skilled pastimes, and as the girls' preference for these activities is increasing, it follows that formal games are becoming less important in general. If this trend should continue with girls becoming more like boys, and boys tending to give up all formal games which have anything to do with girls, the time may come when neither sex shows any strong interest in most of the formal games of childhood (as distinct from the athletic and formal sports of adults). If it is true that such a trend is occurring in childhood away from formalized group activities, then it is interesting to speculate on the causes of this development. One argument might be that children who today live in more permissive, free-communicating, and equalitarian relationships with their parents, have less need for formalized relationships in play. This argument would suggest that the formalities of the traditional children's games, the prestige role-positions, and the power differences invested in the players by the game, were a representation of the hierarchically ordered societies in which the children found themselves. The games were modeled after the formal social interactions which were thought appropriate in the family and in society. Elements of this sort are most obvious in the singing games, team guessing and acting games, dialogue games, co-operative parlor games and couple parlor games, all of which have shown the most striking decrease in importance. When we remember that these games were originally created and played by adults to meet the needs of an older society, the fact of their decay is less surprising.

Today's children by contrast have relatively less need to understand formalized social relations, which makes it understandable that formal group play activities are less meaningful to them. Today's children are said to spend much more time in informal peer group activities both in and out of school. It follows that in their play they would be increasingly interested in such informal group activities as Swimming, Fishing, Hunting, Boating, Bicycle-riding, and Roller skating, which as we have seen, have widespread popularity but are not governed by set patterns of game rules. It has been observed that these children do not show increasing interest in the informal activities that are usually pursued by the individual on his own, such as hobbies.

If these speculations have any foundation, we would expect that the playing of formal games will be of ever decreasing importance in the spontaneous play of children.[22] No doubt numbers of the more competitive of such games will be retained by teachers and playground supervisors for recreational purposes and some will continue to be employed as a subsidiary means of training potential professional athletes. One would expect, too, that children will continue spontaneously to participate in some of these games, in particular chasing, and commercially sponsored board and skill games from time to time; but it is doubtful that a wide range of formal games will continue to be the foundation of peer group activity as it has been traditionally throughout the first forty years of this century.

UNDIFFERENTIATED TEAM GAMES

These are formal games of skill in which the two "teams" are only slightly differentiated in terms of different role behaviors. Each group acts as a pack against the other pack. It is clear that this type of game played mainly by 11-12 year old boys has decreased in importance. Presumably the greater modern attention to major sports has weakened interest in these games. The games that are directly comparable (Fox and hounds or Hare and hounds, Prisoner's base or Base, and Capture the flag or Stealing chips or Eggs) have all lost rank position. Several games, Battle, Stealing chips, Fox and hounds, and Base all have high rankings in the 1890's, whereas the only game today in the first 30 is Tug-o-war where the position is unchanged from 1921.

INDOOR OR BACKYARD GAMES OF PHYSICAL SKILL

The modern list contains a few more games of this sort. Of the comparisons possible, Pick up sticks (Jackstraws) retains about the same rank position today as in 1898. Tiddleywinks loses rank on 1898 and 1921. Billiards loses with both sexes from 1921, Pool loses with girls but holds constant for boys. Croquet seems to have lost importance from the 1890's to 1921 and is not in the 1959 list. Quoits also has lost rank position as between 1896 and 1959. Highest ranking games today are Darts, Ping pong, and Horseshoes, all favored by boys. Highest ranking in the early lists was Croquet, favored by girls. It seems likely that commercial sponsorship will keep some of these games alive for many years to come. The same may be said of the board and card games.

BOARD AND CARD GAMES

There is a tendency for games of this sort to have a slightly higher ranking in the early (1898) list. Old favorites which are not in the current list are Parchesi, Authors, Crokinole, and Lotto. New games of this sort are Bingo, Monopoly, Scrabble, and Clue. Dominoes is less highly ranked than it was. Chess and Snap have maintained their ranking. Checkers and Cards have been in the first twenty in most of the lists. They have been slightly more important to the boys until the 1959 list when they were ranked slightly higher by the girls. Puzzles and Tic Tac Toe have improved their rank positions, but this is more noticeable with the girls. Indications are that these types of games might be increasing in importance for girls and decreasing in importance for boys.

MAJOR SPORTS

In the major sports of Bowling, Football, Basketball, Baseball, Wrestling and Boxing, the girls' preferences are closer to those of the boys in the 1921 list than they were in the earlier lists. However, in the 1959 list, the sexes are again farther apart in these preferences than in the 1921 list. These are several reasons for this. Some games have decreased markedly in popularity with girls since 1921 (or as between San Francisco, 1921 and Ohio, 1959). These are Football, Basketball, Baseball, Wrestling, and Boxing has remained constant with the girls, but has improved rank position with the boys since 1921. The positions of Football and Basketball have improved with boys, while they have lost rank with the girls. Baseball, Wrestling and Boxing have lost rank position with the boys also, but not to the extent that they have with the girls. Tennis, Soccer, and Handball have lost rank position with both sexes, with the difference between the sexes (the boys showing slightly more preference) remaining more or less constant. Football has taken Baseball's place as the number one athletic game.

We might hypothesize that the increase in girls' interest between 1900 and 1920 was due to their greater freedom to play actively and be interested in boys' activities. But that their unwillingness to get closer to boys in these particularly vigorous masculine sports, since that time is due to the realization that these activities, like Cops and robbers, are distinctively masculine.

These trends would indicate that boys are spending more and more time on fewer sports. Bowling, Basketball, and Football improve in rank position, but all the other sports decline (Baseball, Wrestling, Boxing, Volleyball, Tennis, Soccer, Handball). These facts must be kept in mind when rating the disappearance of the undifferentiated team games of yesterday and the decline of the number of individual games of skill. This would appear to be further evidence of the increasing circumscription of the boys' play role.

CO-OPERATIVE PARLOR GAMES

Games of this sort are very important in the list of 1898, but not in subsequent lists. The games no longer found are: Cross questions, Old dame Wiggins, I see a ghost, Consequences, My father had a rooster, Gossip, Key, Table rapping. Borrowed property, Introducing the King and Queen. These games involved the co-operation of two or more players in order to produce a trick on some of the other players, or some absurd result, which was a source of hilarity to all. Apparently the youths of today occupy themselves in other activities as we have noted because these games do not appear on the more recent lists. The games were played mainly by teenagers or older persons in earlier times. They were more highly ranked by girls than by boys.

COUPLE AND KISSING GAMES

Items that are comparable, Dance, Spin the plate (or bottle), and Post office show a decrease in rank position. These games are not as important as they were. Although Spin the bottle is the most favored of kissing games today,[23] its position in the second fifty cannot compare with the 4th ranking of Clap in clap out in 1898. Other games in the earlier lists were: Smiling angel, Goodnight, Pig in parlor, Kiss the pillow, and Last couple out. The rank position of the new kissing games in the 1959 list (Flashlight and Perdiddle) is much lower.

CONCLUSION

This survey of the changes in games over sixty years is based on game lists derived in 1896, 1898, 1921 and 1959. The differences in the sampling techniques used in these various studies implies that considerable caution must be exercised in interpreting differences between their results as differences of an historical sort. Nevertheless, the following conclusions appear warranted.

Some types of games are much less important to children of today than they were to children of the 1890's. These are children's singing games, dialogue games, team guessing and acting games, co-operative parlor games, couple and kissing games, all of which are predominantly girls' games, and team games without role differentiation which are boys' games. Other types of games appear to be played as much today as they were earlier. These are imitative games, chasing games, and central person games of low power. There are other games where the trend is less clear, but that give some evidence of being played less than they used to be. These are individual games of skill, a wide range of organized sports, central person parlor games, and board and card games. Again there is slight evidence that the following types of games are played more often than they used to be: leader games, indoor and backyard games of physical skill, skilled pastimes, and a few selected organized sports.

Perhaps the most important generalizations arising out of this study concern the changing relationships between boys and girls. The finding that the responses of girls have become increasingly like those of the boys as the sixty years have passed is not unexpected, in the light of the well known changes in woman's role in American culture during this period of time. On the other hand, the finding that boys' play roles have become increasingly circumscribed with the passing of the years was unexpected. Yet there is little doubt that boys have been steadily lowering their preference for games that have had anything to do with girl's play. So that it is by implication much more deviant behavior for a modern boy to play at, say, Dolls, Hopscotch, Jacks, Houses, Schools, Cooking, Jump rope, Musical chairs, Simon says, and Singing games than it was for a boy to play at these things in the earlier historical periods covered by these studies. In another sense, too, boys' play is more circumscribed, for it would seem that they have greatly reduced the range of games of individual and team skill and the organized sports to which they will devote their time. This reduction in the range of boys' activities can, of course, be variously interpreted. It contributes to clear-cut role definition of appropriate boys' behavior and perhaps facilitates the development of those boys who have the particular skills required by the games that are in demand. On the other hand it must as surely penalize those many other boys who find that there is a discrepancy between their own abilities and those required in the play roles of their own age sex category.[24] Judging by the few activities that now clearly differentiate a boy from a girl, masculine roughplay (Football, Boxing, Wrestling) and masculine-like intrusiveness (Horseshoes, Throwing snowballs, Marbles, and Darts) have become the residual and central facets of the male sex role.[25]

Of a somewhat more speculative order is the attendant generalization that these historical changes imply that the majority of children's formal games may themselves in due course become anachronistic. The increasing preference of children is for informal group activities, a preference which would appear to be more in accord with the social world in which they now live. Formal games are vestiges of an earlier and more hierarchically arranged society, and they may pass out of spontaneous play as the formalities which they represent become increasingly meaningless to new generations of children. We would not expect such games to disappear completely, but we would expect them to become relatively less important parts of a child's development in this culture.

Notes

[1] Leah Rachel Clara Yoffie, "Three Generations of Children's Singing Games in St. Louis," *JAF,* LX (1947), 1–51.

[2] Brian Sutton-Smith, *The Games of New Zealand Children* (Berkeley, California, 1959).

[3] T. R. Crosswell, "Amusements of Worcester School Children," *The Pedagogical Seminary,* VI (1898–99), 314–371.

[4] Zach McGhee, "A Study in the Play Life of Some South Carolina Children," *The Pedagogical Seminary,* VII (1900) 459–478.

[5] Lewis M. Terman, *Genetic Studies of Genius,* Vol. 1 (Stanford, 1926).

[6] B. G. Rosenberg and B. Sutton-Smith, "A Revised Conception of Masculine-Feminine Differences in Play Activities," *Journal of Genetic Psychology,* 1960, 96, 165–170.

[7] Harvey C. Lehmann and Paul A. Witty, *The Psychology of Play Activities* (New York, 1927).

[8] Josephine C. Foster, "Play Activities of Children in the First Six Grades," *Child Development,* I (1930), 248–254, and Norma Schwendener, "Game Preferences of 10,000 Fourth Grade Children," (New York, 1942).

[9] B. Sutton-Smith, "A Formal Analysis of Game Meaning," *Western Folklore,* XVIII (1959), 13–24; and B. Sutton-Smith, "The Historical and Psychological Significance of the Unorganized Games of New Zealand Primary School Children" (Ph. D. Thesis, University of New Zealand, 1953). A copy is in the library of Victoria University of Wellington, New Zealand, and a microfilm copy is in the library of Ball State Teachers College, Muncie, Indiana.

[10] Mary Cover Jones, "A Comparison of the Attitudes and Interests of Ninth Graders Over Two Decades," a paper presented at the 25th Anniversary Meeting of the Society for Research in Child Development, Bethesda, Maryland, 20 March 1959.

[11] B. G. Rosenberg and B. Sutton-Smith, ibid.

[12] Daniel G. Brown, "Sex Role Preference in Young Children," *Psychological Monographs,* LXX (1956), 1–19.

[13] B. G. Rosenberg and B. Sutton-Smith, "The Measurement of Masculinity and Femininity in Children," *Child Development,* XXX (1959), 373–380.

[14] T. Parsons, *Essays in Sociological Theory* (Glencoe, Illinois, 1949).

[15] Lawrence K. Frank et alia, "Personality Development in Adolescent Girls," *Monographs of the Society for Research in Child Development*, XVI (1951), 195.

[16] Leah Yoffie, p. 50.

[17] T. R. Crosswell, p. 320.

[18] Lehmann and Witty, p. 79.

[19] Schwendener, pp. 38–45.

[20] B. Sutton-Smith, "Peer Status and Play Status," *Recreation*, XLVIII (1955), 172–174; and P. V. Gump and B. Sutton-Smith, "The 'It' Role in Children's Games," *The Group*, XVII (1955), 3–8.

[21] B. Sutton-Smith, "Traditional Games of New Zealand Children," *Folk-Lore*, LXIV (1953), 411–423.

[22] A similar interpretation of game-types as paralleling social life will be found in John M. Roberts, Malcolm J. Arth and Robert R. Bush, "Games in Culture," *American Anthropologist*, LXI (1959) 597–605.

[23] B. Sutton-Smith, "The Kissing Games of Adolescence," *Midwest Folklore*, IX (1959), 189–211.

[24] Leonard S. Cottrell, "The Adjustment of the Individual to His Age and Sex Roles," *American Sociological Review*, VII (1942), 617–620.

[25] E. H. Erikson, "Sex Differences in the Play Configurations of American Pre-Adolescents," *American Journal of Orthopsychiatry*, XXI (1951), 667–692.

Experimental Investigations of Childhood Play

Elizabeth B. Hurlock

Students of child psychology have emphasized the periodicity of the play behavior of children of different ages and have investigated the forms of play which are characteristic of each age. It is the purpose of this paper to bring together in systematic form the studies which relate to the play of the different stages of development from birth to maturity.

Among writers, there is no agreement as to how many play periods there are in the child's development, what names shall be applied to these periods nor how long each one of them lasts. Among the best classifications of age periods in play behavior are those of Baldwin (8), Croswell (31), Curtis (32), Gulick (50), Johnson (66), King (70), Kirkpatrick (71), Lee (72), Lehman and Witty (80), Pyle (103), Puffer (102), Reaney (104), and Wood (128).

Several investigators have attempted to explain the periodicity of play in terms of its causes. Lee (72), Waddle (123), and Norsworthy and Whitley (98) ascribe the different plays of different ages to "instincts." Blanchard (10) and Gulick (50) maintain that the child's play interests depend upon chronological age, physiological age, mental age and environmental situations. Lehman and Wilkerson (78) report that chronological age is more powerful than mental age in determining the child's play

SOURCE. Reprinted from the *Psychological Bulletin*, 1934, **31**, 47–66, with the permission of the author and the American Psychological Association.

behavior. Reaney (104) has subdivided the play of the childhood years into four different periods, based upon chronological age. Many investigators have stressed the fact that the transition from one form of play to another is gradual and often barely perceptible. Curtis (32), Lee (72), and Lehman and Witty (80) point out that the different play periods are not separated by distinct dividing lines.

In the classification of play, the following stages of development have been arbitrarily used by the writer: (1) Babyhood (birth to three years); (2) Childhood (three to six years); (3) Youth (six to eleven or twelve years); (4) Adolescence (eleven or twelve to twenty-one years).

1. Babyhood Play (Birth to Three Years)

For the sake of simplification, the studies summarized here will be classified under different topic heads.

a. TYPES OF PLAY

During the first year the baby, in experimenting with the different sense organs, derives great satisfaction from their stimulation. Major (92) points out that the desire for sensations leads to the baby's earliest play. Fenton (36) has given a month to month summary of the characteristic play at each month level. Freeman (39) divides early babyhood play into three classes. Waddle (123) emphasizes the fact that the play of babyhood is characterized by sensory and motor experimentation. Stern (115) states that to the age of three months, the baby plays almost exclusively with his own limbs; after that age, he begins to play with objects. Norsworthy and Whitley (98) point out that at first the large muscles play a dominant role in the spontaneous play of the baby, while later, the smaller muscles are called into activity. Shirley (111) has divided babyhod play into different levels, each level determined by the motor development.

Appleton (5), Arlitt (6), Bowen and Mitchell (18), Gulick (50), Johnson (66), Lee (72), Wood (128) and others all point out that early babyhood play is simple and subject to constant repetition. From about the age of eighteen months, the play of the baby is largely imitative of the activities he observes in his immediate environment. Furfey (42) and Guillet (48) point out that the rudimentary beginning of dramatic play shows itself during the second year of life.

Norms of play behavior for the babyhood years have been given by Gesell (44) and tests for early play activities have been outlined by him.

b. PLAY MATERIALS

Long and fairly complete lists of toys that appeal to the baby have been given by Arlitt (7), Boehm (14), Heinig (55), Johnson (67), Meek (95), Pyle (103) and others. Ten three-years-olds, observed by Bridges (19) showed a distinct preference for cylinders to be fitted into holes. The favored toys for a group of two-three-year-olds were found by Bott (16) to be mechanical toys.

c. TIME SPENT IN PLAY

There are few studies where an actual record has been made of the duration of the baby's play. Bridges (19) found that the longest median time three-year-olds would give to any one play activity was 15 minutes. The following percentages of time were given by Bott (16) for the play of three-year-olds; raw materials, 29 per cent; locomotor, 25.3 per cent; pattern, 23.2 per cent; and mechanical, 22.5 per cent. Observations by Herring and Koch (57) of 80 babies showed that the interest span increased with age.

d. SOCIAL PARTICIPATION

Lee (72) has pointed out that at an early age the baby shows slight preference for the father as a playmate. Waddle (123) states that play of babyhood is selfish, self-centered and individualistic while Kirkpatrick (71) has stressed the fact that any attempt to direct the baby's play according to set rules will be resented. Bühler's (22 and 23) observations have shown that by the age of nine months, the baby shows real signs of desiring the play companionship of others. Two months later he begins organized coöperative play activities.

Blatz and Bott (11) have found that the two-year-old is solitary in his play while the three-year-old plays with older children and shows the rudiments of team play. Parten (101) found that at two and one-half years there was more solitary play than at any other age level, while the most common form of social participation was parallel play. Salusky (105) has reported the number of children associated in a "collective" to be 2–3 in 67 per cent of the cases, 4–5 in 18 per cent, 6–7 in 9 per cent, and 8–10 in only 6 per cent. Hagman (52) found that there was no definite preference for playmates of the same or of the opposite sex.

2. Childhood Play (Three to Six Years)

The play of childhood, while carrying over some of the characteristic elements of babyhood play, is nevertheless more highly developed and more complex.

a. TYPES OF PLAY

According to Arlitt (6) the child who at three can enjoy an activity as an end in itself, at five finds the end result distinctly more important than the activity. In childhood, Hollingworth (59) explains, "play activities pass from the auto-playful stage, through narcissistic, home, and finally hetero-type interests." Kirkpatrick (71) describes the child's activities as simple, free and imaginative. The transitional aspect of childhood play is brought out by Waddle (123) in the statement that "there is in fact no sudden break, but rather an evolutionary change from period to period."

According to Arlitt (7) "imaginative play reaches its height in the kindergarten and primary grades." Kirkpatrick (71) states that nearly all childhood play is colored by the use of the imagination. Lee (72) explains the dramatic play of children as due to the "impulse to understand their world." Shallit (109) found that dramatic play relating to living conditions, animals and family relationships were most frequent among four-year-olds, while activities involving boats, cars and trains were least frequent.

Imitation of people he admires is common in boys' play according to Angell (4). Children will, Crawford and Menninger (30) have observed, imitate "not only the souls of other people and of animals, but of inanimate objects as well." After the age of three, Forbush (37) has discovered the child adapts the act of the adult to some play idea of his own. Imitating such matter-of-fact actions as going to the store, family life, etc., are very popular, Tanner (117) found, with both boys and girls. Imitation of animals has been observed by Palmer (100) to be common among children.

Play involving skilled movements of the muscles is very popular during childhood. According to Gulick (50) the child "loves to do simple things such as run or jump or climb." By the third or fourth year, Palmer (100) found that children enjoy testing their powers of muscular control in such acts as walking on the edge of curbstones, hopping on one foot, etc. Stern (115) has stated that "even swimming and skating can be managed very happily by many a five-year-old."

Interest in construction is an important element in the play of a child. In the fifth and sixth years, according to Freeman (39), "play with objects develops into simple kinds of construction." Wood (128) points out that the most popular game of childhood is "the ancient and glorious game of mudpies." Hulson's (63) observations showed that the chief activity with blocks was building.

Children begin to collect certain things, such as ribbons, cigar bands, etc., and take pride in the number they are able to accumulate. Hall (53) finds that the "collection of miscellaneous trivial things . . . begins at about three or four years of age and lasts to about seven or eight years." Burk (24) agrees with Hall that collecting begins around the age of three and until eight, it is "crude, groping, undirected."

b. PLAY MATERIALS

Bott (16) found that in three-four-year olds, raw materials such as sand and blocks ranked first as favored toys. For both boys and girls of the four-year level, making simple patterns with colored crayons proved to be the most popular play material, according to Bridges (20). Doll play has been carefully studied by Hall (53). Dolls representing children are favored by the five-year-old, while adult dolls increase in popularity with increase in age. Farwell (35) found that for both sexes, there was a moderate interest in drawing, cardboard and paper construction materials. Hulson (62) has reported that blocks and sand are the favored materials while dolls, blackboards and animals were the least popular with four-year-olds.

The importance of toys, as an accompaniment of dramatic play, has been stressed by Tanner (117) and Crawford and Menninger (30). Forbush (37) believes that "interest in common objects and toys culminates at the close of this period." Benjamin (9) has reported that a girl doll proved to be the favorite toy of girls while an automobile, airplane and cowboy were more often chosen by the boys. Bühler (21) states that after the age of four, the child uses his play materials specifically to make something out of them, in contrast to mere manipulation which is characteristic of earlier years. Hetzer (58) found that below the age of two, construction was merely "unspecific manipulation," while after the age of two, the construction was first in the form of "specific manipulation," and then in the form of "meaningful manipulation." Van Alstyne (120) found that at the ages of two–six years, blocks, clay and doll corner were the most interesting toys.

c. TIME SPENT IN PLAY

Bridges (20), in the case of four-year-olds, found that the median time spent in play with a toy was 6.2 minutes. Farwell (35) found that 31.3 per cent of the 271 children studied, worked with one constructive play material from 50 to 100 per cent of the total working time. Shallit (109) reports that the average length of time spent in dramatic play was 7 minutes. According to Van Alstyne (120), the average attention span for the 8 most popular play materials was 7.0 minutes for the two-year-olds; 8.9 minutes for the three-year-olds; 12.3 minutes for the four-year-olds and 13.6 minutes for the five-year-olds.

d. SOCIAL PARTICIPATION

The child's craving for companionship has been stressed by a number of writers. Crawford and Menninger (30) hold that "after the first few awkward attempts at social play, merely the presence of a little visitor constitutes a sort of game." According to Heinig (55), at "about the age of four, interest in coöperative play becomes paramount." Waddle (123) states that "pleasure in companionship increases, but individual desires dominate."

Much attention has been given to the social organization involved in childhood play. According to Appleton (5), childhood plays are "non-competitive." Blanchard (10) shows that the play of this age consists primarily of unorganized, individualistic play. Bott (16) found that talking and interference were the most common activities while coöperation with other children was least common. Lack of sportsmanship was found by Bush and Rigby (25) to be a common characteristic of childhood play.

In early childhood, Crawford and Menninger (30) have found play to be individualistic. According to Gulick (51) children under seven years of age "care little for the organized games." From two and one-half to four years, Parten (101) found a decided decline in the importance of solitary play, a decrease in parallel play groups and an increase in associative group play.

Salusky (105) has reported that between the ages of two years three months and four years, 40 per cent of the children take part in play groups consisting of 4 or 5 children, 29 per cent in groups of 2 or 3 children, and in large groups of 11 to 20 children, only 5 per cent. Verry (121) has noted 5 distinct social attitudes in the play of preschool children.

The child's choice of play companions has received only a slight amount of attention. Similarity in M.A., I.Q., height, extroversion, personal attractiveness and frequency of laughter were found by Callman (27) to have no influence on friendship. Sex, on the other hand, proved to be a determining factor. Unlike Callman, Chevaleva-Janovskaja (29) reports that the characteristic groups formed between three and five years of age are usually composed of both sexes and that unisexual groups are generally boys' groups. Salusky (105) found a tendency towards one-sex associations among children. Palmer (100) has stressed the fact that children not only enjoy playmates of their own ages but that several years' difference in age is a serious barrier.

Hagman's (52) study indicated that four-year-olds show a decided preference for companions of their own sex while two-year-olds do not. Van Alstyne (120) found that over 50 per cent of the children ranging in age from two to six years, whom she observed, tend to play by themselves when playing with play materials, and in only about 40 per cent of the observations was the gregarious type of grouping found.

The child's craving for play companionship is very apparent in the formation of "imaginary companions" as substitutes for real companions when no real companions exist. Theoretical studies of "imaginary playmates" have been made by Arlitt (6), Green (47), Monroe (97), Norsworthy and Whitley (98), Kirkpatrick (71), Smith (113), and Tanner (117). The most recent study of imaginary companions was a retrospective study made by Hurlock and Burstein (64).

Adelberg (2) studied the leadership of 3 children to determine which traits led to success in their ability to direct others. Blatz and Bott (11) found the beginnings of definite leadership traits in a group of four-year-old nursery school children.

e. DIFFERENTIATION IN PLAY

Much stress has been placed upon the influence of sex as a factor in determining the play of children. Arlitt (6) points out that what sex differences in play are apparent are due to training. Sex differences in play materials favored by children have been noted by Bridges (19 and 20). The favored constructive play materials for boys and girls have been studied by Farwell (35). Shallit (109) reports that the only real sex difference in the dramatic play of four-year-olds was in the case of boats, cars and trains.

Lee (72) explains the sex difference in play interests in soldiers and dolls as due to an "innate basis." Stern (115) notes a sex difference in constructive games. Waddle (123) contends that up to the age of school life, there are no sex differences in play. Van Alstyne (120) found that similarities in the play of girls and boys in childhood are greater than differences.

Gesell and Lord (45) found that children from good neighborhoods stood far above those from poor neighborhoods in initiative and spontaneity in play. Salusky (105) has shown that the games of children from children's homes are reproductions of the life situations of the home, while in the case of peasant children, the games represent family life and the activities of domestic animals.

3. Play of Youth (Six to Twelve or Thirteen Years)

The transitional aspect of the play of youth has been stressed by a number of writers, as Forbush (37), Pyle (103), Hollingworth (59), Tanner (117), and Waddle (123). Gulick (50) and Hall (54) have pointed out that there are two outstanding characteristics of the play of youth: (1) a gradual increase in the number of team games engaged in, and (2) strenuous outdoor play is favored above all others, especially among boys.

a. TYPES OF PLAY

The great variety of play activities characteristic of youth has been pointed out by Lehman and Michie (77). The characteristic play activities for boys and girls of the ages eight to eleven years have been investigated by Lehman and Witty (90). Lists of play activities, together with the frequency of occurrence at each age, have been given by them.

Imaginative play is pronounced during the early part of youth. Furfey (42) found that 67 per cent of a group of eight-year-old boys studied by him indulged in this sort of play. According to Lee (72), imaginative play becomes more creative in form, which shows itself in such activities as drawing and construction. Pyle (103) has found that there is a "gradual decadence of make-believe play." Dramatic play of youth, Johnson (66) has pointed out, is not so spontaneous as before, but simple actions are woven together to form a plot. Doll play has been investigated by Ellis and Hall (34) and was found to be most popular between the ages of seven and ten, with a climax between eight and nine.

The youth's interest in pets has been studied by Lehman (75). Boys showed a marked preference for playing with dogs rather than with kittens. The same preference was shown by girls, only in not so marked a manner.

Collecting is very popular during early youth, especially among boys. Burk (24) found this interest to be most pronounced from the ages of eight to eleven years. The most favored objects collected by boys were cigar tags, stamps, birds' eggs and marbles, while in the case of girls, stamps, shells, picture cards and cigar tags were the first choices. Hall (53) found the favored objects of collection to be similar to those listed by Burk. According to Lee (72) "this is the age of hoarding perfectly useless and dilapidated things." Lehman and Witty (89) found that collecting as a play activity comes to a climax at ten years of age. Whitley (126), on the other hand, finds interest in collecting at its greatest intensity from nine to thirteen years. Durost (33) found that collecting is not related to chronological age but is positively related to mental age.

Johnson (66) has found that the "constructive play of this period will be manifested in large, crude work as in the building of huts, tents, playhouses, etc." Guessing games and games of chance, Hollingworth (59) has pointed out, "become prominent at this stage." At the age of seven or eight, Kirkpatrick (71) has found, games and riddles appeal strongly.

Physical skills, involved in running, jumping, vaulting, etc., are developed at the same time as the mental skills.

Competitive play becomes very popular during youth. After the eighth year, Croswell (31) found that play with a strong element of competition predominates. "Games of low organization," such as the running and chasing, come into popularity at about six years of age, Furfey (42) found, an increase in complexity of form and organization with increase in age. Henderson (56) states that from seven to eleven, games are almost exclusively competitive in character. Games of skill become "almost wholly social games of contest" in the latter part of youth, Palmer (100) contends.

The types of games popular during youth have been investigated by Angell (4), Blanchard (10), Foster (38), and Johnson (66).

Terman and Lima (118) have given a detailed description of the type of reading that appeals to boys and girls at each year of the youth period. Interest in reading, Additon (1) found, is the paramount play interest of girls during this age.

What the youth reads when given a free choice was investigated by Jordon (68). Interest in reading the Sunday "Funny Paper" has been investigated by Lehman and Witty (87). Lippert (91) investigated the reading matter that appeals to girls of the pre-puberty years. Schlotte (106) found that a "rage" for reading develops at the eleven to twelve year period.

Attending moving pictures has been studied on a large scale by Mitchell (96). Lehman and Witty (86) found that 80 per cent of boys and girls between the ages of ten and one-half and fifteen and one-half years of age attended moving pictures.

b. PLAY MATERIALS

Unlike childhood, youth is an age when there is little need for play materials. Ellis and Hall (34) found that adult dolls were preferred to dolls representing children or babies by both boys and girls between the ages of six and twelve years. Interest in making doll clothes does not appear until between seven and nine years.

Interest in pets has been studied by Burk (24). The interest shown in dogs by boys and girls increases rapidly from seven to fourteen years, when it culminates. Girls appear to be more interested in cats than boys and this interest culminates at eleven.

c. SOCIAL PARTICIPATION

Many studies of the social participation in the play life of youth have been made. Among the most famous are the studies by Thrasher (119), Furfey (41), and Puffer (102). Puffer (102), Hall (54), Waddle (123), Lee

(72), and Furfey (41) agree that the "gang" tendency begins around the age of ten and reaches a climax between twelve and fourteen years. The "plays of the eleven-year-old are," Hollingworth (59) finds, "strongly social in the sense that they involve many players."

The play activities of the "gang," Puffer (102) discovered, include games, athletics, card games, etc. Interest in team games and readiness to join gang activities are, according to Furfey (41), characteristics of the play of youth. The activities of gangs, Block (12) found, are ruled by a "mob spirit" which often leads to vandalism and hoodlumism.

Almack (3) found a tendency to select as companions those of like C.A. and M.A. Blanchard (10) explains the similarity of intellectual level in groups of play companions on the grounds that dull children cannot "keep up" with gang activities while gifted children are bored with them. Furfey (40) discovered that contiguity in school or in the neighborhood, was the most important factor in the formation of play companionships. Being a "good sport" and living in the neighborhood, Puffer (102) found to be the two essentials to membership in gangs.

M.A. is responsible, according to Warner (124), for bringing about the grouping of boys into gangs. Wellman (125) found that among girls, chums were most alike in scholarship. In the case of boys, height, C.A. and I.Q. were most similar.

Puffer (102) has listed the following leadership qualities: age, size, skill in play, good fighter, desire to lead, etc. Block (12) holds that ability to "scrap" together with fairmindedness in disputes, is the essential quality of a gang leader. Age and intelligence, Warner (124) found, above that of the other members of the group, are essential in leadership. Caldwell and Wellman (26) hold that the outstanding characteristics of leaders vary with the types of activity engaged in.

d. DIFFERENTIATION IN PLAY ACTIVITIES

The factors influencing the play of youth are:

1. *Sex.* Hall (53) found that 76 per cent of boys and 99 per cent of girls play with dolls. The play of girls is less strenuous than that of boys. This, Hollingworth (59) explains, is due to "social pressure." Croswell (31) has pointed out that boys are less affected by convention in their selection of play interests than are girls, while girls have a larger repertory of play activities. McGhee (94) has stressed the fact that boys have more definite play preferences than girls, while girls engage in a large variety of play activities. Curtis (32) holds that girls do not have the same interest as boys in competitive play, and they are slower in developing the coördinations necessary for most games.

Lehman and Witty (90) found that in the play activities of girls, only 16 of those most often participated in required mechanical ability and motor skill, while in the case of boys, 37 required such abilities. Sex differences in collecting interests were reported by Lehman and Witty (89) for nine, ten and eleven year groups. Only slight sex differences were found by Lehman and Witty (87) in the interest youth displays in looking at the Sunday "Funny Paper." From five and one-half to eight and one-half years of age, Lehman and Witty (90) state that "there is a conspicuous tendency for boys to engage more frequently in extremely active plays and games." In their study of reacting interests, Terman and Lima (118) found that in the case of boys, interest in stories of adventure and mystery was predominant, while girls' first interests were in stories of home and school life.

2. *Intelligence.* How intelligence influences the range of play interests has been investigated by Lehman and Michie (77). In a similar study, Lehman and Witty (81) found that gifted children were solitary in their play and tended to avoid vigorous physical play. How school progress influences social play was also investigated by Lehman and Witty (82). Studies by Shambaugh (108) have revealed that gifted children must have a good understanding of the game to get real satisfaction from it.

Terman and Lima (118) found that gifted boys preferred books dealing with science, history, travel and folk lore while boys of average intelligence preferred adventure and mystery stories. Huber (61) found that dull children preferred the humorous and "familiar experience" type of reading while bright children were more influenced by the literary quality of the reading material and less by its content.

3. *Race.* The play of Negro children, Lehman and Witty (88 and 90) found, is distinctly more social than that of white children at every age from eight and one-half to fifteen and one-half. They also found (83) that Negro children play school more frequently than white children. Scruggs (107) found that to the majority of Negro children, Bible stories were more interesting than any other type. Lehman (74) found that Negro children play more with jacks and marbles than do white children, while in an investigation made by him in collaboration with Witty (83), he reports that Negro children play school more frequently than do white children. Smith (112) made a comparison of the play of Japanese boys with that of American boys.

4. *Environment.* Bobbett (13) has shown that rural boys of the ages of eight to ten indulge in fewer forms of play than do city boys of the same age while the opposite is true for older boys. Chase (28) found that the most popular games of the tenement districts in New York City were those that required little space. Lehman (74) discovered that in a univer-

sity town more football, basketball and marbles were played than in other types studied by him, and (76) that country children attend moving pictures less than town children. In a study by Witty and Lehman (127) it was found that rural children collect many more objects than do city children.

4. Play of Adolescence (Twelve or Thirteen to Twenty-One Years)

Although adolescence is one of the most interesting as well as one of the most vitally important periods of development, fewer scientific studies have been made of the play of this period than any of the others preceding it.

a. TYPES OF PLAY

The most important form of play of adolescence is group play, in the form of games and athletic contests, where strict rules and regulations control the entire play activity. Furfey (42) stresses this love of group play when he states that "whereas a couple of years ago he was satisfied with relatively informal games, he now gives his allegiance to the standard team games." Hollingworth (59) states that "although individual competition is still strong, socialization appears even more markedly than in the plays of the 'Big Injun' age." Furfey (41) found that with the onset of puberty, gang play gives way to organized athletics.

Lehman and Witty (79) found that after the age of nine and one-half years, there was a rapid decline in the percentage of girls of each age group who played with dolls, the most rapid decline coming between eleven and one-half and thirteen and one-half years. Baldwin (8) reported similar results while Hall (53) found that the only interest in dolls which survived puberty was interest in children or baby dolls.

A number of studies have been made of the types of play that lose their interest for the adolescent. Furfey (41 and 42) found that after fourteen, there was a marked decrease in interest in gang play and scouting, and (43) that activities which were predominantly manipulative, dramatic or individualistic were subject to a sudden loss of interest. Lehman and Witty (79) similarly found that the onset of adolescence was accompanied by a waning of interest in youthful activities. Monroe (97) has reported a decline in interest in marbles and hide-and-seek after the age of twelve. McGhee (94) indicates a decline in interest in doll play, make-believe and imitative play. Hall (53) found that from fourteen on, there is a distinct decline in imitative games while dramatic play, if it survives at all, is modified into the vaudeville type. Likewise, collecting wanes in interest.

Wood (128) agrees with Hall, but stresses the fact that it is more pronounced in boys than in girls.

Terman and Lima (118) found that at eleven years, reading interests are very similar to those of the period of youth, but that by twelve, the "climax of the reading craze," there is a pronounced interest in any kind of book, especially those that cater to the "hero-worship" tendency. From fifteen on, less time is given to reading, because of the pressure of school work. Jordon (69) analyzed the reading interests of high school pupils and found a marked increase in adult fiction, towards late adolescence, and a marked decrease in interest in juvenile fiction. Orr and Brown (99) investigated the out-of-school activities of high school students and discovered that 88 per cent of them read books other than those connected with their school assignments. Johnson (66) believes that the reading interest, characteristic of youth, culminates at about the age of thirteen.

Participation in fortune-telling activities was found by Lehman and Witty (84) to be especially popular from the age of twelve and one-half through fourteen and one-half.

Orr and Brown (99) found that in the case of high school girls studied by them, 39 per cent attended theaters or movies as much as once a week. Hollingworth (59) reports that boys attend more than girls. Sullenger (116) investigated the moving picture preferences of 3,295 high school students.

The "favored" plays of adolescence have been investigated by a number of writers. Notably, Monroe (97), Additon (1), Lehman and Witty (90) and McGhee (94).

b. SOCIAL ORGANIZATION OF PLAY

Typically, the adolescent chooses as his play companions individuals of his own age or older, and he develops a marked snobbishness towards his associates.

As this age, according to L. S. Hollingworth (60), tastes in friendship are well established. According to Bonser (15) about 75 per cent of the boys and girls choose their companions from those considerably older or younger than they. Furfey (42) found that the companionship of older boys was more satisfying than that of boys who had formerly been their chums.

Bowden (17) investigated the importance of physical characteristics in leadership and found them to be the least important of all characteristics. The relationship between leadership and college grades was found by Sheldon (110) to be 0.19 and between leadership and intelligence test scores, 0.06. McCuen (93) found that the average of the leaders' scores on intelligence tests was only 3 points above the average of all the scores.

c. DIFFERENTIATION IN PLAY ACTIVITIES

The influence of the sex on adolescent play has received more attention than any other one factor. Hollingworth (59) points out that during adolescence, "there is also a tendency for boys to organize games and enterprises at which girls will be spectators." In adolescence, Freeman (39) holds, boys are conscious of the approval and favor of the girls who are spectators of their combats. In the case of adolescent girls, Wood (128) has found that there is a loss of interest in active games and an awakening of interest in nature and animals.

Sex differences in reading interests have been pointed out by Jordon (68 and 69) and Lehman and Witty (90). Sex differences in reading books, "just for fun," were studied by Lehman and Witty (85). A sex difference in favor of the boys was found by Hollingworth (59) to exist in attendance at moving pictures. Sullenger (116) likewise found sex differences in moving picture preferences.

Terman and Lima (118) have reported that boys and girls in rural and industrial communities read less than those of well-to-do urban communities.

A striking racial difference in writing poetry, " just for fun," was discovered by Lehman and Witty (85) in the case of white and negro adolescents.

Bibliography

1. Additon, H., And What of Leisure? *J. of Soc. Hygiene,* 1930, **16**, 321–334.

2. Adelberg, H., Führertum in Kindergarten. *Zsch. J. Päd. Psychol.,* 1930, **31**, 144–157, 200–203.

3. Almack, J. C., The Influence of Intelligence on the Selection of Associates. *Sch. and Soc.,* 1922, **16**, 529–530.

4. Angell, E. D., *Play.* Boston: Little, Brown and Co., 1910, pp. 100.

5. Appleton, L. E., *A Comparative Study of the Play Activities of Adult Savages and Civilized Children.* Chicago: U. of Chicago Press, 1910, pp. **34**.

6. Arlitt, A. H., *Psychology of Infancy and Early Childhood.* New York: McGraw-Hill Book Co., 1928, pp. 66–70.

7. Arlitt, A. H., *The Child from One to Six.* New York: McGraw-Hill Book Co., 1930, pp. 157–173.

8. Baldwin, B. T., Child Development. *Canadian Nurse,* 1929, **25**, 607–611.

9. Benjamin, H., Age and Sex Differences in the Toy Preferences of Young Children. *Ped. Sem. and J. Genet. Psych.,* 1932, **41**, 417–429.

10. Blanchard, P., *The Child and Society*. New York: Longmans, Green and Co., 1928, Chapter V.

11. Blatz, W. E., and Bott, H., *Parents and the Pre-School Child*. New York: William Morrow and Co., 1929, pp. 128–136.

12. Block, S., *A Psychological Study of Gangs*. Unpublished Master's Essay, Columbia University Library, New York City, 1910, pp. 60.

13. Bobbett, F., *Curriculum Investigations*. 1926, No.31, pp. 150–180.

14. Boehm, E. L., Choosing Play Things. *Child Study*, 1927, **5**, pp. 7–9 and 16.

15. Bonser, F. G., Chums: A Study in Youthful Friendships. *Ped. Sem.*, 1902, **9**, 221–236.

16. Bott, H., Observations of Play Activities in a Nursery School. *Gen. Psych. Monog.*, 1928, No. 4, pp. 44–48.

17. Bowden, A. O., A Study of the Personality of Student Leaders in Colleges in the United States. *J. Abn. and Soc. Psych.*, 1926–1927, **21**, 149–160.

18. Bowen, W. P., and Mitchell, E. D., *The Theory of Organized Play*. New York: A. S. Barnes and Co., 1923, pp. 246–257.

19. Bridges, K. M. B., Occupational Interests of Three-Year-Old Children. *Ped. Sem. and J. Genet. Psych.*, 1927, **34**, 415–423.

20. Bridges, K. M. B., The Occupational Interests and Attention of Four-Year-Old Children. *Ped Sem. and J. of Genet. Psych.*, 1929, **36**, 551–570.

21. Bühler, C., The Child and Its Activity with Practical Material. *Brit. J. Educ. Psych.*, 1933, **3**, 27–41.

22. Bühler, C., The First Social Behavior Patterns of the Child. *Quel. U. Stud.*, 2 Jugkd., 1927, Heft 5, 1–102. (*Child Dev. Abst.*, 1928, Vol. 2, No. 5, p. 379.)

23. Bühler, C., *The First Year of Life*. New York: The John Day Co., 1930, p. 281.

24. Burk, C. F., The Collecting Instinct. *Ped. Sem.*, 1900, **7**, 179–207

25. Bush, R. B., and Rigby, M., The Play Hour. *Psych. Clinic.*, 1929–1930, **18**, 44–51.

26. Caldwell, O. W., and Wellman, B., Characteristics of School Leaders. *J. Educ. Research*, 1926, **14**, 1–13.

27. Callman, R. C., Factors Influencing Friendships Among Pre-School Children. *Child. Devel.*, 1932, **3**, 146–158.

28. Chase, J. H., Street Games of New York City. *Ped. Sem.*, 1905, **12**, 503–504.

29. Chevaleva-Janovskaja, E., Les Groupements Spontanes d'enfants à l'age Pre-Scholaires. *Archiv. de Psychol.*, 1927, **20**, 219–223.

30. Crawford, N. A., and Menninger, K. A., *The Healthy Minded Child*. New York: Coward-McCann, Inc., 1930, pp. 148–167.

31. Croswell, T. R., Amusements of Worcester School Children. *Ped. Sem.*, 1898, **6**, 314–371.

32. Curtis, H. S., *Education Through Play*. New York: The Macmillan Co., 1915, Chapter I.

33. Durost, W. N., Children's Collecting Activity Related to Social Factors. *Teach. Coll. Cont. Educ.*, 1932, No. 535, pp. 115.

34. Ellis, A. C., and Hall, G. S., A Study of Dolls. *Ped. Sem.*, 1896, 4, 129–175.

35. Farwell, L., Reactions of Kindergarten, First and Second Grade Children to Constructive Play Materials. *Gen. Psych. Monog.*, 1930, 8, No. 5 and No. 6.

36. Fenton, J. C., *A Practical Psychology of Babyhood*. New York: Houghton Mifflin Co., 1925, Chapter II.

37. Forbush, W. B., *Manual of Play*. Philadelphia: George W. Jacobs & Co., 1914, Chapter IV.

38. Foster, J. C., Play Activities of Children in the First Six Grades. *Child Development*, 1930, 1, 248–254.

39. Freeman, F. N., *How Children Learn*. Boston: Houghton Mifflin Co., 1917, pp. 56–77.

40. Furfey, P. H., Some Factors Influencing the Selection of Boys' Chums. *J. App. Psych.*, 1927, 11, 47–51.

41. Furfey, P. H., *The Gang Age*. New York: Macmillan Co., 1926, pp. 99–100, 112.

42. Furfey, P. H., *The Growing Boy*. New York: Macmillan Co., 1930, p. 188.

43. Furfey, P. H., Pubescence and Play Behavior. *Am. Jour. Psych.*, 1929, 41, 109–111.

44. Gesell, A., *The Mental Growth of the Pre-School Child*. New York: The Macmillan Co., 1925, pp. 147–155.

45. Gesell, A., and Lord, E. E., A Psychological Comparison of Nursery School Children from Homes of Low and High Economic Status. *J. Genet. Psych.*, 1927, 34, 339–356.

46. Goldberg, B., and Pressey, Q. C., How Do Children Spend Their Time? *Elem. Sch. J.*, 1928, 29, 273–276.

47. Green, G. H., *Psychoanalysis in the Classroom*. London: Univ. of London Press, Ltd., 1921, Chapter IV.

48. Guillet, C., Recapitulation and Education. *Ped. Sem.*, 1900, 7, 397–445.

49. Gulick, E., Some Psychical Aspects of Physical Exercise. *Pop. Sci. Monthly*, 1898, 52, 793–808.

50. Gulick, L. H., *A Philosophy of Play*. New York: Chas. Scribner's Sons, 1920, pp. 83–98, 141–154.

51. Gulick, L. H., Psychological, Pedagogical, and Religious Aspects of Group Games. *Ped. Sem.*, 1898, 6, 135–151.

52. Hagman, E. P., The Companionships of Pre-School Children. *Univ. Iowa Studies; Stud. Child Welfare*, 1933, 7, No. 4, pp. 69.

53. Hall, G. S., and Some of his Pupils, *Aspects of Child Life and Education.* New York: D. Appleton & Co., 1921. Chapters on "The Story of a Sand Pile," "A Study of Dolls," and "The Collecting Instinct."

54. Hall, G. S., *Youth, Its Education, Regimen, and Hygiene.* New York: D. Appleton and Co., 1907, Chapter VI.

55. Heinig, C., Play and Play Material. *Recreation,* 1931, 25, 18–19, 50.

56. Henderson, E. N., *A Text Book on the Principle of Education.* New York: The Macmillan Co., 1915, pp. 383–426.

57. Herring, A., and Koch, H. L., A Study of Some Factors Influencing the Interest Span of Pre-School Children. *Ped. Sem. and J. Genet. Psych.,* 1930, 38, 249–279.

58. Hetzer, H., Kind and Schaffen: Experimente über Konstructive Betätigungen im Kleinkindalters. *Quellen und Studien zur Jugendkunde,* 1931, V. 7; or Jena: Fischer, 1931, pp. 108.

59. Hollingworth, H. L., *Mental Growth and Decline,* New York: D. Appleton & Co., 1927, pp. 129, 179, 200, 210, 245, 300, 355.

60. Hollingworth, L. S., *The Psychology of the Adolescent.* New York: D. Appleton & Co., 1928, p. 259.

61. Huber, M. B., *The Influence of Intelligence Upon Children's Reacting Interests.* New York: Teachers College, Columbia University, 1928, pp. 40.

62. Hulson, E. L., An Analysis of the Free Play of Ten Four-Year-Old Children Through Consecutive Observations. *J. of Juv. Res.,* 1930, 14, 188–208.

63. Hulson, E. L., Block Constructions of Four-Year-Old Children. *J. of Juv. Res.,* 1930, 14, 209–222.

64. Hurlock, E. B., and Burstein, M., The Imaginary Playmate: A Questionnaire Study. *J. Genet. Psych.,* 1932, 41, 380–392.

65. Johnson, G. E., *Education Through Recreation.* Cleveland: The Survey Committee of the Cleveland Foundation, 1916, pp. 46–48.

66. Johnson, G. E., *Education by Plays and Games.* New York: Ginn & Co., 1907, pp. 222.

67. Johnson, H. M., *Children in the Nursery School.* New York: The John Day Company, 1928, pp. 66–80.

68. Jordon, A. M., Children's Interests in Books and Magazines. *Ped. Sem., and J. of Genet. Psych.,* 1925, 32, 455–469.

69. Jordon, A. M., *Children's Interests in Reading.* New York: Teachers College, Columbia University, 1921, pp. 143.

70. King, I., *The Psychology of Child Development.* Chicago: Univ. of Chicago Press, 1904, Chapter XIII.

71 Kirkpatrick, E. A., *Fundamentals of Child Study.* New York: The Macmillan Co., 1922, pp. 179-185.

72. Lee, J., *Play in Education.* New York: The Macmillan Co., 1922, pp. 65–66, 84–101, 107–217, 318–433.

73. Lee, J., The Child's Leisure. *Playground*, 1931, **24**, 13–14.

74. Lehman, H. C., Community Differences in Play Behavior. *Ped. Sem. and J. of Genet. Psych.*, 1926, **33**, 477–498.

75. Lehman, H. C., The Child's Attitude Toward the Dog versus the Cat. *Ped. Sem. and J. of Genet. Psych.*, 1928, **35**, 62–72.

76. Lehman, H. C., The Play Activities of Persons of Different Ages. *Ped. Sem. and J. of Genet. Psych.*, 1926, **33**, 250–272.

77. Lehman, H. C., and Michie, O. C., Extreme Versatility versus Paucity of Play Interests. *Ped. Sem. and J. of Genet. Psych.*, 1927, **34**, 290–298.

78. Lehman, H. C., and Wilkerson, D. A., The Influence of Chronological Age versus Mental Age on Play Behavior. *Ped. Sem. and J. of Genet. Psych.*, 1928, **35**, 312–324.

79. Lehman, H. C., and Witty, P. A., A Study of Play in Relation to Pubescence. *J. of Soc. Psych.*, 1930, **1**, 510–523.

80. Lehman, H. C., and Witty, P. A., Periodicity and Growth. *J. of Applied Psych.*, 1927, **11**, 106–116.

81. Lehman, H. C., and Witty, P. A., Periodicity and Play Behavior. *J. of Educ. Psych.*, 1927, **18**, 115–118.

82. Lehman, H. C., and Witty, P. A., Play Activity and School Progress. *J. of Educ. Psych.*, 1927, **18** 318–326.

83. Lehman, H. C., and Witty, P. A., Playing School—A Compensatory Mechanism. *Psych. Rev.*, 1926, **38**, 480–485.

84. Lehman, H. C., and Witty, P. A., Sex Differences in Credulity. *J. Abn. and Soc. Psych.*, 1928–1929, **23**, 356–368.

85. Lehman, H. C., and Witty. P. A., Sex Differences in Reference to Reading Books, Just for Fun. *Education*, 1928, **48**, 602–617.

86. Lehman, H. C., and Witty, P. A., The Compensatory Function of the Movies. *J. App. Psych.*, 1927, **11**, 33–41.

87. Lehman, H. C., and Witty, P. A., The Compensatory Function of the Sunday "Funny" Paper. *J. App. Psych.*, 1927, **11**, 202–211.

88. Lehman, H. C., and Witty, P. A., The Negro Child's Index of More Social Participation. *J. App. Psych.*, 1926, **10**, 462–469.

89. Lehman, H. C., and Witty, P. A., The Present Status of the Tendency to Collect and Hoard. *Psych. Rev.*, 1927, **34**, 48–56.

90. Lehman, H. C., and Witty, P. A., *The Psychology of Play Activities*. New York: A. S. Barnes & Co., 1927, pp. 235.

91. Lippert, E., *Der Lesestoff der Mädchen in der Vorpubertät*. Erfurt: Stenger, 1931, pp. 132.

92. Major, D. R., *First Steps in Mental Growth*. New York: The Macmillan Company, 1906, pp. 136, 234–235, 236–237, 239–249.

93. McCuen, T. L., Leadership and Intelligence. *Education*, 1929, **50**, 89–95.

94. McGhee, Z., A Study in the Play Life of Some South Carolina Children. *Ped. Sem.*, 1900, **7**, 459–478.

95. Meek, L. H., Play Things for Children. *The Delineator*, 1931, **118**, 25, 73, 74.

96. Mitchell, A. M., The Movies Children Like. *Survey*, 1929, **63**, 213–216.

97. Monroe, W. S., *Play Interests of Children*. Proceedings and Addresses of the National Education Association, July, 1899, pp. 1084–1090.

98. Norsworthy, N., and Whitley, M. T., *The Psychology of Childhood*. New York: The Macmillan Co., 1933, Chapter VI.

99. Orr, A. E., and Brown, F. G., A Study of Out-of-School Activities of High School Girls. *J. Educ. Sociol.*, 1932, **5**, 266–273.

100. Palmer, L. A., *Play Life in the First Eight Years*. Boston: Ginn and Co., 1916, p. 270.

101. Parten, M. B., Social Participation Among Pre-School Children. *J. Abn. and Soc. Psych.*, 1932, **27**, No. 3, pp. 243–269.

102. Puffer, J. A., Boys' Gangs. *Ped. Sem.*, 1905, **12**, 175–212.

103. Pyle, W. H., *The Outlines of Educational Psychology*. Baltimore: Warwick and York, 1912, Chapter VIII.

104. Reaney, M. J., The Psychology of the Organized Group Game. *Br. J. Psych. Monog., Suppl.*, 1916, Vol. 4, pp. 76.

105. Salusky, A. S., Collective Behavior of Children of a Pre-School Age. *J. of Soc. Psych.*, 1930, **1**, 367–378.

106. Schlotte, D., Beobachlungen über den Buchwunsch des jugendlichen Lesers. *Päd. Psychol. Arbeit.*, 1932, **19**, 51–76.

107. Scruggs, S. D., *Reading Interests of Negro Children*. Unpublished Master's Thesis. U. of Kansas, 1925. Reported by Lehman and Witty (**90**).

108. Shambaugh, M. E., The Psychical Education of Gifted Children. *Amer. Phys. Educ. Rev.*, 1929, **34**, 522–525.

109. Shallit, R., The Dramatic Play of Ten Nursery School Children. *Child Development*, 1932, **3**, 359–362.

110. Sheldon, H. D., The Institutional Activities of American Children. *Am. J. of Psych.*, 1898, **9**, 425–448.

111. Shirley, M. M., *The First Two Years*. Minneapolis: U. of Minn. Press, 1931, pp. 227.

112. Smith, P. A., Some Phases of the Play of Japanese Boys and Men. *Ped. Sem.*, 1909, **16**, 256–267.

113. Smith, R. M., *From Infancy to Childhood*. Boston: Atlantic Monthly Press, 1925, pp. 105.

114. Stanforth, A. T., Study of Social Attitudes of a Group of High-School Boys and Girls. *Sch. and Soc.*, 1927, **26**, 723–726.

115. Stern, W., *Psychology of Early Childhood*. New York: Henry Holt and Co., 1924, pp. 95–100, 265–323.

116. Sullenger, T. E., Modern Youth and Movies. *Sch. and Soc.,* 1930, **32,** 459–461.

117. Tanner, A. E., *The Child.* New York: Rand McNally & Co., 1904, pp. 393–415.

118. Terman, A. E., and Lima, M., *Children's Reading.* New York: D. Appleton & Co., 1927, p. 363.

119. Thrasher, F. M., *The Gang.* Chicago, Ill.: The Univ. of Chicago Press, 1927, p. 571.

120. Van Alstyne, D., *Play Behavior and Choice of Play Materials of Pre-School Children.* Chicago, Ill.: Univ. of Chicago Press, 1932, p. 104.

121. Verry, E. E., *A Study of Mental and Social Attitudes in the Free Play of Pre-School Children.* M.A. Thesis, State Univ. of Iowa, 1923, (Reported by M. B. Parten (**101**)).

122. Volobuer, P., Socialny Vsaemovidnosyny on ditey Doshkilnogo Viky. *Dityachy Kollektiv, Kharkov,* 1931, 80–94. (Abstracted in the *Psychological Abstracts,* 1932, **6,** No. 4564.)

123. Waddle, C. W., *An Introduction to Child Psychology.* New York: Houghton Mifflin Co., 1918, Chapter VI.

124. Warner, M. L., Influence of Mental Level in the Formation of Boys' Gangs. *J. App. Psych.,* 1923, **7,** 224–236.

125. Wellman, B., The School Child's Choice of Companions. *J. Educ. Res.,* 1926, **14,** 126–132.

126. Whitley, M. T., Children's Interest in Collecting. *J. of Educ. Psych.,* 1929, **20,** 249–261.

127. Witty, P. A., and Lehman, H. C., Further Studies of Children's Interest in Collecting. *J. of Educ. Psych.,* 1930, **21,** 112–127.

128. Wood, W., *Children's Play.* London: Kegan Paul, Trench, Trubner & Co., Ltd., 1913, pp. 59–92.

4

Street Games of New York City

John H. Chase

Children have been asked what games they liked the best, and from these lists the most popular games have been tabulated. Such lists have been made for Brooklyn children, and for Worcester children.

The trouble with this method is that the most recent games played are apt to be recorded by children as the best, gambling games—like craps—are rarely mentioned, and finally children often record games which they enjoy, but rarely play.

Realizing these defects, and desiring to obtain an accurate list of the most popular out-door games of New York City, I followed the plan, for two years, of walking through the crowded tenement house streets and tabulating (1) the different games being played, (2) the number of children playing each, (3) the amount of seeming interest, (4) the date. The same streets were generally covered each day, but this was varied occasionally to see if different regions were doing the same thing. As a rule, with some variations, the great mass of tenement house children played the same games at the same time the city over. And the ten most popular games during the season when I could watch them, were:

I. Playing with fire—bonfires, fires in buckets, etc.

II. Craps—a gambling game with dice.

III. Marbles—always "for keeps," and a simpler game than in the country; several simple varieties.

SOURCE. Reprinted from the *Pedagogical Seminary*, 1905, **12**, 503–504, with the permission of the Journal Press.

IV. Potsie—a primitive kind of hop scotch.

V. Leap frog—over milk cans and fire pumps, as well as over boys. Commonest contest to see who can leap the farthest before clearing the obstacle. Many varieties—"head and footer," Spanish fly, etc.

VI. Jumping rope.

VII. Baseball. Probably should be nearer head of the list, but my observations did not include the summer.

VIII. Cat. It is probably also played in the summer. A short stick is pointed at one end and placed on the street. The point is tapped with a longer stick or bat. When the short stick bounds into the air it is hit down the street, and the other boy throws it back as near the starting point as possible. There are three ways of scoring, according to which variety of game is being played.

IX. Buttons. Boys throw, or slide, buttons in turn, from street curb toward a wall. The boy coming the nearest throws all the buttons up into the air. They fall in a shower and the ones which land "heads up" are his. Then the boy who came second closest throws the rest up, and keeps those that land "heads up," etc. The same game is played for other things. Cigarette pictures are played for in this way during January; pennies and almost anything flat at different seasons.

X. Tops. They are generally put in a ring, and the game is to split your opponent's top. You may have a poor top for splitting purposes and a good one for spinning.

The dates for different games are as follows:

	Oct.	Nov.	Dec.	Jan.	Feb.	Mar.	April	May
(1)	Leap frog.	Leap frog.	Potsie.	Potsie.	Snow-balling.	Cat.	Base-ball.	Base-ball.
(2)	Craps.	Craps.	Craps.	Craps.		Tops.		
(3)	Buttons.	Buttons.		Cig. Pic.				Cat.
(4)	Fire.	Fire.	Fire.	Fire.	Tops.	Mar-bles.	Mar-bles.	Mar-bles.

Conclusion

1. These ten games are unlike any lists made from the answers of children.

2. The table shows the fire instinct to be very strong.

3. The gambling instinct is very strong.

4. Three popular games are generally going on at the same time.

5. The running games such as tag, prisoner's base, etc., are replaced by cramped games such as leap frog, hop scotch, etc.

5

Play Preference and Play Behavior: A Validity Study

Brian Sutton-Smith[1]

Summary. Studies are reported which compare children's responses to the masculine and feminine items on a play inventory with ratings of the masculinity and femininity of their free play behavior. Systematic but indirect relationships are reported.

A series of studies on the relationship between children's responses to play inventories and their actual free play behavior was planned in collaboration with Vaughn J. Crandall of Fels Research Institute, Ohio.[2] Prior to the death of Dr. Crandall two initial studies were made at the Fels Day Camp during the summers of 1962 and 1963. Each study involved 50 elementary school age children equally divided as to sex and distributed throughout Grades 1 to 6. The play inventory items were derived from a list which had been shown to have discriminating power in a series of earlier studies (3, 4, 5, 6, 8, 9, 10, 11). The children were rated for their competence and participation in masculine and feminine free-

SOURCE. Reprinted from *Psychological Reports*, 1965, **16**, 65–66, Southern Universities Press, with the permission of the author and the publisher.

[1] A full report of these preliminary studies including tables is available from the American Documentation Institute, Auxiliary Publications Project, Photoduplication Service, Library of Congress, Washington 25, D.C. Remit $2.50 for photocopies or $1.75 for 35-mm. microfilm of Document No. 8111.

[2] This research was aided by a grant from U.S.P.H., MH-2238.

play activities. There were problems in establishing an adequately high degree of reliability for some of these ratings. Ratings were also available for other dimensions of free-play behavior (including dependency, aggression, passivity, and achievement) which had been used in Dr. Crandall's large scale studies of children's achievement behaviors (1).

In the first study involving a play scale composed mainly of formal games and mature items (2), there were consistent relations between girls' play preferences and their free-play participation and competence. For boys there was no such general relationship between scale responses and free-play behavior. However, sex inappropriate responses did correlate with dependency behavior toward adults, a finding consistent with those of earlier studies (5, 9). In the second study a more inclusive play scale was employed, involving many informal plays as well as games, and many more immature items (7). In addition, masculine and feminine responses were scored separately rather than combined in one score as in the first study. The results indicated what appeared to be a response set operating for both boys and girls; those who tended to make many responses to the masculine scale also tended to make responses to the feminine scale. In general, the correlates suggested that high responding girls tended to be more intelligent and more masculine in their free-play behaviors, and the high responding boys tended to be younger and more feminine in their free-play behaviors.

The tentative conclusion from these two preliminary studies was that systematic, if not direct, relationships exist between certain types of play preference and play behaviors and that play scales may be a potential diagnostic device for assessing certain types of sex role appropriateness or inappropriateness. The major result of these studies, however, was negative, insofar as they indicated that it is not possible in general to interpret a preference on a play scale as an indicator of real play participation or competence. The meaning of a response to a play scale varies according to the content of the items and to S's sex role identification.

References

1. Crandall, V. Achievement. In H. Stevens (Ed.), *Child Psychology: the sixty-second yearbook of the National Society for the Study of Education.* Chicago: Univ. of Chicago Press, 1963. Pp. 416–459.

2. Roberts, J. M., & Sutton-Smith, B. Child training and game involvement. *Ethnol.*, 1962, 1, 166–185.

3. Rosenberg, B. G., & Sutton-Smith, B. The measurement of masculinity and femininity in children. *Child Develpm.*, 1959, 30, 373–380.

4. Rosenberg, B. G., & Sutton-Smith, B. A revised conception of masculine-feminine differences in play activities. *J. Genet. Psychol.,* 1960, 96, 165–170.

5. Rosenberg, B. G., & Sutton-Smith, B., & Morgan, E. The use of the opposite sex scales as a measure of psychosexual deviancy. *J. Consult. Psychol.,* 1961, 25, 221–225.

6. Rosenberg, B. G., & Sutton-Smith, B. The measurement of masculinity and femininity in children: an extension and revalidation. *J. Genet. Psychol.,* 1963, 104, 259–264.

7. Sutton-Smith, B., & Rosenberg, B. G. *Play and game list.* Bowling Green, O.: Bowling Green State Univer., 1959. (I. B. M. Form I. T. S. 1100 A 6140)

8. Sutton-Smith, B., & Rosenberg, B. G. Manifest anxiety and game preference in children. *Child Develpm.,* 1960, 31, 515–519.

9. Sutton-Smith, B., & Rosenberg, B. G. Impulsivity and sex preference. *J. Genet. Psychol.,* 1961, 98, 187–192.

10. Sutton-Smith, B., & Rosenberg, B. G. Sixty years of historical change in the game preferences of American children. *J. Amer. Folkl.,* 1961, 74, 17–46.

11. Sutton-Smith, B., Rosenberg, B. G., & Morgan, E. Development of sex differences in play choices during preadolescence. *Child Developm.,* 1963., 34, 119–126.

Chapter **III**

Ecological Approaches

Although the empirical work of the 1920s and 1930s did away with the theory that development in children's play followed the course of racial history, practitioners continued, for the most part, with the habit of thinking about play as if it exhibited only one "language" of development. There were no foreign languages. There appears to have been no great felt inconsistency between advocating that a child learns through his play, and at the same time assuming that all children go through the same essential play sequences.

The more striking feature of the 1930s, however, was the quite pragmatic concern, apparent in the Hurlock article in the previous chapter, to know, among other things, what types of toys were most suitable at the various age levels; how long children could be left to play with different materials; what expectations could be held for social and cooperative play; what types of leadership would emerge; how sex differences would influence play; etc. While these were important early approaches to play, it needs to be stressed that like most usage of play and games, both at that time and subsequently, they were not a study of play per se, but of the use of play as a "neutral" field for the study of other matters supposed to be of greater importance.

One group of studies that appeared sporadically from the 1930s onwards and upon which we have chosen to focus this chapter were those in which some measurement was made of a relationship between the types of play material or play activity and the characteristics of the player's responses.

77

While many of these studies were of a correlational character and appeared to have the pragmatic impetus mentioned above, they did represent important first steps towards a manipulative psychology of play. A causal approach is an important complement to the descriptive approaches of the previous chapter.

Under this umbrella, for example, we might include the various studies carried out by investigators within the Lewinian tradition. Although their focus was, in general, more dynamic than ecological (concerned with motivation rather than materials), the spatialized concepts that were a part of the Lewinian system meant that many of the experiments were couched in setting terms. Thus in the famous experiment by Barker, Dembo, and Lewin on the effects of frustration on children's play (1941), frustration was induced first by letting the children play with toys and then by inserting a barrier between the children and their toys. Their subsequent play was less constructive than that which occurred before. While Barker et al. were more concerned with the dynamics of frustration and regression than with the structure of play, their study both scaled play structures in developmental order and showed their proneness to such a setting effect. Similarly, the various studies on what occurs when play is provided as a substitute satisfaction for real needs, or on what occurs when the play is interrupted by other tasks, were pioneering in their use of ecological instrumentation for the underlying dynamics. The ego-psychological orientation of Redl and Gump (mentioned later) with its emphasis on pathways, locomotion, barriers, direct versus indirect attack on opponents, etc. represents a convergence of such setting concepts and psychoanalytic ego psychology.

But to return to the 1930s and the more naive, albeit ecologically focused, work being done with kindergarten children, a typical set of findings were those of Dorothy Van Alstyne, who studied the play behavior and choice of materials of preschool children (1932). She observed the reactions of 112 preschool children to 25 play materials in free-play situations in three nursery schools, two junior kindergartens, and two kindergarten groups. Time records were kept on all children for four months, with ten hours (approximately) of observation on each child. Van Alstyne noted a rise of approximately two minutes in attention span between each age level, amounting to practically double at the fifth year over the second. For the eight most popular materials studied, she reported as follows: two year olds, 7.0 minutes attention span; three year olds, 8.8; four year olds, 12.3; and five year olds, 13.6. The length of the attention span varied from one minute to 45 minutes. In passing we should note that in some more recent work it appears that attention span may not be such a useful index of maturity as was originally thought (Lunzer, 1959).

Continuing with Van Alstyne, sex differences in the appeal made by different types of toys were as follows: Boys preferred materials, assorted blocks, dump carts, wagons, and small cars. Girls preferred materials for passive play, dolls and doll corners, crayons, scissors, clay, colored cubes, beads, wooden animals, and books. Boys chose locomotor toys, girls household materials. Blocks were most popular with boys, and household toys with girls. Both sexes were interested in clay. Ecological suggestions arising out of this study were that materials that foster conversation were dishes, hollow blocks, doll corners, wagons, parallel bars, telephones, blocks, colored cubes, balls, crayons, and clay. Materials highest in the more passive type of cooperations were clay, crayons, scissors, painting, beads, puzzles, books, and balls. Materials highest in active cooperation were wagons, dishes, hollow blocks, assorted blocks, doll corners, colored cubes, dump trucks, and parallel bars. Raw materials were more conducive to longer attention spans than other types. The attention span of clay, painting, doll corners, and blocks was almost twice as great as that for pull toys, balls, dolls, and dishes. Blocks, clay, and doll corners were outstandingly interesting at all four age levels. Over fifty percent of the children of all ages tended to play by themselves when playing with materials.

Of a similar order was the 1933 study by Mildred Parten (reproduced here) or the study by Updegraff and Herbst (1933), in which they found interesting differences between play with clay and play with blocks. For example,

When the two year olds and three year olds played with clay, they watched the play behavior of each other far more than when they played with blocks. For both groups, blocks seem to encourage more mutual activity with the use of the material but less without its use. Partners' suggestions were less accepted with blocks than with clay. Clay encouraged more imitation. . . . Behavior of a sociable and cooperative type occurred more frequently during play with clay, while non sociable and non cooperative behavior had a higher frequency during play with blocks (1933, p. 389).

There are also useful suggestions of this sort in the more recent work *Understanding Children's Play* by Hartley, Frank, and Goldensen (1953). Special note should be made of the seminal role of Lawrence K. Frank in interpreting the importance of play to several generations of parents and psychologists (1951, 1955, 1964).

Johnson's study of playgrounds (1935) represented another early attempt to arrive at an understanding of setting and play relationships. She found that in playgrounds with less equipment there was an increase in both social games and social conflicts, but with more equipment, the reverse occurred. Johnson says:

"In general it would appear that individual behavior is encouraged while social contact and undesirable behavior (teasing, quarreling, crying and hitting) are discouraged by the relatively more extensive equipment. From an immediate point of view it may be that individual endeavour can be increased and undesirable behavior decreased by introducing equipment. From a long term point of view, however, too much equipment may greatly interfere with social development" (1935, pp. 67–68).

This article is interesting because it reflects the traditional dialectic between those who have felt that modern playground equipment has stifled children's spontaneous development, and those who have claimed that without such equipment children engage only in undesirable behavior. Contrast, for example, the quotations from the following writers.

Here is a 1915 statement by Henry Curtis, one of the most important figures in the history of the American playground movement:

In nearly all of our municipal playgrounds at least nine-tenths of all the play is scrub play, which the children make up themselves on coming to it. Many of the children loaf. Play of this kind can never give the training of either body or conduct which organized play should give; for in order to develop the body it must be vigorous, to train the intellect it must be exciting, to train the social conscience it must be socially organized. None of these results come from scrub play.

Those who have shown the most continuing interest in what is here termed "scrub play" have been the folklorists, and they have an almost diametrically opposite view about it. Thus Paul Brewster in his work *American Nonsinging Games* (1953) says of organized play: "Supervised play has taken the place of the earlier spontaneous and hence more enjoyable playing and has made participation in games a mechanical performance instead of the delight which it once was and which it should be still."

Norman Douglas writes even more forcefully of scrub play:

My point . . . my only point was the inventiveness of the children . . . one marvels at the stupidity of the social reformer who desires to close to the children the world of adventure, to take them from their birthright of the streets and coop them up in well regulated and uninspiring playgrounds where under the supervision of teachers their imaginations will decline, their originality wither (1931).

The Gump and Sutton-Smith (1955) article on types of settings and their influence on activity quite explicitly states the relevance of settings as independent variables, only now the emphasis has been extended to include the standard patterns of performance that go along with the physical setting. The most extensive analysis of this sort has been carried out by Gump, Schoggen, and Redl (Barker, 1963). They contrasted the play of a single boy, Wally, in his home setting and at a camp and reported the ecological supports of many types of play. They claim that "the differences obtained were the result of environmental differences" (1963, p. 179), and illustrate this as follows:

The preponderance of watching play time at home was related to the presence of a TV set at home and none at camp. Wally watched a great deal in both situations. Much of the camp watching was directed towards conflicts between other campers or between campers and counselors. At home Wally enjoyed watching competitive encounters between other children in games and between cowboys or soldiers on TV programs. The watching time at camp was less than at home, because camp did not have the necessary behavior objects or props to support extended watching. A by-product of the extended TV watching at home was an increase of manipulative amusement at home. Wally engaged in more episodes and manipulative amusements while watching TV at home than he did during the entire day at camp. So little physical activity was invited by the nature of TV activity that Wally had apparently to develop other outlets for his energies. A number of these outlets were simply restless movements but others involved episodes of "dallying" with strings, bits of upholstery, and odd objects.

The increase in unorganized sport at camp was related to the behavior settings and props in camp which invited vigorous and pleasurable activity; the swimming area, the paths through the woods, the trees for climbing, etc. Dramatics also was related to the behavior setting, woods and to a tree hut in these woods. In the woods were hidden places for pretenses of ambush, or searching or danger in the "wilds." The tree hut also lent itself to much dramatic fantasy. Here, Wally, and his cabin mates were temporarily above the world and acted out fantasies reflective of their commanding position.

Investigation and exploration seemed also related to the availability of the woods. There were 27 such episodes in the camp woods alone; only ten in the entire home day. In the woods were a number of unknowns. What is in a hollow tree? What's that funny looking stuff on the ground? What animals or bugs are in the underbrush? Although the boys had been at camp almost four weeks, the novelty of the woods had not yet worn off; no comparative novelty seemed available in Wally's home neighborhood environment.

Construction play of the reproductive type was supported more emphatically by the camp than by the home, even though materials for such play were available at home. Camp had a craft shop; in the shop were other boys making things and adults who could help. Such a situation was more invitational to construction play than the home situation in which one had to employ initiative and be more alone if a construction project was to result.

Finally, the presence at home of considerable formal and stationary game play forms and their absence at camp seems obviously related to the customs of the children and adults, and to the play possibilities in the two environments. University Boys' Camp deliberately de-emphasized competitive activities, at the same time offering many other possibilities for fun. In Wally's neighborhood, however, traditional games were the custom and served as a major play possibility for children. There were card games at home; baseball games in the street; and carrom, checkers, and horseshoes at the park (and little else significant to do at the park) (1963, pp. 181–182).

The ecological approach of Wright, Gump, Schoggen, etc. can be supplemented by the type of psychological ecology to be found in the works of Irving Goffman (1961). In effect, Goffman carries out a further analysis of the standing patterns of behavior that go with physical settings and reveals that they are themselves game-like rule-controlled structures. One can ask how the players get into these structures, how they prevent them from breaking down, how their roles are transformed by participation, etc. Some of the implications of Goffman's approach to settings are indicated in the Sutton-Smith article on "Boundaries." Within this chapter, then, we have an attempt to understand the ecological determinants of play, beginning with single items (clay or blocks), proceeding to total activities (swimming or crafts) and then, finally, seeking understanding in terms of the rule-systems that are located in any particular physical setting. The implications of this change seem to be that the understanding of the ecological determinants of play requires analysis at a molar as well as a molecular level.

6

Social Play Among Preschool Children

Mildred B. Parten[1]

The material presented in this paper is a part of an extensive observational study of social behavior carried out on nursery school children in the Institute of Child Welfare, the University of Minnesota.[2] Two
earlier papers have dealt quantitatively with the extent of social participation and leadership in preschool groups. This article is concerned with
size of preschool groups, factors influencing the child's choice of playmates, and the social value of various activities, games, and toys.

Data on all these factors were gathered by the time sampling method
of observation. The 34 children were observed daily for one minute each
at the morning free play hour, until 60 or more behavior samples were
obtained. In addition to recording the degree of participation under six
categories: unoccupied, solitary, onlooker, parallel, associative, and organized supplementary play; and degree of leadership under five head-
ings: following, independent pursuit, following some and directing
others, sharing leadership with another, and directing alone. The writer

SOURCE. Reproduced from the *Journal of Abnormal and Social Psychology*, 1933.
28, 136–147, with the permission of the author and the American Psychological
Association.

[1] From the Institute of Child Welfare, the University of Minnesota. Rewritten from
a thesis manuscript for periodical publication by Mary Shirley.

[2] Parten, M. B. Social Participation Among Preschool Children, Jour. of Abn. & Soc.
Psych., 1932, Vol. XXVII, pp. 243–269.

Parten, M. B. Leadership Among Preschool Children. Jour. of Abn. & Soc. Psych.,
1933, Vol. XXVII, pp. 430–440.

made note of the number of children in each group, their names, and the play activity in which they were engaged.

Play Groups

SIZE

Play groups varied in size from two of fifteen children, but small groups were by far the most frequent. Groups composed of more than five children were rarely observed. The data included in Table 1 represent the number of children playing in groups of each size on the basis of percentage frequencies. All the children spent 15 per cent or more of their time in groups of two. The majority of them spent less than 25 per cent of their time in groups of three, less than 20 per cent of their time in groups of four, less than 10 per cent in groups of five, and less than 5 per cent in groups of six or larger.

Table 1

Frequency of Occurrence and Proportion of Time Spent in Play Groups of Various Sizes

Per Cent of Observations	Size of Groups						8 and over
	2	3	4	5	6	7	
0–4	0	0	0	9	24	28	34
5–9	0	0	6	13	8	6	0
10–14	0	4	8	8	2	0	0
15–19	1	9	11	3	0	0	0
20–24	9	13	9	1	0	0	0
25–29	12	6	0	0	0	0	0
30–34	8	1	0	0	0	0	0
35–39	1	1	0	0	0	0	0
40–44	3	0	0	0	0	0	0
Total number of children	34	34	34	34	34	34	34

The most popular size for play groups was two. This was true not only for the nursery school as a whole, but also for every age group except the oldest. (See Figure 1.) No very striking age differences existed in the frequencies of the children's play in groups of three and four, but the tendency to play in groups of five clearly increased with age.

In the course of the study the observer noted six different techniques used by the children to gain entrance into a play group. The most direct

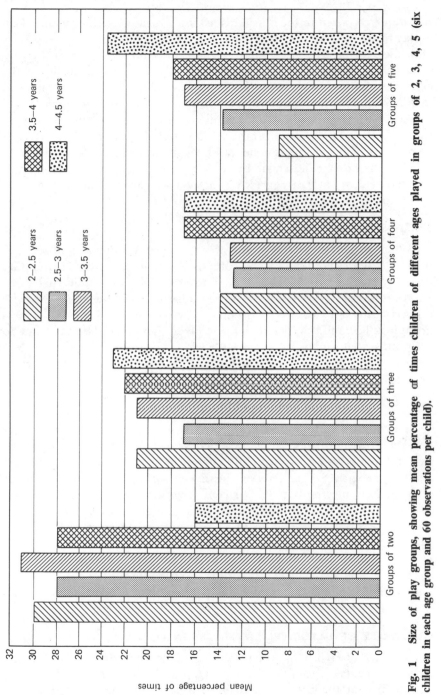

Fig. 1 Size of play groups, showing mean percentage of times children of different ages played in groups of 2, 3, 4, 5 (six children in each age group and 60 observations per child).

85

technique consisted in the outsider's asking a member of the group, "Can I play too?" Somewhat more round-about requests to join the group were addressed to the teacher, "I want a place to paint." Sometimes the outsider gained entrance into the group more subtly by commenting on the activities of some of the members, "My, but that's high. What are you making?" Again the outsider merely presumed that he was accepted and joined the play, perhaps with a comment, "Play I am aunty," or a question, "Shall I be the little brother?" Occasionally the child formed his own group by displaying toys he had brought from home or by assigning rôles to the other children or by inviting others to play, "This chair is for Harriet." The least aggressive method of gaining entrance was by invitation from the group, "Paul, come play with us."

SEX COMPOSITION OF GROUPS

When the 781 two-child groups were analyzed on the basis of sex, 530 or 68 per cent were found to be composed of one sex only. This finding agrees well with that of Chevaleva-Janovskaja, (4) who found that 67.37 per cent of the groups studied were unisexual. Challman (3) likewise reports a marked cleavage in friendship on the basis of sex; out of 718 groupings he found 67 per cent to be of one sex only. The tendency to form unisexual groups increased with age from 61.5 per cent at the two-year level to 79 per cent at the age of four-and-a-half; Even at the earliest ages boys played more often with boys and girls with girls.

SEX OF FAVORITE PLAYMATES

The number of times each child was observed playing with every other child, regardless of the size of the play group, was computed. Thus the five children with whom each child played most frequently were selected. Among the girls 81 per cent of the five favorite playmates were other girls; and among the boys 62 per cent were other boys. The single best playmate for each child was selected from the group of five. Out of the 34 pairs of children thus obtained, 27 were unisexual. Every girl's favorite playmate was another girl; and 12 of the 19 boys had favorites of their own sex. All of the 7 boys who preferred the companionship of a girl were under the median age of the nursery school group; and two of them had as their best playmate an older sister who had been in the school longer and who more or less took charge of the newcomer.

SIMILARITY OF FAVORITE PLAYMATES IN I.Q. AND AGE

The I.Q. of favorite playmates showed little similarity. The differences between friends ranged from 2 to 40 I.Q. points with a mean difference of 19.1 points for the girl pairs, and of 12.9 points for boy pairs. These results are in agreement with Wellman's (6) discovery that boy playmates are more similar in I.Q. than girl playmates. They also are in harmony with Challman's finding that similarity in mental age has little influence on the strength of preschool children's friendships.

In age the playmate pairs differed from 0 to 18 months; but the median age difference was less than 3 months. The average difference for girls was 4.1 months, and for boys 3.5 months. Both Wellman and Challman found similar tendencies for boy chums to be more closely alike in age than girl chums.

The influence of older or younger siblings in the homes showed itself in the children's choice of playmates. Children who had younger brothers or sisters at home averaged 1.1 school playmates who were six months or more their junior, whereas children having no younger siblings averaged .65 younger playmates at school. Similarly children who had older siblings counted among their best friends 1.9 playmates who were six months or more their senior, while children having no older siblings played with .9 older playmates.

Sibling pairs in the nursery school were necessarily omitted from the above calculations. That siblings did show a marked preference for each other is shown in Figure 2. In the chart the top pair of bars compare the older child's companionship with his sib to his friendship with all other children; the second pair compare the younger child's friendship with his sib to his friendship with all other children. Pairs A3-B2, M3-C1, and L2-A1 were sister-brother pairs, with the sister the elder; K3-F2 were boys; and I4-E3 were girls. Two points can be made from these comparisons. First, in the girl-boy pairs the younger brother spends a larger proportion of his playtime with the sister than the sister devotes to him; he apparently depends on her for "mothering". Second, striking differences exist in the unity of the various family pairs. Brothers K3 and F2 were almost inseparable companions; sisters I4 and E3 played almost as frequently with other children as they did with each other.

Choice of Occupations

Whether a child chose a toy or occupation because it brought him into contact with other children or whether he selected the toy for its intrinsic interest regardless of the social situation to which it led, the observer could not ascertain. Nevertheless, 60 records for each of the 34 children were analyzed according to the activities in which the children were engaged.

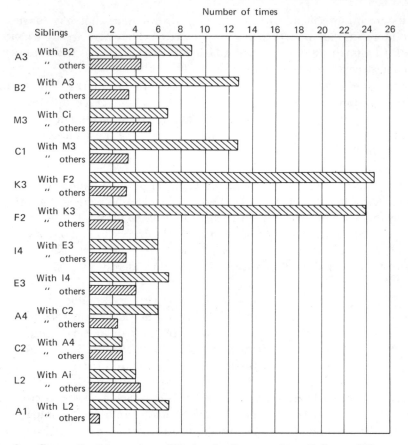

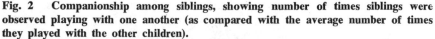

Fig. 2   Companionship among siblings, showing number of times siblings were observed playing with one another (as compared with the average number of times they played with the other children).

FAVORITE ACTIVITIES AND TOYS

In all 110 different activities were noted, 33 of which were observed only once, 79 less than 10 times, 24 from 20 to 100 times, and 12 more than 100 times. The frequency of occurrence of the eleven most popular activities is given on page 89.

The popularity of stringing colored beads and building with blocks among these children is comparable to the preference for fitting cylinders into holes, building with bricks, and arranging wooden color pairs in rows, which Bridges (2) reports for Montreal children. Among the fourteen favorite toys and occupations listed by Bott (1) were big blocks, sectional trains, kiddie-kars, picture books, doll carriages and dolls, and

Occupation	*Number of Times Observed*
Playing at sandbox	330
Playing family, house, and dolls	178
Pulling or hitching sectional train	151
Riding kiddie-kar	146
Cutting paper	122
Molding clay	119
Swinging	102
Building with blocks	99
Looking at object or picture	80
Stringing beads	65
Painting	62
Sitting unoccupied	43

beads. These were also favorites with the Minnesota children. Judging from Bott's statement that "little children play with beans for long periods, emptying them from one vessel to another", the activity is comparable to the sand play in which these children delighted. Skalet (5) in a study of play equipment in the home, found that dolls, garden tools, picture books, sand, scooter, and tricycles were played with for longer periods than other toys. All of these that were available to the nursery school children ranked among their favorites.

AGE DIFFERENCES IN TOY PREFERENCE

Figure 3 shows the popularity of the twelve most preferred toys by age groups. Sand play was the high favorite of the youngest age group and declined in popularity with age, although it remained among the three most preferred activities of the older children. Riding kiddy-kars showed the same trend, but to a less pronounced degree. Idly sitting and idly looking were gradually given up for more active pursuits at the later ages. Family, house, and dolls was the most popular at the three-year age level. The simple motor activity of swinging was also most popular at this age. The more complicated constructive play that utilized clay, paper, or paints became more popular as the children grew older. Play with trains and with beads showed no clear-cut age trends.

SOCIAL VALUE OF TOYS

In order to ascertain what types of social situations accompanied play with each of the toys 50 instances of play with each toy were analyzed for their social participation value. To insure an unbiased sample of 50 instances the last one or two instances of play with each toy were selected from each child's record. Table 2 shows the frequency of each type of

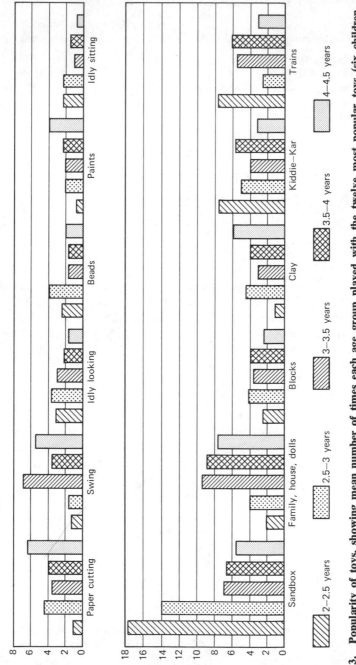

Mean number of times

90

Fig. 3. Popularity of toys, showing mean number of times each age group played with the twelve most popular toys (six children in each age group, sixty observations on each child).

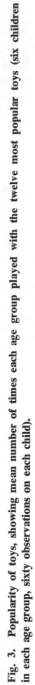

Table 2
Type of Social Participation

	Solitary	Onlooker	Parallel	Asso-ciative	Coop-erative	Total
Sandbox	7	2	32	6	3	50
House and dolls	3	7	1	2	37	50
Trains	18	4	7	17	4	50
Kiddie-kar	1	3	17	16	13	50
Cutting paper	5	4	27	14	0	50
Clay	0	3	40	7	0	50
Swings	9	6	23	12	0	50
Blocks	10	4	12	9	15	50
Beads	8	3	37	2	0	50
Paints	0	8	29	8	0	50

social participation for each toy. House and dolls was the most highly co-operative type of play. Play with sand, paper, clay, swings, beads, and paints was usually participated in as a parallel pursuit. Trains were about equally divided between solitary and associative play activities; and block play occurred with almost equal frequency in every type of social intercourse.

Since the manner of playing with the toys differed from one age group to another it will perhaps be well to describe some of the age differences in the social play with each toy.

SAND

The younger children spent most of their time in pouring the sand from one container to another. Sometimes they packed it solidly into dishes and emptied it out carefully to keep the mold intact; to this accomplishment the child perhaps called an adult's attention with a "See?" Social conflict occasionally arose when one child smashed another's mold or seized his vessel. But as a rule sand play afforded very little social intercourse for the younger child. He was content to stand for long periods, speaking to no one, and completely absorbed in his task.

The older children's sand play was of two types. The first type was very similar to that of the younger children, except that the older children lacked interest in it and were merely passing the time until some more interesting game developed. Their attention was usually drawn to something else in the room and the sandbox was abandoned. In the other type the sand was used for purposes of constructing roads and buildings and for moving truckloads or making choice dishes. This type of play required mental attentiveness and social assistance. Unless the children worked on a co-operative project they divided the sand, with attendant disputes over boundary lines. Competition frequently developed, when the children vied in manufacturing attractive products.

HOUSE

Dramatization of home life, which was the second most popular activity, comprised three types of play. In the first type the younger children were passive participants, allowing themselves to be led around by the older ones who played "mother and daddy" rôles. The "youngsters" apparently did not comprehend their rôles nor modify their behavior to "play up" to their parts. Since it was usually the younger brothers of older nursery school children who were used in this way, their acceptance seemed to be a carry-over from the "tagging along after older brother or sister" that occurred at home.

The second type of play, imitating home situations, consisted in dressing and undressing dolls, rocking them to sleep, and putting them to bed. The little mother seldom directed any conversation to the doll or to other children who were near by. As a rule this type of play was solitary and it occupied the two-to-three-year-old children.

The third type, commonly called "playing house", involved complex social adjustments and was rarely observed in children under three. Events occurring in the home were re-enacted: setting the table and giving a party; telephoning daddy to ask when he was coming home; receiving the doctor for a sick baby; mother's asking daddy for money to shop, and daddy's cautioning her not to spend it all; taking baby for a walk or buggy ride; packing suitcases for a trip; ordering groceries by telephone; spanking baby and putting him to bed; sending daddy off to work. Sex differences in this type of play were obtained by pairing each girl with a boy of approximately the same age. Among the sixteen pairs so obtained 163 instances of playing house were observed; 59 per cent of these instances were recorded for girls. When the activity of playing with dolls, which occurred three times as frequently with girls as with boys, was eliminated, the girl's percentage of playing house was reduced to 53. In dramatization of home and family that did not involve dolls the sex difference was slight. "Baby" rôles were usually played by younger children and male rôles were enacted by boys.

TRAINS

Hitching sectional trains together and drawing them along the floor, which was most popular at the youngest age, seldom involved social contact. Young children would spend the entire play period crawling on hands and knees pulling these trains; occasionally they stopped to rest and glance around the room, but they rarely stood up or moved away from their trains. With the older children train play was an associative or co-operative activity, often involving the building of tracks or stations with blocks. In contrast to the train play of two-year-olds that of the older children was of short duration. Sex preference for the train was more marked than for dolls; of the 120 instances of train play 89 per cent was noted for boys.

KIDDIE-KARS

For the younger children the kiddie-kar was not conducive to social play. They mounted and rode slowly in and out among groups of children, stopping to watch the play of others and moving on when a new group seemed more attractive. The older children usually pretended the kiddie-kars were automobiles and this dramatization resulted in co-operative games of auto parades; auto races; driving to oil stations or garages; having breakdowns and being towed; hauling lumber for building purposes; transporting passengers; and obeying traffic policemen. The last activity often brought into the game children who were mere spectators sitting on kiddie-kars; but the "cop" gave directions to all regardless of their desire to enter the group play. Only 24 per cent of the play with kiddie-kars was observed for girls, and in practically all the instances the girls were under three years. The boys' preference for the toy was equally great at all ages.

SWINGS

Swinging occurred infrequently among the younger children because the swings were difficult to mount. Older children occasionally pushed one another but they were not allowed to "pump" together. Girls occupied the swings 86 per cent of the time they were in use.

CONSTRUCTIVE MATERIALS: PAPER, CLAY, BEADS, PAINT, AND BLOCKS

All children except the youngest group cut paper and molded clay; the younger children used beads in a simple constructive way. Each child obtained these materials from the shelf, seated himself at a table designated for the activity, and occupied himself with his own constructive efforts. Occasionally the older children conversed about the designs they cut or the color patterns they were working out with their beads, but for the most part the social situation was the same for all ages. The girls used paper 63 per cent of the time and beads 78 per cent of the time those toys were used.

Play with water colors was always supervised by a teacher and was offered about once a week. Painting drew a greater number of onlookers than any other activity. The children occasionally conversed about their paintings and were eager to display the finished product. Girls were engaged in painting 59 per cent of the time it was observed.

Blocks afforded all degrees of social participation. They were played with by boys 71 per cent of the time they were used.

IDLY LOOKING AND IDLY SITTING

Examining objects, such as the goldfish, a plant, a new toy, a new dress, or something a child had made involved parallel social participation because the sight of a child intently gazing at an object aroused the curiosity of other children, who then grouped themselves about the object.

Idly sitting on chairs and glancing around the room, or perching upon a high covered radiator overlooking the railroad tracks was most frequently observed among children from two to three years old.

SOCIAL PARTICIPATION SCORE FOR FAVORITE TOYS

Social participation scores were worked out for the ten favorite games and toys by weighting each incidence of play as follows: unoccupied behavior, -3; solitary play, -2; onlooker behavior, -1; parallel play, 1; associative play, 2; co-operative play, 3. The algebraic sum of these scores for each toy were as follows:

House and dolls	103
Kiddie-kar	83
Clay	51
Blocks	51
Scissors and paper	41
Sand	37
Paints	37
Swings	23
Beads	22
Trains	17

Great differences in the social value of each toy exist. Playhouse equipment elicits the most complex social adjustments, whereas trains elicit the least.

Conclusions

Observations of the spontaneous play of nursery school children by the one-minute sampling method indicated that:

1. Preschool children most frequently play in groups of two.
2. The size of play groups increases with age.
3. Two-thirds of the two-child groups are unisexual.
4. The majority of the child's favorite playmates are of the same sex.
5. I.Q. has little influence on the preschool child's friendships.
6. Age and home environment influence friendships.
7. Siblings show a marked preference for each other's society.
8. Playing house is the most social type of play engaged in by nursery school children.
9. Sand play and constructive work with clay, paper, beads, and paints are characteristically parallel play activities.
10. Younger and older children differ in the manner in which they play with toys and hence in the social value the toy has for them.

References

1. Bott, Helen, Observation of Play Activities in a Nursery School. Genet. Psychol. Monog., 1928, 4, 44–88.
2. Bridges, K. M. B., Occupational Interests of Three-Year-Old Children. Ped. Sem. and J. Genet. Psychol., 1927, 34, 415–423.
3. Challman, R. C., Factors Influencing Friendships Among Preschool Children. Child Dev., 1932, 3, 146–158.
4. Chevaleva-Janovskaja, E., Les groupements spontanes d'enfants à l'âge pre-scholaires. Arch. de Psychol., 1927, 20, 219–233.
5. Skalet, Magda, Play Equipment of the Preschool Child. M. A. Thesis, 1927. On file in the University of Minnesota Library.
6. Wellman, Beth, The School Child's Choice of Companions. J. Educ. Res., 24, 126–132.

7

Activity-Setting and Social Interaction: A Field Study

Paul Gump and Brian Sutton-Smith[1]

When the relationship between children and their activities is investigated, interest usually centers upon the question of how children select and use various activities to express their personal and social needs. The present study, and the larger research project from which it derives, attempts to reverse the direction of this interest and ask the question: How do activities limit, provoke, or coerce the expression of children's needs and problems? This form of consideration is based upon the general hypothesis that activities have a reality and a behavior-influencing power in their own right. An activity, once entered, will exclude some potential behaviors, necessitate other behaviors, and, finally, encourage or discourage still other behaviors. This coercive and provocative power of an activity rests upon two subaspects: the behavioral limitations and pos-

SOURCE. Reprinted from *The American Journal of Orthopsychiatry*, Vol. XXV, No. 4, October, 1955.

1 Dr. Fritz Redl developed the basic ideas and the research project from which this study is derived. The study was supported by research grant M-550 from the National Institute of Mental Health, of the National Institutes of Health, Public Health Service. Dr. Fritz Redl was Principal Investigator and Paul Gump, Project Director.

We are also very indebted to the personnel of the University of Michigan Fresh Air Camp, Dr. William C. Morse, Director, for their very generous assistance in providing ideas as well as subjects and facilities for this research.

sibilities in the *physical* setting and its objects, and in the "standard patterns of performance"[1] which constitute the activity. Thus, the activity-setting identified as "making a boat in craft shop" includes the physical objects of shop, wood, saws, etc., and the performances of hammering, sawing, attending to materials, etc. Beyond the performances which are standard in boat making, are behaviors which may become more or less *likely* because a child has entered this particular activity-setting. For example, if the setting should provide one saw and the standard performance should require sawing, conflict interaction may be more likely in such an activity-setting than in one in which tools are plentiful or in which boys are not pressed to use the same tool at the same time.

Those behaviors which are made more likely, although not required, by the physical setting and its standard performances may be labeled *respondent behaviors*. In the present study, the respondent behaviors under investigation were social interactions. The hypothesis tested was that the amount and kind of social interaction is significantly affected by variation of activity-settings. In all, four usual camp activity-settings were investigated: cook-outs, boating, swims, and crafts. Only material from swims and crafts is offered here. The following report, then, deals with a comparison of the amount and kind of social interaction which occurred in the craft and swim activity-settings.

Method

The subjects were 23 boys, aged $9\frac{1}{2}$ to $11\frac{1}{2}$ years, who were campers at the University of Michigan Fresh Air Camp. Most of these boys were referred to camp because of some adjustment difficulties.

Boys went to each activity as members of a cabin group. Therefore, both participants and directly responsible adults (counselors) were similar from activity to activity. This established a natural control over personality, sociometric, and leadership variables which otherwise might have accounted for differences in social interaction between the swim and the craft activity-settings.

Observers took full, on-the-spot recordings of ten minutes of each boy's behavior in each setting. The project director divided the resulting protocols into units so that each interaction of each subject could be coded. (Reliabilities of observation and of coding were checked and were satisfactory; there was 86% agreement on 11 code possibilities.) The

[1] The "standard pattern of performance" idea was stimulated by a similar concept—"standing patterns of behaviors"—employed by Barker and Wright in their excellent book, *Midwest and Its Children*, Row, Peterson and Co., 1955.

Table 1

Relevant Sections of Interaction Analysis Code

Category	Definition and Examples
Sharing	The subject either makes or receives an interaction with the quality of mutuality. Neither the subject nor his associate asks or is asked to serve the purposes of the other but to share an experience or an activity. E.g.: "Hey, look at the boat coming in." "Let's make a submarine."
Helping	The subject asks, or is asked for help (material, information, effort). The subject gives or receives assistance. The interaction is not one of mutuality as in sharing. E.g.: "How do you make this lanyard?" The counselor gives swimming or craft instruction, etc.
Asserting	The subject is involved in an interaction attempt, the intent of which is to gain admiration or interested attention. E.g.: "Hey, look at me! I'm a drunk!" "I know how to do that—that's easy!"
Blocking	The subject is involved in a deliberate "stopping" interaction. The blocker may refuse, ignore, etc. E.g.: "I will not!"
Demanding	The subject makes or receives a forceful request. No autonomy implied to the associate. E.g.: "You give me that!" "Get outa here!"
Attacking	The subject is involved in an interaction attempt, the purpose of which is to "hurt" the recipient—to reduce him, or beat him. E.g.: "You s.o.b.!" One boy physically attacks another or takes something from him.

code was so designed that the number and kind of interactions and the persons (counselor or boys) involved could be tallied. Categories in the code were defined in terms of the *intent* of the *source* of the interaction toward the *target* of the interaction. Categories were abstract enough to be applicable to any setting. The six most relevant of the 11 code categories are briefly defined and illustrated in Table 1.

Results

The effect of activity-setting upon respondent social behavior can be ascertained by checking the amount of over-all interaction, the amount of specific kinds of interactions, and the persons involved in these kinds of interactions. Figure 1 indicates results with regard to amount and kind of interaction.

The difference in amount of interaction in favor of swim is indicated

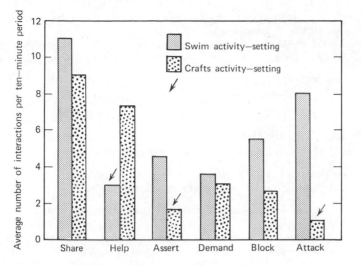

Fig. 1   Amount and kind of social interactions by participants in swim and crafts activity-settings.

by the higher columns for swim interaction in each category except help. The over-all difference is as follows:

Average *swim* interactions	38.8
Average *craft* interactions	26.4
Average difference in favor of swim	12.4

This difference is significant at the .01 level. Other significant differences are indicated by arrows in Figure 1. These differences indicate that the help interaction is more frequent in crafts but that the more

"robust interactions" (assertion and attack) are more frequent in swim. Sharing and blocking tend to be more frequent in swim but differences are significant at only the .10 level.

To determine if the kind of interaction differs between settings, one may compare the percentages of interaction falling in the various categories. In this way the predominant mode or modes of interaction are indicated for each setting. When such a conversion is made, the following results are obtained:

1. One of the most predominant types of interactions in both settings is sharing—about 30 per cent in each.

2. The most predominant nonsharing interaction in crafts is helping—29 per cent (opposed to 8% in swim).

3. The most predominant nonsharing interaction in swim is the aggressive combination of assertion and attacking—33 per cent (opposed to 8% in crafts).

It is also instructive to note which setting generated the greatest *per cent* of interaction between boys and their counselors (and, necessarily, the least *per cent* of interaction among the boys themselves):

Amount of total *craft* interaction which is counselor-involved   46%

Amount of total *swim* interaction which is counselor-involved   26%

The predominant kinds of interaction in which the counselors are involved are shown by the following percentages:

1. The predominant counselor-involved interaction in crafts is help—41 per cent (17% in swim).

2. The predominant counselor-involved in swim, aside from sharing, is conflict combination of demand, block, and attack—34 per cent (17% in crafts).

Discussion

The preceding data demonstrate that activity-settings determine more than the specific activity engaged in by a child. The properties of the activity-setting produce significant and general effects upon the respondent social behavior of its participants. In the settings investigated, these effects were noticeable in the amount and kind of interaction, in the type of person (boy or counselor) involved, and in the types of interaction sought from or offered by these different persons. The results do not seem explicable on the basis of differences in groups or in adult personnel involved—these were similar in each setting.

The general implication for recreational and therapeutic work with children is that choice of activities per se is very important; this choice will markedly affect the children's relations to one another and to the leader or therapist. Specifically, the above results indicate that in the swim setting, the counselor often will be called upon to admire and recognize assertive actions and to settle or supervise conflict interactions; he will be involved in relatively few helping interactions. In crafts, the opposite tends to be true; here the counselor's role involves less admiration and conflict supervision and more helping. Related to setting-produced variations in counselor's role, are the variations in kinds of peer social experiences of the child participants. The counselor learns from such data that a "prescription" of swimming will send a child to a "robust" social climate in which total interaction is high and in which assertion and attacking are highly likely. A crafts "prescription," on the other hand, will place a child in a "mild" social climate in which total interaction is low, assertive and conflict interaction minimal, and dependency (helping—being helped) interaction high.

Findings for this particular camp setting and population cannot be freely generalized to all swim and craft settings. However, a review of the protocols permits one to hypothesize that certain characteristics, *intrinsic* to the physical setting and to the standard pattern of performance of crafts and swims in general, are responsible for the obtained results. These hypothesized intrinsic characteristics are our next concern.

With crafts as a base line, some of the hypothesized characteristics of the two settings may be compared and contrasted.

1. The materials and the standard performances of crafts involve "difficult" goals.

In crafts, one is supposed to "make something." This has several subsidiary effects. Interest and effort tend to go from the child to his project; he is "too busy" to seek interaction. This tends to reduce interaction in crafts. In swim, on the other hand, most of the standard performances are easily accomplished and one has freedom to seek and to respond to interaction. A second effect of the difficult goal is that it leads to need for technical assistance and to need for validation of one's efforts. The latter need is more subtle but important. Boys often ask counselors to approve (not just admire) their progress, although no "real" help is necessary. Thus, the predominance of the help type of interaction in crafts. In swim, the boys need little help or validation for the simple motor acts they accomplish.

2. The materials and the standard performances of crafts are restrictive of the gross motor actions and of "bodily expansiveness."

In crafts, boys have to be careful; running, falling, jumping, etc., are, of course, not a part of the usual craft activity. Swims, however, provide a physical setting with elevations (docks and diving boards) and water (which can break a fall); these, together with standard performances of leaping and diving, lead to novel and "gravity-defying" acts. Cries of "Look at me!" are a likely part of such acts. As one experienced counselor puts it: "They want you to watch the darnedest things—little silly things that wouldn't be possible on land." Protocol material shows that this freedom of bodily action apparently leads to the display reflected by the high incidence of assertive interaction in the swim activity-setting. For some boys, the freedom of bodily actions also seems to lead to a need to test one's physical prowess in competitive or combative interaction; this would account for the high number of conflict interactions in swim.

In the final analysis, the basic characteristics of the activity-setting—

not the activity-settings as such—determine the impact upon participants. The problem for research is the delineation of these characteristics and the discovery of their relationship to the participant's respondent behavior and experience. This problem may be approached by determining what are the major behavioral limitations and opportunities presented by typical settings and by their standard patterns of performances. Then one is in a position to ask what respondent behaviors become more or less likely because children engage in activity-settings with these characteristics.

From here on, the problem may be followed up in two ways: the modal or average effects of certain characteristics can be investigated (as was attempted in the discussion of this study); or, the particular effects upon participants with known personality needs and organizations can be assessed. The first approach is merely a step toward the second; as the second is developed, it becomes feasible to prescribe strategically activities for specific children and groups; it becomes possible to make activity-settings congruent with diagnostic knowledge and with therapeutic aims.

8

Boundaries

Brian Sutton-Smith

This is the problem of the way we get into and out of the play or game. In sports the spatial and temporal boundaries are usually so firmly fixed that they have probably contributed to the illusion that work and play are quite distinct entities. It is a moot point, however, whether the worker dreaming throughout the week of next Saturday's game is at work or at play. And if we step down to young children's games, entry and exit are much looser and the spatial arrangements more pliant. New children can be added or lost from Hide and Seek with little consequence.

But what are the codes that govern these entries and exits? In play we have decades of informal psychoanalytic evidence concerning the ways in which children oscillate in and out of play, going either way to extend their experience or to escape from it. Sometimes the anxiety heightening or anxiety reduction is achieved by a more faithful copy of earlier responses, sometimes by more novelty, and sometimes by an exaggerated and ludicrous rendering of responses. Terence Moore's data suggests that there are probably private schedules and boundaries for this play—nonplay management (1964). Individuals go about their boundary transitions in different ways.

When we move from solitary to group play these matters become more

SOURCE. Address to the Regional Meeting of the Society for Research in Child Development, Clark University, March, 1968. Some parts of this address also appeared in "Games—Play—Daydreams," *Quest,* 1968, **10,** 47–58.

explicit. Bateson has discussed the metacommunications by which animals and humans let each other know that they mean to cross a ludic boundary (1956). They smile, they giggle, they make an exaggerated gesture. In some preliminary studies of my own contrasting children at kindergarten and preadolescent levels, the children at both age levels use mainly ludic techniques to cross such boundaries. That is, they get into each other's play territory by making a play gesture such as a mock attack or a stunt, by inaugurating a fantasy, or by making a ludicrous expression. The younger children use relatively more of these and they are more often egocentric: "Look at me, I'm an aeroplane". About a third of the younger children's gestures and a half of the older children's were social (rather than ludic), that is, invitations, challenges, greetings, requests, and announcements.

Once into the play encounter, Goffman has suggested that it is preserved by various special integrating techniques that prevent its boundaries from breaking down. In an analysis of such techniques, using several day studies (Gump et al. 1955) it became clear that these integrating techniques were more likely to be employed in informal play than in formal games with rules, where the effort goes into clarifying and maintaining the rules. In informal play the techniques were more likely to be needed with intimates than with peer associates, and more likely to be used by girls than by boys. Such techniques included desisting, complying, apologizing, assisting, appealing to an outsider, promising, changing the game, pretending to be hurt oneself after hurting someone else, and humor. In some of the observations an older sibling may harm, hurt, and humiliate younger siblings in play, and yet keep them in the play by a constant shower of such integrating devices. One is almost forced to the conclusion that in these bullying playful encounters, if the older sibling can keep emphasizing the fun, he can get away with murder. To invert William James, war is the moral reward for fun! For the younger sibling, the price of fun is getting hurt.

Approaching play and games in these terms, it becomes apparent that there are differences in the ease with which individuals can initiate and integrate such play encounters. There are people who have difficulty in crossing these boundaries and there are those who do it too easily. People who riot at football matches, or who become possessed by their own reveries (at Puritan prayer meetings or political rallies), or who are game addicts, are examples of persons for whom a great deal of boundary diffuseness (riots) or rigidity (addicts) has developed. Perhaps it is those who have *not* played the sports who are more diffuse about the boundaries between their own mythic identifications and the sport itself.

I have nothing much to say about addicts except that Roberts, Kendon, and I studied chess and bridge players who spent more than 40 hours a week at their games. They were quite uniquely possessed individuals. The chess players were highly disputatious individuals who preferred philosophical and political argumentation with one or two associates, while the bridge players, on the contrary, preferred a large number of nonintensive relationships in which dispute was avoided. In another study, Rosenberg and I found that college individuals claiming to play more than 40 hours of sport a week had an MMPI profile that a clinician would characterize as hysterical. Anyway, my point is that we do have a contrast between individuals who have gone into a fantasy or game world and stay there, and others who, not having been in one, are overwhelmed by their first experience.

But in talking about deviates we are by implication suggesting that there may be a special type of equilibrium that has to be learned. It would be the understanding of the various balances that are involved in the oppositions between work and play, thoughtfulness and spontaneity (Fry, 1963), impulse-control (Redl, 1959), humor and seriousness, and the appropriateness of each of these to different people in different settings. In Piaget's theory play and imitation are contrasted as two disequilibrial states within the equilibrium of thought. From the present perspective we might regard seriousness and "funfulness" as two disequilibrial states within an equipoise that contains them both. One can be a dedicated bore, or a flippant dilettante; an addict of work or play. But what is it if one can ignore both extremes and yet do his business? In Lieberman's work on playfulness in young children, her young subjects who were highly playful did not restrict themselves to play, but were spontaneous and humorous in all settings and were able to pass easily from one to the other (1965). They had boundary facility. Here her playfulness and "equipoise" are similar. Perhaps, following Piaget, we are looking for a developmental series of equipoise operations identified by the subject's ability to move easily in and out of the polarities mentioned above and with adequate involvement in all, yet without breakdown into embarrassment or boredom.

In sum, although talking about socially provided boundary systems, I am also implying there may be some immediate psychological functions that are directly relevant to the maintenance of these structures. Which is to say that what begins as a study of ecology may be impossible to pursue without a parallel study of the psychic structures that exist concordantly within the individual players.

References

Most of the references are contained in the Bibliography at the end of this volume. Those of special relevance to this article are as follows:

Fry, W. F. *Sweet Madness: A Study of Humor.* Palo Alto: Pacific Books, 1963.

Gump, P. V., Schoggen, P. H. Sutton-Smith, B., Schoggen, M., and Goldberg, T. *Wally O'Neil at Home* (Vol. I), *Wally O'Neil at Camp* (Vol. II), Wayne State University Library Manuscript, 1955.

Chapter IV

The Psychoanalytic Tradition

In the previous section it was noted that after the early 1930s there was a substantial decrease in quantitative studies of play. The interest in play, however, did not decrease, it was now largely channelled by psychoanalytic interpretations and implemented through doll-play techniques. While the use of such techniques was in the first place largely for diagnostic and therapeutic purposes, increasingly these were subjected to a variety of forms of quantitation, as indicated by the Lewin and Wardwell article.

Some preliminary remarks concerning the play theories of Freud and others seem in order. Since the 1930s and 1940s, the dominant theoretical interpretation of play has emanated from Freudian sources. In *Beyond the Pleasure Principle*, Freud gave several explanations of play, but the most important of these and the most often repeated was the following:

We see that children in their play repeated everything that has made a great impression on them in actual life, so that they thereby abreact the strength of the impression and so to speak make themselves masters of the situation (1955).

Freud illustrated the argument by his oft-quoted story of the well behaved boy of 18 months who, while strongly attached to his mother, had to contend with the fact that she repeatedly left him for hours on end. He did not cry when she went, but did develop the troublesome habit of flinging into the corner of his room or under the bed all the little things on which he could lay his hands, accompanying this action by an expression of interest and gratification, and emitting a loud, drawn out noise that in the judgment of the mother meant "go away." Freud explained this behavior in several ways, by and large favoring the view quoted above that through his dramatizations the child was gaining mastery over his anxiety at his mother's absence. This formulation had the virtue of explaining why the child's behavior might become rewarding once it was adopted. The symbolic response repeated in the absence of the anxiety-inducing circumstances might actually contribute to a reduction of anxiety through repetition. Freud was sufficiently impressed by the way in which his subjects persistently reintroduced the unpleasant past that he termed the phenomenon the repetition-compulsion and provided it with an instinctive basis in his metabiological system. A learning theorist might remark in passing that these illustrations and arguments permit symbolism to be construed as a process whereby a human subject can initiate his own extinction series.

Freud had another interpretation for the same phenomena. He said:

The flinging away of the object so that it is gone might be the gratification of an impulse of revenge supressed in real life but directed against the mother for going away, and would then have a defiant meaning.

Here we have play behavior originating in a set of impulses that are incompatible with the child's major orientation. Had the small boy, for example, been openly defiant towards the mother, this would have been a rejection of her, and at the same time psychologically at his undifferentiated age, tantamount to having her reject him. We may assume that the latter would be intolerable to such a young and dependent child. He wished to continue his dependent responses but also wished to express defiance. The solution was the compensatory expression in symbolic terms that few would take seriously and that might be so ambiguous that few would understand.

Menninger's interpretation of play and games follows this second line. For him the child's play gives vent to aggression that cannot be released elsewhere:

The most important value of this unrealistic nature of play is the opportunities that it affords for the relief of repressed aggressions (1942, p. 172).

Frequently as we all know, the aggressions and hostilities which the games are supposed to absorb, break through the repression into consciousness and quarreling ensues. . . . This applies not only to child's play but to the more symbolic contests such as table games (1942, p. 173).

The very fact that the little girl plays with dolls at all—which the mother takes to be such a sweet and natural act of imitation—is in the child's unconscious an aggression against the mother. It is an aggression in that it is a way of saying, 'It is I who should have the children, not you.' . . . it is a way of saying, 'Mother you are no longer necessary; I am a big lady now, and it is I who should have the long dresses and babies, not you; you can be dispensed with (1942, pp. 176–177).

The whole point of the doctor game is the erotic fantasy of being the victim of a powerful man who has access to all parts of the body, with a concomitantly acted hostile fantasy directed against the parent's prohibitions (1942, p. 178).

Play behavior originating thus in conflict, providing a mastery of anxiety, and yielding the subject some compensatory value appears to have been the most-often repeated explanation of play in subsequent psychoanalytic writings, although there are varying formulations and the terms "catharsism," "tension reduction," "wish fulfillment," "passivity to activity," and "leave of absence from reality" are often made use of (Waelder, 1933).

With Erikson, however, we move beyond this relatively narrow emphasis on the part play takes in anxiety reduction and compensatory wish fulfillment, to an emphasis also on the growth functions it may serve. Thus in *Childhood and Society* (1950) he says:

To grow means to be divided into different parts which move at different rates. A growing boy has trouble in mastering his growing body as well as his divided mind. . . . I would look at the play act, as vaguely speaking, a function of the ego, an attempt to bring into synchronization the bodily and the social processes of which one is a part even while one is self. . . . The emphasis, I think, should be on the ego's need to master the various areas of life, and especially those in which the individual finds his self, his body, and his social role wanting and trailing. To hallucinate ego mastery is the purpose of play—but play . . . is the undisputed master of only a very slim margin of existence (pp. 184–185).

The playing adult steps sideward into another reality; the playing child advances forward to new stages of mastery. I propose the theory that the child's play is the infantile form of the human ability to deal with experience by creating model situations and to master reality by experiment and planning (p. 186).

In this chapter we include an article by Peller that is particularly insightful with respect to children's play though in a fairly traditional psychoanalytic manner. This is followed by a summary version of one of Erikson's most memorable studies into children's play configurations, and finally, a review of research into doll play by Lewin and Wardwell. This chapter would not, however, be complete without some reference to recent systematic studies that derive some of their major concepts from the Freudian tradition, in particular, those by Moore (1961, 1964), Gilmore (1966), and Collard (1967).

9

Models of Children's Play

Lili E. Peller

Children's play, and especially the various rôles and characters incorporated by them in their "dramatic" play, have been the subject of many comments both inside and outside of the psychoanalytic school.

Until recently, academic psychology assumed an "instinct" to imitate that prompted a child to copy whatever he chanced to observe frequently enough and long enough. Freud pointed out, in *Beyond the Pleasure Principle*, that it is not necessary to assume a special instinct to imitate. There is no imitation without an emotional motivation. A child's play is not like a mirror which necessarily reflects what is within its "sight." The child is highly selective in the behavior he imitates. His choice of a rôle follows certain principal lines.

This paper presents a number of "models" or formulas of play activities, and illustrates them with examples culled from our experience and from literature. Undoubtedly this survey is incomplete. Even so, it may stimulate further observations and new interpretations of the material at hand.

CHOICE BASED ON LOVE, ADMIRATION

A child pretends to be some one whom he admires and loves and whom he would like to resemble. By and large, admiration and wishful antici-

SOURCE. Peller, Lili E. "Models of children's play. *Ment. Hygiene.* Stks. **36**: 66–83, 1952. Reprinted with the permission of the National Association for Mental Health.

pation of his own adult rôle determine the rôle he chooses. This is the type of children's play that adults find most amusing and that has been most frequently described, not only in psychological literature, but also in novels and poems. The child plays at being mother, father, or teacher; he pretends to be a king, a queen, or a fairy. At play he recaptures a fragment of his ancient belief in the omnipotence of wishes. He enjoys a power and prestige denied to him in reality.

When adults speak of "happy childhood," they probably have in mind the child who hobbles around in high-heeled shoes or who has draped around himself some piece of adult clothing and thus has jumped with great ease the gulf between wishing and being.

On closer investigation, however, the situation is not quite so carefree and happy. Admiration alone is seldom the basis for the child's choice; as a rule, there is an admixture of frustration, deprivation, or fear.

Michael, aged three years and eight months, has refused to go to nursery school, although all his friends are going there, and he thus remains without playmates in the park. Whenever a passer-by starts a conversation, asking his name, and so on, he answers, "My name is Michael Schoolboy," saying it with so much assurance that people are inclined to believe him.

There can be little doubt that Michael would like to go to school and be with his friends. But he cannot bring himself to leave his mother. In his playful change of name, the conflict is solved. He *is* a schoolboy. In fact, in almost every instance of such play one finds an element of fear or of envy accompanying the obvious admiration and love.

A RÔLE ASSIGNED TO AN INANIMATE OBJECT

In a variation of the type of play discussed above, the child does not himself assume a rôle, but appoints a doll or a toy animal—or it may well be a pillow, a piece of wood—to the rôle of the child, the baby. To have some one depending on him indirectly changes the child's status. Or the child pretends to have an imaginary companion—a brother, a sister, or a dog.

Popsy made his appearance when Billy was about three and a half. We first became conscious of him when driving in the car. Billy always urged his father to pass other cars on the road and get to the "head of the line." But when a car passed us and sped ahead, Billy would chuckle, "My Popsy is driving that car. Doesn't he go fast?" Sometimes Popsy rode on the roof of our car. Sometimes he jumped from treetop to treetop beside the roadside as we went by.

Once when we commented on an attractive new schoolhouse, Billy remarked, "My Popsy is a teacher in that school." That same night he got uncovered and called. As his mother tucked the blankets around him again, he whispered, "Popsy pulled those blankets off of me. Isn't Popsy a nuisance?"

The wishes, peculiarities, and possessions of this imaginary family member have to be respected. In a casual, apparently unintentional way this may give the child a chance to retaliate for some of the things he experiences. In a disturbed child, this mechanism is intensified and thus more obvious.

"David, aged two and a half, a very nervous child with a highly nervous mother, seemed quiet and comparatively happy in the first two days in the residential nursery. He was inseparable from a toy dog, Peter, whom he had brought from home. Peter slept with him, ate with him, was in his arms even when he was bathed and dressed, and David insisted that Peter should be taken care of as if he were another child in the nursery.

"When his mother visited him after two days, David had his first temper tantrum. He insistently demanded that she should kiss Peter on the mouth and hug him as if he were her baby. From then on and for quite a while he reacted with, temper to any imaginary slight done to Peter. He would cry whenever another child would knock against the toy and would throw himself on the floor with despair whenever the dog inadvertently fell out of his arms. Peter is evidently a symbol for himself and has to be treated as he himself wants to be treated. His mother has to make up in affection to the dog for the wrong she had done to David by sending him away from home."[1]

The pleasure a child derives from his doll or Teddy bear stems largely from this source. The young child who is not under severe emotional pressure will play in this way intermittently, now feeding the Teddy with remarkable patience and carrying it with great care and a little later flinging it around carelessly. He assigns a rôle and forgets about it with equal ease. The significance of this type of play changes with the child's age. The five-year-old may play the maternal rôle all day long, but the two- or two-and-a-half-year-old, who is consistently gentle with his dolls, has in our experience been a person burdened by too many worries.

Barbe, aged three, lost her father in the war. Her grief-stricken mother has not been able to explain the father's absence to the child and consequently B. has a number of fears. For instance, she is terrified of the Santa Claus in the department store and does not even want to go near the store.

The consultant who sees mother and child presents Barbe one day with a chocolate Santa Claus, whom she takes with evident pleasure and no fear. Before leaving for home the mother wants to put the chocolate figure into a box, explaining that otherwise it might get broken, but Barbe objects. The mother proceeds to put it in anyway. Barbe is in tears. Her mother is highly annoyed with her unreasonable behavior. Barbe is alternately screaming and imploring her mother not to put Santa into the box.

At this point the consultant suggests making slits for air in the box and that

---

[1] See *War and Children*, by Anna Freud and Dorothy T. Burlingham. New York: Medical War Books, 1943. pp. 133–34.

solves the situation. Barbe calms down and permits her to put Santa Claus into the box. The child would rather dare her mother's anger than risk displeasing the chocolate figure.

CHOICE BASED ON FEAR

Whenever the child takes on the rôle of some one whom he fears, anxiety or frustration determines his impersonation. Several of Freud's classical examples follow this line: a child plays at being the doctor, after the doctor has administered a painful treatment or performed a minor operation. Anna Freud reports the case of the child who conquers the fear of crossing the dark hall by pretending to be the ghost she dreads to encounter. By choosing the rôle of the doctor or the ghost, the child can switch from the passive to the active rôle and inflict upon another person —be it a child or a doll—what has previously been done to him. The change from a passive to an active rôle is the basic mechanism of many play activities both of children and of adults. It mitigates the traumatic effect of a recent experience and it leaves the player better equipped to undergo the passive rôle again, when necessary. This accounts for a great deal of the healing power of play.

THE LOSING PARTY

In observing children at play, we see that while the dominant aggressive rôles are preferred, there is always some child willing to submit to the assault, to take the rôle of the sick child who has to swallow medicine and is sent to bed, or, in war play, to take the rôle of the hated enemy soldier who is invariably defeated. How can this be explained?

Several explanations suggest themselves. The very simple and non-psychological one is that a younger or less popular child fears that he will be excluded from the play altogether unless he takes such a rôle. Another explanation is that we have here early passive or masochistic tendencies. Finally the behavior can be explained by giving a broader meaning to the mechanism of "turning from the *passive* to the *active* experience." A child who himself chooses or consents to be the passive, the victimized party and knows that he can terminate this rôle whenever he pleases is not really passive. Even in the inactive rôle, he is self-steered and not a play ball.

INCOGNITO INDULGENCE

In contrast to the rôles described so far, which in the child's scale of values go in a direction "beyond and above" his present status, the child also chooses rôles that are distinctly "passed and below" him. For instance, he plays at being an animal or a baby. Freud states: "The wish which dominates childhood is the wish to be big and adult and do as the adults are doing." Why, then, should a child slip into a rôle that limits the powers he actually possesses?

Such a play rôle provides a convenient disguise for enjoying pleasures that are no longer compatible with the youngster's sense of his own dignity and grown-upness. This motivation can be understood if we consider how the young child is torn between two worlds. His superego takes its standards from his parents and teachers, whom he wants to please. Often, however, he cannot give up childish pleasures as quickly as he is expected to. Aware of the "subversive" elements in his own house, the superego of the early latency years is especially strict. Yet by announcing, "This is not me. It's a puppy dog," the child can permit himself to enjoy sniffing, crawling, getting dirty. By declaring, "I am a baby now," he can cuddle up, suck his fingers, insist on being carried around, talk gibberish. A child living under great pressure to be sensible and grown-up is more likely to select a rôle along this line. In one and the same play situation, a forbidden wish can be simultaneously expressed and disclaimed.

L., not quite five years old, insists for weeks and months daily on the following morning ritual: Her mother must greet her, "Good morning, Bambi." L. replies: "Good morning, Feline! You know, Feline, my mother died. Will you be my friend now?" To this her mother must answer: "Yes, Bambi. I'll always stay with you."

Often L. continues this rôle all day long. She has borrowed this scene from the Bambi film. There Bambi's mother is shot and killed by the hunter and the lonely and distressed Bambi finds Feline in the forest and lives with her forever after. L. is a girl with many problems and her death wishes against her mother and the consequent fear that they will come true are particularly strong. About a year ago her baby brother was taken to the hospital where he died suddenly. Now L.'s mother is pregnant again and L. is terribly afraid and pleads with her not to go to the hospital.

In the past month the rôle of Bambi has provided L. with an excellent outlet for her own double-barreled wishes.

Bambi's mother was a deer, and people don't take it so seriously when a deer dies. After that sad event Bambi felt lost and lonely, but he got over the loss; so a human child would get over it, too, and find other friends, should his mother die. In the Bambi camouflage, loss and consolation can be lived through in phantasy without feelings of guilt.

It must be remembered that a child frequently assigns a rôle to an animal completely different from the one discussed here. A wolf, a horse, sometimes also a dog or a rooster may be symbols of great power and ferocity. In our examples, animals are a kind of "second rate" human beings. They feel and talk like human beings, yet they may indulge in actions that the child would consider beneath his dignity. After all, they are "only" animals and it is not upsetting when they lack the restraint expected in *homo sapiens*. On the other hand, it is permissible to do things to them that would be unthinkable with humans.

This type of play might be called "incognito indulgence." The child lends his motor apparatus to one part of his self and holds his superego in abeyance by declaring: "That's not really me. You don't have to interfere." As in any make-believe, there is the implicit assurance, "All this is for a limited time only."

The prototype of this play mechanism is the dignitary, the Caliph Harun-al-Rashid or the Emperor Joseph II, who, shrouded in a cloak that provides convenient incognito, can visit all kinds of lowly places where he could not be seen if recognizable as himself.

An animal can enjoy feelings or show character traits that would be repulsive or cause feelings of guilt and shame in a human being. He can also be treated in a way that would be punishable if used toward a person. It works conveniently both ways, whether the animal is the subject or the object. The heroes of some of our most beloved children's stories are animals and thus can go through dangers and ordeals that would be outrageous in the human world.

Take Peter Rabbit. He really is a disobedient and greedy little boy who runs away from home. At the climax of the story, after stuffing himself with forbidden delicacies, Peter is chased by the old gardener who wants to kill him and put him into a mince pie. It would be outrageous in our day and age to tell such a story about a child. But story-teller and listener agree to call the hero a rabbit, and the plot can become more dramatic and much truer to the young child's hidden anxieties.

In more than one way this story follows the line of archaic childish reasoning: the impending punishment fits the crime. Peter is in a predicament because he ate forbidden things and now the gardener is going to eat him. It is tit for tat. As the story draws to its close, this horrible punishment is mitigated to one that is more likely to befall a naughty little boy: Peter is sent to bed without supper. But even this punishment still fits the crime. The characters in *The Wind in the Willows*, in Dr. Doolittle's books, and in many children's classics act in accordance with this "logic."

Seeing only the superficial, conscious aspect of a story, educators have at times objected to the unbiological thinking that is fostered as animals strut on their hind legs, talk, and are dressed like human beings. Yet more than 2,000 years ago when Æsop wanted to chide and deride human vices and weaknesses, he hit upon the same device; greed, vanity, and stupidity are somehow less offensive when encountered in animals. The implied accusation becomes less direct and loses its sting. After all, what can one expect from a fox, a peacock, or an ant?

The most recent and possibly the most popular addition to the long list of animal masks for human follies and foibles are Donald Duck, Mickey Mouse, and their consorts. In five minutes flat, the hero of an animated strip undergoes a series of atrocities that no exaggeration and no colorful details could make funny if they were happening to a human being.

CLOWNING

Another mask that provides a convenient incognito is *clowning*. For instance, a child in a kindergarten has put on his cap the wrong way. He could correct it quickly and hope that none of his playmates noticed his blunder. (He would not be playing then.) Instead, he chooses another road: he repeats his mishap deliberately and in an exaggerated form, putting it, so to say, between quotation marks. Now he draws everybody's attention to his mistake, and he does not feel bad about it any more— just the opposite. After all, it is plain that he *chooses* to act this way.

The observation of a clowning child shows that there is more than one way of turning the tables, of switching from the passive to the active rôle. The clown does to himself what fate tried to do to him. That he gets plenty of attention may be called a secondary gain. The primary gain is that he need not admit—either to himself or to others—that he committed a blunder the first time. By deliberately repeating and paraphrasing it, he makes himself master of the situation.

A group of seven-to-nine-year-old campers stand on the platform near the train. Suddenly the locomotive releases steam with a loud hissing noise. H., who stands near it, almost jumps with fright. He notices that the others are looking at him, about to laugh. An embarrassed smile comes on his face and as the hissing recurs a few seconds later, he repeats and exaggerates his former movements. He throws his arms up, shrieks, and almost tumbles over. He repeats these antics with every blast of steam. Now he has the laughers on his side; he is the hero who parodies getting scared. He is not the victim of the situation, but the victor.

Clowning differs from the other models of play in that it requires an audience. It is as if the clown were saying to fate: "You thought you could lick me by showing me up as clumsy (or stupid, or ugly, or queer-looking). All right, I am not just a little clumsy (or ugly), I am very much so, but on my own choosing. You did not do it to me." Contrary to the other make-believe changes—"I am not envious or afraid. I myself am the giant, the king, the bogeyman"—this reversal cannot be enjoyed without the appreciative mirror of an audience.

Hiding one's own identity under the cloak of a clown, an animal, or a baby differs also in another aspect from the other paradigms of play discussed here. The others may be called *pre-stages of identification.* Being unable to achieve in reality a happy ending, an active rôle, or the strength of the aggressor, the child brings, at least in his play, things "into another order, more satisfying to himself." But in the incognito mechanism, the child adopts a way of acting not in order to incorporate it into his own person—as, for instance, in the identification with the aggressor —but in order to accentuate the distance, the veritable gulf between himself and such behavior. *"Facio quia absurdum,"* seems to be the principle of his actions. He rids himself of childish and ostracized impulses by acting them out drastically and copiously. He lends his motor apparatus to one part of his self while the other part—or his superego—pretends to be an uninvolved observer.

There are other instances in which we treat our own self as if it were another person and deal with another person as if it were our own self. There is, for instance, the mechanism that Anna Freud has called "altruistic secession," whereby we grant to and even encourage in another person an indulgence that our own conscience does not permit us.

Another example is the young child who tattles to his mother or teacher about the misdeed of a brother or a playmate. His denunciation of the other is not primarily malicious, as it might be in the case of older children or adults. Well enough does the young child know that he himself harbors similar "bad" desires. He uses his playmate to gain relief from his own guilty conscience.

In clowning, the child's superego disclaims what his bodily self does, while in tattling he clamors for the punishment of another person's misdeeds in order to atone for his own similar desires. In all these phenomena the gulf between superego and ego is temporarily wider than the distance between superego and another ego.

Thus far we have discussed *whose rôle* the child takes over and *why* he does so. Now we will follow another lead: to what extent do elements of the child's play copy a recent exciting or traumatic experience and to what extent are they *variations* of or *additions* to the past event. From the actor we turn to the plot.

DEFLECTED VENGEANCE

A child may suffer severe frustration without showing hostility against the person who disappoints or thwarts him. Instead, he vents his feelings on another person or on an object, often on his toys. Here the hostility is *deflected,* as in the classical example of the play with the bobbin.

The child (about eighteen months old) used all his toys only to play "gone" with them. He had a bobbin with a piece of cord fastened to it. He never thought of pulling it, for instance, along the floor, playing cart with it. Instead, he threw it with great dexterity into his crib which was covered so that the bobbin disappeared, saying his ominous "O-O-O-O" and then he pulled the cord so that the bobbin reappeared. . . . He greeted its appearance with a joyous "da."

Now the interpretation of this play was not difficult. It was connected with the great cultural achievement of the child, with his successful renunciation of instinctual gratification in permitting his mother to leave without remonstrating. Now he got even, so to say, by enacting the same disappearing and returning with the objects within reach. . . . The throwing away of an object, so that it was gone, could be the gratification of an impulse of vengeance against the mother for her leaving which in real life was suppressed. It could have the defiant meaning: "Go away! I don't need you. I even send you away."[1]

Since it is impossible to avoid frustrations and disappointments in the child's daily life, this type of play can be observed in every nursery.

In a variation of this formula, only the *mood,* the general *feeling* tone, is taken from a recent traumatic experience, but the child's play actions do not copy the action to which he has been subjected.

Anna Freud has given an illustrative example of a six-year-old boy who had undergone dental treatment and came to his analytic hour in a very bad mood.

The dentist had hurt him. He is angry and unfriendly and starts maltreating the things in my room. His first victim was an eraser. He wants me to give it to him as a present. I refuse and so he wants to cut it in half with a knife. Then he turns to a big role of cord and wants this as a present, explaining to me how well he could use it as a leash for his animals. Again I refuse and so he gets a knife and at least cuts off a long piece for himself. But he does not use it. Instead, he cuts it all up into small pieces. Then he rejects the cord, turns to the pencils, and starts sharpening them indefatigably with a knife, breaking off all the points and sharpening them again and again. It would be wrong to say that he plays at being a "dentist." The image of the dentist does not enter his behavior. *His identification does not concern the person of his adversary, only his aggression.*[2]

In our work with nursery schools, we frequently observed the following behavior: A little girl mercilessly spanks her dolls, puts them to bed for punishment, pushes them around, and so on. The teacher, naïvely assuming that the child's behavior mirrors the treatment she received at home, takes the first opportunity to talk to the mother. When the mother asserts that the child has never been spanked, and that the parents believe in lenient and progressive methods of education as sincerely as the teacher, the latter is nonplused.

[1] Sigmund Freud in *Beyond the Pleasure Principle.*
[2] *The Ego and the Mechanisms of Defense,* by Anna Freud. New York: International Universities Press, 1946.

The child's play in such a case reflects the feeling, not the treatment she experienced. The little girl felt her mother's impatience, anger, or hostility and uses "poetic license" in finding actions to express it in her doll play. She treats her dolls as her mother may at times *wish* to treat her.

ANTICIPATORY RETALIATION

The actual situation may be even further removed from the impression we gain from the play in the doll corner. The mother is unaware of any conflict or strain. Yet the child may be angry with her for one or the other reason. The child is the one who harbors hostile feelings against her mother and, therefore, expects her to retaliate. Indeed, with some children an unwarranted outburst of hostility against parent or teacher is a fairly reliable indication that they have done something forbidden. The underlying reasoning (conscious or unconscious) is, " I am justified in doing this to you as you plan to do it to me." The child's attitude may be called "anticipatory retaliation." (Credit for coining this seemingly self-contradicting term goes to *Time* magazine. It was used in 1948 in a discussion of our relations with Russia.) This mechanism was discussed by B. Bornstein, who calls it a "prophylactic aggressive attitude" and described several instances in which a child "takes over an aggression that he anticipates."[1]

Conversely, a little girl may be extremely gentle and kind with her dolls—not because her mother treats her this way, but because she would like her mother to be so kind and loving with her.

This indicates how careful we must be before drawing any inference about a mother's attitude. The child's play with her dolls may follow any one of these formulas: This is the way mother treats me, or this is how she *should* treat me or, this is the way she *feels* toward me, or, this is the way she will treat me once she finds out what I have done.

HAPPY ENDING

In other instances, the child's play mirrors and repeats a former experience except that the ending has been reversed from an unhappy to a happy one.

Shortly after Jonathan had moved from the city to a farm, he was playing with a visiting girl cousin in the yard when suddenly the lid of the dug-out on which the children were standing caved in and Eileen fell into the pile of manure it had covered. She struggled, yet sank deeper into the oozy mass. Jonathan stood petrified, torn between the desire to run for help and his unwillingness to leave her. Fortunately, somebody soon happened to pass by and rescued the girl. Months later, his mother overheard him repeating the incident with his toys.

[1] See "Clinical Notes on Child Analysis," in *Psychoanalytic Study of the Child*, Vol. I. New York: International Universities Press, 1945.

His commentary ran: "The boy fell in splash! . . . But he is a big boy. He can get out all by himself."

Many of the ambitious daydeams of latency and later years follow the same formula.

MAGIC (NO RISK)

In another variation, the child repeats an everyday experience in order to gain the assurance that there will *always* be a happy ending, or, possibly, that it is within the child's power to bring about the happy ending.

"Hide and seek," the favorite game of most children between eighteen months and two years of age, is a case in point. The child "hides" in a nook or under the table and the mother has to look for him. He enjoys endless repetitions. At first sight this may seem a simpler version of the more skilled hide-and-seek play of older children. The real difference becomes obvious only after the adult, feeling that the act has been repeated in the same form often enough and is getting monotonous, tries to improve it by introducing variations. For instance, the mother begins to "seek" the child in places where she has not looked before and takes a longer time in finding him. But the youngster gets impatient and darts out from his hiding place, pointing at himself. "Look! Here I am!" Or the mother suggests that he hide in another corner, in a place where it will be more difficult to find him. This does not appeal to the child and he is apparently deaf to the remark that mother already *knows* the place where he had been hiding before. It does not matter to him, or it is more correct to state that this is exactly what he wants.

Thus the young child's hide-and-seek play follows a formula different from the game of older children. With them, it consists in pitting against each other skill and cunning in hiding and seeking, each player trying to outsmart the other. Each one hopes to win, but knows his risk of losing, and this suspense provides the spice of the game. The younger child's hide-and-seek game is but a pantomimic assurance: "Whenever mother is out of sight, I can reunite with her in a short time. *I* am the one who brings about our separation, and *I* can bring about our reunion. His hide-and-seek play resembles a square dance in which the couples part and weave their way in traditional figures through the dancing group to meet again.

> Goodbye, farewell, my dear old friend.
> We'll meet again, you may depend.
> We'll meet again ere long
> In merry dance and song.

There is nothing new or unexpected in the stanzas and steps of a folk dance, yet the dancers enjoy the familiar sequence as the child relishes his well-worn pattern of play.

MANIPULATION AND PLAYFUL REPETITION

In every type of play discussed thus far, some feature of reality is "canceled"—in fact, this cancelation seems to be the purpose of the play. From the actor's point of view, his version of his assigning of rôles improves reality. Now we come to forms of play that apparently have no intention of undoing events or of changing the status of players; their only purpose is to broaden and to vary contact with reality, as in manipulative play, or to prolong an experience, as in playful repetition. Everyday examples are throwing a ball, letting sand run through the fingers, opening and closing a faucet, and so on.

Do these activities belong to true *play?* Are they not either plain enjoyment or rational forms of learning, aiming directly at the goal of acquiring a skill or gaining information? For the time being, let us note that to exclude them is to ignore an important and at times revealing segment of the child's interests. Later we may discover additional reasons that favor their inclusion in a survey of play.

There is no plot in these activities. The child does not step into any rôle; there is no drama, no climax, as there is in play instigated by Œdipal tensions, and the child's actions do not seem to have a symbolic value. In a way, these activities are the direct precursors of later experimentation, of the physical, chemical, geographical explorations of the older child.

But they are forerunners only, and they are to a large extent evoked or accentuated by the child's emotional problems.

Martin, five years old, habitually visits his grandmother several times a week. One day he notices an egg-timer which had been within his reach all the time. For a long time he sits still and watches the thin trickle of fine sand run, turning the small hourglass over and over again. This simple manipulation and observation fascinates him and he repeats it on several visits. This is in contrast to his usual active and roving behavior. For the last couple of weeks Martin had heard many allusions about a baby brother or sister who will arrive after Christmas, and this is the month of July.

L., aged two years and three months, builds for height with extraordinary perseverance and skill. She has wooden cylinders, $3\frac{1}{2}$ inches long and with a base the size of a nickel, and she succeeds in putting four or five on top of one another before the structure collapses. It would be a skilful performance for a seven-year-old.

She has a blackboard which she uses but little for scribbling. Instead, she makes a wet spot on it—then blows on the wet spot and watches it disappear. This, too, she repeats many times, showing an unusual patience.

L. has been seen by a consultant because she has outbursts of rage, and attacks her mother, biting and scratching her. Her difficulties could be traced to a traumatic castration experience. Her only playmate and the only person she ever saw naked was a cousin, a year older, a very wild and aggressive boy. She also had very early and strict toilet training.

These are instances of seemingly purely manipulative play. The activity runs on and on in a rather monotonous way or possibly with a crescendo or diminuendo. Yet when the child's emotional problems become known, it appears that the manipulative activity carried out with innumerable repetitions was not chosen at random.

Of course, in a young child's day there is much playful manipulation that has no deeper emotional roots. It is characterized by less persistence, and the child does not become so oblivious of his surroundings, of other toys, of the ridicule of other people, or of parental prohibitions.

On the other hand, in children's so-called dramatic play with dolls, and so on, there are frequent interludes in which the ideational content runs low or gets confused and hazy and only the pleasure in some kind of manipulation or repetition keeps the children going.

Written records of children's family and household play have a tendency to gloss over its incoherences and sudden shifts. Adults are prone to read into the children's doings a progressive movement from one episode into the next. Yet the play of children under five usually resembles less a stage play and more a dream. There are duplications of persons and episodes, sudden changes of locality—all of which just don't make sense, not even to the observer who knows the players well. It is amazing how children can apparently enjoy playing "together" for a long time, their ideas clicking for a while—then go far apart.

The child may modify his handling of a material, using it in many different ways and thus exploring it, or he may just repeat what he has already been doing. The doing as such seems to be pleasant enough to induce repetition. K. Bühler has termed this kind of activity with no goal *"Funktionslust."* The mere functioning, the activity in itself, brings pleasure. This method of play belongs to the youngest age group. It includes the child's babbling monologues in which he pronounces sounds and syllables, listens and repeats and varies them; the long spells of playing with his fingers, his toes, or a rattle. If any imagery accompanies this play, he may have vague hallucinations of gratification and grandeur. There cannot be any plot, as there is no risk, no competition. In a sense, intending and carrying out coincide.

Manipulative play that is chosen with great persistence is related to the child's emotional tensions; it has symbolic value and merges into dramatic play. In later years, manipulative play—for instance, doodling

—may return chiefly in stages of fatigue, or when a person is deeply pre-occupied with an emotional or intellectual problem—in short, when part of his resources are drained off.

In academic child psychology, one often finds the statement that the younger the child, the shorter the span of attention. This is correct only when we try to force upon a young child materials and play methods that would be more suitable for older children. A child of eighteen months or two years when permitted to handle and explore mud, sand, or water will show remarkable perseverance and an even longer span of fully con-centrated attention than older children with the same media and tools.

A play activity can belong to several models at the same time. For instance, Goethe's earliest childhood memory of how he threw all his doll dishes, one by one, out of the window and then let his mother's plates and cups follow because he enjoyed the cheerful clang of their breaking on the pavement outside, reads like an account of manipulative play. However, Freud's analysis shows that it was also an act of magic—namely, the symbolic eviction of a brother, who was about three years his junior. It was also an act of deflected vengeance. This shows that there is no rigid dividing line between various forms of play. Many of the things said here about the playing child are, with minor variations, equally true for the playing adult.

In conclusion, we may point out some of the teleological aspects of play. What are the benefits of play for the child? Several earlier play theories, especially Charles Darwin's, emphasized the acquisition of skills useful for the future adult, skills essential for survival in a certain en-vironment. Playful repetition helps in the retention of knowledge and skill.

The psychoanalytic interpretation so far has stressed the emotional release gained through play. Children play in order to mitigate, to deny, or temporarily to solve a conflict. In play the child recaptures for a while the omnipotence he once believed he possessed. He repeats and gradually assimilates an experience that was traumatic or a narcissistic insult. Play may help him to overcome a specific fear. And, of course, play is a source of pleasure. In addition to these emotional values, we would like to dis-cuss the benefits of play for the child's intellectual growth, benefits that are certainly not the cause of play, yet are inherent in it. Let us go to the very simplest quality of play: the playing child *repeats* an experience he has had, or a part of it. *Repeating it, he divests it of its uniqueness.* An event that has no precedent will overwhelm even the best equipped adult. Such events happen seldom to grown-ups. We can usually classify an occurrence in terms of past events or at least draw an analogy. The adult can in his thoughts go over the event that upset him or that he did not quite grasp. Reliving it in thought, he *reduces* it from a unique experience to one that can be classified with previous experiences.

The young child, however, meets "unprecedents" all the time. He has only a limited ability to recapture an image by repeating its verbal label or by repeating it in thought. Impressions that are unique are not amenable to laws. Play enables the child to reëxperience, to remold past impressions and events and their accompanying moods and emotions. *Playful repetition provides essential, possibly indispensable steps toward concept formation.* Freud defines thinking as test-acting (*Probehandeln*) carried out with a minimum of expenditure of energy. By pointing out the similarities between thought processes and direct action, by looking for their common denominator, we gain a better understanding. Can anything be gained by comparing formulas of *play* with the act of thinking? At first this seems a ridiculous comparison, almost blasphemous.

Thinking is a way of acting that respects the laws of reality. Play is largely wishful thinking, and as such ignores the laws of reality and poses as a "cheap" substitute for reasoning. Moreover, in play the expenditure of energy is big. Indeed, the overflow of useless energy has been considered the cause of play (Schiller-Spencer's theory of play).

Solving a problem through play thus appears the opposite of seeking a solution through reasoning. Yet the two share also certain features, above all the absence of direct and immediate consequences in the outer world. In thinking we pick out elements of reality and vary them; the same is done in play. Thinking is far quicker than direct action; steps taken in play can be instantaneous. Thinking requires imagination; so does play. Things that in reality are far apart in space or time can be brought into juxtaposition in the process of reasoning, but play also overcomes the obstacles of time and space with great facility. Play, as well as reasoning, is caused by an experience that was not concluded to our complete satisfaction. It was either too short, too sudden, unpleasant, or an insult to our ego, or we were not able to understand what was going on. Therefore, we are "at it," going over its various aspects in thought or play to be better equipped when it recurs or when we decide to seek it again.

Tentatively, we may say that a good deal of children's play is a crude kind of test action. In comparison to scientific thought, its tools are clumsy and inefficient. The adult in possession of the versatile symbolism of words can hardly estimate what it means for the young child to bring situations back by casting himself into different rôles, by play and pantomime. Play not only helps the child in his emotional adjustment; play activities are also the matrix of future realistic action and reasoning.

In conclusion, let us revert to the mechanism that seems to be at the root of most play: the turning from the passive to the active rôle. Being "passive" has several distinct meanings. It may, for instance, signify being physically inactive; it may also mean not knowing what to expect, being at the mercy of forces that the passive person cannot understand or predict, or being overwhelmed by a force or a person. Conversely, being in the active rôle may have any of the following meanings: being physically active, being informed and able to anticipate the next step, being superior in strength, leading.

The various types of passivity may befall a person separately or jointly and their traumatic effect varies accordingly. For instance, a tonsillectomy can be a shocking event if the child does not know what to expect—e.g., that he will go to sleep, wake up with pains, be unable to swallow, and so on. If the child has been told about these things beforehand, he will still be physically inactive and a person much stronger than he will give the orders and inflict pain, yet the shock is likely to be far less severe. The child who has been taken by surprise, who has not had the chance to go over the event beforehand in thought, is more likely to play it out persistently afterwards in an effort at *adjustment and self-cure. Again, play seems to substitute for reasoning.* We can also put it in the short formula: play stands for pre-event anxiety, and anxiety for post-event play.

While the various formulas of play discussed here merge and overlap, certain groupings emerge. There are the play formulas that tell a story and in which several people interact. *Dramatic play,* as it is often called, may be instigated either by the child's wish to be grown-up—presto! And then it seems to say: "It's so hard to wait so long. At least make believe these things." Or possibly: "If I pretend it ardently, maybe it will come true." The rôles the child chooses are pre-stages of identification. Then there are play models based on the opposite formula: "I pretend to be the baby (or clumsy, and so on) in my play; then it's obvious that I am not really clumsy (babyish)." Or: "If I make believe these things, they will not cling to me in real life." The child takes a rôle in order to accentuate the distance between himself and such behavior.

In either case, the child enjoys a gratification denied to him in reality or given in too small a measure. This kind of play helps the child to cope with the frustrations, the fears, the unfulfilled hopes, the disappointments, and the envy rooted in his situation in the family.

Manipulative play and play based on magic are basically different from the above. They are variations and ramifications of body skills and body controls, of oral and anal activities and of the one human relationship that precedes all others—e.g., the infant's need for his mother. They are instigated by his efforts to derive gratifications from his own body or from his mother—not from his broader human environment. With the child's entrance into the Œdipal phase, these play patterns do not disappear, but they lose their prominence.

10

Sex Differences in the Play Configurations of American Pre-Adolescents

Erik H. Erikson

In previous publications[1] the writer has illustrated the clinical impression that a playing child's behavior in space (i.e., his movements in a given playroom, his handling of toys, or his arrangement of play objects on floor or table) adds a significant dimension to the observation of play. And, indeed, three-dimensional arrangement in actual space is the variable distinguishing a play phenomenon from other "projective" media, which utilize space either in two-dimensional projection or through the purely verbal communication of spatial images. In an exploratory way it was also suggested that such clinical hints could be applied to the observation of older children and even of adults; play constructions of college students of both sexes[2] and of mental patients were described and first impressions formulated.[3] In all this work a suggestive difference was observed in the way in which the two sexes utilized a given play space to dramatize rather divergent themes; thus male college students occupied themselves to a significant degree with the representation (or avoidance of) an imagined

SOURCE. Adapted from a larger paper published in the *American Journal of Orthopsychiatry*, XXI, No. 4 (1951), 667–692. Reprinted with the permission of the author and the American Orthopsychiatric Association. Figures are to be found in the original source but are not included here.

danger to females emanating from careless drivers in street traffic, while female college students seemed preoccupied with dangers threatening things and people in the interior of houses, and this from intrusive males. The question arose whether or not sex differences could be formulated so as to be useful to observers in a nonclinical situation and on a more significant scale; and whether these differences would then appear to be determined by biological facts, such as difference in sex or maturational stage, or by differences in cultural conditioning. In 1940 the opportunity offered itself to secure play constructions from about 150 California children (about 75 boys and 75 girls), all of the same ages.[4] The procedure to be described here is an exploratory extension of "clinical" observation to a "normal" sample.[5] The number of children examined were, at age eleven, 79 boys and 78 girls; at age twelve, 80 boys and 81 girls; at age thirteen, 77 boys and 73 girls. Thus the majority of children contributed three constructions to the total number of 468 (236 play constructions of boys and 232 constructions of girls), which will be examined here.

On each occasion the child was individually called into a room where he found a selection of toys such as was then available in department stores (122 blocks, 38 pieces of toy furniture, 14 small dolls, 9 toy cars, 11 toy animals) laid out on two shelves. There was no attempt to make a careful selection of toys on the basis of size, color, material, etc. A study aspiring to such standards naturally would have to use dolls all made of the same materials and each accompanied by the same number of objects fitting in function and size, and themselves identical in material, color, weight, and so on. While it was not our intention to be methodologically consistent in this respect, the degree of inconsistency in the materials used may at least be indicated. Our family dolls were of rubber, which permitted their being bent into almost any shape; they were neatly dressed with all the loving care which German craftsmen lavish on playthings. A policeman and an aviator, however, were of unbending metal and were somewhat smaller than the doll family. There were toy cars, some of them smaller than the policeman, some bigger; but there were no airplanes to go with the aviator.

The toys were laid out in an ordered series of open cardboard boxes, each containing a class of toys, such as people, animals, and cars. These boxes were presented on a shelf. The blocks were on a second shelf in two piles, one containing a set of large blocks, one a set of small ones. Next to the shelves the stage for the actual construction was set: a square table with a square background of the same size.

The following instructions were given:

I am interested in moving pictures. I would like to know what kind of moving pictures children would make if they had a chance to make pictures. Of course,

I could not provide you with a real studio and real actors and actresses; you will have to use these toys instead. Choose any of the things you see here and construct on this table an *exciting* scene out of an *imaginary* moving picture. Take as much time as you want and tell me afterward what the scene is about.

While the child worked on his scene, the observer sat at his desk, presumably busy with some writing. From there he observed the child's attack on the problem and sketched transitory stages of his play construction. When the subject indicated that the scene was completed, the observer said, "Tell me what it is all about," and took dictation on what the child said. If no exciting content was immediately apparent, the observer further asked, "What is the most exciting thing about this scene?" He then mildly complimented the child on his construction.[6]

The reference to moving pictures was intended to reconcile these preadolescents to the suggested use of toys, which seemed appropriate only for a much younger age. And, indeed, only two children refused the task, and only one of these complained afterward about the "childishness" of the procedure: she was the smallest of all the children examined. The majority constructed scenes willingly, although their enthusiasm for the task and their ability to concentrate on it, their skill in handling the toys, and their originality in arranging them varied widely. Yet the children of this study produced scenes with a striking lack of similarity to movie clichés. In nearly five hundred constructions, not more than three were compared with actual moving pictures. In no case was a particular doll referred to as representing a particular actor or actress. Lack of movie experience can hardly be blamed for this; the majority of these children attended movies regularly and had their favorite actors and types of pictures. Neither was the influence of any of the radio programs or comic pictures noticeable except in so far as they themselves elaborated upon clichés of western lore; there were no specific references to "Superman" and only a few to "Red Ryder." Similarly, contemporary events of local or world significance scarcely appeared. The play procedure was first employed shortly before the San Francisco World's Fair opened its gates —an event which dominated the Far West and especially the San Francisco Bay region for months. This sparkling fair, located in the middle of the bay and offering an untold variety of spectacles, was mentioned in not more than five cases. Again, the approach and outbreak of the war did not increase the occurrence of the aviator in the play scenes, in spite of the acute rise in general estimation of military aviation, especially in the aspirations of our boys and their older brothers. The aviator rated next to the monk in the frequency of casting.

It has been surmised that in both groups the toys suggested infantile play so strongly that other pretensions became impossible. Yet only one girl undressed a doll, as a younger girl would; she had recently been involved in a neighborhood sex-education crisis. And while little boys like to dramatize automobile accidents with the proper bumps and noises, in our constructions automobile accidents, as well as earthquakes and bombings, were not made to happen; rather their final outcome was quietly arranged. At first glance, therefore, the play constructions cannot be considered to be motivated by a regression to infantile play in its overt manifestations.

In general, none of the simpler explanations of the motivations responsible for the play constructions presented could do away with the impression that a play act—like a dream—is a complicated dynamic product of "manifest" and "latent" themes, of past experience and present task, of the need to express something and the need to suppress something, of clear representation, symbolic indirection, and radical disguise.

It will be seen that girls, on the whole, tend to build quiet scenes of everyday life, preferably within a home or in school. The most frequent "exciting scene" built by girls is a quiet family constellation, in a house without walls, with the older girl playing the piano. Disturbances in the girls' scenes are primarily caused by animals, usually cute puppies, or by mischievous children—always boys. More serious accidents occur too, but there are no murders, and there is little gun play. The boys produce more buildings and outdoor scenes, and especially scenes with wild animals, Indians, or automobile accidents; they prefer toys which move or represent motion. Peaceful scenes are predominantly traffic scenes under the guiding supervision of the policeman. In fact, the policeman is the "person" most often used by the boys, while the older girl is the one preferred by girls.[7] Otherwise, it will be seen that the "family dolls" are used more by girls, as follows functionally from the fact that they produce more indoor scenes, while the policeman can apply his restraining influence to cars in traffic as well as to wild beasts and Indians.

The general method of the study was clinical as well as statistical; i.e., each play construction was correlated with the constructions of all the children as well as with the other performances of the same child. Thus *unique elements* in the play construction were found to be related to unique elements in the life-history of the individual, while a number of *common elements* were correlated statistically to biographic elements shared by all the children.

In the following three examples, the interplay of manifest theme and play configuration and their relation to significant life-data will be illustrated.

Deborah,[8] a well-mannered, intelligent, and healthy girl of eleven, calmly selects (by transferring them from shelves to table) all the furniture, the whole family, and the two little dogs, but leaves blocks, cars, uniformed dolls, and the other animals untouched. Her scene represents the interior of a house. Since she uses no blocks, there are no outer walls around the house or partitions within it. The house furniture is distributed over the whole width of the table but not without well-defined groups and configurations: there is a circular arrangement of living-room furniture in the right foreground, a bathroom arrangement along the back wall, and an angular bedroom arrangement in the left background. Thus the various parts of the house are divided in a reasonably functional way. In contrast, a piano in the left foreground and a table next to it (incidentally, the only red pieces of furniture used) do not seem to belong to any configuration. Taken together, they do not constitute a conventional room, although they do seem to belong together.

Turning to the cast, we note, within the circle of the living-room, a group consisting of a woman, a boy, a baby, and the two puppies. The woman has the baby in her arms; the boy plays with the two puppies. While this sociable group is as if held together by the circle, all the other people are occupied with themselves: clockwise, in the left foreground, the man at the piano, the girl at the desk, the other boy in the bed in the left background, and the second woman in the kitchen along the back wall.

Having arranged all this slowly and calmly, Deborah indicates with a smile that she is ready to tell her story, which is short enough: "This boy [in the background] is bad, and his mother sent him to bed." She does not seem inclined to say anything about the others. The experimenter (who must now confess that, at the end of this scene, he permitted himself the clinical luxury of one nonstandardized question) asks, "Which one of these people would you like to be?" "The boy with the puppies," she replies.

While her *spontaneous story* singled out the lonely boy in the farthest background, an *elicited afterthought* focuses, instead, on the second boy, who is part of the lively family circle in the foreground. In all their brevity, these two references point to a few interpersonal themes: punishment, closeness to the mother and separation from her, loneliness and playfulness, and an admitted preference for being a boy. Equally significant, of course, are the themes which are suggested but not verbalized.

The selective references to the boy in disgrace and to the happier boy in the foreground immediately point to the fact that in actual life Deborah has an older brother. (She has a baby brother, too, whose counterpart we may see in the baby in the arms of the mother.) We have ample reason to believe that she envies this boy because of his superior age, his sex, his sharp intellect, and his place close to the mother's heart. Envy invites two intentions: to eliminate the competitor and to replace, to become him. Deborah's play construction seems to accomplish this double purpose by splitting the brother in two: the competitor is banished to the lonely background; the boy in the foreground is what she would like to be.

We must ask here: Does Deborah have an inkling of such a "latent" meaning? We have no way of finding out. In this investigation, which is part of a long-range study, there is no place for embarrassing questions and interpretations. Therefore, if in this connection we speak of "latent" themes, "latent" cannot and does not mean "unconscious." It merely means "not brought out in the child's verbalization." On the other hand, our interpretation is, as indicated, based on life-data and test material secured over more than a decade.

But where is Deborah? The little girl at the desk is the only girl in the scene and, incidentally, close to Deborah's age. She was not mentioned in the story. She is, as pointed out, part of a configuration which does not fit as easily and functionally into a conventional house interior as do the other parts. The man at the piano, closest to the girl at the desk, has in common with her only that they share the two red pieces of furniture. Otherwise, they both face away from the family without facing toward each other; they are parallel to each other, with the girl a little behind the father.

In life, Deborah and her father are close to each other temperamentally. Marked introverts, they are both apt to shy away in a somewhat pained manner from the more vivacious members of the family, especially from the mother. Thus they have an important but negative trend in common. Just because of their more introvert natures, they are unable to express what unites them in any other way than by staying close to each other without saying much. This, we think, is represented spatially by a *twosome in parallel isolation.*

In adding this theme to the two verbalized themes (the *isolated bad boy* and the identification with the *good boy in the playful circle*), we surmise that the total scene well circumscribes the child's main life-problem, namely, her isolated position between the parents, between the siblings, and (as yet) between the sexes. In a similar but never once identical manner, our clinical interpretation arrives at a theme representative of that life-task which (present or past) puts the greatest strain on the present psychological equilibrium. In this way, the play construction often is a significant help in the analysis of the life-history because it singles out one or a number of life-data as the *subjectively most relevant* ones and adds a significant key to the dynamic interpretation of the child's personality development.

We may ask one further question: Is there any indication in the play constructions as to how deeply Deborah is disturbed or apt to become disturbed by the particular strain which she reveals? Here a clinical impression must suffice. Deborah uses the whole width of the table. She does not crowd her scene against the background on into one corner, as according to our observations, children with marked feelings of insecurity are apt to do; neither does she spread the furniture all over the table in an amorphous way, as we would expect a less mature child to do. Her groupings are meaningfully and pleasingly placed; so is her distribution of people. The one manifest incongruity in her groupings (father and daughter) proves to be latently significant; only here her scene suffers, as it were, a symptomatic lapse. Otherwise, while there is a simple honesty in her scene, there certainly is no great originality and no special sparkle in it. But here it is necessary to remember the surprising dearth of imagination in most constructions and the possibility that only specially inclined children may take to this medium with real verve.

In one configurational respect Deborah's scene has much in common with those produced by most of the other girls. She places no walls around her house and no partitions inside. In anticipation of the statistical evaluation of this configurational item, we may state here an impression of essential femininity, which, together with the indications of relative inner balance, forms a welcome forecast of a personality potentially adequate to meet the stresses outlined.

In addition to the arrangement on the table and its relation to the verbalization, clinical criteria may be derived from the observation of a child's general approach to the play situation. Deborah's approach was calm, immediate, and consistent; her selection of toys was careful and apt. Other typical approaches are characterized by prolonged silence and sudden, determined action; by an enthusiasm which quickly runs its course; or by some immediate thoughtless remark such as, "I don't know what to do." The final stage of construction, in turn, can be characterized by frequent new beginnings; by a tendency to let things fall or drop; by evasional conversation; by the need to find room for all toys or to exclude certain types of them; by a perfectionist effort at being meticulous in detail; by an inability to wind up the task; by a sudden and unexplained loss of interest and ambition, etc. Such time curves must be integrated with the spatial analysis into a spacetime continuum which reflects certain basic attributes of the subject's way of organizing experience—in other words, the ways of his ego.

In the spatial analysis proper, we consider factors such as the following:

   1. The subject's approach, first, to the shelves and then to the table, and his way of connecting these two determinants of the play area.

   2. The relationship of the play construction to the table surface, i.e., the area covered, and the location, distribution, and alignment of the main configurations with the table square.

   3. The relationship of the whole of the construction to its parts and of the parts to one another.

Let us now compare the construction of calm and friendly Deborah with that of the girl most manifestly disturbed during the play procedure. This girl, whom we shall call Victoria, is also eleven years old; her intelligence is slightly lower than Deborah's. She appears flushed and angry upon entering the room with her mother. A devout Catholic, Victoria had overheard somebody in the hall address this writer as "Doctor." She had become acutely afraid that a man had replaced the Study's woman doctor at this critical time of a girl's development. This she had told her mother. The mother then questioned the writer; he reassured both ladies, whereupon Victoria, still with tears in her eyes but otherwise friendly, consented to construct a scene in her mother's protective presence.

Victoria's house form (she called it "a castle") differs from Deborah's construction in all respects. The floor plan of the building is constricted to a small area. There are high, thick walls and a blocked doorway; and there is neither furniture nor people. However, there seems to be an imaginary population of two: "The king," says Victoria, letting her index finger slide along the edge of the foreground, "walks up and down in front of the castle. He waits for the queen, who is changing her dress in there" (pointing into the walled-off corner of the castle).

In this case the "traumatic" factor seems to lie, at least superficially, in the immediate past; for the thematic similarity between the child's acute discomfort in the anticipation of having to undress before a man doctor and, in the play, the exclusion of His Majesty from Her Majesty's boudoir seems immediately clear. High walls and closed gates, as well as the absence of people, all are rare among undisturbed girls; if present, they reflect either a general disturbance or temporary defensiveness.

One small configurational detail in this scene contradicts the general (thematic and configurational) emphasis on the protection of an undressed female from the view even of her husband. In spite of the fact that quite a number of square blocks were still available for a high and solid gate, Victoria selected the only rounded block for the front door. This arrangement, obviously, would permit the king to peek with ease if he were so inclined, and thus provides, for this construction, the usual (but always highly unique) discrepant detail which reveals *the dynamic counterpart to the main manifest theme* in the construction. Here the discrepant detail probably points to an underlying exhibitionism, which, in this preadolescent girl, may indeed have been the motivation for her somewhat hysterical defensiveness; for her years of experience with the Study had not given her any reason to expect embarrassing exposition or wilful violation of her Catholic code. We note, however, that Victoria's construction, overdefensive as it is in its constricted and high-walled configuration and theme, is placed in the center of the play table and does not, as we have learned to expect in the case of chronic anxiety, "cling" to the background; her upset, we conclude, may be acute and temporary.

Lisa, a third girl, has to deal with a lifelong and constant problem of anxiety: she was born with a congenital heart condition. This, however, had never been mentioned in her interviews with the workers of the Guidance Study. Her parents and her pediatrician, although in a constant state of preparedness for the possibility of a severe attack, did not wish the matter to be discussed with her and assumed that they had thus succeeded in keeping the child from feeling "different" from other children.

Lisa's scene consists of a longish arrangement, quite uneven in height, of a number of blocks close to the back wall. On the highest block (according to the criteria to be presented later, a "tower") stands the aviator, while below two women and two children are crowded into the small compartment of a front yard, apparently watching a procession of cars and animals. Lisa's story follows. We see in it a metaphoric representation of a moment of heart weakness—an experience which she had never mentioned "in that many words." The analogy between the play scene and its suggested meaning will be indicated by noting elements of a moment of heart failure in brackets following the corresponding play items.

"There is a quarrel between the mother and the nurse over money [anger]. This aviator stands high up on a tower [feeling of dangerous height]. He really is not an aviator, but he thinks he is [feeling of unreality]. First he feels as if his head was rotating, then that his whole body turns around and around [dizziness]. He sees these animals walking by which are not really there [seeing things move about in front of eyes]. Then this girl notices the dangerous situation of the aviator and calls an ambulance [awareness of attack and urge to call for help]. Just as the ambulance comes around a corner, the aviator falls down from the tower [feeling of sinking and falling]. The ambulance crew quickly unfolds a net; the aviator falls into it, but is bounced back up to the top of the tower [recovery]. He holds on to the edge of the tower and lies down [exhaustion]."

Having constructed this scene, the child smilingly left for her routine medical examination, where, for the first time, she mentioned to the Institute physician her frequent attacks of dizziness and indicated that at the time she was trying to overcome them by walking on irregular fences and precipitous places in order to get used to the dizziness. Her quite unique arrangement of blocks, then, seems to signify an uneven fencelike arrangement, at the highest point of which the moment of sinking weakness occurs. That the metaphoric expression of intimate experiences in free play "loosens" the communicability of these same experiences is, of course, the main rationale of play therapy.

These short summaries will illustrate the way in which configurations and themes may prove to be related to whatever item of the life-history, remote or recent, is at the moment most pressing in the child's life. A major classification of areas of disturbance represented in our constructions suggests as relevant areas: (1) family constellations; (2) infantile traumata (for example, a twelve-year-old boy, who had lost his mother at five but had seemed quite oblivious to the event, in his construction revealed that he had been aware of a significant detail surrounding her death; this detail, in fact, had induced him secretly to blame his father for the loss); (3) physical affliction or hypochrondriac concern; (4) acute anxiety connected with the experiment; (5) psychosexual conflict. Naturally these themes interpenetrate.

II

We shall now turn to a strain which is by necessity shared by all pre-adolescents, namely, sexual maturation—a "natural" strain which, at the same time, has a most specific relation to the clearest differentiation in any mixed group, namely, difference in sex.

Building blocks provide a play medium most easily counted, measured, and characterized in regard to spatial arrangement. At the same time, they seem most impersonal and least compromised by cultural connotations and individual meanings. A block is almost nothing but a block. It seemed striking, then (unless one considered it a mere function of the difference in themes), that boys and girls differed in the *number* of blocks used as well as in the *configurations* constructed.

Boys use many more blocks, and use them in more varied ways, than girls do. The difference increases in the use of ornamental items, such as cylinders, triangles, cones, and knobs. More than three-quarters of the constructions in which knobs or cones occur are built by boys. This ratio increases with the simplest ornamental composition, namely, a cone on a cylinder; 86 per cent of the scenes in which this configuration occurs were built by boys. With a very few exceptions, only boys built constructions consisting *only* of blocks, while only girls, with no exception, arranged scenes consisting of furniture exclusively. In between these extremes the following classifications suggested themselves: towers and buildings, traffic lanes and intersections, simple inclosures, interiors without walls, outdoor scenes without use of blocks.[9]

The most significant sex differences concern the tendency among the boys to erect structures, buildings and towers, or to build streets, among the girls, to take the play table to be the interior of a house, with simple, little, or no use of blocks.

The configurational approach to the matter can be made more specific by showing the spatial function emphasized in the various ways of using (or not using) blocks. This method would combine all the constructions which share the function of *channelizing* traffic (such as lanes, tunnels, or crossings); all elaborate buildings and special structures (such as bridges, boats, etc.) which owe their character to the tendency of *erecting* and *constructing;* all simple walls which merely *inclose* interiors; and all house interiors, which are without benefit of inclosing walls and are thus simply *open interiors.*

In the case of *inclosures,* it was necessary to add other differentiations. To build a rectangular arrangement of simple walls is about the most common way of delineating any limited area and, therefore, is not likely to express any particular sex differences. But it was found that, in the case of many boys, simple inclosures in the form of front yards and back yards were only added to more elaborate buildings or that simple corrals or barnyards would appear in connection with outdoor scenes. In this category, therefore, only more detailed work showed that (1) significantly more boys than girls build inclosures only in conjunction with elaborate structures or traffic lanes; (2) significantly more girls than boys will be satisfied with the exclusive representation of a simple inclosure; (3) girls *include* a significantly greater number of (static) objects and people within their inclosures; (4) boys *surround* their inclosures with a significantly greater number of (moving) objects.

Height of structure, then, is prevalent in the configurations of the boys. The observation of the unique details which accompany constructions of extreme height suggests that the variable representing the opposite of elevation, i.e., *downfall,* is equally typical for boys. Fallen-down structures, namely, "ruins," are exclusively found among boys,[10] a fact which did not change in the days of the war when girls as well as boys must have been shocked by pictorial reports of destroyed homes. In connection with the very highest towers, something in the nature of a downward trend appears regularly, but in such a diverse form that only individual examples can illustrate what is meant: one boy, after much indecision, took his extraordinarily high tower down in order to build a final configuration of a simple and low character; another balanced his tower very precariously and pointed out that the immediate danger of collapse was in itself the exciting factor in his story, in fact, *was* his story. In two cases extremely high and well-built façades with towers were incongruously combined with low irregular inclosures. One boy who built an especially high tower put a prone boy doll at the foot of it and explained that this boy had fallen down from its height; another boy left the boy doll sitting high on one of several elaborate towers but said that the boy had had a mental breakdown and that the tower was an insane asylum. The very highest tower was built by the very smallest boy; and, to climax lowness, a colored boy built his structure *under* the table. In these and similar ways, variations of a theme make it apparent that *the variable high-low* is a *masculine variable.* To this generality, we would add the clinical judgment that, in preadolescent boys, extreme height (in its regular combination with an element of breakdown or fall) reflects a trend toward the emotional overcompensation of a doubt in, or a fear for, one's masculinity, while varieties of "lowness" express passivity and depression.

Girls rarely build towers. When they do, they seem unable to make them stand freely in space. Their towers lean against, or stay close to, the background. The highest tower built by any girl was not on the table at all but on a shelf in a niche in the wall beside and behind the table. The clinical impression is that, in girls of this age, the presence of a tower connotes the masculine overcompensation of an ambivalent dependency on the mother, which is indicated in the closeness of the structure to the background. There are strong clinical indications that a scene's "clinging" to the background connotes "mother fixation," while the extreme foreground serves to express counterphobic over-compensation.

In addition to the dimensions "high" and "low" and "forward" and "backward," "open" and "closed" suggest themselves as significant. Open interiors of houses are built by a majority of girls. In many cases this interior is expressly peaceful. Where it is a home rather than a school, somebody, usually a little girl, plays the piano: a remarkably tame "exciting movie scene" for representative preadolescent girls. In a number of cases, however, a disturbance occurs. An intruding pig throws the family in an uproar and forces the girl to hide behind the piano; the father may, to the family's astonishment, be coming home riding on a lion; a teacher has jumped on a desk because a tiger has entered the room. This intruding element is always a man, a boy, or an animal. If it is a dog, it is always expressly a boy's dog. A family consisting exclusively of women and girls or with a majority of women and girls is disturbed and endangered. Strangely enough, however, this idea of an intruding creature does not lead to the defensive erection of walls or to the closing of doors. Rather, the majority of these intrusions have an element of humor and of pleasurable excitement and occur in connection with open interiors consisting of circular arrangements of furniture.

To indicate the way in which such regularities became apparent through exceptions to the rule, we wish to report briefly how three of these "intrusive" configurations came to be built by boys. Two were built by the same boy in two successive years. Each time a single male figure, surrounded by a circle of furniture, was intruded upon by wild animals. This boy at the time was obese, of markedly feminine build, and, in fact, under thyroid treatment. Shortly after this treatment had taken effect, the boy became markedly masculine. In his third construction he built one of the highest and slenderest of all towers. Otherwise, there was only one other boy who, in a preliminary construction, had a number of animal intrude into an "open interior" which contained a whole family. When already at the door, he suddenly turned back, exclaimed that "something was wrong," and with an expression of satisfaction, rearranged the animals along a tangent which led them close by but away from the family circle.

Inclosures are the largest item among the configurations built by girls, if, as pointed out, we consider primarily those inclosures which include a house interior. These inclosures often have a richly ornamented gate (the only configuration which girls care to elaborate in detail); in others, openness is counteracted by a blocking of the entrance or a thickening of the walls. The general clinical impression here is that high and thick walls (such as those in Victoria's construction) reflect either acute anxiety over the feminine role or, in conjunction with other configurations, acute oversensitiveness and selfcenteredness. The significantly larger number of open interiors and simple inclosures, combined with an emphasis, in unique details, on intrusion into the interiors, on an exclusive elaboration of doorways, and on the blocking-off of such doorways seems to mark *open and closed* as a feminine variable.

The most significant sex differences in the use of the play space, then, add up to the following picture: in the boys, the outstanding variables are height and downfall and motion and its channelization or arrest (policeman); in girls, static interiors, which are open, simply inclosed, or blocked and intruded upon.

In the case of boys, these configurational tendencies are connected with a generally greater emphasis on the outdoors and the outside, and in girls with an emphasis on house interiors.

The selection of the subjects assures the fact that the boys and girls who built these constructions are as masculine and feminine as they come in a representative group in our community. We may, therefore, assume that these sex differences are a representative expression of masculinity and of femininity for this particular age group.

Our group of children, developmentally speaking, stand at the *beginning of sexual maturation*. It is clear that the spatial tendencies governing these constructions closely parallel the morphology of the sex organs: in the male, *external* organs, *erectible* and *intrusive* in character, serving highly *mobile* sperm cells; *internal* organs in the female, with vestibular *access*, leading to *statically expectant* ova. Yet only comparative material, derived from older and younger subjects living through other developmental periods, can answer the question whether our data reflect an acute and temporary emphasis on the modalities of the sexual organs owing to the experience of oncoming sexual maturation, or whether our data suggest that the *two sexes may live, as it were, in time-spaces of a different quality*, in basically different fields of "means-end-readiness."[11]

In this connection it is of interest that the dominant trends outlined here seem to parallel the dominant trends in the play constructions of the college students in the exploratory study previously referred to. There the tendency was, among men, to emphasize (by dramatization or avoidance) potential disaster to women. Most commonly, a little girl was run over by a truck. But while this item occurred in practically all cases in the preliminary and abortive constructions, it remained a central theme in fewer of the final constructions. In the women's constructions, the theme of an insane or criminal man was universal: he broke into the house at night or, at any rate, was where he should not be. At the time we had no alternative but to conclude tentatively that what these otherwise highly individual play scenes had in common was an expression of the sexual frustration adherent to the age and the mores of these college students. These young men and women, so close to complete intimacy with the other sex and shying away only from its last technical consummation, were dramatizing in their constructions (among other latent themes) fantasies of sexual violence which would override prohibition and inhibition.

In the interpretation of these data, questions arise which are based on an assumed dichotomy between biological motivation and cultural motivation and on that between conscious and unconscious sexual attitudes.

The exclusively cultural interpretation would grow out of the assumption that these children emphasize in their constructions the sex roles defined for them by their particular cultural setting. In this case the particular use of blocks would be a logical function of the manifest content of the themes presented. Thus, if boys concentrate on the exterior of buildings, on bridges and traffic lanes, the conclusion would be that this is a result of their actual or anticipated experience, which takes place outdoors more than does that of girls, and that they anticipate construction work and travel while the girls themselves know that their place is supposed to be in the home. A boy's tendency to picture outward and upward movement may, then, be only another expression of a general sense of obligation to prove himself strong and aggressive, mobile and independent in the world, and to achieve "high standing." As for the girls, their representation of house interiors (which has such a clear antecedent in their infantile play with toys) would then mean that they are concentrating on the anticipated task of taking care of a home and of rearing children, either because their upbringing has made them want to do this or because they think they are supposed to indicate that they want to do this.

A glance at the selection of elements and themes in their relation to conscious sex roles demonstrates how many questions remain unanswered if a one-sided cultural explanation is accepted as the sole basis for the sex differences expressed in these configurations.

If the boys, in building these scenes, think primarily of their present or anticipated roles, why are not boy dolls the figures most frequently used by them? The policeman is their favorite; yet it is safe to say that few anticipate being policemen or believe that they should. Why do the boys not arrange any sport fields in their play constructions? With the inventiveness born of strong motivation, this could have been accomplished, as could be seen in the construction of one football field, with grandstand and all. But this was arranged by a girl who at the time was obese and tomboyish and wore "affectedly short-trimmed hair"—all of which suggests a unique determination in her case.

As mentioned before, during the early stages of the study, World War II approached and broke out; to be an aviator became one of the most intense hopes of many boys. Yet the pilot shows preferred treatment in both boys and girls only over the monk, and—over the baby; while the policeman occurs in their constructions twice as often as the cowboy, who certainly is the more immediate role-ideal of these Western boys and most in keeping with the clothes they wear and the attitudes they affect.

If the girls' prime motivation is the love of their present homes and the anticipation of their future ones to the exclusion of all aspirations which they might be sharing with boys, it still would not immediately explain why the girls build fewer and lower walls around their houses. Love for home life might conceivably result in an increase in high walls and closed doors as guarantors of intimacy and security. The majority of the girl dolls in these peaceful family scenes are playing the piano or peacefully sitting with their families in the living-room: could this be really considered representative of what they want to do or think they should pretend they want to do when asked to build an exciting movie scene?

A piano-playing little girl, then, seems as specific for the representation of a peaceful interior in the girls' constructions as traffic arrested by the policeman is for the boys' street scenes. The first can be understood to express *goodness indoors;* the second, a guarantor of safety and *caution outdoors.* Such emphasis on goodness and safety, in response to the explicit instruction to construct an "exciting movie scene," suggests that in these preadolescent scenes more dynamic dimensions and more acute conflicts are involved than a theory of mere compliance with cultural and conscious ideals would have it. Since other projective methods used in the study do not seem to call forth such a desire to depict virtue, the question arises whether or not the very suggestion to play and to think of something exciting aroused in our children sexual ideas and defenses against them.

All the questions mentioned point to the caution necessary in settling on any one dichotomized view concerning the motivations leading to the sex differences in these constructions.

The configurational approach, then, provides an anchor for interpretation in the ground plan of the human body: here, sex difference obviously provides the most significant over-all differentiation. In the interplay of thematic content and spatial configuration, then, we come to recognize an expression of that interpenetration of the biological, cultural, and psychological, which, in psychoanalysis, we have learned to summarize as the *psychosexual.*

In conclusion, a word on the house as a symbol and as a subject of metaphors. While the spatial tendencies related here extend to three-dimensionality as such, the construction of a house by the use of simple, standardized blocks obviously serves to make the matter more concrete and more measurable. Not only in regard to the representation of sex differences but also in connection with the hypochrondriac preoccupation with other growing or afflicted body parts, we have learned to assume an unconscious tendency to represent the body and its parts in terms of a building and its parts. And, indeed, Freud said fifty years ago when introducing the interpretation of dreams: "The only typical, that is to say, regularly occurring representation of the human form as a whole is that of a house."[12]

We use this metaphor consciously, too. We speak of our body's "build" and of the "body" of vessels, carriages, and churches. In spiritual and poetic analogies, the body carries the connotation of an abode, prison, refuge, or temple inhabited by, well, ourselves: "This mortal house," as Shakespeare put it. Such metaphors, with varying abstractness and condensation, express groups of ideas which are sometimes too high, sometimes too low, for words. In slang, too, every outstanding part of the body, beginning with the "underpinnings," appears translated into metaphors of house parts. Thus, the face is a "façade," the eyes "front windows with shutters," the mouth a "barn door" with a "picket fence," the throat a "drain pipe," the chest a "bone house" (which is also a term used for the whole body), the male genital is referred to as a "water pipe," and the rectum as the "sewer." Whatever this proves, it does show that it takes neither erudition nor a special flair for symbolism to understand these metaphors. Yet, for some of us, it is easier to take such symbolism for granted on the stage of drama and burlesque than in dreams or in children's play; in other words, it is easier to accept such representation when it is lifted to sublime or lowered to laughable levels.

The configurational data presented here points primarily to an unconscious reflection of biological sex differences in the projective utilization of the *play space;* cultural and age differences have been held constant in the selection of subjects. As for *play themes,* our brief discussion of possible conscious and historical determinants did not yield any conclusive trend; yet it is apparent that the material culture represented in these constructions (skyscrapers, policemen, automobiles, pianos) provides an anchor point for a reinterpretation of the whole material on the basis of comparisons with other cultures. In such comparisons *houses again mean houses;* it will then appear that the basic biological dimensions elaborated here are utilized at the same time to express different technological space-time experiences. Thus it is Margaret Mead's observation that in their play Manus boys who have grown up in huts by the water do not emphasize height, but outward movement (canoes, planes), while the girls, again, concentrate on static houses. It is thus hoped that the clear emphasis in this paper on the biological will facilitate comparative studies; for cultures, after all, elaborate upon the biologically given and strive for a division of labor between the sexes and for a mutuality of function in general which is, simultaneously, workable within the body's scheme and life-cycle, meaningful to the particular society, and manageable for the individual ego.

Notes

1. Erikson, 1937, 1938, 1940.
2. Erikson, 1938.
3. Erikson, 1937; see also Rosenzweig and Shakow, 1937.
4. The author is indebted for this opportunity to Dr. Jean W. Macfarlane,

director of the Guidance Study, Institute of Child Welfare, University of California, Berkeley. The Guidance Study, in the words of its director, is "a 20-year cumulative study dedicated to the investigation of physical, mental, and personality development" (Macfarlane, 1938). Its subjects were "more than 200 children arbitrarily selected upon the basis of every third birth during a given period in Berkeley, California." The children were matched at birth on certain socioeconomic factors and divided into a guidance group and a control group. The study thus provided for "cumulative observation of contemporaneous adjustments and maladjustments in a normal sample."

5. At the time of this investigation, the author was not familiar with the much more comprehensive "world-play" method of Margaret Lowenfeld in England (Lowenfeld, 1939).

6. The emphasis on the element of "excitement" warrants an explanation. In the exploratory study mentioned above (Erikson, 1938), Harvard and Radcliffe students had been asked to build "a dramatic scene." All English major educated in the imagery of the finest in English drama, they were observed to build scenes of remarkably little dramatic flavor. Instead, they seemed to be overcome by a kind of infantile excitement, which—on the basis of an extensive data collection—could be related to childhood traumata. Conversely, a group of psychology students in another university, who decided to employ a short cut by asking their subjects to build "the most traumatic scene of their childhood," apparently aroused resistance, and produced scenes characterized by a remarkable lack of overt excitement of any kind, by a dearth in formal originality, and by the absence of relevant biographic analogies. These experiences suggested, then, that we should ask our preadolescents for an exciting scene in order to establish a standard against which the degree and kind of dramatic elaboration could be judged, while this suggestion as well as the resistance provoked by it could be expected to elicit lingering infantile ideas.

7. Honzik, 1951.

8. All names are, of course, fictitious, and facts which might prove identifying have been altered.

9. An analysis of the sex differences in the occurrence of blocks and toys in the play constructions of these preadolescents has been published by Dr. Marjarie Honzik. For a systematic configurational analysis and for a statistical evaluation see the original article (Honzik, 1951). The writer is indebted to Dr. Honzik and also Drs. Frances Orr and Alex Sheriffs for independent "blind" ratings of the photographs of the play constructions.

10. One single girl built a ruin. This girl, who suffered from a fatal blood disease, at the time was supposed to be unaware of the fact that only a new medical procedure, then in its experimental stages, was keeping her alive. Her story presented the mythological theme of a "girl who miraculously returned to life after having been sacrificed to the gods." She has since died.

11. For an application of the configurational trends indicated here in a masculinity-femininity test cf. Franck, 1946. See also Tolman, 1932.

12. Freud, 1922.

List of References

Erikson, Erik Homburger. 1937. "Configurations in Play," *Psychoanalytic Quarterly,* VI, No. 2, 139–214.

———. 1938. "Dramatic Productions Test." In *Explorations in Personality,* ed. H. A. Murray, New York: Oxford University Press.

———. 1940. "Studies in the Interpretation of Play. I. Clinical Observation of Play Disruption in Young Children." *Genetic Psychology Monographs,* XXII, 557–671.

———. 1951. "Sex Differences in the Play Configurations of Preadolescents," *American Journal of Orthopsychiatry,* XXI, No. 4, 667–92.

Franck, K. 1946. "Preference for Sex Symbols and Their Personality Correlation," *Genetic Psychology Monographs,* XXXIII, No. 2, 73–123.

Freud, S. 1922. *Introductory Lectures on Psychoanalysis.* London: Allen & Unwin.

Honzik, M. P. 1951. "Sex Differences in the Occurrence of Materials in the Play Constructions of Preadolescents," *Child Development,* XXII, 15–35.

Lowenfeld, M. 1939. "The World Pictures of Children: A Method of Recording and Studying Them," *British Journal of Medical Psychology,* XVIII, Part I, 65–101.

Macfarlane, J. W. 1938. *Studies in Child Guidance. I. Methodology of Data Collection and Organization.* ("Society for Research in Child Development Monographs," Vol. III, No. 6.)

Rosenzweig, S., and Shakow, D. 1937. "Play Technique in Schizophrenia and Other Psychoses," *American Journal of Orthopsychiatry,* VII, No. 12, 32–47.

Tolman, E. C. 1932. *Purposive Behavior in Animals and Men.* New York: Century Co.

11

The Research Uses of Doll Play

Harry Levin and Elinor Wardwell[1]

The history of science offers many examples of potentially useful theories that did not realize their promise until appropriate methods had been devised. Once methodology becomes available, a flood of research often follows, which in turn tries the theory and results in new formulations that in their turn wait on experimental devices. Such progress may falter either because of an absence of theoretical speculation or the lack of methods, and it is futile to assign prior importance to one or the other.

Such interdependence becomes clear when we compare the influence that Binet's scales had on the theories of intellective behavior in children to the relative dearth of systematic research on early personality development, although there is certainly no lack of theories concerning the latter problem. However, standardized methods for appraising personality variables in preliterate children are in short supply.

Reasons for the dearth of methods are not hard to find. Research with preschool children presents certain special problems. The instructions and operations must be simple enough for young children to understand. The subjects must have the physical abilities to perform whatever acts are

SOURCE. Republished from the *Psychological Bulletin*, 1962, Vol. 59, No. 1, 27–56, with the permission of the authors and the American Psychological Association.

[1] We are indebted to the participants in the workshop on doll play methods at the 1957 American Psychological Association meetings for many suggestions which appear in this paper. We especially thank Mary Ford, Clara Melville, Judy Rosenblith, and Richard Walters for their comments on the manuscript.

demanded by the method. Perhaps most important, the tasks must entice and maintain interest against a brief span of attention. Further, for personality research minimal determination of the child's behavior as artifacts of measuring devices is desirable.

Few extant methods meet these criteria. Bellaks' CAT (1950) and the Rorschach (e.g., Ames, Learned, Metraux, & Walker, 1952) are widely and profitably used but present problems. They rely solely on children's language responses and are, in the writers' opinions, too dependent on passive, nonacting out, behavior. Likewise, interviews with children, because they depend on the child's understanding of language may introduce many idiosyncratic factors.

Doll play has offered the promise of range and flexibility in personality research. It is the purpose of this paper to summarize the research uses of doll play and to assay the results of the promise which this method offers.

Doll play started as a clinical device. Anna Freud (1928) attributes its first use to Melanie Klein who employed it as a procedure both for the diagnosis and treatment of disturbed children. However, the concern of this survey is with the *research* rather than the clinical uses of doll play. By "research uses" we shall mean that variables have been measured by this method and related to other variables. The studies reviewed cover the period 1933 to 1960.

What is doll play? There are numerous variations, but essentially the young child is presented with a set of dolls—such as a family—and a setting in which dolls are to operate—such as a home—and told to manipulate the dolls while he tells a story about them. The child has an opportunity here to talk as well as to act. Endless changes can and have been rung on this basic theme: the composition of the dolls, the nature of the setting, the amount and kinds of interaction with the researcher, the directions and structure presented to the child, etc. A host of variables has been scored from the children's protocols. Chief among them are aggression, stereotypy, and prejudice. The method appears to be more useful for some of these variables than for others.

Although doll play was used in research before their work, a strong impetus to doll play as a method in the study of personality development was the work of R. R. and Pauline S. Sears at the Iowa Child Welfare Research Station in the mid-1940's. The original studies, after Bach (1945) indicated the potential value of the method, were methodological and will be discussed below. The serendipitous occurrence of marked sex differences in doll play led to more recent work by these investigators and their co-workers on identification in children, providing one case where a characteristic of a method led to new theory, rather than the converse textbook ideal.

Because of the theoretical dispositions of the early investigators, the most frequent variables measured were derived from behavior theory and were indices of acquired drives in children. Hence, more than any other behavior, fantasy aggression has been measured by this technique, and it was the happy confluence of theory and method that this particular behavior is frequently elicited in doll play.

A host of differences exist among the subjects, equipment, and procedures in the studies which will be reviewed. The following sections are organized to indicate the modal findings or procedure and to sketch the range of variations from the typical occurrence.

Method

SUBJECTS

The usual subjects in doll play research have been preschool children. However, children between the ages of 5 and 10 have been used in many investigations, and in three studies the subjects were up to 13 years old (Honzik, 1951; Levy, 1933; Witkin, Lewis, Hertzman, Machover, Meissner, & Wapner, 1954). Subjects at the extremes of the age range have usually required procedural adaptations. Heinicke (1956), in his study of 2-year-olds, found that children of this age did not use dolls as agents of actions. He felt that he gathered meaningful data about his subjects by putting them in a doll play situation, but in view of the types of variables which yielded results—rate of play, calling for parents, seeking the observer's affection, hostility to dolls and other play objects—it would seem that the findings were incidental to the doll play method. At the upper age levels subjects usually have been instructed to regard the dolls as characters in a play or movie. Only one study has used adult subjects—Rosenzweig and Shakow (1937) compared the constructions of play materials by adult psychotics to those of normal adults, and concluded that their subjects responded favorably to the technique.

Most research with doll play has employed white subjects. Occasionally, in studies of racial identification and prejudice Negroes have been used (Goodman, 1952; Graham, 1955; Radke & Trager, 1950; Stevenson & Stewart, 1958). The method has also been used successfully with American Indian groups (Gewirtz, 1950) and with children in a primitive society (Henry & Henry, 1944).

Both boys and girls have served as subjects. The only indication that there might be sex differences in willingness to play with dolls comes from Finch (1954), who reported that among her subjects, aged 3–8, those from all-boy families refused to participate. However, since her procedure involved doll play in the home as well as in the laboratory, the findings may not be typical.

EQUIPMENT

There is no standard material for the construction of dolls—they may be made of plastic, wood, clay, celluloid, rubber, stuffed fabric, or pipe cleaners and cardboard. Their clothing may be nonexistent, simple or elaborate, removable or permanent. However, in the majority of studies reported, the dolls were 1.5"–6" tall, realistically dressed, and were flexible so that they could be bent to standing or sitting positions. The "standard doll play family," to the extent that it exists, consists of father, mother, boy, girl, and baby. This number can either be reduced or expanded to study particular interactions—e.g., restricted to mother and child (Isch, 1952); to mother, baby, and older brother or sister (Levy, 1933); or expanded to include maid (Bryan, 1940); teacher (Bach, 1945; Melville, 1959); grandparents (Halnan, 1950; Johnson 1952); or additional siblings (Bryan, 1940). Sometimes the subject is given dolls which duplicate his own family (Bremer, 1947; Halnan, 1950; Holway, 1949; Johnson, 1952; Radke, 1946; Ryder, 1954), or he is presented with a large number of dolls of different age-sex categories, and given his choice (Goodman, 1952; Henry & Henry, 1944; Korner, 1949).

The dolls are typically presented in, or in front of, some indoor setting. Most common is the use of a five- or six-room house which has fixed wooden or cardboard walls, but no roof. The house is usually filled with realistic, movable doll furniture which has few manipulatable parts. Sometimes no house is used—instead, the child is given furniture which is either organized into "rooms" or lined up in rows (Bryan, 1940; Finch, 1954; Goodman, 1952; Halnan, 1950; Holway, 1949; Johnson, 1952; Korner, 1949; Phillips, 1945; Pintler, 1945; Radke, 1946; Robinson, 1946; Ryder, 1954). Occasionally blocks are available, making it possible for the child to construct walls if he desires them (Bryan, 1940; Pintler, 1945). Settings other than houses have been employed in rare instances—e.g., a complete neighborhood (Meister, 1948), a school room (Bach, 1945; Melville, 1959), or a scale model of a backyard filled with play equpiment (Bremer, 1947).

PROCEDURE

Typically, the subject is brought into an experimental room, shown the dolls and other equipment, and told that he may play with them in any way he wishes. Sometimes it is suggested that he make up a story (Bach, 1945, 1946; Bach & Bremer, 1947; Hollenberg, 1949; Johnson, 1951; Krall, 1953; Levin, 1955) but even in these cases the direction of the fantasy is left completely to the child.

The interaction between experimenter and subject is usually controlled to some extent—the experimenter may avoid interaction whenever possible (Bryan, 1940; Honzik, 1951); he may limit the frequency of interaction, usually according to the levels established by Pintler (1945), which will be discussed later; or he may control the situation only in the sense of adopting a constant attitude of noninterfering permissiveness and attentiveness (Bach, 1946; Bach & Bremer, 1947; Holway, 1949; Levin, 1955; Ryder, 1954).

In studies whose primary aim is to compare the results of free doll play with results of other measures of personality (Ryder, 1954; Simpkins, 1918; Witkin et al., 1954) one session of play may be all that is used. Most experiments, however, provide for the analysis of session-to-session changes, usually with two 20-minute sessions a few days apart. Some studies have used more than two sessions (Bremer, 1947; Heinicke, 1956; Hollenberg & Sperry, 1951; Isch, 1952; Johnson, 1951; Phillips, 1945; Pintler, 1945).

In most cases, the session length is determined beforehand, but even though measures are taken only during the standard time, the subject may be allowed to continue playing as long as he wants (Bremer, 1947). Some workers have not limited the session time, but have recorded all responses until the child lost interest (Goodman, 1946; Ryder, 1954). The latter procedure, of course, makes imperative the use of response proportions instead of response frequencies as measures.

In studying specific variables which would be unlikely to occur with sufficient frequency to give useful results under the free play procedure outlined above, investigators have used a more directive approach in which the setting of the story is specified. The measurements may be mainly in terms of the dolls' actions, as when Levy (1933) records what the subject has the older doll do when it sees its baby sibling at the mother's breast, or doll play may frankly be used as an aid to make it easier to talk to children. In the doll play interview used by Ammons and Ammons (1952), the movement of the dolls is often only an adjunct to enable children to express feelings when they are having difficulty in verbal expression. The same seems to be true of Conn's (1938) study of carsickness, and of Levy's (1940) and Conn's (1940) studies of reactions to the discovery of genital differences.

Studies of prejudice (Goodman, 1946; Radke & Trager, 1950) have confronted subjects with direct choices between white and Negro dolls to reveal their concepts of the status of the racial groups and their preferences for them. In addition, Goodman used a story completion technique, in which the subject decided which doll won in cases of conflict.

The story completion technique is not necessarily restricted to the study of one variable. Since the completion of a prestructured story takes only a short time, a variety of situations can be presented, offering the advantage of overall scores as well as specific ones. Stamp (1954) and Walsh (1956) had their subjects complete a number of stories, including one free story which the child made up himself. Several other studies have used a combination of free play and story completion (Halnan, 1950; Johnson, 1952; Winstel, 1951; Wurtz, 1957).

D. B. Lynn (1955) has developed a Structured Doll Play Test (SDPT) which presents the child with 10 situations in a given order, each with a prescribed arrangement of dolls and furniture. The child completes the story, which in some situations involves a clear-cut choice—e.g., between bottle and cup, crib and bed, mother and father—thus facilitating objective scoring. The SDPT has already been used in investigating age and sex differences (R. Lynn, 1955) and the effects of father absence in Norwegian sailor families (Lynn & Sawrey, 1959), and an extensive program of research using the test is planned (Lynn & Lynn, 1959).

Certainly the effort to get a more standardized procedure to insure comparability among studies is worthwhile. At present, the great variety of materials and procedures which have been employed make such comparisons of unknown significance. One way to overcome this difficulty is to follow the line suggested above—i.e., to develop a standard procedure and use it throughout an extended research program. However, it is readily apparent that no one method can fit the needs of every research. For example, Wurtz (1957), after trying to use responses to incomplete stories as an index of guilt, concluded that the technique was too highly structured for his purposes. It seems that in addition to standardization an attempt should be made to clarify the effects of variations in equipment and procedure in order to help explain results already obtained, and to offer the prospective research worker information that will allow him to select the best for his purposes.

To a large extent, the worker currently faced with a choice of doll play procedures is offered very little advice. The best way to learn how to do a good doll play study still seems to be to collect the "lore" from someone with experience in the area. Some of this information is given as hints in research reports, but it is scattered and because of its dependence on the specific conditions may not be generally useful. For example, Ammons (1950) found that there were significantly fewer refusals to respond in a doll play interview when simple alternatives were given, when the subject was asked what the doll would do rather than what it would say, when the items were affect-loaded, and when the subject was asked to verbalize the feelings of child, rather than adults, dolls. These kinds of "hints" will be useful to anyone planning to use a doll play interview with a sample similar to Ammons' (boys, aged 2–6), but we cannot say whether they have application to free doll play or to other age-sex groups. Similarly, it would be valuable to be able to predict how much the child will identify the dolls with his own family members, but no attempt has been made to find ways of influencing this variable. Bach (1945) reports that among his nursery school subjects, any insistence by the experimenter that the child identify with the dolls led to resistance by the subject. Within the same approximate age range, Despert (1940) found 14 out of 15 subjects who made at least some specific identification of the dolls with their own families, while Finch (1955) reports little success in getting children to act out parental roles in relation to dolls in the laboratory.

The major attempts to evaluate the effects of equipment and procedure have been made in research under the influence of R. R. Sears. Phillips (1945) found that the only effects of giving the subject highly realistic dolls and furniture rather than having him play with unclothed dolls and "furniture" of simple wooden blocks were increased exploratory behavior and less time spent in organizing the materials. Pintler's (1945) study of the effect of organization of the equipment disclosed that when the furniture and walls of the house were arranged in irregular rows instead of being organized into rooms, children spent more time in organizational behavior. Giving the subject a doll family that duplicates his own has been shown to produce more identification with the dolls than does the use of a standard family (Robinson, 1946). In a study comparing yard and house settings, Bremer (1947) found that the use of a house led to more inappropriate organizational behavior, whereas having the dolls placed in a yard setting with picnic, garage, sandbox, slide, and swing produced more nonstereotyped thematic fantasies, more theme changes, and more total aggression.

In the investigation of the effectiveness of the experimenter in maintaining rapport and stimulating the child to elaborate themes in play within the experimental situation (Pintler, 1945) it was found that high interaction between experimenter and child (between 15 and 20 of such stimulating interacts in 5 minutes of play) produced more nonstereotyped fantasies, more theme changes, more aggression, and an earlier onset of aggression play than did a low interaction level (less than 5 interacts in 5 minutes). Studying the effect of the length and number of experimental sessions, Phillips (1945) found no differences between the fantasy material produced in three 20-minute sessions and that in a single hour-long session.

The sex of the experimenter also seems to affect results. Subjects show more aggression in the presence of an experimenter of the same sex (Caron & Gewirtz, 1951).

The above summary represents our total substantive information about the effects of procedural variations. Even our information about those variables that have been investigated is limited, since most of them have been studied in isolation or in combination with only one other manipulated variable. Each is tied to the particular age group on which it was used, and has been tested only with respect to a limited number of dependent variables. For example, perhaps the most widely used reference of those in the above discussion is the work of Pintler (1945). Several studies (Bremer, 1947; Jeffre, 1946; Krall, 1953; Phillips, 1945; Robinson, 1946; Scott, 1954; Sears, 1951; Sears, Pintler, & Sears, 1946; Yarrow, 1948) used "Pintler's high interaction level" or "Pintler's low interaction level" as standards which have been demonstrated to have certain effects. There is no doubt that this work is a valuable contribution; however, it appears that there is much knowledge still to be gained on interaction level before complete understanding of its role is reached. Pintler's study used only preschool children, and there are indications that the levels she used may be less successful with older children. For example, Simpkins (1948), using 5–9 year old subjects, tried to use Pintler's high interaction level, but decided that the fantasy material was being directed by the experimenter too much, so she employed a more nondirective attitude. E. Z. Johnson (1951) found that neither of Pintler's levels was satisfactory for third graders, and ended up using an intermediate level.

The effects of many potentially influential variables have never been studied. Thus far, all the studies that have varied the behavior of the experimenter have revealed differences as a consequence. Since it appears that the experimenter is necessary to encourage verbalization of the subjects, his role becomes crucial. Is there a way to standardize "the doll play experimenter? Or is it more profitable to partial out his influence on the results? It seems to us that the answer to these questions awaits the demonstration of significant differences—e.g., attributable to the "warmth" of the adult, a dimension suggested by workers in the field to be of importance. Only after such characteristics have been identified objectively can a decision be made as to how best control them.

Reliability and Validity

CONSISTENCY OF BEHAVIOR

In this section it is not our intention to discuss scoring reliability, since this form of reliability, as in all observational procedures, depends on the explicitness of the definition of the observation categories and on the adequacy of observers' or coders' training. Nevertheless, it surprised the reviewers how often researchers neglected the common research protocol of reporting observer reliability. In many cases, this simple omission make the appraisal of results difficult.

Two kinds of information exist about the consistency of a subject's behavior in doll play: the comparison of scores across two or more sessions (analogous to test-retest reliability) and comparisons between early and later portions of a single session (as in split-half reliability). As with so much of doll play data, most information exists for the aggression variable. The session-to-session correlations in either amount or per cent aggression varies from .50 to .85 with a median intersession correlation of about .65 (Ammons & Ammons, 1949; Gewirtz, 1950; Levin & Sears, 1946; Sears, 1951; Stamp, 1954; Yarrow, 1948). These correlations when interpreted against a background of varying observer reliabilities and session-to-session changes in the incidence of aggression (see below) indicate quite acceptable reliability. It should be kept in mind that test-retest reliabilities of more highly standardized tests of intelligence are within the same range for children of this age.

Ammons and Ammons (1949) in a structured doll play situation, report corrected split-half reliabilities for aggression of .77 for the first session and .75 for the second.

For other than doll play aggression, Bryan (1940) reports a more holistic appraisal of behavioral consistency in doll play, wherein a graduate student matched protocols for two sessions at better than chance level. The intersession period in Radke's study (1946) was 4–5 weeks. The consistency in specific categories ranged from 29% for dominant themes to 67% for such variables as attitude toward the mother.

There are, unfortunately, too few reports of the consistency of behaviors other than aggression to appraise the reliability of other variables.

VALIDITY

Doll play shares with expressive-projective techniques certain serious problems in the determination of validity. Take aggression as an example. Since aspects of this behavior are disapproved in real life and since doll play presumably reduces these social restraints it may be expected that children high in the inhibition of real aggression may be especially aggressive under make believe circumstances. Were the result a substantial negative correlation between real life and fantasy aggression, the purposes of validity would still be well served. However, in any group of children we may expect variations among children in the amount of aggression anxiety and so there may be no negative or positive relationships between real and fantasy aggression.

The problem is the ubiquitous one of whether doll play behavior is replicative of real life or wish fulfilling in relation to real life. Bach

(1945) estimates that more than 75% of children's doll play responses is replicative and the writers' experiences tend to support this contention. This further complicates matters because the validity problem would be more amenable to solution if a child were consistent in one mode or the other whereas he probably varies even within a single session. These problems will be taken up again later.

Against this pessimistic backdrop, we may inspect the validity of doll play behavior against the following criteria: observation of real life behavior, teacher's ratings, other measuring techniques, and questioning the child.

Observation of real life behavior. Several impressionistic accounts do not agree. Despert (1940) reports that doll play home life had "associated emotional expressions not in all cases in accordance with the observations made on their overt social behavior (family or group)" (p. 25). By contrast, Miller and Baruch (1950) and Henry and Henry (1944) say that various types of aggression and sibling rivalry are congruent between doll play and real life.

In a well worked-out study, Isch (1952) compared behavior in doll play during four sessions with the observations of mother-child inter-action in two half-hour sessions. The correlations tended to be low for equivalent categories—around $r = .20$—but Isch believed that fantasy tended to reproduce real life. For example, when the mothers were highly rejecting and highly aggressive the children represented the mother doll as aggressive. In general, aggression was more severe in fantasy than in real life, e.g., burning a doll in the stove.

Two other studies are relevant. R. R. Sears (1947), relating several studies, reports a complicated relationship between aggression in nursery school and in doll play. Children who were least aggressive in preschool exhibited both extremes in doll play aggression, the determining factor being how severely the subjects were punished at home for aggression. Heinicke (1956) says that there is a generally good correspondence be-tween nursery school behavior and actions in doll play by 2-year-olds, a younger group than is usually employed in doll play research. However, it should be remembered that 2-year-olds do not engage in doll play, in the usual sense.

Teacher's ratings. The relationship between teacher's ratings and doll play behavior is unclear for several reasons. For one, the results them-selves are contradictory. For another, where the teacher is not rating actions similar to those manifested in doll play but is providing data for predicting doll play behavior, the findings are usually rationalizable, post hoc, by common sense or by one theoretical scheme or another. In line with the latter point, for example, Bach (1945) reports that children rated as "compliant" by their teacher had, in doll play, more fantasies about school, more stereotyped fantasies, and were less aggressive toward the teacher doll. These, and other findings like them, seem reasonable, but before we accept them as evidence of formal validity, the specifications for the rejection of the hypothesis are necessary. Unfortunately, the state of theory in personality development is not yet able to provide such specifications.

The problem of replication versus wish fulfillment particularly troubles the interpretation of the relationships between aggression in the classroom and in the fantasy situation. One prediction, based on a theory of displacement, is that docile children in the classroom will be aggressive in the fantasy situation, but the prediction must further involve the manner in which the child's real life aggressions are handled. Restrictive classrooms appear, for instance, to depress fantasy aggression (Levin, 1955).

As with so much of the doll play data, the findings of different researchers do not agree. Bach (1945) found that children rated as "normally aggressive" showed *less* thematic aggression than did either of the extreme groups. Isch (1952), at least during the first three of four doll play sessions, found just the opposite. By the fourth session, subjects rated as "strongly aggressive" showed the most fantasy aggression. Korner (1949) found no relationships between teacher ratings of hostility and the manifestation of hostile actions in doll play. Bach (1945) may have a resolution to this dilemma when he reports that there is a closer correspondence between rated and fantasy behavior for those children who "identified" with a doll—called it "I," or protected it, etc.

Two impressionistic attempts at validation disagree so completely that they do little more than confuse the issue. In Bryan's study (1940) teachers could match complete protocols of doll play with the appropriate children accurately only in one out of 20 attempts. By contrast, Walsh (1956) reports 90% agreement between doll play and teachers' ratings on such variables as freedom of action, freedom and adequacy of emotional expression, and response to environmental stimuli.

Relationship of doll play to other measuring techniques. The several studies of predictive validity give a generally more hopeful account of the validity of various doll play measures. Ryder (1954) reports that behavior in doll play agrees with that in balloon play and blocking; Simpkins (1948) found that when the Ames picture stories and doll play were scored on the same categories the agreement was high, although there were more responses—many of them nonthematic—in doll play than in the story situation. Witkin et al. (1954) in a study different from most using doll play, found that children who exhibited much organization in fantasy play tended to be able to resist field influences in perception as ascertained by tilting-room-tilting-chair tests and by rod and frame tests.

Radke (1946) strikes the only dissident note in this rubric of validity, among the authors who treat predictive validity. She failed to find relationships between doll play and projective picture identifications which she used as part of a large battery of measures on preschool children.

Doll play and direct questioning of children. Many of the same factors which make doll play data difficult to understand also influence the ways in which children answer interview questions, so that the relationships— or lack—between the two must be treated cautiously. The agreement in responses to the two questions, Which parent do you like best? and Which one does the little boy (doll) like best? ranges from 25% to 63%. When the inquiry is phrased as "Which *doll* loves other most often?" the agreement between the answer and nonstereotyped doll play goes up to 68.4% (Graham, 1955). The closer correspondence of the second study is reasonably attributed to the likelihood that the child was reporting about his doll play performance itself rather than about the antecedents of the fantasy.

In summary, the findings on validity are not substantial, if by validity we mean the correspondence between doll play and nonfantasy behavior. On theoretical grounds, strong congruence should not be expected. More definitive tests of validity must take the form of construct validity which in turn waits on clear and unequivocal hypotheses.

Areas of Research

One of the qualities of doll play which has made it attractive to researchers is the flexibility with which it can be adapted to different content areas. Modifications of equipment and procedure have made it possible to study a great variety of human problems "in miniature." Among the areas of doll play research are the following: constructive-destructive tendencies (Ackerman, 1937), father fantasies of delinquent children (Bach & Bremer, 1947), evaluation of play therapy (Bixler, 1942), car sickness (Conn, 1938), concepts of parental roles (Finch, 1955), sibling rivalry in American (Levy, 1936) and in Pilaga Indian children (Henry & Henry, 1944), aggression and aggression anxiety in accident repeaters (Krall, 1953), hostility in allergic children (Miller & Baruch, 1950), adult schizophrenia (Rosenzweig & Shakow, 1937), reactions to the discovery of genital differences (Conn, 1940; Levy, 1940), self-concepts of underarchievers (Walsh, 1956), and achievement and work fantasies of industrious children (Melville, 1959).

In fact, the number of variables that have been educed from doll play

is so great that we cannot catalog all of them. Instead, five problems which
have been investigated extensively will be discussed below in an attempt
to summarize the present state of information about them and to illustrate some measuring problems commonly found in the use of the doll
play technique. The areas are aggression, stereotypy, doll preference,
father absence, and prejudice.

AGGRESSION

Far more than any other behavior, aggression has been investigated by
doll play techniques. The investigator has assurance that at some point
in the doll play procedure, a substantial number of children will evidence
some aggressive acts. The behavior may be verbal, or acting out the aggression, or a combination. Conceptually, aggression has been defined as
any act whose intent is to injure, physically or psychologically, another
doll or equipment. Operationally, this common definition presents certain
difficulties. First is the inference of intent. This part of the definition is
designed to eliminate accidental aggressive acts. Since the child is manipu-
lating dolls and furniture in a small space, he will from time to time
knock over a doll or a piece of equipment without apparently meaning
to. Investigators often want to ignore such fortuitous acts, and, in fact, it
is not difficult to distinguish such accidental acts from "intended" aggression. It seems to us that the problem in operation is far less serious than
is the inclusion of intent in the formal definition.

Another category of events not covered by the definition but often
scored as aggression is the attribution of motives or traits by the subject to
a doll; e.g., the boy is bad, the mommy is mean. One way of handling
this contingency is to include the subject as a scorable agent of aggression
and to count the above two examples as aggression from the subject to the
appropriate doll.

In fact, a major virtue of doll play is the freedom it provides the investigator to design a scoring system that fits his problems. The many
specific categories which have been scored under the general aggression
rubric are illustrated in the middle column of Table 1. They include total
aggression, verbal and physical aggression (often interpreted as indirect
and direct), mischief, scolding, tangential, displaced, projected, etc. The
latency of the first aggressive act in the session has been studied, and
usually interpreted as an index of aggression anxiety. The agents and
objects of aggressive acts are popular topics of study. A generalization,
though, is that when many subcategories of aggression are scored, the
incidence in any one category is so small that they are combined for
purposes of analysis into large groupings such as "total aggression" or
"direct" and "indirect" aggression, etc.

Table 1

Summary of Studies on Aggression[a]

Author	Measures of Aggression	Independent Variables
Ammons & Ammons, 1953	Reactions to aggression 　Counter-aggression 　Leaving field 　Verbal expression 　Appeal to adult 　Inhibition of aggressive 　feelings Outcome of aggression 　Success 　Failure Objects of aggression 　Negro doll 　White doll	Age of subject
Bach, 1945	Hostility-aggression (% of 　non-stereotyped)[a] Agent of aggression Object of aggression[a]	Sex of subject[a] Teacher ratings on aggression 　and compliance in school[a] Frustration before doll play[a]
Bach, 1946	Total aggression (% of total 　acts) involving father doll[a] Agent of aggression[a] Object of aggression	Father separation[a] Sex of subject[a] Mothers' reports of their de- 　scriptions of absent fathers 　to children
Bach & Bremer, 1947	Fantasy aggression (fre- 　quency)[a] 　Killing 　Justification of hostile 　aggression 　Defensive rationalization 　Aggression in response 　to commands Father doll as agent or object[a]	Delinquency of subjects 　(home for prepsychopathic 　children)[a]
Bremer, 1947	Total aggression (frequency)[a] 　Nonstereotyped aggression 　Stereotyped aggression 　Suffered aggression (ex- 　pressing suffering in 　pain) 　Chasing or escaping 　Justification of aggression	Doll house setting compared 　to yard setting[a] Sex of subject[a]

Table 1—Continued

Author	Measures of Aggression	Independent Variables
	Nonthematic aggression *Agents of aggression Objects of aggression	
Caron & Gewirtz, 1951	Total aggression (% of total acts)[a] Latency of aggression[a] Projection of aggression Agent of aggression Object of aggression	Sex of experimenter[a] Sex of subject[a] Age of subject[a]

Gewirtz, 1950	Total aggression (% of total
	acts)[a]
	Direct
	  Physical injury
	Indirect
	  Verbal aggression
	  Discipline
	  Discomfort-causing
	Acts of aggression
	Object of aggression
	Projection of aggression
	Displacement of aggression
	Response attenuation (ratio
	of direct to indirect)
		Sac and Fox Indians com-
		pared to white children[a]
		Age of subject[a]
		Sex of subject[a]
		Session-to-session changes[a]

Gewirtz & Caron, 1954	Physical injury (% of total acts)[a] Latency of aggression Agent of aggression Object of aggression	Sex of experimenter[a] Sex of child[a] Session-to-session changes
Hollenberg & Sperry, 1951 Hollenberg, 1949 Sperry, 1949	Total aggression (% of total acts)[a] Aggressive mischief, dis- obedience Verbal discipline & aggres- sion feelings—scold, threaten derogation Physical discipline Physical injury to person Physical injury to equip- ment States of uncomfortable feeling	Frustration at home (mother interview) Punishment for aggression at home (mother interview)[a] Sex of child[a] Session-to-session change[a] Disapproval of aggression dur- ing experimental session[a]

Table 1—Continued

Author	Measures of Aggression	Independent Variables
	Projection of aggression Intensity of aggression	
Holway, 1949	Total aggression (frequency)	Mother interview data on (a) Strictness of feeding schedule (b) Mothers feeling tone on feeding schedule (c) Number of months breast fed (d) Age begin toilet training
Jeffre, 1946 Isch, 1952	*Total aggression (frequency) *Total aggression (% of total acts) Agent of aggression *Object of aggression	Teacher ratings on aggression[a] Session-to-session changes[a] Observed mother-child interaction (rejection, aggression)
Johnson, 1951	Total aggression (frequency)[a] Aggression mischief[a] ⎫ Verbal aggression[a] ⎬ Contra-social[a] Physical injury to person or equipment[a] ⎭ States of uncomfortable feeling[a] Verbal discipline ⎫ Physical discipline ⎬ Prosocial[a] Agent of aggression[a] Object of aggression[a]	Age of subject[a] Sex of subject[a] Session-to-session changes[a]
Korner, 1949	Total aggression (frequency) (Listing of types of aggression observed)	Content of incomplete story Hostility ratings based on parent & teacher ratings
Krall, 1953 Krall, 1951	Total aggression (frequency)[a] Action aggression Verbal aggression[a]	Accident prone compared to accident free children[a] Sex of subject[a]

Table 1—Continued

Author	Measures of Aggression	Independent Variables

	Aggressive anxiety
	  Differences between verbal aggression & action aggression
	  Latency of aggression[a]
	  Inhibition of aggression
	  Displaced aggression
	  Projected aggression
		Session-to-session changes

Levin, 1953	Total aggression (% of total acts)[a]	Sex of subject[a] Severity of punishment of aggression at home (mother interview)[a] Session-to-session changes[a] Quarreling & fighting in class (teacher judgment)[a]
Levin, 1955	Total aggression (% of total acts)[a]	Sex of subject[a] Dominance control of classroom teacher (observed)[a] Session-to-session changes
Levin & Sears, 1956	Total aggression (% of total acts)[a]	Sex of subject[a] Identification with parent (mother interview)[a] Sex of usual punisher (mother interview)[a] Severity of punishment for aggression toward parents (mother interview) Session-to-session changes[a] Ordinal differences[a] Socioeconomic status
Levin & Turgeon, 1957	Total aggression (% of total acts)[a]	Mother's presence at doll play session[a] Stranger's presence at doll play session[a]
Levy, 1936	Prevention of hostility Direction of hostility (order of attack on different objects) Forms of hostility Mild	Sibling rivalry problems of subjects

Table 1—Continued

Author	Measures of Aggression	Independent Variables
		Sex of subject[a]
	Simple assault Primitive hostility Self-punishment & retribution	
Miller & Baruch, 1950	Presence-absence of *Direct hostility *Indirect hostility Displaced hostility *Hostility against self	*Allergic compared to nonallergic problem children
Phillips, 1945	*Total aggression (frequency)	Realism of materials Session length *Session-to-session changes
Pintler, 1945	*Total aggression (frequency) Latency of aggression	*Experimenter-subject interaction *Organization of materials *Session-to-session changes
Pintler, Phillips, & Sears, 1946	*Total aggression (frequency)	*Sex of subject
Robinson, 1946	Total aggression (frequency) Stereotyped Nonstereotyped Agent of aggression *Object of aggression	*Type of doll family: standard or duplicate of subject's family Presence or absence of sibling in subject's family
Ryder, 1954	*Rating of aggressive feeling Rating on inhibition of aggressive feeling Total aggression (frequency)	*Father separation *Sex of subject
Scott, 1954	Total aggression (frequency) *Agent of aggression *Object of aggression	*Separation from parents
Sears, 1951	*Total aggression (frequency) Nonthematic Thematic *Bodily injury *No bodily injury Nonpersonal aggression (by dolls toward nonpersonal objects)	*Sex of subject *Age of subject *Sibling status *Father absence *Session-to-session changes

Table 1—Continued

Author	Measures of Aggression	Independent Variables
	Trouble as result of demons, catastrophes, or imaginary characters *Latency of aggression Agent of Aggression *Object of aggression	
Sears & Pintler, 1947	Agent of aggression *Object of aggression Content of aggression	*Sex of subject
Sears, Pintler, & Sears, 1946	*Total aggression (frequency) Agent of aggression *Object of aggression	*Sex of subject *Age of subject *Father separation *Session-to-session changes
Stamp, 1954 (story complications)	*Direct (% total aggression: self doll → parent) *Indirect (% total aggression: self doll, with implied intention; or → parent but not by self) Directed → self (% total aggression) *Displaced (remaining % total aggression)	*Teacher ratings of subjects as "rebellious" or "submissive" *Sex of subject Session-to-session changes

Yarrow, 1948	Agent of aggression
	Object of aggression
	*Total aggressive acts
	  *Nonstereotyped aggression
	  *Stereotyped
	*Tangential aggression
	*Latency of aggression
		*Sex of subject
		Experimentally induced frustration, antecedent to doll play
		(a) Failure
		(b) Satiation
		*Session-to-session changes

a Asterisk indicates involvement in relationships significant at .05 or better.

The tendency to proliferate basic categories and to recombine them into various indices presents a difficult problem for comparing and evaluating studies. Since a large number of combinatorial indices are possible from a few basic variables and since experimenters choose for theoretical or other reasons to form different combinations, studies which should be comparable are not. The evaluator is also tempted to think that many of the combinations and arithmetic manipulations of scores were reached post hoc and to wish for replications of findings.

As illustrative of the large amount of research on aggression, only a few topics will be discussed in detail: sex and age influences; session-to-session changes; and the child rearing antecedents of total, displaced, and projected aggression.

Age, sex, and aggression. The single best documented finding using the play technique is that boys are more aggressive than girls. Still, in spite of the overwhelming evidence on this point there are a few contradictory or nonconfirmatory results. Krall (1951) reported more aggression among the girls in her sample, but a careful check on her data is best interpreted as no rather than reversed sex differences. Likewise, Henry and Henry (1944) reported no sex differences in aggression for Pilaga Indian children, and Hollenberg and Sperry (1951) found none among Iowa City nursery school subjects. Since the findings are so overwhelmingly in the other direction the burden of explaining the dissenting results must fall on these few investigators.

E. Z. Johnson (1951) adds an important result to the repetitive "boys more than girls" data. She found that boys do exceed girls in physical aggression, but that girls show more verbal aggression than do boys. This finding is reasonable in light of the findings on overt—nonfantasy—aggression.

Johnson's finding in regard to age of the subjects is also provocative. Younger children show more of what she calls "contrasocial" aggression, while older children's aggression is more "prosocial," usually depictions of the parents punishing the children. As one compares the 5- with the 8-year-olds, the usual sex difference in aggression decreases. Caron and Gewirtz (1951) confirm this finding. P. S. Sears (1951), on the other hand, found that the sexes become more different in this respect as they are older, but it must be remembered that her subjects ranged in age from 3 to 5, which is younger than the youngest group in the other two studies citing age differences in fantasy aggression.

Session-to-session changes in doll play aggression. Second only to the consistent finding that boys are more aggressive than girls, is the ubiquitous result that children are more aggressive in the second compared to the first session of doll play (e.g., Hollenberg & Sperry, 1951; Levin & Sears, 1956; Sears, 1951). Although the amount of aggression increases, children tend to maintain their relative rank order in aggressiveness (Sears, 1951). The above findings apply to the first two sessions. When children participated in more than two sessions, aggression in the later sessions presented a more complicated picture. For example, Jeffre (1946) reported that across four sessions, aggression toward the experimenter and equipment increased, which seems a likely reflection of a child's frustrated boredom with the doll play task. Pintler (1945), using three sessions, found that the latency of the first aggressive act decreased in the later sessions.

The increase in aggression appears to be related to amount of experience in doll play and not particularly to the interval between sessions. Phillips (1945) compared doll play performance in a single one-hour session to three 20-minute sessions. The changes that occurred between the first and final thirds of the massed session were similar to those between the first and last distributed sessions.

A reasonable explanation of this common finding is that the child learns with time that the restraints against the expression of aggression are not operative in doll play and hence he may vent his impulses more freely. The fact that when a stranger is introduced into a second session the usual increase in aggression does not occur lends experimental credence to this interpretation (Levin & Turgeon, 1957).

Child rearing antecedents of doll play aggression. The hypotheses relating certain child rearing practices to aggression in doll play have come from psychoanalytic and behavior theory. The setting of doll play is thought of as a situation relatively free from real life restraints and so appears on a similarity dimension with home and school, but different enough from the real life settings so that the restraints against aggressive expression are less potent. If, therefore, aggression is punished at home, such actions are less likely to occur at the point of punishment but will be manifest in the safety of doll play. The general hypothesis has been that there is positive correlation between severity of punishment at home and the incidence of aggression in doll play. One shortcoming of the displacement hypothesis is that it does not predict a higher frequency of incidence in doll play than the less severely punished condition—only that such denied behaviors will appear in fantasy but not in real life. A conflict drive hypothesis has been added to the original displacement one to cover this lack (Whiting & Child, 1953, p. 353). This additional hypothesis postulates a drive increment due to the subject's desire to express aggression and his fear of such expression. Since drive operates multiplicatively, the combination of hypotheses covers the prediction of severe parental punishment leading to high fantasy aggression.

What is the evidence for this hypothesis? Hollenberg and Sperry (1951) reported confirmation. In an earlier summary report of research performed under his direction, R. R. Sears (1947) found the predicted state of affairs: those children who were most severely punished at home were most aggressive in doll play.

An attempt to replicate this finding further entailed fairly elaborate changes in the hypothesis (Levin & Sears, 1956). On a larger and more varied sample—the previous studies were done with university nursery school groups—the simple "punishment leading to aggression" hypothesis did not hold. Rather, doll play aggression was shown to be predictable from a combination of the sex of child, the real life agent of punishment, and the nature of the child's identification with his parent, as well as the severity of punishment. In general, these findings lend themselves more easily to a replicative rather than to a displacement interpretation. Taken in the light of E. Z. Johnson's (1951) finding that older children evidenced more prosocial aggression, the more mature, identified children may be portraying the parental punishment that they have experienced. It is interesting to note that real life aggression among primary school children was predictable from much the same variables as the fantasy behavior in the Levin and Sears' study (Eron, 1958).

One other study based on the displacement hypotheses obtained completely contradictory results (Levin & Turgeon, 1957). The prediction that the presence of the mother at the doll play session would redintegrate aspects of the home and reduce the freedom of doll play was not borne out. The opposite finding emerged; aggression was more frequent before the mother compared to the control condition. The investigators called the original hypothesis into question and suggested that there are characteristics of the doll play situation which make doubtful its use as a point on a simple freedom-from-inhibition dimension.

Wurtz (1960) in a recent theoretical statement argued that mild aggression anxiety should facilitate attenuated aggression in doll play. He found some confirmation for this notion in a reanalysis of earlier data reported by P. S. Sears (1951) and Sears, Pintler, and Sears (1946), when the index of attenuation is based on the use of child compared to adult dolls as agents and objects of aggression.

In addition to thinking of total doll play aggression as a manifestation of displacement, the same phenomenon has been studied within the doll play situation itself. If a child has been punished for aggression, the depiction of this punishment in doll play should arouse more anxiety than in cases of aggression toward a doll less similar to the performer. This conceptualization creates substantial difficulties. It implies that although doll play in general is not very inhibiting, there is still sufficient anxiety to influence the choice of dolls that act as the objects of hostility. We might expect, therefore, a mild and not very consistent effect on the choice of objects of aggression. The unreliability should be compounded by the low incidence of acts which determine any displacement score. For example, if 15% of all doll play units are aggressive and this percentage is divided among five dolls equally, we are dealing with expected displacement scores of 3% of the total number of acts, and the unreliability of this miniscule proportion is obvious.

The implications of the displacement hypothesis for understanding pro- and contrasocial aggression are especially difficult to justify. If severely punished, highly identified children accurately replicate their parents' punishment in doll play, they would showing little displacement although they have experienced severe punishment.

The final comment on doll play analysis of displacement is, to our thinking, most serious and applies equally below to the discussion of projection. How are the doll agents or objects of aggression to be ordered for the analysis of the two defense mechanisms? Most often, the assumption is made that the child uses the doll most similar to himself as the point of origin on the similarity continuum. For children who are strongly identified with their parents, this assumption is suspect. Granted this point, however, the additional points create greater difficulties. Should the grouping be by sex or age? Does the dimension for a girl go: girl (G), mother (M), boy (B), father (F), baby (bb); or G, B, M, F, bb; or, perhaps, G, M, F, B, bb; etc.? All of these are empirically answerable, albeit difficult, questions. One possibility is that the dimension is an idiosyncratic, response mediated one. Another tack may be that the nature of the dimension varies depending on the behavior being studied; i.e., one sequence of dolls for aggression, another for dependency, etc. As will be pointed out in the final section of this paper, there is little evidence that can be brought to bear on these questions.

An analog to displacement within the doll play session is "projection," which is defined in terms of the doll agents of aggression. Presumably, a doll most similar to the child carrying out hostile acts represents projection of the child's hostile impulses to the doll. The above comments on displacement also apply to this mechanism.

A number of studies relate the agents and objects of aggression to demographic characteristics of the child, as can be seen in Table 1. However, a direct test of the displacement or projection formulations requires information about the nature of the child's aggression anxiety as well as the dolls he chooses to initiate and receive hostile acts. Only one study yields this information directly (Hollenberg, 1949). She found that children who were severely punished for aggression at home projected aggression more in doll play than did less severely punished children. Comparable data on displacement are not available.

In summary, the demographic and practice correlates of doll play aggression are clear and substantial. However, the problems of greater theoretical interest—the child rearing correlates of doll play aggression—must, because of their conceptual unclarities and inconsistent results, remain open questions. A thorough test of the displacement model would require information about the anxiety attached to the expression of aggression at home, the amount of such behavior actually exhibited at home, the instigation to aggression, and the amount of aggression shown in doll play. A questionable assumption is that the instigation to aggression is more or less the same in doll play as in the home—that it is a characteristic of the person independent of the situation. No single study fulfills more than one or two of these requisites.

STEREOTYPY

Many doll play studies have categorized routine, habitual actions, "doll action appropriate to the time, place, situation, and characters involved" (Phillips, 1945). These behaviors are most often termed "stereotyped," although they sometimes have been labeled "realistic" or "routine role." Such doll actions usually constitute a considerable part of the total acts in a session. Krall (1953) reports that stereotyped thematic responses constitute 45% of all responses made in doll play, and Bach (1945) and E. Z. Johnson (1951) report that 59% and 66% of thematic responses are stereotyped actions.

The most consistent finding with regard to stereotypy is a sex difference: girls show more stereotyped behavior than do boys (Bach, 1945, 1946; Bremer, 1947; Honzik, 1951; Pintler, Phillips, & Sears, 1946; Yarrow, 1948). This finding might be attributable to the greater familiarity of girls with doll playing, but since it occurs from age 3 onward, it would seem more likely to be related to greater inventiveness of young boys. As a case in point, Tuddenham (1952) reports that first, third, and fifth graders recognize that the "typical girl" is less daring than the "typical boy."

The amount of stereotypy decreases from session to session (Bach, 1945; Phillips, 1945; Yarrow, 1948), a fact which may be explained in several ways. The higher incidence of aggression in later doll play sessions may displace stereotyped responses. Also, the relaxation of restraints in the second session which yields more aggression may also lead to more nonstereotyped, nonaggressive behaviors. It seems natural that a child faced with a new situation would first represent the most highly practiced behaviors—the routine acts of the home.

Attempts have been made to relate stereotypy to adjustment. Bach (1945) reported that children whom teachers rated as being "well adjusted" showed a higher rate of decrease of stereotypy over sessions than did "poorly adjusted" children. Holway's (1949) findings on "realistic" play, which seems to be closely related if not identical to stereotyped play, show that at the end of therapy, children play more realistically using less fantasy, aggression, or tangential (nondoll) play. Holway's study attempted to relate doll play to child rearing variables. She found that realistic play was positively related to the amount of early self-regulation in feeding and the number of months the child was breast fed.

In Holway's (1949) sample of 3–5 year olds, there was no correlation between realistic play and either CA or IQ. However, Graham (1952), comparing seven "bright" primary school children with seven "dull" ones found that the brighter children used more stereotyped responses.

Aside from the sex differences, session-to-session changes, and possible IQ differences, there have been no other substantial findings with regard to stereotyped play. In studies of delinquents (Bach & Bremer, 1947), accident repeaters (Krall, 1953), and various methodological explorations reported above (Phillips, 1945; Pintler, 1945; Robinson, 1946), no significant differences in the amount of stereotyped behavior were found between experimental and control groups. In the area of parent separation, the results are not consistent—Bach (1946) found that father-separated children showed more stereotyped fantasies about home life, whereas Scott (1954) reported that institutionalized children indulged in less stereotyped play than did children living with their parents.

The stereotype category is usually regarded as a residual category rather than as a major interest. A recent study indicates that it may have some predictive value if further analyzed. Melville (1959) found that children who spend a large proportion of their school time working industriously use the "work routine" category (that portion of stereotyped behavior which is work oriented) in fantasy more than do less industrious children. Note that this is a more or less direct replication in doll play of observed real life behavior. Melville's study suggests that a finer breakdown of the stereotypy category might be profitable.

DOLL PREFERENCE

Although many doll play studies record which dolls were used as agents and objects of fantasy acts, few of them report analysis of doll usage in any detail. The greatest interest in this variable has been evidenced by researchers in the areas of aggression and the effects of separation from parents, and the results are presented in the appropriate parts of this paper.

Probably the best substantiated generalization to be made about this topic is that subjects tend to prefer the same sex parent doll to the parent doll of the opposite sex. This tendency shows some increase with age. The finding has not appeared in every study—e.g., Graham's (1952) subjects, regardless of sex, tended to use the mother doll more than the father doll —but significantly greater use of the opposite sex parent has not been reported. E. Z. Johnson (1951) found that while in portrayal of routine (stereotyped) behavior all subjects used the mother more often than the father doll, the greatest session-to-session increase in the use of the father occurred among older boys. In a nursery school sample (Sears et al., 1953), the girls used the mother doll more than the father, while the boys used the two dolls equally, thereby employing the father doll more than the girls did.

Five studies which have used relatively structured situations to lead the child to make a direct choice also report same sex preference. Ammons and Ammons (1949) found a father preference among 3- and 4-year-old boys, and a mother preference among 4- and 5-year-old girls, and R. Lynn's (1955) 6-year-old subjects showed a greater preference for the same sex parent doll than did her 4-year-old subjects. Emmerich (1959) had his subjects complete stories using first the adult and then the child dolls. Correspondence between the two sets of behaviors was taken to indicate high identification. He found that preschool children—especially boys— tended to identify more with parents of the same than with parents of the opposite sex. Similarly, highly sex-typed boys depict more nurturance, punishment, and power via the father than via the mother doll (Mussen & Distler, 1959). To get at sex role identification, Rabban (1950) asked children aged 3–9 to select the doll that "looks most like you." Starting at the age of 4, the choices were correct as to sex.

Preschool children who have been reared permissively emphasize the adult dolls in their fantasy productions (Levin, 1958). This finding may be interpreted in several ways: permissive parents interact more with their children and thereby provide a more frequent adult model, parents who rear their children permissively permit them to explore and practice adult-like behaviors more than do nonpermissive parents, and permissiveness is one of the antecedents of identification with parents which is reflected in the child's preoccupation with adult actions in doll play.

EFFECTS OF SEPARATION FROM PARENTS

Interest in this area grew out of the problems of wartime father separation, and the majority of studies have been concerned with the absence of the father rather than the mother from the home. The studies of father absence can conveniently be divided into two groups: those concerned with children currently separated from their fathers, and those of children whose fathers had been absent during the first year or two of the child's life but were living with the family at the time of the study. Bach (1946) studied children aged 6–10 whose fathers were in the service abroad and had been away for 1–3 years. He found that father-separated children, compared to a control group whose fathers were at home, produced fewer doll actions that involved the father doll; enacted a more stereotyped view of family life; and made the father doll more aggressive, less authoritarian, and more affectionate, than did the control group. Using a smaller group of subjects, he found that where the mother described the absent father to the children in deprecatory terms, the children portrayed the father as being more aggressive to his doll children, but as receiving more affection from them; i.e., unfavorable typing of the absent father seemed to produce ambivalent feelings in the children. Another study (Sears et al., 1946; Sears, 1951) found that nursery school children whose fathers were absent from the home did not show the session-to-session increase in aggression that is usually found. In addition, boys (but not girls) whose fathers were absent were less aggressive in their fantasies (Sears et al., 1946). The father-present control group of boys showed most aggression in doll play toward the father doll and the boy doll (sex category), while the boys without fathers showed most aggression toward the father and mother dolls (age category) (Sears, 1951).

Lynn and Sawrey (1959), using the Structured Doll Play Test, have investigated absence of fathers in children of Norwegian sailor families. They found that girls (but not boys) whose fathers were gone were more dependent than the control children. However, on a measure of "maturity" (choice of sleeping in a crib or bed), boys without fathers were less mature than boys whose fathers were at home. In contrast to other studies of father absence, this one also investigated the child's relationships with mother, and concluded by doll play and other techniques that the mothers of father-absent children were more overprotective than were control group mothers.

Studies of homes where the father is currently absent do, then, find substantial results. Positive results have not been so easy to find in studies in the second group—those in which a previously absent father is present in the home at the time of the investigation. Halnan (1950), L. C. Johnson (1952), and Ryder (1954) performed doll play studies as part of the Stanford University research on father relations of war-born children. Only one difference was found between responses of control groups and those of children aged 4–7 who had been separated from their father during the first 2 years of life. In Ryder's study the doll play of the previously father-separated children was rated as revealing more aggressive feeling. Since this was an inferred measure rated by the experimenter and an observer, and since measures of overt aggression in doll play did not show any significant differences in this or either of the other two studies, it must be concluded that there is little evidence of marked effects on the doll play of children temporarily separated from their fathers in early life.

In view of the recent great interest in the effects on the child of separation from his mother, it is surprising that doll play has not been used to investigate this area. So far as is known, there has been no study using this technique with children living in households where the mother is absent. However, there are two investigations of children separated from both parents. Heinicke (1956) studied 2-year-olds living in residential nurseries because their parents were on vacation, sick, or having another child. He found results which agreed with observations of the subjects in their nursery life—e.g., they sought the affection of adults by crying—but, as has been observed before, most of his results were not specifically concerned with doll play responses. Scott (1954) studied children separated from their parents because they had been institutionalized because of neglect, mental illness in the family, etc. He found that the subjects showed a much greater than average tendency toward "metamorphosis," i.e., the subject himself acted as an authority figure and treated all the dolls as children. It is doubtful that this result should be attributed to parent separation as such; it seems just as reasonable to relate it to the effects of institutionalization.

REACTIONS TO RACIAL AND RELIGIOUS DIFFERENCES

Of the studies of children's reactions to Negro-white differences, several (Goodman, 1952; Graham, 1955; Radke & Trager, 1950; Stevenson & Stewart, 1958) have used both Negro and white subjects, while one used only white subjects (Ammons, 1950; Ammons & Ammons, 1953), and another (Clark & Clark, 1947) used Negro subjects exclusively. In this area unstructured doll play, compared to structured, has not produced meaningful results. Graham (1955) recorded the free play of Negro and white subjects with both Negro and white dolls, but made only intraracial analyses of his data. There were no outstanding differences between the two groups. Goodman (1946) used only 24 subjects in the part of her study involving free play, and found no statistically significant differences between Negroes and whites. However, she did uncover several trends which seem worthy of follow-up with a larger group—e.g., Negro subjects tended to assign main roles to white dolls, and seldom revealed positive evaluations of negro dolls. In her later studies (Goodman, 1952), where no statistical evaluations were made, she reported that doll play was a successful technique, but it is difficult to tell how much success is attributable to the free play method itself since it was used mainly as the introduction to a doll play interview.

It has been much more common, and apparently more profitable, to use controlled methods of exploration like direct questioning about preference for dolls of different color (Clark & Clark, 1947; Goodman, 1952; Radke & Trager, 1950; Stevenson & Stewart, 1958), identification of race (Ammons, 1950; Ammons & Ammons 1953; Clark & Clark, 1947), requiring the child to pair dolls which "go together" (Goodman, 1952), pairing dolls with middle class or slum houses, and with dress-up or work clothes (Radke & Trager, 1950), and various incompleted stories which offer an opportunity for a doll of one color to "win" over a doll of another color (Ammons, 1950; Ammons & Ammons, 1953; Goodman, 1952).

Results obtained from these techniques, sometimes used in connection with more extensive interviewing (Ammons, 1950), are in fair agreement with one another. Negro and white nursery school children appear to be well aware of racial physical differences (Ammons, 1950; Clark & Clark, 1947; Goodman, 1952). Both racial groups are likely to identify with the white doll when asked "Which looks most like you?" (Clark & Clark, 1947; Goodman, 1946), although with increasing age there is more correct identification until at age 7 a slight majority of Negroes identify with the Negro doll (Stevenson & Stewart, 1958). In addition, some of the Negroes show either confusion or wish fulfillment by insisting that although they are now dark skinned, they had white skins as babies (Goodman, 1946). There have been consistent reports that white dolls are preferred esthetically by white children, while Negro children do not show a clearcut preference for Negro dolls, but instead may either choose the white doll (Clark & Clark, 1947; Goodman, 1946), show only a slight preference for the Negro doll (Radke & Trager, 1950), or show reluctance to make any choice (Goodman, 1952). Interpretation of this result is not unequivocal, since it may reflect past experience with dolls and story book characters who are more often white than colored. More important would seem to be Radke and Trager's (1950) finding that, even when subjects are equated for social class, 5–7 year olds of both races accept the idea that Negroes belong in poorer housing.

While it seems to have been demonstrated clearly by the method of doll play that children are capable of making discriminations on the basis of color, it has not been shown that these discriminations are reflected in fantasy behavior in any consistent way. Ammons (1950) reported that white boys showed a tendency with increasing age to use Negro dolls as scapegoats. On the other hand, analysis of the same data did not reveal any differences in the success of Negro vs. white dolls in conflict—whichever doll the subject was using at the moment tended to be successful in aggression (Ammons & Ammons, 1953). Stevenson and Stewart's (1958) Southern Negro subjects chose the white doll as the one with whom they would like to play, except at the oldest age level—7 years—where a small majority chose the Negro doll. Goodman (1946) found no social acceptability differences among subjects who had chosen the white doll esthetically. The white doll might be "prettier," but the Negro doll was just as acceptable as a birthday party guest. In further studies, Goodman's (1952) subjects mixed the races indiscriminately in free doll play.

This lack of consistent discriminatory behavior in doll play is paralleled by a similar unconcern in observed behavior. Goodman (1946) found no consistent prejudice in nursery school behavior of her mixed racial group. The results of doll play are congruent with those of other methods in finding a poor correspondence between beliefs and the development of interracial behavior. The evidence on this point has been reviewed by Harding, Kutner, Prochansky, and Chein (1954).

Hartley and Schwartz (1951) described materials and procedures for studying attitudes toward religious groups. Subjects were given three doll families, each of which stands in front of a montage background of photographs, one suggesting a Jewish religious context, one Catholic, and the other a middle class home without any religious symbols. The investigator notices what spontaneous identification the subject makes of the backgrounds, and uses these as a lead-in to a doll play interview with the child. The only data available from the use of this technique are some protocols, but it appears to be easily adaptable to the analysis of group differences.

EXPERIMENTAL MANIPULATIONS

It is obvious, at this point, that the bulk of the studies has employed doll play to measure naturally existing characteristics of the subjects, with no attempt to influence these characteristics. By contrast, projective studies of adults have recently used experimental variations both to test specific hypotheses for which manipulation is relevant as well as to ascertain the validity of the measurement (e.g., McClelland, Atkinson, Clark, & Lowell, 1953).

The four experimental studies of doll play divide into two groups: either some experiences of the child prior to doll play or experiences during the course of the procedure are varied. In the first category, Bach (1945), testing a frustration-aggression hypothesis, subjected some of his preschool subjects to a longer rest period than others just before a doll play session. Since a long rest was presumably frustrating, these children elaborated the rest theme in their fantasy output more often and more aggressively than did the short rest group. Yarrow's (1948) results are less clear. He had one group of subjects play with a difficult tinker toy before doll play and compared them to a group who were given an easy task. The frustrated subjects tended to show increased aggression, more tangential play, and distorted thematic play than the other subjects but the results were not statistically significant. When the children experienced antecedent satiation—putting pegs into boards until they refused to continue—they gave more inappropriate thematic units—e.g., sleeping in the kitchen.

To test the effects of aggression anxiety on fantasy aggression, Sperry

(1949) compared three groups of children, each of whom participated in four sessions. For one group the experimenter disapproved of the subject's aggression in the second session. The experimenter disapproved of the subject's aggressive acts in the second and third sessions for another group and expressed no disapproval to the control group. Only the group punished in the second session decreased their disapproved acts in the third period (Hollenberg & Sperry, 1951).

Working also with a model of aggression inhibition, Levin and Turgeon (1957) compared two groups of subjects. The first group's second doll play session was observed by their mothers; in the other group a strange adult female was present. Mothers facilitated the children's aggression whereas the stranger inhibited socially disapproved acts.

In general, doll play has suffered from a dearth of experimental treatment. Some experimental operations relevant to the variables being measured would add to the validity of the method and, to judge from other projective techniques, would provide more discriminating measures of individual differences.

Discussion

What can we say now about the doll play technique, which two decades ago appeared so promising? Certainly an overall body of sensible, interrelated findings is not apparent. Where doll play was used in a connected group of studies from one laboratory, coherent results do appear. Otherwise, single investigators performing one or two studies using the method occasionally report interesting results but there are almost as many islands of findings as there are investigators. One might hope that the common method would provide the links between studies, but the flexibility of doll play, both in procedure and scoring of variables, makes the connections among findings tenuous.

In the area of aggression there are results that have been replicated. However, their very redundancy makes them appear trivial in comparison to what might have been discovered in the years of effort. We may take as fact that young boys are more aggressive than young girls and that children are more aggressive in the second than in the first doll play session. Most other doll play findings have to be hedged with boundary conditions, and restrictions must be put on general statements.

To understand this state of affairs it may be useful to review the virtues and shortcomings of doll play. We believe that the meager payoff comes not from the technique itself, but from the assumptions which underlie the method. First, what should any method of assessing personality provide? Objectivity has not often been a problem in doll play so long as the variables are carefully defined and the scorers are well trained. Reliability has been looked at both in terms of the consistency of behavior and in terms of categorizing agreement among scorers. Besides, the method is not heavily dependent on verbalization, which recommends it for use with young children, and it is interesting to them. The major difficulties appear in understanding what the method is measuring.

REPLICATION AND WISH FULFILLMENT

The basic question that has influenced the understanding of doll play is whether the child is telling about events and hopes and plans which are available to him in his day-to-day world or whether his acts in this setting are otherwise unavailable. The criterion for identifying wish fulfilling fantasies is that nonfantasy expression of the behaviors is prohibited and they are then expressed in fantasy. The prohibitions may be actually imposed on the child or may result from natural conditions: e.g., his color or sex or size. Therefore, the specifications for wish fulfilling fantasies are four: evidence that there are in "real life" some restraints against the expression of the behavior in question, a desire for such expression, little overt manifestation of the behavior, and the appearance of the behavior in fantasy.

Few research studies include all of the requirements of the wish fulfillment model. The studies of parental punishment and fantasy aggression make certain assumptions about the model, but both the results and the assumptions must be questioned since no study clearly replicates another. For example, it is assumed that severe parental discipline inhibits overt expression, yet there is some evidence that punishment and overt aggression are positively correlated (Sears, Maccoby, & Levin, 1957).

In the studies of racial identification and prejudice, the assumptions, although not usually specified, are often reasonable. For example, a substantial number of Negro children indicate in doll play that they want to play with white children (e.g., Clark & Clark, 1947). To take this as wish fulfilling behavior we need to know that such interracial play is not possible and actually does not occur. These inferences may be based on sociological characteristics of the child's neighborhood, although it is preferable to test these assumptions directly.

The inclusion of "wishes" under the replication rubric requires some explanation. If the child's wishes are not denied real expression, this category of behavior does not fit our wish fulfillment model. One way of thinking about doll play behavior is that it gives the child an opportunity to express his current experiences and preoccupations. The correspondence between real life and fantasy need not be uninteresting for research

purposes. In this type of fantasy the child may give the researcher a picture of his thoughts and actions which would be much more difficult to
elicit in an interview. Also, so far as the child's functioning is concerned,
replicative fantasy may well provide him an opportunity to practice and
develop skills which are transferable to his nonfantasy life.

To take advantage of the wish fulfillment-replication distinction in
research, it would be most helpful if a child consistently acted either one
or the other type of fantasy. Unfortunately, such is probably not the case.
A child may change his emphasis from session to session or may vary the
proportions of fantasy within a session. The ideal condition would allow
the researcher to categorize a sequence of doll play as wish fulfillment
or replicative. Our current knowledge about children's fantasies preclude
any such simple procedure although, as we suggest below, there may be
some guides in making this decision within doll play itself.

Some researchable problems which would aid in distinguishing and
making use of the differences between replication and wish fulfillment
are suggested below:

1. Without exception in the doll play studies reviewed the fantasies
have been categorized in terms of simple counts of units. Molar sequences
of behavior and units of interaction which are now common in observations of adult interaction have not been applied to children's fantasies.
For example, if the sequence is "the father spanks the boy and then the
boy hits the father" we might be more justified in tolerating the notion
for future tests that this is a wish fulfilling episode compared to the "father spanks the boy and the boy cries."

Likewise, doll play actions that indicate that inhibitions are being
overcome may be discernible. The two indices that have been used are
latency of the first aggressive act and the occurrence of tangential behavior. The latter may be promising if analyzed in a sophisticated fashion.
Tangential actions such as looking out the window or engaging the experimenter in conversation which appear irrelevant to doll play may
indicate a variety of states. The child may be bored, or unable to think
of more actions to portray, or he may indeed be experiencing anxiety over
some impulse which is at the threshold of experience. These possibilities
could be studied within the doll play protocol. It would be interesting to
see if the precursors to boredom are a sequence of redundant acts by the
subjects. On the other hand, signs of disinhibition may be succeeded by
behaviors we assume to be generally prohibited or have been specifically
prohibited for the subject.

In summary, we are saying that there exist in the usual doll play data,
possibilities for more elaborate and potentially more profitable analyses
than have so far been made.

2. The above approach to the wish fulfillment and replication problem focuses on response measures. It is our belief that the study or manipulation of antecedent conditions also may be a fruitful tack.

Our first suggestion is to make use of detailed naturalistic information. A log of the child's experience for a day or two prior to doll play might be kept and the fantasy protocol compared with what we know occurred in the child's life. A very detailed log is represented by *One Boy's Day* (Barker & Wright, 1951). Such an approach is clearly inductive and simply provides a mass of data which may be scrutinized for simple correspondences or for more complex transformations between real life and doll play fantasy. For example, one could look at the ways in which an objectively described situation is filtered through the child's perceptions, and the results might provide clues to types of experiences which form the raw materials for wish fulfillment compared to those types of experiences which are replicated with a high degree of fidelity.

The above naturalistic approach may point up variables, which, through experimental variation, will provide more substantial causal relationships between experiences and fantasy. For example, will a series of successes followed by a failure be fantasied as a success or failure? Does strongly goal oriented action that is not permitted consummation appear in doll play as goal achieved? Can a child be given a set to portray either wish fulfilling or replicative events?

In essence, we are suggesting that an experimental approach to the antecedents of children's fantasies has been tried very little and may provide substantial payoff. If significant antecedent manipulations are found, and their effects are potent and consistent across subjects, a more convenient response index to the two types of fantasy may appear. A case in point is the empirically derived scoring scheme for n Ach, which includes those categories of fantasy that respond consistently to experimental manipulation of arousal compared to neutral instructions.

NATURE OF INSTIGATION IN DOLL PLAY

One of the presumed virtues of doll play is that the amorphousness of the stimulus situation would permit wide expression of "person" variables. Consequently, the preoccupations of the subject would be the major determinants of his fantasy responses. Recently, the contribution of the instigating stimulus itself has received serious attention in projection theory. For example, in the TAT measurement of need achievement the pictures were found to vary in the degree to which they elicited achievement imagery.

In doll play, we get the impression that the situation may be too broadly instigating for the purposes for which the technique is often used. Since this projective method is used to measure a wide variety of child behaviors, it is questionable if it is an equally appropriate measuring device for all of the variables. The data imply quite certainly that doll play is a useful device for measuring fantasy aggression. Beyond that, the incidence of other actions which may be coordinated to such motivational systems as dependency and achievement appear to be meagre. In other words, the home as the miniature situation is associated with so many kinds of behavior that the researcher cannot be sure that the actions in which he is interested will appear with sufficient frequency to be useful.

We can suggest two devices to narrow the spectrum of instigation. The first is to arrange a doll play setting which calls forth the specific behaviors upon which the study focuses. For example, several studies have used a school room rather than a house when the researcher was interested in school related behavior (Bach, 1945; Melville, 1959) and one study used a play yard setting (Bremer, 1947) to study play related behavior.

The second procedure focuses doll play even more narrowly, and may be thought of as analogous to the story completion technique. The experimenter presents the child with a problem and then permits the child to complete the action when the dolls are given to him. Lynn's recent structured doll play test follows this procedure; and the studies of prejudice in which the child is asked to make a choice of a doll is a second example of the focused method.

Summary

This paper surveyed the development and uses of doll play as a research tool. Besides methodological studies the findings in five areas of investigation which have used doll play were summarized: aggression, stereotypy, doll preference, effect of separation from parents, and prejudice. Although certain groups of studies yield interrelated results, the use of this research tool has been so varied that the overall impression is of many disparate findings, in spite of the basic similarity in method. It is suggested that a conceptual difficulty underlying the studies has been the lack of distinction between wish fulfilling and replicative fantasies in children.

References

Ackerman, N. W. Constructive and destructive tendencies in children. *Amer. J. Orthopsychiat.*, 1937, **7**, 301–319.

Ames, Louise B., Learned, Janet, Métraux, Ruth W., & Walker, R. N. *Child Rorschach responses: Developmental trends from two to ten years*. New York: Hoeber, 1952.

Ammons, Carol H., & Ammons, R. B. Research and clinical applications of the doll-play interview. *J. Pers.*, 1952, **21**, 85–90.

Ammons, Carol H., & Ammons R. B. Aggression in doll-play: Interviews of two- to six-year-old white males. *J. genet. Psychol.*, 1953, **82**, 205–213.

Ammons, R. B. Reactions in a projective doll-play interview of white males two to six years of age to differences in skin color and facial features. *J. genet. Psychol.*, 1950, **76**, 323–341.

Ammons, R. B., & Ammons, H. S. Parent preferences in young children's doll-play interviews. *J. abnorm. soc. Psychol.*, 1949, 44, 490–505.

Bach, G. R. Young children's play fantasies. *Psychol. Monogr.*, 1945, **59** (2, Whole No. 272).

Bach, G. R., Father fantasies and father-typing in father-separated children. *Child Develpm.*, 1946, **17**, 63–80.

Bach, G. R., & Bremer, Gloria. Projective father fantasies of preadolescent, delinquent children. *J. Psychol.*, 1947, **24**, 3–17.

Barker, R. G., & Wright, H. F. *One boy's day.* New York: Harper, 1951.

Bellak, L., & Bellak, Sonya S. *Children's Apperception Test, manual.* (Rev. ed.) New York: CPS Co., 1950.

Bixler, R. Nondirective play therapy. Unpublished master's thesis, Ohio State University, 1942.

Bremer, Gloria. The effect of two fantasy environments on children's doll-play responses. Unpublished master's thesis, State University of Iowa, 1947.

Bryan, Carol. An experimental study of the dramatization of family life situations by young children. Unpublished master's thesis, University of Minnesota, 1940.

Caron, A. J., & Gewirtz, J. L. An investigation of the effects of the sex category of the interacting adult, chronological age (6, 8 and 10), and sex of child on aggressive (hostile) behavior in doll-play. *Amer. Psychologist*, 1951, **6**, 307. (Abstract)

Clark, K. B., & Clark, Mamie P. Racial identification and preference in Negro children. In T. M. Newcomb & E. L. Hartley (Eds.), *Readings in social psychology.* New York: Holt, 1947. Pp. 169–178.

Conn, J. H. A psychiatric study of car sickness in children. *Amer. J. Orthopsychiat.*, 1938, **8**, 130–141.

Conn, J. H. Children's reactions to the discovery of genital differences. *Amer. J. Orthopsychiat.*, 1940, **10**, 747–754.

Despert, J. L. A method for the study of personality reactions in preschool age children by means of analysis of their play. *J. Psychol.*, 1940, 9, 17–29.

Emmerich, W. A study of parental identification in young children. *Genet. psychol. Monogr.*, 1959, **60**, 257–308.

Eron, L. D. The use of theory in developing a design. Paper read at American Psychological Association, Washington, D. C., August 1958.

Finch, Helen M. Young children's concepts of parental roles. Unpublished doctoral dissertation, Florida State University, 1954.

Finch, Helen M. Young children's concepts of parent roles. *J. home Econ.*, 1955, 47, 99–103.

Freud, Anna. Introduction to the technic of child analysis. *Nerv. ment. Dis. Monogr. Ser.*, 1928.

Gewirtz, J. L. An investigation of aggressive behavior in the doll-play of young Sac and Fox Indian children and a comparison to the aggression of midwestern white preschool children. *Amer. Psychologist*, 1950, 5, 294–295. (Abstract)

Goodman, Mary E. The genesis of race awareness and attitude. Unpublished doctoral dissertation, Radcliffe College, 1946.

Goodman, Mary E. *Race awareness in young children*. Cambridge, Mass.: Addison-Wesley, 1952.

Graham, T. F. Doll-play phantasies of Negro and white primary-school children. Unpublished doctoral dissertation, University of Ottawa, 1952.

Graham, T. F. Doll-play phantasies of Negro and white primary-school children. *J. clin. Psychol.*, 1955, 11, 29–33.

Halnan, Helen H. A study of father-child relationships using a doll-play technique. Unpublished master's thesis, Stanford University, 1950.

Harding, J., Kutner, B., Prochansky, H., & Chein, I. Prejudice and ethnic relations. In G. Lindzey (Ed.), *Handbook of social psychology*. Vol. 2. Cambridge, Mass.: Addison-Wesley, 1954. Pp. 1021–1061.

Hartley, E. L., & Schwartz, S. A pictorial doll-play approach for the study of children's intergroup attitudes. *Int. J. Opin. attitude Res.*, 1951, 2, 261–270.

Heinicke, C. M. Some effects of separating two-year-old children from their parents: A comparative study. *Hum. Relat.*, 1956, 9, 105–176.

Henry, J., & Henry, Zunia. Doll-play of Pilaga Indian children: An experimental and field analysis of the behavior of the Pilaga Indian children. *Res. Monogr. Amer. Orthopsychiat. Ass.*, 1944, No. 4.

Hollenberg, Eleanor. A study of some effects of child-training practices on doll-play behavior. Unpublished master's thesis, State University of Iowa, 1949.

Hollenberg, Eleanor, & Sperry, Margaret. Some antecedents of aggression and effects of frustration in doll-play. *Personality*, 1951, 1, 32–43.

Holway, Amy R. Early self-regulation of infants and later behavior in play interviews. *Amer. J. Orthopsychiat.*, 1949, 19, 612–623.

Honzik, Marjorie P. Sex differences in the occurrence of materials in the play constructions of preadolescents. *Child Develpm.*, 1951, 22, 15–35.

Isch, Maria J. Fantasied mother-child interaction in doll-play. *J. genet. Psychol.*, 1952, 81, 233–258.

Jeffre, Maria F. D. Fantasied mother-child interaction in doll-play. Unpublished doctoral dissertation, State University of Iowa, 1946.

Johnson, Elizabeth Z. Attitudes of children toward authority as projected in their doll play at two age levels. Unpublished doctoral dissertation, Harvard University, 1951.

Johnson, L. C. The effect of father absence during infancy on later father-child relationship using a doll-play technique. Unpublished master's thesis, Stanford University, 1952.

Korner, A. F. *Some aspects of hostility in young children.* New York: Grune & Stratton, 1949.

Krall, Vita. Personality factors in accident-prone and accident-free children. Unpublished doctoral dissertation, University of Rochester, 1951.

Krall, Vita. Personality characteristics of accident-repeating children. *J. abnorm. soc. Psychol.,* 1953, **48**, 99–107.

Levin, H. Effects of parental punishment on young children's overt and fantasy aggression. *Amer. Psychologist,* 1953, **8**, 387. (Abstract)

Levin, H. The influence of classroom control on kindergarten children's fantasy aggression. *Elem. sch. J.,* 1955, **55**, 462–466.

Levin, H. Permissive child rearing and adult role behavior. In D. E. Dulany, Jr., R. L. DeValois, D. C. Beardslee, & Marian R. Winterbottom (Eds.), *Contributions to modern psychology.* New York: Oxford Univer. Press, 1958.

Levin, H., & Sears, R. R. Identification with parents as a determinant of doll-play aggression. *Child Develpm.,* 1956, **27**, 135–153.

Levin, H., & Turgeon, Valerie F. The influence of the mother's presence on children's doll-play aggression. *J. abnorm. soc. Psychol.,* 1957, **55**, 304–308.

Levy, D. M. Use of play technique as experimental procedure. *Amer. J. Orthopsychiat.,* 1933, **3**, 266–277.

Levy, D. M. Hostility patterns in sibling rivalry experiments. *Amer. J. Orthopsychiat.,* 1936, **6**, 183–257.

Levy, D. M. "Control-situation" studies of children's responses to the difference in genitalia. *Amer. J. Orthopsychiat.,* 1940, **10**, 755–762.

Lynn, D. B. Development and validation of a Structured Doll-Play Test for children. *Quart. Bull. Ind. U. Med. Cent.,* 1955.

Lynn, D. B., & Lynn, Rosalie. The Structured Doll-Play Test as a projective technique for use with children. *J. proj. Tech.,* 1959, **23**, 335-344.

Lynn, D. B., & Sawrey, W. L. The effects of father-absence on Norwegian boys and girls. *J. abnorm. soc. Psychol.,* 1959, **59**, 258–262.

Lynn, Rosalie. A study of the responses of four- and six-year-olds to a structured doll-play test. Unpublished master's thesis, Purdue University, 1955.

McClelland, D. C., Atkinson, J. W., Clark, R. A., & Lowell, E. L. *The achievement motive.* New York: Appleton-Century-Crofts, 1953.

Meister, D. Adjustment of children as reflected in play performance. *J. genet. Psychol.,* 1948, **73**, 141–155.

Melville, Clara P. A study of overt and fantasy expressions of variables related to young children's motivation toward working industriously in school. Unpublished doctoral dissertation, Stanford University, 1959.

Miller, H., & Baruch, Dorothy W. A. study of hostility in allergic children. *Amer. J. Orthopsychiat.*, 1950, **20**, 506–519.

Mussen P., & Distler, L. Masculinity, identification, and father-son relationships. *J. abnorm. soc. Psychol.*, 1959, **59**, 350–356.

Phillips, Ruth. Doll-play as a function of the realism of the materials and the length of the experimental session. *Child Develpm.*, 1945, **16**, 123–143.

Pintler, Margaret H. Doll-play as a function of experimenter-child interaction and initial organization of materials. *Child Develpm.*, 1945, **16**, 145–166.

Pintler, Margaret H., Phillips, Ruth, & Sears, R. R. Sex differences in the projective doll-play of preschool children. *J. Psychol.*, 1946, **21**, 73–80.

Rabban, M. Sex-role identification in young children in two diverse social groups. *Genet. psychol. Monogr.*, 1950, **42**, 81–158.

Radke, Marian J. The relation of parental authority to children's behavior and attitudes. *Inst. Child Welf. monogr. Ser.*, 1946, **22**.

Radke, Marian J., & Trager, Helen G. Children's perceptions of the social roles of Negroes and whites. *J. Psychol.*, 1950, **29**, 3–33.

Robinson, Elizabeth F. Doll-play as a function of the doll family constellation. *Child Develpm.*, 1946, **17**, 99–119.

Rosenzweig, S., & Shakow, D. Play technique in schizophrenia and other psychoses. *Amer. J. Orthopsychiat.*, 1937, **7**, 36–47.

Ryder, Joyce M. Aggression with balloons, blocking, and doll-play. In Lois M. Stolz and collaborators, *Father relations of warborn children*. Stanford: Stanford Univer. Press, 1954. Pp. 212–243.

Scott, R. G. Projective parental fantasies of parent-separated children and children in families. Unpublished EdD dissertation, Teachers College, Columbia University, 1954.

Sears, Pauline S. Doll-play aggression in normal young children: Influence of sex, age, sibling status, father's absence. *Psychol. Monogr.*, 1951, **65**(6, Whole No. 323).

Sears, Pauline S., & Pintler, Margaret H. Sex differences in doll-play aggression. *Amer. Psychologist*, 1947, **2**, 420. (Abstract)

Sears, Pauline S., & Staff of the Laboratory of Human Development, Harvard University. Child-rearing factors relating to playing of sex-type roles. *Amer. Psychologist*, 1953, **8**, 431. (Abstract)

Sears, R. R. Influence of methodological factors on doll-play performance. *Child Develpm.*, 1947, **18**, 190–197.

Sears, R. R. Relation of fantasy aggression to interpersonal aggression. *Child Develpm.*, 1950, **21**, 5–6.

Sears, R. R., Maccoby, Eleanor E., & Levin, H. *Patterns of child rearing*. Evanston, Ill.: Row, Peterson, 1957.

Sears, R. R., Pintler, Margaret H., & Sears, Pauline S. Effect of father separation on preschool children's doll-play aggression. *Child Develpm.*, 1946, **17**, 219–243.

Simpkins, Vera A. A comparison of verbal and motor fantasies in children. Unpublished master's thesis, Clark University, 1948.

Sperry, Margaret. An experimental study of the effects of disapproval of aggression on doll-play. Unpublished master's thesis, State University of Iowa, 1949.

Stamp, I. M. An evaluation of the Driscoll Playkit used with incomplete stories as an instrument for the diagnosis of personality. Unpublished Ed D dissertation, Teachers College, Columbia University, 1954.

Stevenson, H. W., & Stewart, E. C. A developmental study of racial awareness in young children. *Child Develpm.*, 1958, **29**, 399–409.

Tuddenham, R. D. Studies in reputation: I. Sex and grade differences in school children's evaluation of their peers. II. The diagnosis of social adjustment. *Psychol. Monogr.*, 1952, **66**(1, Whole No. 333).

Walsh, Ann M. *Self-concepts of bright boys with learning difficulties.* New York: Teachers Coll., Columbia Univer., Bureau of Publications, 1956.

Whiting, J. W. M., & Child, I. L. *Child training and personality.* New Haven: Yale Univer. Press, 1953.

Winstel, Beulah. The use of a controlled play situation in determining certain effects of maternal attitudes on children. *Child Develpm.*, 1951, **22**, 299–311.

Witkin, H. A., Lewis, H. B., Hertzman, M., Machover, K., Meissner, P. B., & Wapner, S. *Personality through perception.* New York: Harper, 1954.

Wurtz, K. R. The expression of guilt in fantasy and reality. Unpublished doctoral dissertation, Stanford University, 1957.

Wurtz, K. R. Some theory and data concerning the attentuation of aggression. *J. abnorm. soc. Psychol.*, 1960, **60**, 134–136.

Yarrow, L. J. The effect of antecedent frustration of projective play. *Psychol. Monogr.*, 1949, **62**(6, Whole No. 293).

Chapter V

Comparative Approaches

This section begins with the excellent 1945 view by Frank Beach of the state of theory and observation on the subject-matter of animal play at that time. His approach to the possibilities of understanding animal (or human) play in terms of most of the concepts that had been proposed for it was predominantly pessimistic. A further paper by Schlosberg suggests, in fact, that the category of play is hardly necessary. It can be subsumed under the rubrics of stimulus-response psychology. Despite Beach's pessimism and Schlosberg's "reductivism," students of animal behavior have continued to observe and discuss animal play, and because of the improved techniques of observation and more careful conceptualization, the adequacy of the descriptive record has increased considerably over the past 20 years. Among the best current accounts of this record are Welker's "An Analysis of Exploratory and Play Behavior in Animals" (1961), Berlyne's "Laughter, Humor and Play" (1969) and Jewell and Loizos' "Play, Exploration and Territory in Mammals" (1966).

In her introduction, Loizos says:

Play in animals has generally been thought to be without function. This attitude has possibly arisen from a false analogy with the use of the word as it applies to human behavior where play is opposed to work. Animals do not work and therefore cannot be said to play, at any rate in the human sense of the word. It is suggested that it might be a more fruitful approach to start with the assumption that animal play does have survival value, in view of the time and energy spent in play by, in particular, the carnivores and the primates (1966, p. 1).

The paradox with play is that it has usually been thought to be nonproductive, while at the same time is has been declared to increase in extent as one ascends the evolutionary scale. Part of the problem, apparently, has lain in the rather restrictive definition applied to the term productive, and by implication to the assumptions about adaptation that underlay it. The deterministic assumptions prevalent in the life sciences have placed the heaviest weight on those animal and human responses that clearly made a direct contribution to survival. Response systems of a play or expressive sort have been somewhat anomalous within this system and have been regarded generally as epiphenomena with no clear role in human survival.

However, if one focuses attention on the more voluntary (less determinable) responses of animal and human organisms and concedes that their development is important, then the functional role of play becomes more explicit. It might be argued that traditional scientific definitions of adaptation give insufficient emphasis to the development of voluntary control in behavior. Such voluntary control implies various forms of mastery such as the anticipation of outcomes, the choice of instrumental behaviors, freedom from immediate sensory controls, a capacity to sustain the direction of behavior over a number of responses, sequential organization, and skill in mobilizing resources. All of these phenomena are often included among traditional definitions of play. From a biological point of view, therefore, it might make sense to regard play as an exercise of voluntary control systems. Presumably on a psychological level, it is the freedom and "as if" quality of play that guarantees the exercise of such controls.

Unfortunately, few recent studies have had a framework of this character. Instead they have focused on the types of antecedent phenomena that appear to instigate play, but seldom on the response systems or structures that might be said to characterize the nature of that play itself. There is attention to instigating stimuli; to relationships between exploration and play; instigating motivational states and to instigating properties of other species members, adults and peers. In turn, play is discussed in terms of species differences and ontogenetic sequences, but there is only slight reference to the way in which these are transformations of activities found in nonplay behavior. There follows some brief examples of these current approaches.

First, when the focus is upon *instigating ludic signals*, the concern is with those stimuli or cues responsible for the initiation and maintenance of the ludic system. In a fascinating article entitled "The Message, This is Play," partly reproduced in the next chapter, Bateson (1956) has suggested that given suitable circumstances, humans use a variety of social signals to trigger off this type of response system. There are involuntary signals (such as smiling or a twinkle in the eye); there are simulated signals in which the pretence is indicated in some gestural way, by an exaggeration of action or appearance; there are stock play signals in which the individual is invited or challenged to play; and there are postplay signals when one individual assures another that he was only joking, etc. In animals, likewise, there may be particular signals for the onset of play, though these observations are, of course, most susceptible to faulty inference. Howling monkeys trigger off play with soft twittering squeaks to each other, and dog mothers do the same by rubbing faces, gently biting, mouthing, or pawing at the pup (Rheingold, 1963). Dogs may signal to each other similarly by wagging their tail, which is perhaps the canine equivalent of a smile. There are possibly many such species-specific signals, though whether they are always present at the initiation of play is a matter for research. The question is important, however, because these signals have a somewhat ritualized quality, whereas in most of the current study when play and exploration have been bracketed together, it has been said that novelty alone is sufficient to instigate them both. Because much of the recent interest in play has to do with its classification as an intrinsic motivational system along with exploration, it seems worthwhile at this point to indulge in a fairly lengthy excursus on the interrelationships between *play and exploration* with an eye to identifying the similarities and differences between their instigating circumstances and response properties.

Both exploratory behavior and play have been described as self-motivated activities whose rewards lie in the gratifications that they bring directly to the participants (Berlyne, 1960; Welker, 1961). Typical research findings from this work that generalize across many animal and some human studies are as follows. (1) Novel properties in the ecology (blocks, puzzles, colors, and games) increase the response levels of the subjects exposed to those properties. As subjects cease to be able to do new things with objects, however, their response to them decreases. Berlyne has indicated that other properties of objects that have similar effects are their complexity, their surprisingness, their uncertainty, and their capacity to induce conflict. (2) The greatest increases in response levels are recorded for those objects with which the subjects can do most things; that is, that can be handled, moved, seen, touched, etc. (3) Exploratory and play behavior, like other response systems, is susceptible to increase or diminution in response level as a result of appropriate parental reinforcements (Marshall, 1966). (4) Exploratory and play behavior in child subjects correlates highly with information seeking in general (Maw and Maw, 1965).

Unfortunately, because play and exploration are categorized together in most of these studies, it is not possible to state what proportion of the increased responsivity is due to one or the other. But attempts have been made to distinguish between the two. On the basis of his observations of infants, for example, Piaget casts them into a temporal relationship, with exploration preceding play. He says:

We find, indeed, though naturally without being able to trace any definite boundary, that the child, after showing by his seriousness that he is making a real effort at accommodation, later produces these behaviors merely for plea- sure, accompanied by smiles and even laughter, and without the expectation of results, characteristic of the circular reactions through which the child learns (1951, p. 90).

Welker, on the other hand, in his study of play in animals (1961) sees the difference mainly in terms of a passivity-activity dimension. Thus, he says:

exploration "consists" of cautiously and gradually exposing the receptors . . . to portions of the environment. The goals or incentives consist of sensory stimulation, and novel stimuli in any modality are especially important. Play consists of a wide variety of vigorous and spirited activities: those that move the organism or its parts through space such as running, jumping, rolling . . . and vigorous manipulation of body parts or objects in a variety of ways (1961, p. 176).

Berlyne's definition varies slightly. He says "Much, possibly most, play is exploratory behavior. We are, however, in no position to identify all play as exploration, because exploration is best defined in terms of intrinsically rewarding or biologically neutral sensory consequences. While much playful behavior is apparently aimed at satisfying or 'entertaining' sensory con- sequences" (1970). Along similar lines again but with a more operant flavor, Goldberg, Godfrey, and Lewis have recently written: "We shall call behavior 'play' when the subject shows free emission of responses such that choice of response and rate of emission are determined solely by the organism" (1967).

We note that in all these differentiations attention is given mainly to the response differences between exploration and play. It seems to be assumed that novelty is equally important for both. Our earlier reference to ludic signals, however, raises some doubt about this. There is some possible resolution of these paradoxes in Mason's extensive studies of clinging and play behavior in chimpanzees. The outcomes are fairly con- sistent. When the infant chimpanzees were subjected to real novelty, sepa- ration from other, or drug-induced arousal, they almost always sought the support of others in clinging activity. As novelty waned, and when the others were familiar, then the chimpanzees themselves gradually increased their rates of play activity. The intensity of play rose gradually as a func- tion of familiarity and of mild novelty within that familiar situation. "Play characteristically is directed towards the novel, variable, or mildly stimu- lating features of the environment, and it probably serves to increase arousal rather than to reduce it. . . . The thesis that clinging reduces arousal and play augments it suggests a loose homeostatic relation between these social response patterns and motivational variables" (1967, p. 115). Putting together Mason's findings with the above quotations from Piaget, Welker, Berlyne, and Lewis et al., we can perhaps talk of a continuum of novelty. At one end the very novel or strange leads to avoidance (clinging responses), the mildly novel leads to exploration involving searching activities by the organism, but when the setting is thoroughly familiar, then play can ensue. Whether it occurs because the novelty occurs within a familiar setting, or because it is accompanied by a play signal and is thus changed in some qualitative fashion requires further research.

To raise questions of this nature is to reveal the paucity and grossness of the observations usually made of young organisms. There has not been the careful and molecular observation of the sequences leading to ludic behavior that is necessary for definitive statements about the matter of instigating "stimuli" or "signals." Again, even with respect to the differences in responsivity where agreement seems greater among those quoted above, it is also very clear from Piaget's observations that distinctions are difficult to make because exploration and play are both polarities within self-motivated activity, with the child often changing rapidly from one to the other, so that it is difficult to classify an activity as one or the other. There may well be "playful exploratory behavior" and "exploratory playful behavior." It is only in older subjects, in fact, who themselves categorize their activities as one or the other, as hobbies or games, that we become reasonably certain of the difference.

Students of both animal and human play are very clear that play, like other *intrinsic motivational systems* (Berlyne, 1960), usually occurs only in the absence of painful stimulation or intense homeostatic drives—although there are entriguing exceptions, as when toddlers become so engaged in play that they urinate in their clothes rather than stop playing, and sportsmen become so engrossed in their games that they continue despite painful injuries. These latter exceptions, however, seem to refer to conditions that occur *after* the players have become involved and are under the sway of the ludic system. In general, play is postponable. It is instigated lightly by play signals, playful agents, or its own intrinsic seductive cues (the playground, the chess board) or play times (recess) rather than arising irrevocably out of the ordinary flow of circumstances.

It is difficult in this light, therefore, to know what to make of those theories of play that declare its instigating conditions to be various states of anxiety, aggression, and sex, or conflicts between these and other drives. And yet, the record of play therapy is clear enough. Children obsessed by mild anxieties about aggression often symbolize aggression compulsively over a long series of play sessions—though if their anxieties are too great, there can be play disruption. In addition, the records of projective literature seem to suggest that high motivational states may obtain direct expression in fantasy when not accompanied by anxiety, and may obtain indirect or disguised expression when they are accompanied by anxiety. Again, cross-cultural studies have given ample evidence of systematic relationships between the presence of games in culture and the existence also of antecedent child-training conflicts. The fewer the types of games found in tribal cultures, the greater the degrees of child-training indulgence. Obversely, the more types of games, the greater the degrees of socialization anxiety and pressure (Roberts & Sutton-Smith, 1962).

So, on the one hand, there is evidence of connections between play contents and antecedent drive states, and on the other a variety of phenomena suggesting that play does not commence until such drive states are not at a high level. Even Piaget's statement that play succeeds exploration is subsumable to the generality that play does not commence until other behavior systems are sated. From the materials on ludic signals above, we might infer that the norm of play, motivationally speaking, is a moderate degree of arousal. Play signals are used to maintain "an even temperature," "a good spirit," and when this is done, then important drives can be introduced. So it is perhaps proper to speak of such motivational states as being assimilated into the ludic behavior system and thus determining its content, rather than to speak of them as "causing" the play itself.

But to return once again to the question of ludic signals, it is probably unwise to attempt to isolate the matter of ludic signals from *the character of those who do the signalling*. Animal observations indicate that elk mothers will initiate splash-and-run games with their calves. The calves initially show fear and are reluctant to enter the water, but after a few such experiences become eager to follow her. While this is going on, there are vocalizations back and forth between mother and calf. Observations on dogs also indicate considerable differences between breeds in the amount of play instigated by the mothers (Rheingold, 1963).

While parents can and do have an important role in the development of play, there is no question that the great bulk of play and game behavior receives its social instigation from peers. Mothers may be particularly important at the very beginning, however, perhaps setting up norms for play or a readiness for play. Call and Marschak have observed that human mothers may initiate playfulness in the first days of life by playing with the baby's fingers as he feeds at the breast or bottle (1966). What is most characteristic of human or animal young such as elks, pups, or primates is that most play solicitation comes from other animals of the same age group. Perhaps the most important single demonstration anywhere of the importance of peers and the power of their play instigations for each other is to be found in Harlow's contrast between the play activities of monkeys who lived alone with their mothers, and monkeys who had no mothers but had other monkeys to play with. We quote in extenso:

Another pilot experiment has shown that even normal mothering is not enough to produce socially adequate offspring. We isolated two infants in the exclusive company of their mothers to the age of seven months, and then brought the mother-infant pairs together in a playpen unit. The female infant took full advantage of the play apparatus provided, but in three months the male was never seen to leave its home cage, and its mother would not permit the female to come within arm's reach. Social interaction of the infants was limited to an occasional exchange of tentative threats. For the past two months they have been separated from their mothers, housed in individual cages, and brought together in the playroom for 15 minutes each day. In this normally stimulating environment, they have so far shown no disposition to play together. Next to the infants that have been raised in total isolation, these are the most retarded of the infants tested in the playroom. . . .

The opportunities afforded by the playroom were most fully exploited by two groups of four infants that otherwise spent their days housed alone in their cages with a cloth surrogate. These animals were released in the playroom for 20 minutes a day from the first month of life through the eleventh, in the case of one group, and through the second year in the case of the other. In contrast with all the other groups observed in the playroom, they did their "growing up" in this environment. Even though their exposure to the room and to one another was limited to 20 minutes a day, they enacted with great spirit the entire growth pattern of the rhesus-monkey play behavior.

They began by exploring the room and each other. Gradually over the next two or three months they developed a game of rough-and-tumble play with jumping, scuffling, wrestling, hair-pulling, and a little nipping, but with no real damage, and then an associated game of flight and pursuit in which the participants are alternately the threateners and the threatened. While these group activities evolved, so did the capacity for individual play exploits, with the animals running, leaping, swinging, and climbing heedless of one another and apparently caught up in the sheer joy of action. As their skill and strength grew, their social play involved shorter but brisker episodes of free-for-all action, with longer chases between bouts. Subsequently, they developed an even more complex pattern of violent activity, performed with blinding speed and integrating all objects, animate and inanimate, in the room. Along with social play, and possibly as a result of by-product, they began to exhibit sexual posturing in an immature and fleeting form in the first six months and more frequently and more adult in form by the end of the year. The differences in play activity that distinguish males and females became evident in the first two or three months, with the females threatening and initiating rough contact far less frequently than the males and withdrawing from threats and approaches far more frequently.

Thus in spite of the relatively limited opportunity for contact afforded by their daily schedule, all the individuals in these two groups developed effective infant-infant play relations. Those observed into the second year have shown the full repertory of adult sexual behavior. At the same chronological age these motherless monkeys have attained as full a maturity in these respects as the infants raised with their mothers in the playpen (1962, pp. 136–146).

About the only thing on a human level that remotely resembles this demonstration of the effectiveness of peers as instigators for play and for growth (as in the case of these primates) is the group case study by Freud and Dann (1944), and perhaps some of the studies of children of the kibbutz (Rabin, 1965). An important conclusion that can be drawn from Harlow's work and these other items is that what may be most important in "releasing" a ludic response or ludic system, is to have this response modeled by another agent of similar identity, and, therefore, possessing response capacities similar to the subject, a process which, following Scott, might be termed allelomimetic modeling behavior (1963). The great hunger of young children for each other and the long periods of play they can spend together, would appear to attest to the particularly suitable character of peers as releasers, perhaps because they provide facilitative models of ludic behavior systems.

A more biological approach is to seek an evolutionary perspective on play, which is the procedure followed by Welker (1961). First, he finds that there is ample evidence for play activities in birds and mammals, but that it may be lacking in the lower vertebrates. It seems to be present in rats but not in mice. Exploratory behaviors have been noticed in invertebrates. Second, the higher the phylogenetic scales (complexity, social organization, infant protection, and delayed motivation), the greater the amount of time spent in play, and the greater the variety of play and the more complex its character. Which of these scales is the most relevant is unfortunately not discussed by Welker. Third, both Welker and Berlyne stress the key roles of novelty and complexity in inducing exploratory and play responses in experimental studies with rhesus monkeys, chimpanzees, hyenas, and rhinoceroses; also, such investigatory and manipulatory behavior is stronger in animals with more complex nervous systems. Fourth, each species has its own characteristic type of exploratory and play behavior, and even different breeds of dogs may vary greatly in their amounts and types of playfulness. Whether or not such playfulness relates to other characteristics of the breeds, we do not yet know. Is it because the cockers play less than the shelties that they are also less sensitive?

Yet another approach to the definition of play is in terms of the ontogenetic sequences found in different species. There are several major characteristics of ontogenetic sequences in play that should first be mentioned. There is a transition from infant to juvenile play, a distinction more marked in the primates and humans than with other species. With dogs and cats there seems to be more typically social infant-infant interaction at the very beginning of play behavior. We might surmise that play responses may be increasingly endogenous to the organism, given certain phylogenetic conditions such as delayed motivation and infant protection, but there are exceptions, and these interrelationships require more careful examination than have yet been given.

Secondly, play seems to be conspicuously an activity of the young, directed towards the immature others or towards features of the physical environment. The lower the species (that plays), the more true is this generality. As we move upwards through the species, the period of play activity extends for an increasing period of the life span. It is arguable that in humans it never completely ceases to be an important response system. Thirdly, in the very young the optimum level of arousal that seems to parallel play is very low, and the young organism may find even slight increases in arousal aversive. With increased growth and familiarity with the environment, the degrees of arousal that can be regarded as "moderate" or "optimal" by the organism increase greatly in intensity. A football game fought through with fierce intensity by adults but with adherence to the rules and a sporting spirit, is a good example of the way in which there can be a developmental incrementation of the arousal system relevant to ludic behavior.

Examples of the infant-animal play usually involve the mother and other members of the litter. Kittens jump over the mother, toy with her tail, and paw her. Pups mouth and bite the mother's ears, legs, and tail, then they proceed to biting play with objects. From here they go to pawing, jumping, and tumbling over each other. Infant langur monkeys play between the mother's legs in the first few weeks and climb over her, but generally do not go more than two or three feet from the mother. If they do, she may pull them back by the tail. By three months they are still playing mainly by themselves or climbing about on adult females. The mothers chase others away. By the age of six months the infants are permitted to play with each other, but not with juveniles. Play groups may include as many as sixteen young monkeys, but average two to four; and half of all play groups have fewer than three members. Running, jumping, chasing, wrestling, and tail pulling are supplemented by more complicated forms of play, sometimes oriented towards objects; but play is usually interpersonal and exploratory. By ten months the infant spends four to five hours a day in such group play and may move with his age mates when the total group travels. By fifteen months he is weaned from the mother and he sleeps, eats, and plays with other juveniles.

Play is the most important activity in the life of the male juvenile, and it is pursued with great abandon for as many as four or five hours a day. Even the most active and boisterous play is usually silent. The juvenile occasionally squeals or grunts if he falls from a tree or is hit by a play partner, but unless they are prolonged and intense, these sounds do not draw the attention of the adults. After the play group is disrupted by adults or by too violent activity, it reassembles within two or three minutes. Since male play groups cover great distances rapidly, most groups stay on the edge of the troop away from adult females with young infants. Although male and female juveniles often begin to play together, males quickly form all-male groups leaving the female juvenile behind with the infant-twos (Jary, *ibid.*, p. 301).

A somewhat similar series of events has been recorded for other primate groups (baboons and gorillas). Chimpanzees in captivity are said to display considerable play ingenuity; given sticks, they experiment with them, pole-vaulting; they somersault; they ride on each other's backs, move rhythmically together in a line, dab clay over their bodies and other objects, etc. Lions hide and stalk each other. Elks, moose, bison, and boars are reported to play rushing and biting games. But like the observations of the infant play of these species, we really lack detailed observations on the nature of the ludic behavior systems as such (what triggers them, exactly what behaviors they include, etc.).

We have been dealing with the various stimuli that are antecedent to play, and to some extent with the types of play that are characteristic both phylogenetically and ontogenetically. In addition to these concerns, however, any understanding of animal play must deal with the way in which the play structures parallel, reproduce, or present transformations of the nonplay structures. For even if play is characterized biologically as an exercise of voluntary control systems (thus giving it a novel adaptive significance), it is never only a straightforward exercise. Play structures have their own special character and quality. The response transformations we observe in infant-animal play seem to be often a replication of behavior that is more fully expressed by older animals outside of play. The infants or juveniles chase but do not assault, hunt and capture but do not destroy, attack and mouth but do not bite, and mount but do not copulate. Partial forms of hunt-flight-fight and sexual behavior are the most obvious components of such animal play. Children's play also appears to contain a great deal that is partially replicative of their own activities elsewhere, or the activities of others.

Recently Eibl-Eibesfeldt has made the following case for the transformations in animal play. First, he says, the action patterns are not carried through to their usual ends. Second, many patterns are combined in play in ways that are not found outside of it. "Play may even combine behavior patterns of functional cycles that normally operate in mutual exclusion, for example, hunting, fighting, and sexual behavior" (1967, p. 138). Third, "it is free of the usual tensions of instrumental behavior, and yet it is not without intensity. . . . Play fighting can occur with great intensity and still show all the friendly attributes such as tail-wagging and biting inhibition;

a serious encounter even on the lowest intensity, looks completely different" (*ibid.*, p. 139). Fourth, "during play the animal may invent new motor patterns. All the described play behavior involves experimentation with the organism's own body and abilities, or experimental interactions with another species member . . . we may consider play as an experimental dialogue with the environment. . . ." (*ibid.*, p. 139).

Having claimed that play is a distinctive type of transformation and activity (partially replicative and partially novel), and that it is not to be reduced to exploration or inadequate observation, the task of indicating what is to be included and what not is nevertheless quite formidable. If one deals only with lower organisms, it is easy to label something as playful that on subsequent investigations turns out to be strictly functional, such as the leaping of the fishes described by Beach in this chapter. Berlyne even suggests that "there seems to be a great deal of justice to the view that our ignorance is the main factor that holds together the category of play" (1970), though Berlyne then proceeds to follow this dramatic statement with an extended discussion of the sports of humans, games of children, and the continuing observations of play by biologists, indicating that there is still considerable substance within this recalcitrant category.

The various descriptions given above help to allay the pessimism about the reality of play with which this chapter began and which is reflected in the two readings. They do suggest some of the essential components, contextual, ontogenetic, phylogenetic, and transformational, of any systematic description of play. They also show the way in which a dominantly stimulus-response approach is being altered to permit ludic phenomena to be reckoned with. There is recognition of novel classes of stimuli (instigating stimuli and agents); and there is recognition of novel responses (transformational responses). What is now required perhaps, is the development of a sequential account of these "transformations," or of the ludic structures that evolve ontogenetically, within each species. A study of play structures and their relationship to the development of voluntary control systems might also be instructive.

12

Current Concepts of Play in Animals

Frank A. Beach

Present-day understanding of animal play is regrettably limited, and current views on the subject are considerably confused. On the one hand, there are the hundreds of observations made by naturalists, by animal breeders and by nearly every one who has kept a household pet to indicate that animals of many species do exhibit various types of behavior which, if they were observed in humans, would undoubtedly be called play. On the other hand stands our undeniable ignorance as to the essential nature of play, its causes and its results. The richness of the observational evidence is in sharp contrast to the poverty of scientific knowledge.

It is significant that authors of several recent American text-books on comparative or physiological psychology have failed to make any mention of play in animals, or have skipped over the subject as lightly as possible (Warden, Jenkins and Warner, 1936; Maier and Schneirla, 1935; C. T. Morgan, 1943). Their reluctance or inability to treat the topic undoubtedly derives from the exclusively observational character of available data and the obvious inadequacy of existing interpretations.

It is not the purpose of this paper to present new data pertinent to the problem under consideration, or to propose any original, all-inclusive theoretical interpretation. Instead it is hoped that a survey of existing knowledge and an evaluation of the theories presently available may

SOURCE. Republished from *Amer. Naturalist*, 1945, **79**(785), 523–541, with the permission of the author and the publisher.

point the way toward profitable lines of future work which will lead to a more complete understanding of the subject.

Commonly Accepted Characteristics of Play

Play is generally regarded as differing from non-playful activities in several ways. Whether or not it is possible to discern any pervasive characteristics common to all forms of behavior which are commonly listed under this rubric depends upon the definition of play. At this point, however, we shall overlook this source of difficulty and list the outstanding characteristics of playful behavior as set forth by most students of the subject.

(1) It is commonly stated or implied, although it can not be objectively demonstrated, that playful behavior in animals as in man carries an emotional element of pleasure. Not all pleasant activities are playful; but all play is assumed to be pleasurable. (2) Play is usually regarded as characteristic of the immature animal rather than the adult. Grown individuals may play; but they do so less frequently than juvenile members of their species. (3) It is usually supposed that play differs from non-playful responses in having no relatively immediate biological result which affects the continued existence of the individual or the species. In other words, play is customarily regarded as non-utilitarian. (4) The outward forms of play are relatively species-specific. Dogs play in certain ways, horses in others, and apes in still others. (5) The amount, duration and diversity of play in a given species is related to its phylogenetic position. In general, play is more frequent, more variable, and occurs during a longer portion of the life span in higher animals than in lower. The play of fishes appears infrequent and stereotyped when compared with that of lower mammals; while the play of dogs is less diversified and prolonged than that of monkeys and apes.

Types of Behavior Which Have Been Called Play

A wide variety of animal responses are frequently lumped together under the general heading of play. The categories are not clear cut, but may merge insensibly one into another; and sometimes several kinds of play may be combined in an integrated series of reactions. In listing the main types of play we shall temporarily refrain from any evaluation of the validity of the classification.

GENERAL BODILY ACTIVITY

Many young animals display a great deal of bodily activity, chiefly of a locomotor character, in which vast amounts of energy are expended and no obviously useful result is achieved. Fishes of some species periodically leap above the surface of the water; some birds indulge in elaborate aerial acrobatics; colts gallop about the pasture; puppies race back and forth in the yard; kittens scamper widly across the room over the sofa and under the chair; in addition to climbing, sliding and jumping, chimpanzees execute complicated bodily actions such as turning somersaults, or revolving rapidly in pinwheel fashion while lying at full length on the ground (Kohler, 1931). Some writers regard these reactions as a form of play (Mitchell, 1912; Haigis, 1941; Gudger, 1944).

YOUTHFUL PRACTICE OF ADULT ACTIVITIES

Young animals of many species exhibit various behavior patterns which also appear in the repertoire of the adult individual; but when executed during immaturity the responses are often incomplete, and seem to lack any practical outcome. Well-known examples of such behavior, which is generally interpreted as play, are the mock battles of puppies, the pursuit and capture of any small, moving object by kittens and the infantile or juvenile sex reactions of many species (Groos, 1898).

EXPLORATION AND EXPERIMENTATION

Responses falling in this category may range from very simple investigatory reactions to highly complex and original types of experimentation (C. L. Morgan, 1900). The tendency of young birds and mammals to peck, scratch, claw, pull and bite at objects in their environment is illustrative of the relatively simple exploratory reactions which some observers regard as play. In contrast stand the knottying and pole vaulting of chimpanzees, which are also examples of manipulative or experimental behavior albeit of a higher order.

SOCIAL RESPONSES

Certain inter-individual reactions which seem to lack any practical outcome are often listed as play. The "tilting matches" of young British warblers (Pycraft, 1912), "king-of-the-mountain" games of lion cubs (Cooper, 1942), "follow-the-leader" games of young monkeys (C. L. Morgan, 1900) fall in this general category.

Social play is prominent among chimpanzees according to the descriptions of Kohler (1931). He states that when several young apes were given a large sack, one crept into the container and the others pulled it about on the ground. Small chimpanzees sometimes rode pickaback on the shoulders of older animals and then slid downward, grasping the bearer's trunk with the hind legs and walking on the ground with the hands.

The "dancing" of young apes would probably come under the heading of social play. This activity is highly variable and ranges from spinning round and round in a solo performance to participation in rather complicated group performances. Several chimpanzees may start to march single file around a post or box. Gradually their pace increases and they trot, often with emphasis upon one foot so that a primitive kind of rhythm emerges; and as they trot and stamp, the animals may wag their heads in time with the pedal rhythm. A direct quotation from Kohler will serve to illustrate the complexity and group character of the behavior.

As the whole group were joyously trotting round a box, little Konsul stepped to one side outside the circle, drew himself up to his full height, swung his arms to and fro in time to the trotting, and each time that fat Tschego passed him, caught her a sounding smack behind.

INTER-SPECIES REACTIONS

Although animals of one species occasionally respond to those of a foreign species in what might be regarded as a playful manner, play between species is not common. The outstanding exception to this generalization is the play which takes place between man and his pets. If one is to accept any of the characteristics or criteria of play which are accorded common usage, it must be admitted that the dog plays with his master (Russell, 1936). The animal may engage in sham hunts or battles with the man in much the same manner as with another dog. On the other hand he may with equal readiness participate in a "learned" game such as "fetch," or perform various tricks without any material reward. It is particularly significant to note that the animal may take the initiative in beginning the interspecies play, and signalize in a variety of ways his eagerness to tease his master into a game. In similar fashion young chimpanzees play with human companions (Wolfe, 1936); and the desire to do so is so strong that opportunity to play has successfully been used as an incentive in certain learning experiments (Yerkes and Petrunkevitch, 1925).

Criteria and Causes

The majority of interpretations purporting to define or explain play are speculative in nature, deductively derived and completely untested.

SURPLUS ENERGY

The poet Schiller is reputed to have suggested that play is an expression of overflowing energy which can find no other outlet. Actually, as Curti (1930) has pointed out, Schiller merely noted that playful behavior usually occurs when an ample supply of energy is available; but later writers have reinterpreted the original suggestion to form a theory stating that certain types of play constitute a release of extra physical, and perhaps mental or emotional energy.

A variation of this hypothesis, in modern dress, has been restated by Tolman (1932) in the suggestion that men and perhaps some of the lower animals have a need under certain conditions to achieve "mild harmonious fatigues." It is proposed that when the organism is in a "neutral sort of metabolic condition," and other needs or appetites are not strongly engaged, there is a condition of unspent energy. This state is regarded as one of physiological disequilibrium requiring complementary fatigue for neutralization. In defining play, Tinklepaugh (1942) states as one criterion the fact that play is a type of activity which occurs under conditions of surplus time and energy.

Suggestions of this sort have little to recommend them. In the first place they are base upon the most obvious sort of circular reasoning. The catch lies in the definition of the term "surplus." When a cat chases, catches and devours a mouse, a certain amount of energy is expended; but no one suggests that this is extra, or surplus energy. Now, when the same cat chases, catches and chews on a rubber ball, an equal energy loss may occur; but in this case it is said to be surplus energy which has been released. Catching and eating mice is serious business for the cat (or at least the human observer thinks that it *should* be); whereas pursuit of a rubber ball serves no obvious, immediate and practical end (in so far as the observer can tell). Therefore ball chasing must be play, whereas mouse chasing is not play. Refraining for the moment from commenting upon the anthropomorphic reasoning involved, we can see that the decision as to whether or not the expended energy is surplus energy, depends upon the interpretation of the behavior as playful or serious. Therefore to set up as one criterion or explanation of play the condition that it involves the release of surplus energy is to do no more than complete the circle.

As far as mental and emotional energy are concerned, our concepts in this field are so fuzzy and debatable that it is sheer nonsense to predicate explanations of behavior upon the supposed accumulation and discharge of these hypothetical forces. Definition of one unknown in terms of a second unknown is good algebra but poor psychology.

Present-day knowledge of physiology does not support the belief that physical energy is something which can be stored up in the organism like water in a reservoir. There is no known process whereby unexpended energy "backs up" and creates a pressure, demanding release. To be sure certain sources of potential energy, such as liver glycogen, may be accumulated; but this is quite a different matter; and, thus far at least, no one has suggested that play occurs because the liver feels the need of discharging stored glycogen.

Instead of referring to energy, surplus or otherwise, it seems best to conceive of a muscle, nervous unit or organism as being either completely rested and ready to respond maximally to stimulation, or as being partially or almost completely exhausted, in need of rest and repair. Under conditions of partial or total exhaustion the organism may be expected to react weakly, incompletely, or to fail entirely to respond to stimuli from the external environment. Such a concept would lead us to anticipate that play, which, like any other type of behavior, constitutes a response to stimulation, would occur most frequently and readily when the animal is rested and in a state of readiness to react. This is exactly what happens; but be it noted that non-playful activities also occur most frequently under the same conditions. Thus, the tired animal is less apt to play than is his rested fellow; but he is equally less likely to "work."

Several writers, including Mitchell (1912), have objected to the interpretation of playful activities as the mere discharge of a waste product; and have insisted that the energy employed in play is expended upon "the business of youth." C. L. Morgan (1900) also states that "normal" rather than "surplus" energy is involved in the play of animals.

Finally, as Groos (1898) and others have observed, superabundant energy is not always a condition of play. Young animals can often be seen to play to the point of apparent exhaustion, lie panting with fatigue, and suddenly respond to the advent of a play-inducing stimulus with the abrupt resumption of their energy-draining games.

It is generally recognized that young animals are often more active than adult members of their species (Cooper, 1942), and perhaps the observation of this difference has given illusory support to the surplus energy criterion of play .

GENERAL EXUBERANCE, OR JOIE-DE-VIVRE

It is often stated that playful behavior is "enjoyed for purely its own sake" (Tinklepaugh, 1942), "expresses a joy of living" or "manifests a general exuberance" (Pycraft, 1912). Some writers combine this criterion with the surplus energy criterion, and conclude that play grows out of a pleasure in being active (Haigis, 1941). From this point it is but a step to the conclusion that animals play because playing is pleasant.

Before criticizing this theory let us state unequivocally that the comparative psychologist does not look upon all animals other than man as machines which automatically carry out their life functions without intelligence, without conscious purposes and without any emotional involvement. On the contrary, many if not all of the lower mammals, the birds, reptiles, amphibians and fishes manifest varying degrees of intelligence and adaptability. To be sure, their behavior is less variable than that of man, and their ability to profit from experience may be relatively limited; but many observers believe that the differences are more of degree than of kind. There is, furthermore, little reason to deny to animals various kinds and degrees of emotional experience. Accordingly, the most militant and objective "behaviorist" can not seriously object to the statement that the dog which romps through the snow, barking, leaping, dashing wildly hither and yon, or plays at "fetch" with his master, is enjoying the experience.

Having done our feeble best to disarm the critical reader who promptly and scornfully cries, "Mechanist!" at any one daring to speak out against anthropomorphic interpretations of animal behavior, let us proceed to examine the purported explanation of animal play as a form of activity which is engaged in solely for the pleasure it brings the performer.

The first and most obvious objection is that this so-called interpretation does not interpret nor explain. It is directly comparable to the explanations of sixteenth century theologicians who interpreted all natural phenomena as manifestations of divine will, or to the animalistic beliefs of more ancient "explainers." One might with equal accuracy state categorically that a plant grows toward the sun, a cloud moves across the sky or a stick floats on the surface of the stream, because the plant, the cloud and the stick derive pleasure from behaving as they do. Here is no explanation, no advance in the understanding of basic causal relationships responsible for the outward activity.

Explaining a playful response by referring its occurrence to one (assumed) character common to all forms of play is equivalent to explaining that water boils because it is hot. To be sure, boiling water is usually quite hot (although its temperature may vary considerably as any tenderfoot who has tried to cook at high altitudes will ruefully attest); but the explanation for boiling is to be found in the elucidation of the relationship between the atmospheric pressure and the vapor pressure of the liquid.

Another indictment against the *joie-de-vivre* hypothesis as an explanation of animal play is that its uncritical adoption tends to discourage and render apparently unnecessary any further attempt to examine in detail the real nature of the reactions thus "explained."

NON-UTILITARIANISM

In defining play the majority of writers have agreed that one of the criteria for this form of behavior is that it is not directly useful, although the possibility of eventually practical results is not denied. There are several practical and theoretical objections to this criterion.

Very often the conclusion that a particular act performed by an animal has no directly practical value is actually no more than a confession of the observer's ignorance. An example will illustrate this point. Various fishes, including members of the family *Belonidae*, exhibit a curious habit of "leaping" over free-floating objects such as sticks and straws. As described by Breder (1932) for *Tylosurus raphidoma* the reaction of the fish is as follows:

First the fish will swim up slowly to the stick so as to be nearly at right angles to it (in a horizontal plane) and gently protrude the beak through the surface of the water, sliding the tip over the stick. Usually if the stick is too small and gives away too easily, or too large and gives away too little, the fish will withdraw. If it is of the proper buoyancy and sinks ever so little under the weight of the beak, a violent tail action follows and the fish clears the water, but in such a manner that usually part of the body rubs against the stick in passing and the fish falls to the other side, from which it may turn and leap back again.

Many naturalists who have seen this behavior have concluded that it is a playful response lacking in any practical outcome (Gudger, 1944). Other observers have noted that fishes which persistently leap over floating sticks are often heavily infested with ectoparasites that are easily scraped off. It has been suggested that leaping across solid objects may serve to dislodge the parasites, and thus to free the fish of the infestation (Breder, 1932). The validity of this surmise has yet to be established by additional observation or by experimental approach; but the significant point would seem to be that it is susceptible to objective verification or disproof. In contrast, it is a very difficult if not impossible task to establish beyond reasonable doubt the absence of utilitarian function for any type of animal response.

Adoption of the non-utilitarianism criterion in its pure form reflects a certain degree of naiveté. As has been noted, young animals often perform, incompletely, various actions which will be executed in their totality during adult life. In the mature animal the behavior in question can be shown to serve an obvious and biologically useful end, such as mating and reproducing, securing food, self-defense, etc. In the young animal the behavior pattern does not terminate in the same result. Accordingly it is sometimes concluded that the reactions of the youngster are without any immediate result or purpose.

This is obvious sophistry. There is no reason to assume that a given pattern of behavior must serve one and only one end under all conditions and at all stages of development. The flight of a bird may assist it to elude a predacious foe, to secure necessary food, to charm its mate, to transport it to a different environment or to bring about any one of several other equally "practical" results. Furthermore, the scientific study of animal behavior, if it has taught us nothing else, should have impressed upon us the folly of trying to define *a priori* the motives and ends of animal conduct. It is unadulterated nonsense to assume that, in the absence of intensive and prolonged study, the human observer is capable of discerning the presence or absence of a "useful" result consequent to a complex response. (The eating of bones by pregnant female mammals of non-carnivorous species was thought useless until advanced understanding of the physiology of pregnancy revealed the need for extra supplies of calcium.)

The practicality or usefulness of a course of action is a function of a multiplicity of variables. A man transported suddenly into a new and strange cultural setting would be at a loss to recognize the motives for certain response patterns, and might be quite incapable of discriminating between utilitarian and non-utilitarian modes of conduct. The building up of a comfortable financial reserve in anticipation of future emergencies is a practical and utilitarian bit of behavior in our culture. The same behavior would be highly impractical not to say socially dangerous among Mexicans of the Sinaloa region; for in their culture a man is responsible for the support of all relatives whose resources are inferior to his own. Therefore the individual with wealth or a new house is perpetually parasitized by less fortunate relatives who continue with him as long as the money lasts or the house stands. Thus the accumulation of "excess" worldly goods is practical in one social setting and quite the opposite in another.

If, without extensive study, man can not differentiate between "useful" and "useless" behavior in fellow members of his own species, how can he expect to make such a discrimination in connection with the reactions of animals of an entirely different genus, and even class?

Results of Play

Although many writers agree that playful acts must be performed because of the pleasure or satisfaction which they engender, and can not have any immediate, utilitarian outcome, it is nevertheless often stated that certain types of play do possess important, long-term effects.

Youthful practice for adult life. It is common knowledge that immature animals frequently perform incompletely or imperfectly, and without apparent useful outcome, certain patterns of behavior which will be exhibited during adulthood in complete and biologically effective form. This observation has so impressed many writers that they interpret one function of the play of young animals as "an irresponsible apprenticeship to the serious business of life" (Pycraft, 1912; Mitchell, 1912).

Adherents of this view usually make several basic assumptions. (1) The type of play to which this theory pertains is held to be determined largely by heredity, since it is believed to appear without opportunity for learning or imitation, and takes approximately the same form in all members of a given species. (2) Although instinct accounts for its broad outlines, the response is regarded as being imperfectly organized upon a purely genetic basis, so that each individual must perfect the inherited reactions by practice and repetition. (3) An intriguing ramification of the theory is stated in the further postulate that the types of behavior under consideration are all of great biological importance, since each is essential to the life of the individual and thus to the perpetuation of the species. It is pointed out that the play period of infancy permits the practice of these vital responses under conditions where error and incompleteness are not fatal. The extension or modification of inherited tendencies is thus possible before the animal is subjected to the exigencies of an independent existence, wherein the forces of nature selection are constantly operating to weed out inefficiency, and the penalty for error may be sudden death (C. L. Morgan, 1900).

It is not impossible that experience gained during the practice of certain activities during youth increases the efficiency with which the same responses will be performed in maturity. However, the observation that the acts are performed incompletely or inexpertly by the young animal, and appear in more complete and biologically-effective form in the behavior repertoire of the adult, does not justify the conclusion that the perfection of the adult's reaction is a result of the practice during immaturity. If we are to prove, rather than assume, that the kitten's repeated chase and capture of the ball of string is later reflected in improved mousing, it must be shown that kittens which have had no opportunity to play at chasing and catching are poorer mouse catchers in adult life than are other cats which have had normal opportunities for such practice during kittenhood. The same comparison holds true for all other types of play which have been assumed to "polish and perfect imperfect instincts."

Unfortunately, objective proof of this nature is almost completely lacking.[1] Perhaps a puppy which is kept in isolation from all other animals, and thus prevented from indulging in sham fights, will, upon the

[1] As a matter of fact, young kittens which "play" with rats are less likely to become rat killers when they mature than are kittens that fail to exhibit mock chases or capture responses (Kuo, 1930).

attainment of maturity, be equally as ferocious and successful a fighter as other dogs which participated in countless mock battles during puppy-hood. These suggestions run counter to the interpretation of play as a form of essential training and preparation for adult life; but the impor-tant point is that we simply do not know which supposition most closely approximates the facts. Only direct test will settle the question.

In a few instances there is good reason to believe that the "playful" execution of a behavior pattern during immaturity is without effect so far as the performance of the same response in adulthood is concerned. For example, during their wrestling, chasing and mock-fighting immature rats often execute large portions of the adult mating pattern (Small, 1899; Beach, 1942a). If, however, rats are raised in individual cages, so that they have no opportunity for any such practice, they mate during adult life in exactly the same fashion and with the same effectiveness as do their brothers which have been raised with females (Stone, 1922; Beach, 1942b).

This is not to say that the infantile practice of various behavioral reactions is always without effect upon the efficiency with which the responses are executed later in life. The conditions under which a kitten is raised have a powerful effect upon its tendency to kill rats (Rogers, 1932; Kuo, 1938). Some kittens fail to develop rat-killing behavior when raised in isolation but display such reactions after they have observed rat-chasing and killing on the part of another cat (Kuo, 1930).

The play period of some primates is prolonged, and involves the ex-ecution of many activities later indulged in by the adult (Yerkes and Tomlin, 1935). It is known that sexually inexperienced adult male chim-panzees often are incapable of mating effectively with the receptive fe-male. Apparently a great deal of experimentation and practice is neces-sary before this vital part of the animal's behavior repertoire can be carried out efficiently; and Bingham (1928) has found that immature chimpanzees exhibit sex play very frequently during childhood. It is not too much to assume that this practice has it beneficial effects upon adult performance. However, to assume is not to know, and in this case, as in every other, direct test of the hypothesis offers the only means of arriving at a final answer.

A point sometimes overlooked by adherents to the theory that play serves a preparatory function is the occurrence of similar responses in adult animals. Cooper (1942) has described the play of mature African lions as consisting chiefly of hiding behind objects and then creeping forth to stalk and perhaps leap upon another adult. Presumably the grown animal has no need to practice such activities (although it would un-doubtedly be suggested by some authors that this behavior is a means of keeping the responses in good working order!); but of course the fact that such playful reactions occur in adult life does not prevent them from serving a preparatory function in the juvenile animal.

EXPLORATION AND EXPERIMENTATION

Exploratory play is sometimes held to familiarize the animal with the properties and potentialities of the world about it. An eventually practical outcome of such play has been thought to lie in its tendency to promote the development of new modes of conduct and to inhibit biologically dangerous reactions. From the psychiatric point of view, Masserman (1944) has suggested that exploratory responses represent one expression of an anticipatory need to determine the relative safety and potentialities of the environment. Although these assumed functions of exploratory play are based upon *a priori* reasoning more than controlled observation, there are some instances in which they can be shown to exist.

Köhler (1931) reports that captive chimpanzees given stout sticks or poles soon devised a crude form of vaulting or jumping, using the stick as a crutch. Originally this response was indulged in apparently as a form of amusement, and was not used as a means of achieving any secondary objective as far as the observer could determine. Although further test and observation would be necessary to establish the point, it seems probable that the pole-vaulting response was a form of play, and the outgrowth of experimentation with the stick. Later, however, when the apes were confronted with the problem of obtaining a banana which was suspended above their reach they quickly put the vaulting technique to good use, employing it as a means of getting the fruit.

SOCIALIZATION

Some kinds of play have been assumed to encourage particular types of inter-individual reactions. It will be recalled that chimpanzees engage in various social activities which involve participation by several individuals. Tinklepaugh (1940) has proposed that such behavior early in life enhances the individual's adaptability and cooperativeness, both of which are essential characteristics of the species.

SELF-EXPRESSION OR DIVERSION

Yerkes (1943) states that play in chimpanzees is one form of self-expression, self-amusement or diversion. He has observed animals draping themselves and wearing strips of cloth or paper, fruit skins, flowering plants or leafy branches. (Whether or not such reactions can be interpreted as self-adornment is a moot point; but the element of diversion is held to be obvious.) Apes often "paint" or smear objects or flat surfaces with feces, and this too is a form of activity which Yerkes regards as self-expressive, and perhaps playful.

Köhler (1931) describes the manner in which chimpanzees moistened white clay with saliva and then proceeded to daub the resulting mixture on their own bodies and upon all sorts of objects in their environment.

The proposed socialization and diversion functions of certain kinds of play appear reasonable and logical, but must be regarded as speculative until further evidence is forthcoming.

Potential Methods of Approach

If it is apparent that current understanding of play in animals is limited, and that presently accepted criteria and explanations are inadequate, it should be equally obvious that there are various steps which could be taken to improve the situation.

CONTROLLED OBSERVATIONS

The most pressing need is for controlled observation of those activities which are customarily regarded as play. To replace the anecdotal, impressionistic or romanticized descriptions of animal behavior there must be provided detailed, objective accounts based upon repeated observation. Information is needed, not only concerning the observable reactions of the animal, but also regarding various aspects of the environmental situation. So far we know practically nothing as to the probable stimulus patterns which elicit playful responses.

A beginning in this direction has been made by a few workers. For example, Cooper (1942) reports that the play of lions occurs most commonly following a major change in the environment, such as release of the animals from an inside cage, the introduction of new individuals into the pride or the sudden appearance of the attendant. It is added that play frequently takes place just before feeding time, is more common on cool days, and is shown by females more than males.

Studies of the ontogenetic development and regression of play in a single species would be valuable, and would supplement the vague generalization that play is essentially an infantile activity.

In so far as possible records gathered under field conditions should be checked in a setting permitting systematic variation of the stimulus situation.

DEFINITIONS AND CRITERIA

In attempting to define or set up criteria for play it should first of all be recognized that no single hypothesis can be formulated to explain all forms of play in every animal species. The types of activity which are commonly termed playful are so variable in form and complexity that a different interpretation is indicated at least for each major category. Secondly, it must be apparent that many playful and non-playful pursuits differ in subtle and elusive fashion. There is no sharp borderline between play and work for animals, any more than for man. The two types of activity are often difficult to distinguish, and some complex responses may be partly play and partly work (Kollarits, 1940).

This means that any serviceable definition of play must be based upon a number of predominating characteristics which combine to set it off from non-playful behavior; and can not be derived from adherence to one or two rigid criteria such as imperfect, juvenile performance or non-utilitarianism. It may eventually prove helpful, if the facts warrant, to state that playful reactions as a class tend to lack the immediate, biologically useful results which normally accompany non-playful responses; but it is definitely inadvisable to set up as an inflexible rule the dictum that no activity is play if it achieves a useful end.

Thirdly, the conclusion is inescapable that play must eventually be defined in objective terms. If no such definition has yet been forthcoming its absence may be traced directly to the lack of essential data. In connection with other, equally complex types of animal behavior, workers are building interpretations founded on recognized, demonstrable physiological and psychological processes and functions. Learning, maternal behavior, courtship and mating, territory defense, social dominance and a host of equally important categories of response have proven susceptible to an objective approach. There is no reason to believe that play is unique in this respect.

EXPERIMENTAL VALIDATION OF THEORIES

We have previously indicated the necessity of subjecting to direct test certain currently accepted interpretations of the functions of play. There is no need to limit ourselves to speculation in this field. If they actually exist, the "preparatory" function, the "experimental" function and the "socialization" function which have been assigned to play can be objectively demonstrated, quantitatively measured and operationally defined. Furthermore, as new evidence justifies their formulation, new theories can and should be exposed to the "test-revise-retest" process of critical analysis.

HUMAN APPLICATIONS

In closing it may be worth while to comment on the fact that play in humans, although it has been studied more extensively than play in animals, is only partially understood (Alverdes, 1932; Blumenfeld, 1941; Britt and Janus, 1941; Curti, 1930; Dever, 1917; Watson, 1919). An evolutionary approach has proven fruitful in advancing our knowledge of many phases of human behavior; and it is not too much to hope that the careful study of animal play will offer potentially significant results in the increased understanding of similar behavior in man.

References

Alverdes, F.
    1932. "The Psychology of Animals." Kegan Paul, Trench, Trubner & Co., London.

Beach, F. A.
    1942a. *Jour. Comp. Psychol.*, 34: 285–292.
    1942b. *Jour. Genet. Psychol.*, 60: 121–136.

Bingham, H. C.
    1928. *Comp. Psychol. Monogr.*, 5: 1–161.

Blumenfeld, W.
    1941. *Phil. and phenomenol. Res.*, 1: 470–478.

Breder, C. M.
    1932. *Papers Tortugas Lab., Carnegie Inst. Wash.*, Publ. no. 435, 28: 8–9.

Britt, S. H. and S. Q. Janus.
    1941. *Jour. Soc. Psychol.*, 13: 351–384.

Cooper, J. B.
    1942. *Comp. Psychol. Monogr.*, 17: 1–48.

Curti, M. W.
    1930. "Child Psychology." Longmans, Green & Co., New York.

Dever, J.
    1917. "Instinct in Man: A Contribution to the Psychology of Education." Cambridge Univ. Press, London.

Groos, K.
    1898. "Play of Animals." Appleton Co., New York.

Gudger, E. W.
    1944. Am. Nat., 78: 451–463.

Haigis, E.
    1941. *Zeit. Psychol.*, 150: 92–167.

Kohler, W.
    1931. "The Mentality of Apes." 2nd ed. Harcourt, Brace, New York.

Kollarits, J.
    1940. *Ach. Psychol. Genève*, 28: 73–79.

Kuo, Z. Y.
  1930. *Jour. Comp. Psychol.*, 11: 1–35.
  1938. *Jour. Comp. Psychol.*, 25: 1–18.
Maier, N. R. F. and T. C. Schneirla
  1935. "Principles of Animal Psychology." McGraw-Hill, New York.
Masserman, J. H.
  1944. "Behavior and Neurosis." Univ. Chicago Press, Chicago.
Mitchell, C. P.
  1912. "The Childhood of Animals." Frederick A. Stokes, New York.
Morgan, C. L.
  1900. "Animal Behavior." Edward Arnold, London.
Morgan, C. T.
  1943. "Physiological Psychology." McGraw-Hill, New York.
Pycraft, W. P.
  1912. "The Infancy of Animals." Hutchinson and Co., London.
Russell, E. S.
  1936. *Quart. Rev. Biol.*, 11: 1–15.
Small, W. S.
  1899. *Am. Jour. Psychol.*, 11: 80–100.
Stone, C. P.
  1922. *Jour. Comp. Psychol.*, 2: 95–153.
Tinklepaugh, O. L.
  1942. "Social Behavior of Animals," Ch. XIII in "Comparative Psychology."
    2nd ed. F. A. Moss, ed. Prentice Hall, New York.
Tolman, E. C.
  1932. "Purposive Behavior in Animals and Men." Century, New York.
Warden, C. J., T. N. Jenkins and L. Warner
  1936. "Comparative Psychology." Ronald Press, New York.
Watson, J. B.
  1919. "Psychology from the Standpoint of a Behaviorist." J. P. Lippincott
    Co., Philadelphia.
Wolfe, J. B.
  1936. *Comp. Psychol. Monogr.*, 12: 1–72.
Yerkes, R. M .
  1943. "Chimpanzees: A Laboratory Colony." Yale Univ. Press, New Haven.
Yerkes, R. M. and A. Petrunkevitch
  1925. *Jour. Comp. Psychol.*, 5: 99–108.
Yerkes, R. M. and M. I. Tomlin
  1935. *Jour. Comp. Psychol.*, 20: 321–358.

13

The Concept of Play

Harold Schlosberg

In a recent paper (1) Dr. Beach published a critical examination of past and present concepts of play. In it he pointed out that "recent American text-books on comparative or physiological psychology" have neglected the topic, and attributed the neglect to "the exclusively observational character of available data and the obvious inadequacy of existing inter-pretations." Beach then presented the better-known theories of play, and urged the necessity of testing these theories by controlled observation.

In the present writer's opinion, Beach does not go far enough in his criticisms. The program Beach suggested could scarcely be carried out, and it would be of little value even if it were practicable. The basic dif-ficulty is found in the definition of the concept 'play.' Beach does not define the term, but states that "Any serviceable definition of play must be based upon a number of predominating characteristics which combine to set it off from non-playful behavior." Nevertheless, he believes that play can eventually be defined in objective terms, as can other complex activities (among others, he mentions maternal behavior, courtship and mating, and social dominance).

Unfortunately, play is a concept of a type different from that of ma-ternal behavior or courting. One can define maternal behavior fairly well in terms of an integrated pattern of stimuli and responses of a particular type. But behavior is generally called playful only if it seems useless in

SOURCE. Republished from the *Psychological Review*, 1947, **54**, 229–231.

the eyes of an observer. Thus, maternal behavior, mating, and social dominance are primary categories that describe fairly specific behavior sequences, while 'play' is simply a descriptive term that may be applied to behavior in any one of the primary categories, as long as the behavior seems incomplete or otherwise useless. It is obvious that behavior may be incomplete or inadequate for a number of reasons. These reasons may be phrased in the conventional terminology of stimulus-response psychology, without any reference to such a vague concept as 'play.'

1. GENERALIZATION

If an organism already responds to one stimulus in a certain fashion, it will respond to similar stimuli in a similar way. The mechanism and limits of generalization have not been worked out in detail, but it seems to be a fairly basic characteristic of our receptor-neuro-muscular system. A puppy chasing a rolling ball is an excellent example of generalized response to small moving objects. It would seem gratuitous to ask whether or not he is practicing skills necessary for future hunting! Of course such activity *may* develop necessary skills, and it may be worth-while to investigate the question, but it would seem likely that we would find more about the activity of chasing a ball by studying the conditions which determine the act itself.

2. THRESHOLDS

The strength of a stimulus necessary to evoke a response varies with the condition of the organism. One factor which influences the threshold is fatigue. This factor would seem to be closely related to the 'excess energy' theory of play. A rested animal will respond to many stimuli which are too weak or unimportant to elicit behavior in a tired animal. A rested condition is neither essential nor peculiar to play, as Beach pointed out, but it is probable that a rested condition makes the animal more responsive to stimuli which are not closely related to a strong drive, or to partial stimuli. To this extent the 'excess energy' theory of play is valid, as long as we do not put the cart before the horse and say that the animal plays to use up excess energy.

Thresholds also vary as a result of external or internal changes of a general sort. For example, the male Siamese Fighting Fish (*Betta splendens*) will desert the bubble nest containing eggs if the temperature drops a few degrees. Or he may carry out other partial activities, such as building the nest but not mating with the female, if the diet has been inadequate. Presumably hormonal and neural factors are of great importance, but they have not been studied adequately in this species. Do we understand these partial patterns better if we say, "The male is only playing at breeding"?

Beach himself has contributed much to our knowledge of the neural and hormonal factors which control sex behavior in the rat. For example, he finds that immature males will show complete mating behavior considerably before the normal age of puberty, if they are treated with testosterone proprionate. In discussing his results he says (2, p. 290):

It appears that the neuromotor mechanisms mediating copulatory behavior are well organized and ready for functioning long before puberty; and they do function at a relatively low level prior to the occurrence of postpubertal testicular activity. That the resultant behavior is incomplete and infrequent may be due to the presence of high thresholds in the circuits in question. The function of androgen is thus interpreted as a lowering of these thresholds. The hormone does not organize the behavior, but does facilitate its appearance by reducing thresholds in the essential neuromotor circuits.

It would seem that this sort of research is more fruitful than wondering why animals exhibit sex play, or play at hunting, or fighting, or what you will.

3. LEARNING

If we forsake our interest in the 'practice for later life' explanation of play, and instead examine specific cases of partial or generalized behavior, we find many interesting problems that are related to learning. For example, extensive generalization is characteristic of the early stages of many conditioned responses. It is only after considerable training, often by the method of differential reinforcement, that conditioned responses become precise and differentiated. It may well be true that early initial generalization is at least a partial explanation of the frequently reported 'playfulness' of young animals. The relative importance of maturation and of practice in cutting down this early generalization is in great need of investigation.

Learning comes into the picture in another way. Often apparently useless activity is reinforced by obscure means, so that it is continued for a long time. For example, a dog may bring a ball to his master, who will throw it, and then pat the dog for retrieving it. Whether the pat on the head acts as reinforcement in its own right, or through functional autonomy, is not the question here; certainly the pat serves as a reward, and reinforces the sequence of behavior that was set off either by the sight of the ball or of the dog's master. Many of our adult forms of play (as bridge) are reinforced by even more obscure methods, but they are undoubtedly reinforced in some fashion if they continue. The current emphasis on children's play as a diagnostic and therapeutic tool shows most clearly that this apparently aimless behavior is often highly motivated. Incidentally, it furnishes an excellent example of the advantages of studying specific behavior in a direct fashion, instead of armchair theorizing. The technique could scarcely have evolved on the basis of general theories of play, or from our knowledge of play in young animals.

One could go on in this fashion for many more pages, showing how the facts subsumed under the term 'play' can be handled more effectively in specific stimulus-response terms. But enough has been said to indicate that the category 'playful activity' is so loose that it is almost useless for modern psychology.

References

1. Beach, F. A. Current concepts of play in animals. *Amer. Nat.*, 1945, **79**, 523–541.
2. —. Sexual behavior of prepuberal male and female rats treated with gonadal hormones. *J. comp. Psychol.*, 1942, **34**, 285–292.

Chapter VI

Cognitive Approaches

In a great deal of current research, and as an important part of the contemporary rehabilitation of play as a serious subject matter, it has been identified with exploratory and competence-motivated behavior. While both of these characteristics of play were taken for granted in earlier biologically based approaches to the study of child behavior and thus were presumed to be grounded in instinctive appetites, there has been little mention of them in the past thirty years. The most nearly "cognitive" emphases were the "attention span" of the 1930s;[1] the view that the young child fails to differentiate between his wishes and reality within Lewinian psychology, and Erikson's statement that the young child's play is the equivalent of the adult's planning activity. Much earlier (in 1895, for example), James Mark Baldwin was saying of child's play:

The child is constantly bringing his thoughts, interpretations inventions, to the social tests represented by the judgments and sentiments which his creations meet with in society about him . . . this testing essential to growth as it is, finds a field for exploitation in games (1895, p. 154).

The child's originalities are in great part the new ways in which he finds his knowledge is falling together in consequence of his attempts to act to advantage on what he already knows (p. 123).

Psychologists are more familiar with the view that children gain understanding through taking roles in play in the relatively more recent works of

[1] We are indebted to Dr. Millie Almy for this point.

George H. Mead (1934) and Norman Cameron (1947), a view reiterated in the introductory article by Gregory Stone above.

In the modern era, Piaget has been the primary exponent of play as a cognitive activity. As Piaget's work with play is more theoretical than empirical, his work on the subject will be presented and discussed in the theoretical chapter.

For Piaget play is a polarity of thought, and thought processes precede and underly language processes. Russian psychologists, however, have typically given the language processes themselves a more fundamental role in development than has Piaget. In a classic study by Luria and Yudovich, for example, the authors demonstrated that a pair of twins, retarded in speech and without the objective necessity for developing language, manifested play behaviors of a most simple kind.

To this primitive speech, interlocked with action, there corresponded a peculiar, insufficiently differentiated structure of consciousness; as has been shown, the twins were unable to detach the word from the action, to master orienting, planning activity, to formulate the aims of activity with the aid of speech and so to subordinate their further activity to this verbal formulation. Therefore, even at the age of five to five and a half years our twins could not master skills nor organize complex play of a kind proper to children of this age, and were unable to engage in productive, meaningful activity. Their intellectual operations thus remained very limited. . . . We therefore, removed the "twin situation" by separating the children and placing them in separate, parallel groups in kindergarten and then observed the changes that took place . . . (1959, p. 121).

Under the pressure of the need to speak to other children, Luria and Yudovich report that the twins quickly developed a normal language system along with the appropriately complex play behaviors.

In the article by D. El'Konin we have again an emphasis upon the formative role of both language and adult example in the development of children's play. A recent and compelling document that appears to provide support for the Russian view is "The Effects of Sociodramatic Play on Disadvantaged Children," by Sara Smilansky (1968). For some time various psychologists working in Head Start programs have been pointing out that such children tend not to play imaginatively. Their play is dominated by sensory-motor and kinetic activity. Smilansky, working in Israel with immigrant groups from Asia and North Africa, now appears to have documented this fact extensively within these groups. Unlike middle-class children, these children do not indulge extensively during preschool years in role playing, dramatic play, or imaginative activity. They proceed from motor play, through circumscribed and realistic imitative play, to rule games without the diverse imaginative activities that have usually been assumed to mediate between these. So not only are competitive games not universal (as Roberts and Sutton-Smith have shown), but also it now appears that imaginative sociodramatic play is not universal either. This is a surprising conclusion, because most psychologists have for years been immured within the assumptions and data provided by middle-class nursery schools. It was assumed that every child played imaginatively, and that play was biologically instigated and hence universal. These assumptions now stand challenged, and it becomes necessary to study both the learning procedures and the differential types of play structure that are present in different groups. Elsewhere, in an article entitled "The Games of Two Cultures" (Sutton-Smith, 1969), the argument has been presented that the type and development of imaginative play that we have regarded as universal is actually a recent emergent on the human scene, and that the type of play described by Smilansky, and also recorded in works of folklore, is the more general form. Smilansky's findings contribute considerably to the view of D. El'Konin, that the members of the adult culture play a determining role in children's play.

Unfortunately, although the above arguments are intriguing and appear to contain some merit, Eifermann, also working in Israel, appears to have established that disadvantaged children over five years, practice *more,* not less, sociodramatic play (See the article in Chapter VII "Social Play in Childhood"), which means either that Smilansky's observations were not valid (perhaps the children were too frightened to play naturally in the unfamiliar nursery situation), or that there is an age difference in the way in which these children, as compared with the control groups, participate in sociodramatic play. In the latter case, the disadvantaged children may have developed their imaginative play at a slower pace. It may not have been very apparent from two to four years of age, but have become more evident thereafter. We have argued elsewhere: "This raises the question whether there may be some critical interdependencies between the time at which imaginative activity is most abundant and its availability for the development of abstract processes. It is possible, for example, that the integration of imagery and action through solitary imaginative play during the preoperational period leads to relatively neutralized capacities for internalization by school age, so that the "as if" attitude, rid in part of its object cathexes, is free for the imaginative enterprises of reading and number. Whereas the same development, occurring later in more peer-oriented times, acquires the object-related vigor of that age period and lends itself more readily to the Lordship of the Flies than to such solitary processes as reading." (Sutton-Smith, 1970, 1970a).

The cognitive focus within psychology has usually followed more directly from the type of interests mentioned in the prior chapter on animal play. The studies have both been more molecular and more experimental in orientation. An example is the paper of Corinne Hutt reproduced here, in which she provides a careful experimental examination of some of the transitions between exploration and play.

Given that with sufficiently molecular behavioral observations, play can be generally discriminated from exploration, then thinking about its functions and structure follows several lines. The article by Sutton-Smith suggests that the play may itself be a source of novel responses and novel concepts, and some evidence from Lieberman is advanced in partial support of that premise. Again, it is suggested that the representational set or "as if" attitude required by play has larger implications for cognitive development. This "symbolic attitude" may be a precursor not only for play but also for logic. Bateson extends this point in the extract from his article "The Message 'This Is Play,' " in which he points to some of the logical involvements required by the discrimination between things that are included in the play and things that are not so included.

We complete this chapter with reference to articles in which the question of exploration and play, sometimes in learning-theory terms and sometimes in competence terms, is being examined with a new and welcome degree of precision (Goldberg, Godfrey and Lewis, 1967; Friedlander, 1966; Pepitone et al., 1967).

14

Symbolics and its Functions in the Play of Children

D. El'Konin

Investigators of play, whatever their psychological orientation (Keira [?], Groos, Klaparede [?], Stern, Buhler [?], Koffka, Levin, Thorndike, Piaget, Rubinshtein, Vygotskii and others) point to the creation of the play situation as one of the characteristic signs of the play of small children. From outward appearances this situation is characterized by the fact that in it the child uses some objects to designate and replace others.

In the words of L. S. Vygotskii, the behaviorist would describe play and its characteristic property as follows: "The child designates ordinary things by unusual names (words), his ordinary actions by unusual designations, in spite of the fact that he knows the real names." The psychological literature of the recent past characterizes the fact as *symbolism;* and the play itself, in which such use of objects and actions occurs, is called symbolical (see Piaget). An original conception of the symbolism of the play of children of this age led Koffka to the theory of "two worlds" (the world of reality and the world of play) and to an interpretation of play as the world of children's freedom, in which the child leaves the world of restraint and reality. It is precisely the symbolism of play that led Piaget to the conception of it as an activity which is dominated by the child's assimilation of the external world into his ego, to the representa-

SOURCE. *Soviet Education.* Vol. 8 (Part 2), No. 7 (May, 1966); 35–41.

tion of symbolic play as the manifestation of egocentric thought in pure form.

We gave these examples in order to show the importance of the investigation of the symbolism in children's play. Such investigation is necessary both from practical and theoretical considerations. By revealing the actual nature and function of play symbolics, it is possible to penetrate more deeply into the life and development of preschool children and to outline ways of guiding play.

In some investigations (Getzer [?], Kotetishchvili [?], Piaget) the question of symbolization is considered only in relation to the substitution of one object for another. Such a method of examining this form of symbolization is permissible in experimental investigations, but it cannot disclose the general functions of symbolism in play. In extensive symbolic play, at least two forms of symbolization occur: first, the assumption by the child of the *role* itself (the child identifies himself with another person) and the fulfillment of play *activities* which substitute for and, consequently, symbolize real activities; second, the substitution, or symbolization, of one *object* for another.

Thus, the substitution of one object for another is included in the structure of symbolization of another person by children, and in the system of play activities which designate his real activities. We believe that the examination of each of these elements in the overall structure and in their interconnections can reveal the functions of symbolization and their development.

*   *   *

The origin of the role in play, i.e., the child's likening of himself to another person, has not been studied adequately. Even in Piaget's fundamental research, which was especially devoted to the emergence and development of the symbol in the child, this question was not singled out or analyzed.[1] Moreover, Piaget believes that from the moment when the identification of the child with the other person and the reproduction of the activities are very clearly revealed, there begins a regress of symbolics, of the symbolical assimilation. (Analysis of these views of Piaget's is given later.)

In explaining the genesis of the role and its development in the play of preschool children, we shall rely on the research of F. I. Fradkina[2] and on some of her experimental work. Preconditions for the origin of the role are formed in the process of development of object activities in early

[1] J. Piaget, *La Formation du symbole chez l'enfant*, 1945.

[2] F. I. Fradkina, *Psikhologiia igry v rannem detsve (geneticheskie korni doshkol'noi igry)*, Dissertation, Moscow, 1946.

childhood, mainly in the second and third years of life. These activities, i.e., the socially developed methods of using definite objects, cannot be acquired by the child by means of a simple transfer to new objects of the sensorimotor schemes which were formed in the first year. They are formed only in the joint activity of the child with adults. At first these activities are closely connected with those objects upon which they were formed. This refers not only to everyday objects, whose use is taught to the child by adults, but also to playthings. For the child the plaything is still not separate from other objects.

Fradkina makes special note of the following: "As many times as I observed Tanya (1 year, 20 days) at play, she always lulls to sleep, feeds only the animals, i.e., only those playthings with which these activities were shown to her. She still does not transfer them to other objects." Generalizing the materials obtained from her systematic observations, Fradkina writes: "For the child there is as yet no significance in the presence or absence of a resemblance of the plaything with the object of which it is a model or copy; for her it is immaterial whether the toy cup resembles the cup from which the child herself drinks, in order for her to give her doll a drink from it. It is important only that it was *the cup itself* or the *same kind* of a cup from which adults gave a drink to the doll. We observed how children gave a drink to a doll or animals from casks, pots, wine glasses, cups, pitchers, tureens, etc., because these play- things were used by adults in their joint games with the children."

Ia. Z. Neverovich[3] suggested to young children that they transfer a learned object activity to other objects and under other conditions (to carry it out without an object or with an imagined object; with the help of a stick, i.e., with an object which does not have a strictly fixed method of operation; with the help of another object which has a strictly defined method of operation). Young children (from one to two years) were not able to carry out the activity without an object or with another object. To these children the activity was not yet separate from the object with which it was assimilated.

At the beginning stages of its formation, the activity is connected with a definite object and is not independently transferred by the child to another object. This constitutes its principal difference from senso- motor manipulative schemes, in which assimilation of the object by motions clearly appears (it is a well-known fact that in the first year of life children make one and the same movements with the most diverse playthings). Somewhat later, children begin to reproduce actions shown

[3] Ia. Z. Neverovich, "Ovladenie predmetnymi dvizheniiami v preddoshkol'nom i doshkol'nom vozraste," *Izvestiia APN RSFSR*, No. 14, 1948.

to them with different playthings. They "feed" not only those animals which they fed together with adults, but also others. Later, the limits of such transfer expand. Games appear that represent not the reproduction of actions shown to the child earlier with definite playthings but that reflect individual moments of the child's life. This becomes possible when mere observation of the activities of adults is sufficient for learning an activity.

Gradually, the range of object activities and the extent of transfer possible for the child widen. However, there is still not any symbolization of one object by another. If the child carries out identical actions with a cup, a cask, a wine glass, an egg shell, an orange rind, and other objects which have a depression and thereby permit performing the activity of "feeding," it still does not follow from this that the cask or wine glass is a *substitute* for the cup. Here they are only objects with which it is possible to carry out the very same action. This is especially obvious when the child carries out identical actions with diverse subject [*siuzhetnye*] playthings: he gives a drink, feeds or puts to sleep the doll, horse, rubber dog, plastic fish, etc. Not one of these objects substitutes for or symbolizes another. In such cases the child reproduces not a separate action, but the entire situation of feeding, putting to sleep, taking for a walk, etc.

Such a transfer of activity from one object to another during reproduction of the entire situation is of interest because it involves a disintegration of the close connection of the activity with one definite object. This is the first stage toward the *generalization* of the activity. Such generalization occurs because, remaining the same in terms of meaning, the activity is constantly changing in terms of the composition of the specific operations, in terms of its operational-technical embodiment. The next stage in the separation of the activity from the object ensues during a reproduction of the situation in which all the objects necessary for this are absent. This includes, for example, the feeding of imaginary food, the bathing of dolls in imaginary water, feeding without plates and dishes, etc.

Simultaneously with this, as Fradkina notes, some objects begin to be used as substitutes for others. Playing with subject playthings or with everyday objects, children also acquire sticks, pebbles, blocks, etc., using them as subsidiaries—as soap during bathing, as a spoon during feeding, as a thermometer during bathing or medical treatment. These objects were always merely subsidiary. The fundamental objects were those from the surrounding environment or playthings similar to these. It is important to point out that these supplementary objects do not have a strict functional significance; they are semifunctional. Using them during the recreation of definite situations, children at the first stages of such substitution did not give these objects play names. For example, Lida (2 years,

23 days) sits on the carpet and holds a caster and a nail in her hands. The teacher gives her a doll and suggests that she feed it. Lida brings the nail to the doll's mouth and feeds it, using the nail as a spoon. On being asked, "What is that?" Lida replies: "A pin" (nail).

Sometimes the impression is created that the child calls such subsidiary objects by play names. But as Fradkina writes concerning this, if you know the "history" of the use of this brick, stick, or pebble in previous play, the illusion of independence disappears. It becomes clear that this is a name acquired from adults and forgotten with time. Observations that follow the play of the child day after day confirm this. A stick which the child calls a thermometer was given to her shortly before by the teacher for a plaything and she called it a thermometer several times. The pebbles were often offered by the teacher at a time of playing at bathing and were then called soap. The imitative character of the play name is clearly displayed when the child, in play that has new content, uses an object given a definite name earlier by the teacher. The child does not substitute it for the object which was substituted with the teacher and, consequently, it is used differently, but he gives it the same name as the teacher did earlier.

It is only at the next stage of development of play that semifunctional subsidiary objects acquire completely independent play names. At this time, in the third year of life, there occurs a widening of the sphere of objects used as substitutes. The demands that the substitutes resemble the substituted objects become minimal. One and the same object may substitute for the most diverse things, and at the same time one and the same thing may be substituted for the most diverse objects. In the course of such constantly expanding transfer, the activity is, as it were, separated from the object upon which it was formed and undergoes essential changes. It becomes more and more generalized and is converted into an original scheme that gives only the general sense of the activity and expresses either its results or the general method of fulfillment. It is namely these, one might say, microscopic changes of the activity, its transformation into an *imitative* activity, in a certain sense into a *symbolizing* activity, that lead to the destruction of the "object fetishism" peculiar to the initial stage of formation of activities, to the original separation of the activity from its object. This constitutes a decisive step toward connecting the activity with the person who produced it, toward seeing behind each activity the *person* to whom it belongs.

In contrast to play of an earlier age, children now do not simply operate with one or another object, do not simply reproduce separate aspects of the life surrounding them, but imitate the activities of specific adults: teachers, nurses, the doctor, plumbers, etc. Any object activity is bipolarly oriented in its internal structure. On the one hand, it is connected with the object and, on the other, it is a human action, connected with the person who carries it out. The destruction of "object fetishism" creates only the preconditions for reorientation of the activity from the object to the person who stands for each action.

However, the child cannot make such a reorientation independently. This is shown especially in the fact that the children, when reproducing the chain of activities which characterize the conduct of a definite adult person, nevertheless do not independently call themselves by the name of this adult, and consequently still do not identify their activities with the activities of the adult. The child may call himself by such a name only after the teacher does so. Fradkina gives many examples of this. Piaget describes similar observations. We shall give one example from Fradkina's work. During play at medical treatment, when Anya (2 years, 3 months, 19 days) treats her doll, the teacher turns to her and says: "You will be Aunt Olya (the physician's name) and the doll is your patient." Anya repeats many times: "Anya is Olya, Anya is Olya," and swabs the heads of dolls and animals with cotton. It is characteristic that such naming is observed not only in play, but also in many other situations of the child's life.

The dual designation of oneself simultaneously with one's own name and with the name of the adult whose activities the child reproduces has great psychological significance. This is an act of identification of his activities with the activities of another person and, thereby, a comparison of them and a reorientation of the activities from the object to the adult. Fradkina called this stage in the development of the play of the young child the "role in action," emphasizing by this the identification by the child of his actions with the actions of an adult.

Thus are created the preconditions for the emergence of role playing proper, the development of which occurs already in the preschool age. The assumption by the child of the role of an adult is an original form of symbolization. The question arises as to what are the conditions under which the child takes upon himself the role of the adult, and how much his actions during this acquire the character of that which is being symbolized. In order to elucidate certain conditions of the assumption by the child of a role, we conducted an experiment which resembled in content the play described by J. Selli [?] of two little sisters in the game "Sisters." The children were asked to play "themselves," "some specific friends," and finally "the teacher." As a rule, playing "themselves" is not undertaken by young and medium-age children. Older children suggest as the content of such play one of their usual occupations. Realizing this content, they construct their relationship with the experimenter not as play but as "serious." It is interesting to note that only the older children justify their refusal to play "themselves." They say: "This is not playing. How can I play Nina when I am Nina?" Thus, only toward the end of preschool age do children begin to recognize play as the portrayal of *another* person.

Playing "a friend," during which the child must perform the role of another of the children, is resisted by the youngest preschool children. Only the older preschoolers assume such roles. During this they articulate either typical actions or pursuits of a given child, or certain characteristic behavioral traits. We may assume that the youngest and medium-age preschool children, not being able to single out characteristic traits of conduct of their friends, are therefore unable to carry out similar roles.

The role of the teacher is willingly assumed both by young and older children. Only among some older boys is the role of teacher resisted, and they suggest other roles instead of it. Boy teachers seem unreal to them. The small children are not confused by this incongruity and portray this role successfully.

Observations of play enable us to explain change in the content of the roles of adults. For the young preschool children, performing the role of the teacher means to feed the children, to put them to sleep, to take them for a walk. The child acts as though the other children are only the background for the performance of his role (the teacher acts—the children obey). However, for medium age and older preschoolers, the role of the teacher is increasingly concentrated around the "teacher-child" relationships themselves. Comments and instructions are given with respect to carrying out one or another action, the logic of their development, the interrelations of the children. "Teacher" not only places the "cup" on the table, pours the "coffee," gives the "rolls," but also *governs* the children.

Materials of these and analogous observations permit the conclusion that the content of play changes as follows: the children pass from play, the basic content of which is reproduction of object activities of adults, to play whose basic content becomes the reproduction of relationships between adults or between adults and children.

Change in the content of play is closely connected with change in the nature of the activities that are carried out by the child. These activities become increasingly more curtailed and generalized, being converted into figurative activities that communicate only the general sense of the original activities. The child shows only that he has carried out some activity demanded in the course of play. The demonstration acquires a symbolic nature—it only resembles the activity carried out by an adult or child in a real situation. It is more an expressive gesture accompanied by speech than an object activity proper.

Before determining the functions of symbolism at various stages of development of play, we must consider the question of the symbolization of objects, which, as we have already pointed out, arises comparatively early, even before the appearance of role playing proper, and is an important precondition of it.

Jean Piaget, in considering questions of the origin of symbolization, completely excludes *speech* from this process. He solves the problem of symbolization only within the relationship of the object and the activity with it. Piaget attempts to understand the development of symbolism as a purely assimilative process, independent of the process of socialization, of the intercourse of the child with the adults who are in his environment and teach him, as a process of spontaneous development that occurs as a result of the direct collision of the child with objective reality. Such an abstraction seems improper to us and is not in conformity with the actual course of development. As a matter of fact, if speech in no way participated in the process of formation of symbolics, then we could assume that the symbolical function will develop in children with speech impediments or in deaf-mute children just as it does in children with normal speech.

However, as investigations show, symbolization is closely connected with the development of speech. Thus, the investigation by A. R. Luriia and F. Ia. Iudovich[4] showed that speech impediments at the level of so-called autonomous speech are accompanied by impediments in the development of symbolism of play, and progress in the development of speech in these children leads to the elimination of impediments in the formation of symbolization. G. L. Vygotskaia's study of deaf-mute children with various degrees of development of phonetic speech showed that children who do not possess speech cannot substitute one object for another in play and that as speech is mastered, the transfer of the meaning of one object to another is greatly facilitated.[5] Moreover, this investigation showed that it is necessary for deaf-mute children to be specifically taught the transfer of the meaning of one object to another. We have already presented facts from Fradkina's investigation which showed that even in the case of the normally developing child it is necessary, if not to teach him directly, then in any case to suggest the possibility of play utilization and the renaming of the object. In the light of these data the idea of the spontaneous development of symbolism in the child seems at least debatable.

The relationships of speech, the object, and the activities have their

[4] A. R. Luriia and F. Ia. Iudovich, *Rech' i razvitie psikhologicheskikh protsessov u rebenka*, RSFSR Academy of Pedagogical Sciences Press, 1956.

[5] G. L. Vygotskaia, *Razvitie siuzhetnorolevykh igr glukhikh detei i rukovodstvo imi v detskom sadu*, author's abstract of dissertation, 1963.

own history. At the beginning stages of development, speech follows the activity with the object. This is shown clearly, for example, in N. Kh. Shvachkin's work.[6] In his investigation, preschool children were offered a set of playthings and they learned their names and purposes by mastering the activities in the process of specially organized play. After the names and methods of operation with the objects were mastered, those same objects, painted another color, were introduced into the play. It was found that the children did not immediately name these new (actually old, but differently painted) playthings, and only after they were included in play and the children performed the same actions with them were the playthings called by their appropriate names.

Later the situation changes essentially. The renaming of objects begins to anticipate the activity with them. This change is connected with the appearance of the role. L. S. Slavina's research is of interest here.[7] In her experiments, young preschool children were given for play some objects that do not have a rigidly fixed method of activity, for example, blocks and small plates. The child began to manipulate these objects as he was prompted to by their physical characteristics: he laid them out according to color and shape, added or took away something from the plate, etc. When asked what they were playing, the children replied: "With blocks," "With pebbles," "It is so simple" [*Tak prosto*]. Not one of the children performed actions that were characteristic of role playing. Then playthings were introduced into the play situation which suggested a definite subject to the children and the possibility of playing a role. The introduction of these new objects immediately changed the character of the play, although the child did not use them directly, but continued to work with the playthings which he had at his disposal earlier. However, the activities with these playthings acquired a different meaning. The immediate relationship of the child to the objects, which had been determined by their physical qualities, was changed into a relationship mediated by the role adopted by the child. The manipulation was changed into "preparation of dinner," the blocks or pebbles—into diverse "food," the frying pans—into a "plate," and the child himself into a "cook" or a "mama." The objects were given new names, and the activities with them were now determined by these new names, and through this by new functions.

Thus, the original relationship *object-action-word* is changed into a fundamentally new relationship: *word-object-action*.

In the development of play we encounter symbolization at least twice,

[6] N. Kh. Shvachkin, "Eksperimental'noe izuchenie rannikh obobshchenii u rebenka," *Izvestiia APN RSFSR*, No. 54, 1954.

[7] L. S. Slavina, "Razvitie motivov igrovoi deiatel'nosti rebenka," *Izvestiia APN RSFSR*, No. 14, 1948.

the first time during the transfer of an activity from one object to another, with the renaming of the object. Here the function of symbolization consists in the destruction of the rigidly fixed nature of the object activity, in the "separation" of it from a definite object. Symbolization functions as a *means of simulating human activities.*

The second time we find symbolization is when the child assumes the role of an adult, with the reproduction of the meaning of human activity by means of generalized and curtailed activities which acquire the nature of an imitative gesture. Symbolization functions as a *means of simulating social relationships* which exist *between adults.* The play itself, due to these functions, emerges as a powerful means of the child's penetration into reality.

But this is only the aspect of the matter which concerns the structure of play activity. In addition, the symbolization that occurs in play is most closely connected with the development of a series of psychic processes. Without stopping to examine this aspect of the question in detail, we shall confine ourselves to citing some of L. S. Vygotskii's considerations on this question (the verbatim report of an unpublished lecture is cited). He said: "I would say that in play the child operates with meaning that is isolated from a thing, but not from a real activity with a real object."

Thus, there arises an extremely interesting contradiction which involves the fact that the child operates with meanings that are divorced from things and their activities, but operates with them in relation to some real activity and some other real thing. This is the transitional nature of play, which makes it an intermediate link between the purely situational relatedness of the young child and thinking that is isolated from a real situation. In play the child operates with things as things having meaning; he operates with the meanings of words which substitute for the thing; therefore, in play there occurs the emancipation of the word from the thing.

Play leads to internal processes at school age—to endophasia, logical memory, abstract thought.

In his notebook, discussing this very question, L. S. Vygotskii movingly wrote: "The path from play to internal processes in school age—endophasia, association [*vrashchivanie*], logical memory, abstract thinking (without things, but in concepts)—is the main path of development; one who understands this connection understands the main element in the transition from preschool to school age."

15

Exploration and Play in Children

Corinne Hutt

Synopsis

Exploration and play are concepts often used synonymously. Exploration itself is seen to be at least two different classes of behavior, viz. specific exploration and diversive exploration. Discrepancies in the literature are shown to be due to a failure to make this distinction. It is suggested that play may be similar to the latter but contrasts with the former. A study of exploratory behaviour in 3–5-year-old nursery school children is reported. The primary aim of the study was the investigation of exploratory activity elicited by a novel object and the habituation of this activity with repeated exposure. The results also threw some light on the determinants and genesis of "play" activities. Auditory feedback was found to be more potent than visual feedback in eliciting and maintaining "play" responses. It was thus possible to distinguish investigative or specific exploration from play on several grounds. By reference to the probable ontogenetic course of these behaviours, an explanation is offered for the traditional view of them as synonymous activities. It is not fruitful to label behaviours as "playful" simply because they are performed by young and immature animals.

Introduction

Exploration and play are often regarded as one class of behaviour. Welker (1956a, b) in describing some determinants of exploration and play in chimpanzees, as well as the variability manifested in these behaviours,

SOURCE. *Symp. zool. Soc. Lond.* (1966) No. 18, 61–81.

treats them as indistinguishable. More recently (1961) he has acknowledged this more explicitly: "the term play is often used in conjunction with, or in place of, the term exploration. In other instances play is used as the generic term, exploration being only one type of play". On the grounds that a distinction between play and exploration is not always ready-made, he justifies a perfunctory attempt to define these behaviours. Hayes (1958) in studying the maintenance of play activities in children, included games with marbles as well as visual exploration of pictures. Thorpe (1963), too, implicitly assumes the equivalence of exploration and play; he states that where appetitive behaviour and consummatory behaviour are not too strictly tied, we may begin to get general exploration of the environment which often takes the form of play, and he sees learning deriving from this process of play or exploration. Berlyne (1960) has discussed the perceptual and intellectual activities which are engaged in for their own sake, and calls them comprehensively "ludic behaviour", defining this category as "any behaviour that does not have a biological function that we can clearly recognize".

At the same time, it is clear that these authors are aware of this conceptual confusion and of the need for clarification and distinction. Thorpe says "there are various possible explanations for behaviour which can be described as play, and it would be a mistake to think that at present they can all be brought together in one category". Berlyne states "ludic behaviour forms such a motley assortment that it is highly unlikely that all of it has just one function . . . so far it is mainly our ignorance that binds them all together". But in general theories of exploration have subsumed play and theories of play have failed to take cognisance of exploratory activities. Since these two classes of behaviour are likely to differ in terms of their determinants, morphology and function, we might consider briefly the empirical data and theoretical arguments concerning them.

Exploration

Most definitions of exploratory behaviour have tended to be over-inclusive: exploratory behaviour is defined as "any behaviour which tends to increase the rate of change in the stimulation falling on the animal's receptors which is not impelled by homeostatic or reproductive need" (Barnett, 1963), or "those responses that alter the stimulus field" (Berlyne, 1960). These are hardly operationally useful definitions, but attempts have been made to classify these behaviours more precisely in terms of the receptors involved, e.g. orienting, locomotor, and investigatory responses (Berlyne, 1960; Hayes, 1960; Welker, 1961). Whatever the measure of behaviour used it is generally accepted that novel situations and objects elicit exploratory behaviour (Berlyne, 1950; Montgomery, 1953; Carr and Brown, 1959a), that this responsiveness shows a decrement with continued exposure (Adlerstein and Fehrer, 1955; Inhelder, 1955; Welker, 1956b; Glanzer, 1961), and a recovery after a period of non-exposure (Montgomery, 1951; Berlyne, 1955). This habituation of exploratory behaviour has been interpreted in terms of Hullian principles of reactive and conditioned inhibition by Berlyne (1950); in terms of the Pavlovian theory of inhibition by Danziger and Mainland (1954); in terms of stimulus satiation by Glanzer (1958); and in terms of the weakening of the exploratory drive elicited by novel stimuli by Montgomery (1953). This type of behaviour directed at particular features of the environment and showing the properties mentioned above, has been termed *specific exploration* by Berlyne (1960).

On the other hand, workers from the Wisconsin Laboratory have shown that visual exploration persists in the monkey over a long period of time (Butler and Harlow, 1954) and shows a non-decremental steady pattern from day to day (Butler and Alexander, 1955). Similar results were reported for manipulatory investigation by Harlow et al. (1956), and Carr and Brown (1959b). At first sight, these two sets of results appear contradictory, and Harlow's (1956) conclusion that "manipulatory behaviour is self sustaining", adds little to the description of the behaviour. If, however, one examines the conditions under which the animal is reported as showing a maintenance or increase in exploratory activity with time, these are in general those we would describe as sensorily depriving or at least unstimulating; typically, small bare cages were used. The animal was therefore deprived of the opportunity of alternative activities other than those directed towards himself or to the predetermined stimulus objects. Under these conditions, the animal strives to vary sensory input: rats press a lever for no other "reward" than microswitch clicks and relay noises (Kish and Antonitis, 1956); monkeys bar press for a change in brightness (Moon and Lodahl, 1956), or show increasing manipulation and chewing of a door which is the only variable object in its restricted environment (Symmes, 1959); children in an empty room engage in bodily manipulations and gestural patterns (Hutt et al., 1965); adults in sensory deprivation experiments talk and whistle to themselves (Bexton et al., 1954). Moreover, since we are usually told *how much* of an activity is performed, and not *in what manner,* the interpretation of the behaviours in restricted environments as specific types of exploration needs to be questioned. For example, in the Butler and Harlow study the monkey was said to be visually exploring when the trap door was held open for relatively long periods of time. Symmes, however, reports that in a similar situation, the monkeys "very commonly sat near the door holding it open with one hand, and moving it against the spring resistance, and only occasionally turning to look through the opening". The animals continued to do this even if there was complete darkness outside the door. Such efforts to vary stimulation are similar in effect to, and differ only in complexity from, human recreational and entertainment activities. It is this behaviour that Berlyne (1960) terms *diversive exploration*, to distinguish it from specific exploration.

Play

The term "play" covers a heterogeneous assortment of activities from the darts and gambols of young birds and mammals to the extremely ritualized games of adult humans. In his review, Beach (1945) lists five characteristics of play, only three of which are relevant to its definition. These are: (1) that it carries an emotional element of pleasure: (2) that it is characteristic of the immature animal rather than the adult: (3) that it differs from non-playful responses in having no relatively immediate biological result.

The first characteristic has clearly impressed many authors: Bally (1945) refers to play as appetitive activity in a "relaxed field" ("im entspannten Feld"), Bertalanffy (1960) as activities which are accompanied by "functional pleasure", Meyer-Holzapfel (1956) as activities which are characterized by the "disinterested" atmosphere concerning the consummatory act, and Lorenz (1956) comments that "the usual opposition between play and being serious has a very real background". Although, as Beach points out, systematic studies of play activities and the environmental factors that elicit them are lacking, theories to explain the occurrence and function of this behaviour in young mammals have always been forthcoming.

Perhaps the earliest of them is that of Spencer in 1855, who regarded play as an outlet for surplus energy. In 1891 Stanley Hall, influenced by evolutionary principles and Haeckel's biogenetic law, stated that the play of children passed through a series of stages comparable to those appearing in the evolution of the social group (see Rogerson, 1939). Hall (1904) stated "I regard play as the motor habits and spirit of the past of the race, persisting in the present, as rudimentary functions sometimes of and always akin to rudimentary organs. The best index and guide to the stated activities of adults in past ages is found in the instinctive, untaught, and non-imitative plays of children . . .". Groos (1898, 1901) regarded play activities as incomplete in themselves, i.e. lacking a consummatory act, but as a rehearsal of patterns which would be of future biological significance. McDougall (1931) questioned Groos's assumption of an instinct to play, and disputed the notion that motor patterns associated with specific instincts were being exercised. He argued that play was non-purposive and involved the expenditure of surplus neural energy. Schlosberg (1947) has argued that play can more parsimoniously be conceptualized in S–R terms, that is as responses initially readily elicited by certain stimulus configurations, but which gradually acquire more specificity by differential reinforcement. Thomae (1956) has formulated the hypothesis that inner, organismally determined behaviour has periodicity or rhythm whereas outer, environmentally determined behaviour is aperiodic and sporadic, an hypothesis that underlies the studies of children's play by Lehr, Erfmann, and Schapitz; from Lehr's work it is concluded that with maturation the focus of young children's play shifts from movement periodicity, through object and location periodicity, to "activity level" periodicity. Brownlee (1954) has reiterated the postulate of a play drive and Haldane (1956) has suggested that games or play may result in the loss of negative entropy.

The category of play commonly includes bodily activities, activities involving inanimate objects (investigation or games), animate objects (social play), and competitive sports. When to this heterogeneous category is added yet another, such as exploration (which in turn includes topographical, object and social exploration), there seems little likelihood of arriving at general principles governing the nature, occurrence and function of these behaviours. It seems essential therefore that we attempt a more precise conceptualization and inquiry of these behaviours.

The study to be described here, although primarily designed to investigate specific exploration in children, does throw some light on those behaviours customarily called play.

Experiment

The main aim of the experiment was the study of curiosity or exploratory behaviour elicited in young children by the presentation of a novel object, and the habituation of this behaviour with time. Since we were concerned with the attraction of novelty to the child, rather than a forced responsiveness, it was decided to allow it alternative choices. These consisted of five familiar toys.

SUBJECTS

The subjects were all nursery school children between the ages of 3 and 5 years. They were seen in a small room in the school which was relatively familiar to them. The furniture was stacked against one wall,

Fig. 1 The novel object: a red metal box on four brass "legs" and a lever ending in a blue wooden ball. The directional manipulations of the lever are registered on four counters which could be left open as here, or covered up.

leaving most of the floor area free for the child to move around in. Altogether thirty nursery school children were studied under the conditions to be described. Five children of friends were also seen in a playroom specially constructed to enable film records to be made (Lee and Hutt, 1964).

APPARATUS

The novel object was designed to allow for the assessment of both novelty and complexity variables, although the latter was not parametrically varied. The object consisted of a red metal rectangular box on four brass legs (Fig. 1). On the top was mounted a level at the end of which was a blue wooden ball. The four directional movements of the lever were registered by four Post Office counters which could be made visible to the child. It was also possible to allow the child differential auditory feedback contingent upon specific manipulatory movements (a bell in one of the horizontal directions and a buzzer in one of the vertical). Four conditions of relatively increasing complexity were thus available:

(i) No sound or vision: the bell and buzzer switched off and the counters covered up.

(ii) Vision only: noises off, but counters visible.

(iii) Sound only: bell and buzzer on, but counters covered.

(iv) Sound and vision: noises on and counters visible.

PROCEDURE

The six experimental sessions were preceded by two pre-exposure sessions which additionally served to familiarize the child with the room and the five toys. These pre-exposure sessions were procedurally identical to the experimental sessions, except for the presence of the novel object. All sessions were of 10 min duration. An experimental design was used that ensured that the week-ends were equally distributed over the experimental sessions under each condition. The experimental sessions were otherwise 48 h apart. In the nursery school observations were entered in check-lists, an entry being made every 10 sec by the observer who sat in a corner of the room. The child was asked if he would like to play for a few minutes while the observer finished off some work. Further details were recorded at the end of each session. The four children seen in the film unit were left to play by themselves, but knew the observer was in the adjoining room. The counters on the object were read at the end of each session.

Results

In general, when the children entered the room they looked at the novel object immediately, or approached it, often asking the observer what it was. They would then examine the object manually or inspect it visually while holding the lever, and finally engage in active manipulation of the lever.

The amounts of time spent exploring the object under conditions (i) and (ii) are shown in Fig. 2. There is a progressive decrement of exploratory activity with repeated exposure. If the counter readings are used as a measure of investigatory manipulation, a similar trend is seen under both these conditions (Fig. 3).

These decay curves, whether of time or manipulatory activity, are exponential functions of time, and if a Naperian logarithm transformation of the number of manipulations is used to plot manipulations against trials, the two lines of best fit are seen to have different slopes (Fig. 4). The regressions of manipulations on trials are significant under both conditions (i) (variance ratio = 11·5, d.f. = 4, $P < 0·05$), and (ii) (variance ratio = 27·56, d.f. = 4, $P < 0·01$). Thus, addition of the visual feedback slightly decreased the rate of habituation to the novel object.

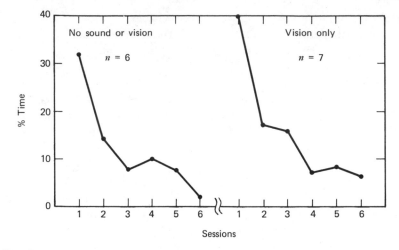

Fig. 2   Proportions of time spent exploring the novel object on successive trials under (i) no sound or vision, and (ii) vision only, conditions (n = number of subjects).

The initial amount of exploration was greater with the visual incentive, than with no such incentive.

Under both conditions (iii) and (iv) the object was increasingly manipulated, and only after the fifth exposure was there a decrease in this responsiveness (Fig. 5). It appeared that simply making noise contingent

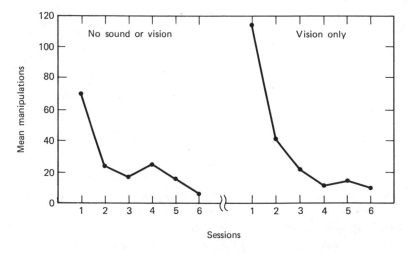

Fig. 3   Mean amounts of manipulatory exploration under (i) no sound or vision, and (ii) vision only, conditions.

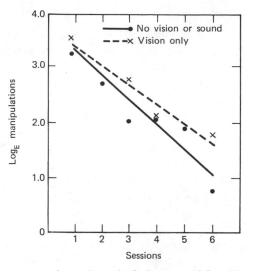

Fig. 4   Linear regressions of manipulations on trials under (i) no sound or vision, and (ii) vision only, conditions, when a Naperian logarithmic transformation of manipulations is used.

upon certain manipulatory responses completely altered the temporal pattern of activity towards the object. Addition of the visual to the auditory feedback only served to enhance this pattern.

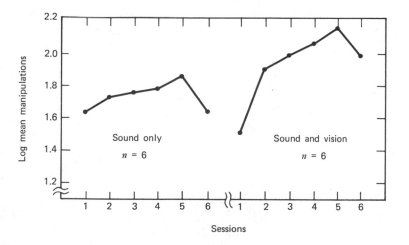

Fig. 5   Manipulatory exploration of the novel object on successive trials under (iii) sound only, and (iv) sound and vision, conditions ($n =$ number of subjects).

ANALYSIS OF ACTIVITIES

It was clear that under conditions (iii) and (iv) the nature of activities engaged in changed markedly over the six sessions. Investigative responses gave way to other behaviours, and it was decided to separate the time spent investigating the object from other activities involving it. Investigative responses were those responses that involved visual inspection, and feeling, touching or other manipulations accompanied by visual inspection. These had in common the characteristic of "learning the properties" of the object. Whereas under the two no-sound conditions nearly all the activity directed towards the object was of this kind, this was not so under the sound conditions. The time spent in investigatory responses decreased progressively from session 1 to 6 under both conditions (iii) and (iv) (Fig. 6); Grant's analysis of variance (1956) involving the use of orthogonal polynomials indicates that the linear components of these trends are significant ($F = 557 \cdot 5/31 \cdot 24$, d.f. = 1 and 30, $P < 0 \cdot 001$; $F = 1457/94 \cdot 5$, d.f. = 1 and 30, $P < 0 \cdot 001$ respectively).

As investigation of the object decreased other activities involving it increased. When analysed these consisted of repetitive motor movements, manipulations of long duration accompanied by visual inspection of other objects, and a sequence of activities incorporating both the novel object and other toys—in other words a "game". Examples of these were respectively: patting the lever repeatedly, leaning on the lever making the bell ring continuously while looking around the room, and running round with the truck ringing the bell each time the object was passed. There is another group of responses which can be termed "transposition-of-function"—those responses which resulted in the object explicitly fulfilling another function, e.g. something to climb, a bridge, or a seat. All these

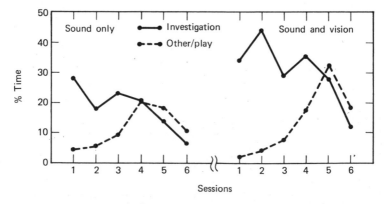

Fig. 6 **Proportions of time spent in (a) investigating and (b) other activities involving the novel object under conditions (iii) and (iv).**

Fig. 7   Characteristic patterns of exploration. Note synchrony of visual and manual receptors, and "intent" facial expressions and postures.

activities (i.e. repetitive movements, "games" and "transposition-of-function" responses) are those which an observer would recognize and label as *play*. They occurred hardly at all under the no-sound conditions, and when they did they were entirely of the "transposition-of-function" kind. By the sixth session, however, even "play activities" directed towards the object decreased and it seems likely that these responses are a quadratic function of time, though more results are required to demonstrate this.

In all children, once active investigation had commenced, it generally proceeded vigorously, all aspects of the object being explored. It was only once the child had apparently learned all there was to know about the object that it was incorporated in play activities, and any further learning was purely incidental. In fact one boy who started a "game" after a relatively brief period of investigation failed to find the buzzer. However, if during play a new property or aspect of the object was chanced upon, a further spell of investigation would follow.

The transition from investigative exploration to playful activities was marked by certain features: during investigation all receptors were oriented towards the object, the general expression being one of "concentration" (see Fig. 7); at a later stage (intermediate between investigation and

Fig. 7 (continued)

play), manipulation might occur with simultaneous visual exploration of other stimuli, and the intent facial expression changed to a more relaxed one. Finally in play for much of the time, the receptors were desynchronized (i.e. vision and manipulation were no longer simultaneously directed towards the object) and the behaviour towards the object might almost be described as "nonchalant" (see Fig. 8).

The relative amounts of time spent on other activities from session to session are shown in Figs. 9 and 10. Under the no-sound conditions gestures increased with continued exposure to the same situation; this was probably a reflection of the child's boredom, particularly as yawning and stretching figured prominently in the latter sessions. That the situation had become less attractive under these conditions was indicated by two children who showed some reluctance to being exposed to it for the fifth or sixth time. Under the sound conditions, however, locomotion progressively increased over the sessions; presumably once the children had started moving about as they did when playing a game, they continued to do so, even when they had tired of the object. On the whole, orienting responses towards the adult were most frequent in the first and last experimental sessions, i.e. at the initial presentation of the novel

Fig. 7 (concluded)

object, and when the child had become more or less tired of the situation. In the first case the adult provided assurance, in the second the possibility of further stimulation when other objects had lost their attraction.

PATTERN OF APPROACH

There was a marked difference in the pattern of initial approach towards the object between the nursery school children and the children seen in the film unit. The presence of the adult in the room appeared to make the nursery school children more adventurous and less apprehensive of novelty; they approached and investigated the object readily. The latency of approach for the two groups of children is given below.

School (adult present)	Film unit (no adult)
30·0 sec	108·0 sec

Fig. 8 **The characteristic pattern of play: in this case of the "transposition-of-function" kind. Note desynchrony of different receptors: child looks around the room while sitting on the object, holding the lever, and cuddling another toy.**

The children who were by themselves showed more neophobia and even when they did approach the object their early responses were tentative. All of them also first approached the object with a familiar toy—the boys with the truck and the girls with the panda.

NON-EXPLORERS

The children discussed so far are those who sooner or later engaged in active exploration of the novel object. There was another subgroup of

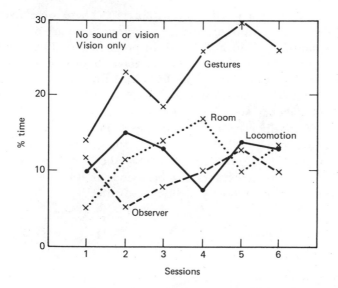

Fig. 9 Proportions of time spent gesturing, exploring the room, looking at the observer, and in locomotion, from session to session under conditions (i) and (ii).

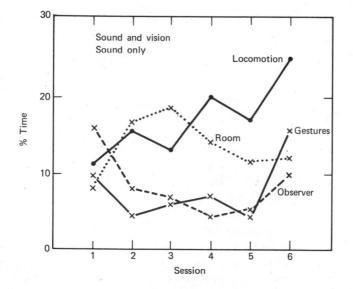

Fig. 10 Proportions of time spent gesturing, exploring the room, looking at the observer, and in locomotion, from session to session under conditions (iii) and (iv).

children who might be termed "non-explorers". There were five such children under these conditions, and three in another part of the study using other conditions (Hutt and Level, in preparation). These children appeared distinctly inhibited: they moved about hardly at all, watched the adult and smiled at her for a good deal of the time, and often engaged in stereotyped activities like twining a piece of string round their fingers. When they did make any approaches to the object, these were of a tentative nature, and hardly ever led to active exploration. In general these children were described by other adults in the school as "good" and "obedient". It would be of interest to know whether these children would be less inhibited in their exploratory behaviour in the absence of the adult, and this question is shortly to be investigated.

Discussion

Consideration has primarily been given to specific exploration of a novel object and its habituation as well as those responses which might be termed play. By restricting myself to those responses directed towards the same stimulus object, I have tried to draw some distinction between exploration and play. These behaviours can be differentiated on a number of grounds. Investigative, inquisitive or specific exploration is directional, i.e. it is elicited by or oriented towards certain environmental changes. Its decay is a monotonic function of time, and any overall response measure would mask this. The goal is "getting to know the properties", and the particular responses of investigation are determined by the nature of the object.

Play, on the other hand, only occurs in a known environment, and when the animal or child feels he knows the properties of the object in that environment; this is apparent in the gradual relaxation of mood, evidenced not only by changes in facial expression, but in a greater diversity and variability of activities. In play the emphasis changes from the question of "what does this *object* do?" to "what can *I* do with this object?". While investigation is stimulus-referent, play is response-referent. In this respect an observation of Mead's (1956) is pertinent: "you will find with children who are spinning a top or bouncing a ball that stopping the action is the deprivation, not taking the ball away". Again, while investigative exploration demonstrably results in the acquisition of information, in play such learning is largely incidental (see also Jackson and Todd, 1946). Haldane's hypothesis quoted earlier thus seems a valid one. Indeed, by being repetitive, play is by definition a highly redundant activity, and can actually prevent learning as was illustrated by one of our subjects. Schiller (1957) too describes how his chimpanzee Don failed to learn to use a stick to solve a problem because he was preoccupied with the play activity of "weaving".

It is of interest then to enquire why play has traditionally been regarded as an exploratory activity. In infancy and early development most of the animal's environment is novel, and it has also an inadequate memory store against which to match new objects; thus, much of its behaviour is likely to be investigatory. Harlow (1953) is less equivocal about this in his observations of a young child: "Perhaps the most striking characteristic of this particular primate has been the power and persistence of her curiosity-investigatory motives". At the same time, many of the young animal's responses are of a repetitive nature—a pattern which commonly characterizes play (see, for example, primary, secondary and tertiary circular reactions described by Piaget, 1953). Thus, in infancy it is perhaps difficult to distinguish between investigatory responses and play responses. During ontogeny, however, these two activities diverge, and become more easily separable, until in the adult there is a sharp distinction between investigatory activities on the one hand, and play activities on the other, which are often of an extremely ritualized kind. There may indeed be many instances where both features of exploration and play are present, but these should not prevent us from attempting to make the distinction. It may be that many of the young animal's responses are investigatory rather than playful. Certainly, so-called play activities in the developing organism may be a preparation for future skills in the sense that any motor activity is, e.g. walking. Lorenz (1956) points out that such activities in any animals cannot be regarded simply as a rehearsal of instinctive or innate behaviour patterns, since "play is most prominent in species which combine a minimum of equipment of instinctive movements with a maximum of exploratory learning". They may also utilize much energy, but to consider this as "surplus" is to regard the organism as a closed system (Bertalanffy, 1960). It does seem, however, that play is relatively low in the motivational hierarchy, i.e. it can be inhibited by fear, hunger, curiosity or almost any other drive. Morris (1956) makes a similar point more neatly: he suggests that in play "the mechanisms of mutual inhibition and sequential ordering", evident in other drive states, are not operational and hence there is less control over the nature and sequence of motor patterns.

In the human species there are many kinds of play that are not engaged in by other mammals. Certain forms of imitative play and dramatic play are associated with a greater degree of conceptual sophistication in the human, and it may be that for a better understanding of these activities, which have their analogies more on the stage than in the cot, we need an analysis of their linguistic content as well. My concern up to the present has been with less symbolic forms of play.

A difference between the determinants of exploration in children and in lower mammals, chiefly rodents, may be noted *en passant*. Rodents will explore a new environment but not a new object in a familiar setting (Chitty and Southern, 1954; Shillito, 1963). Children, on the other hand, will not readily explore a new environment on their own, but will explore a new object if placed in a relatively familiar environment. This difference may represent a shift in biological emphasis from prey to predator.

Conclusions

Studies of exploration have been concerned with *at least* two different kinds of behaviour having somewhat contrary functions. In psychophysiological terms diversive exploration has been seen by Hebb (1955) as an attempt to avoid states of monotony or low arousal; by Fiske and Maddi (1961) as an attempt to vary stimulation in order to sustain a certain level of activation; and by Berlyne (1960) as an effort to increase sensory input so as to avoid a state of boredom or high arousal. Investigative or specific exploration, on the other hand, seeks to reduce uncertainty and hence arousal or activation produced by the novel or complex stimulation. Play in its morphology, determinants and functions often appears to be more similar to diversive exploration than specific exploration. Extending Bertalanffy's (1960) model of the psychophysical organism as an open system tending to a steady state and allowing for "anamorphosis" (i.e. spontaneous transition toward higher order), we might suggest that play represents a steady state, and exploration a process of anamorphosis. At other times, by its repetitive nature and practice effects, play may more parsimoniously be considered conceptually in the category of skills. Until we are able to use a more precise terminology, it may be premature to conclude as Thorpe (1963) does that true play, both in a phylogenetic and an ontogenetic sense, can lead "to the development of exploratory drive". In certain cases the opposite can be true. In the human species a systematic investigation of play is still lacking and a satisfactory understanding of this class of behaviour awaits, as Beach (1945) has pointed out, an analysis of the motor patterns, their situational determinants and ontogenetic development. We must beware too of the danger of circularity in describing an activity as play simply because a young animal performs it.

Acknowledgments

I am indebted to Miss Megan Level for invaluable help at every stage of the study. I acknowledge with thanks the co-operation of the Chief Education Officer, Oxford, and in particular the help and encouragement we have received from Miss Joan Lawrence and her staff at The Slade Nursery School, Oxford. My thanks are also due to S. J. Hutt for valuable criticism and statistical help, and to Dr. C. Ounsted for comments on the manuscript. The work was supported by grants from the Nuffield Foundation, Smith, Kline & French Foundation, and the British Epilepsy Association.

References

Adlerstein, A. and Fehrer, E. (1955). The effect of food deprivation on exploratory behaviour in a complex maze. *J. comp. physiol. Psychol.* **48**, 250–253.

Bally, G. (1945). "Vom Ursprung und den Grenzen der Freiheit". Schwabe, Basel.

Barnett, S. A. (1963). "A Study in Behaviour." Methuen, London.

Beach, F. A. (1945). Current concepts of play in animals. *Am. Nat.* **79**, 523–541.

Berlyne, D. E. (1950). Novelty and curiosity as determiners or exploratory behaviour. *Br. J. med. Psychol.* **41**, 68–80.

Berlyne, D. E. (1955). The arousal and satiation of perceptual curiosity in the rat. *J. comp. physiol. Psychol.* **48**, 238–246.

Berlyne, D. E. (1960). "Conflict, Arousal and Curiosity." McGraw-Hill, New York.

Bertalanffy, L. von. (1960). *In* "Discussions on Child Development" (J. M. Tanner and B. Inhelder, eds.), p. **73**. Tavistock Publications, London.

Bexton, W. A., Heron, W. and Scott, T. H. (1954). Effects of decreased variation in the sensory environment. *Can. J. Psychol.* **8**, 70–76.

Brownlee, A. (1954). Play in domestic cattle in Britain: an analysis of its nature. *Br. vet. J.* **110**, 46–68.

Butler, R. A. and Alexander, H. M. (1955). Daily patterns of visual exploratory behaviour in the monkey. *J. comp. physiol. Psychol.* **48**, 247–249.

Butler, R. A. and Harlow, H. F. (1954). Persistence of visual exploration in monkeys. *J. comp. physiol. Psychol.* **47**, 258–263.

Carr, R. M. and Brown, W. L. (1959a). The effect of the introduction of novel stimuli upon manipulation in rhesus monkeys. *J. genet. Psychol.* **94**, 107–111.

Carr, R. M. and Brown, W. L. (1959b). Manipulation of visually homogeneous stimulus objects. *J. genet. Psychol.* **95**, 245–249.

Chitty, D. and Southern, H. N. (1954). "Control of Rats and Mice," Vols. 1 and 2. Clarendon Press, Oxford.

Danziger, K. and Mainland, M. (1954). The habituation of exploratory behaviour *Aust. J. Psychol.* **6**, 39–51.

Fiske, D. W. and Maddi, S. R. (1961). A conceptual framework. *In* "Functions of Varied Experience" (D. W. Fiske and S. R. Maddi, eds.). Dorsey Press, Homewood, Illinois.

Glanzer, M. (1958). Curiosity, exploratory drive and stimulus satiation. *Psychol. Bull.* **55**, 302–315.

Glanzer, M. (1961). Changes and interrelations in exploratory behaviour. *J. comp. physiol. Psychol.* **54**, 433–438.

Grant, D. A. (1956). Analysis-of-variance tests in the analysis and comparison of curves. *Psychol. Bull.* **53**, 141–154.

Groos, K. (1898). "The Play of Animals" (E. L. Baldwin, trans.). Appleton, New York.

Groos, K. (1901). "The Play of Man" (E. L. Baldwin, trans.). Appleton, New York.

Haldane, J. B. S. (1956). Discussion on plays and vacuum activities. *In* "L'Instinct dans le comportement des animaux et de l'homme". Masson, Paris.

Hall, G. S. (1891). "Pedagogical Seminary." Worcester, Mass.

Hall, G. S. (1904). "Adolescence: Its Psychology and Its Relations to Physiology, Anthropology, Sociology, Sex, Crime, Religion, and Education." Vol. 1, p. 202. Appleton, New York.

Harlow, H. F. (1953). Mice, men, monkeys and motives. *Psych. Rev.* **60**, 23–32.

Harlow, H. F., Blazek, N. C. and McClearn, G. E. (1956). Manipulatory motivation in infant rhesus monkeys. *J. comp. physiol. Psychol.* **49**, 444–448.

Hayes, J. R. (1958). The maintenance of play in young children. *J. comp. physiol. Psychol.* **51**, 788-79.

Hayes, K. J. (1960). Exploration and fear. *Psychol. Rep.* **6**, 91–93.

Hebb, D. O. (1955). Drives and the C.N.S. (conceptual nervous system). *Psychol. Rev.* **62**, 243–254.

Hutt, C., Hutt, S. J. and Ounsted, C. (1965). The behaviour of children with and without upper C.N.S. lesions. *Behaviour* **24**, 246–268.

Inhelder, E. (1955). Zur Psychologie einiger Verhaltensweisen—besonders des Spiels—von Zootieren. *Z. Tierpsychol.* **12**, 88–144.

Jackson, L. and Todd, K. M. (1946). "Child Treatment and the Therapy of Play." Methuen, London.

Kish, G. B. and Antonitis, J. J. (1956). Unconditioned operant behaviour in two homozygous strains of mice. *J. genet. Psychol.* **88**, 121–129.

Lee, D. and Hutt, C. (1964). A play-room designed for filming children: a note. *J. Child Psychol. Psychiat.* **5**, 263–265.

Lorenz, K. (1956). Plays and vacuum activities. *In* "L'Instinct dans le comportement des animaux et de l'homme". Masson, Paris.

McDougall, W. (1931). "Introduction to Social Psychology." Methuen, London.

Mead, M. (1956). *In* "Discussion on Child Development". (J. H. Tanner and B. Inhelder, eds.), p. 139. Tavistock Publications, London.

Meyer-Holzapfel, M. M. (1956). Uber die Berichschaft zu Spiel und Instinkthandlunge. *Z. Tierpsychol.* 13, 442–462.

Montgomery, K. C. (1951). Spontaneous alternation as a function of time between trials and amount of work. *J. exp. Psychol.* 42, 82–93.

Montgomery, K. C. (1953). Exploratory behaviour as a function of "similarity" of stimulus situations. *J. comp. physiol. Psychol.* 46, 129–133.

Moon, L. E. and Lodahl, T. M. (1956). The reinforcing effect of changes in illumination on lever-pressing in the monkey. *Am. J. Psychol.* 64, 288–290.

Morris, D. J. (1956). Discussion on plays and vacuum activities. *In* "L'Instinct dans le comportement des animaux et de l'homme". Masson, Paris.

Piaget, J. (1953). "The Origin of Intelligence in the Child." Routledge and Kegan Paul, London.

Rogerson, C. H. (1939). "Play Therapy in Childhood." Oxford University Press, London.

Schiller, P. H. (1957). Innate motor action as a basis of learning: manipulative patterns in the chimpanzee. *In* "Instinctive Behaviour" (C. H. Schiller, ed.). Methuen, London.

Schlosberg, H. (1947). The concept of play. *Psychol. Rev.* 54, 229–231.

Shillito, E. E. (1963). Exploratory behaviour in the short-tailed vole. *Microtus agrestis. Behaviour* 21, 145–154.

Spencer, H. (1855). "Principles of Psychology." Longmans, Green, London.

Symmes, D. (1959). Anxiety reduction and novelty as goals of visual exploration by monkeys. *J. genet. Psychol.* 94, 181–198.

Thomae, H. (1956). "Die Periodik im kindlichen Verhalten." Verlag für Psychologie Dr. Carl-Jürgen Hogrefe, Göttingen.

Thorpe, W. H. (1963). "Learning and Instinct in Animals." Methuen, London.

Welker, W. I. (1956a). Some determinants of play and exploration in chimpanzees. *J. comp. physiol. Psychol.* 49, 84–89.

Welker, W. I. (1956b). Variability of play and exploratory behaviour in chimpanzees. *J. comp. physiol. Psychol.* 49, 181–185.

Welker, W. I. (1961). An analysis of exploratory and play behaviour in animals. *In* "Functions of Varied Experiences" (D. W. Fiske and S. R. Maddi, eds.). Dorsey Press, Homewood, Illinois.

16

The Role of Play in Cognitive Development

Brian Sutton-Smith

Our interest here is in research investigations of play as form of cognitive variation seeking. A useful lead is provided by the work of Lieberman (1965). She was interested in relations between children's playfulness and their creativity. Her subjects were 93 kindergarten children from middle-class homes attending five kindergarten classes in three New York schools. The children were rated on playfulness scales which included the following characteristics:

1. *How often does the child engage in spontaneous physical movement and activity during play?* This behavior would include skipping, hopping, jumping, and other rhythmic movements of the whole body or parts of the body like arms, legs, or head, which could be judged as a fairly clear indication of exuberance.

2. *How often does the child show joy in or during his play activities?* This may be judged by facial expression such as smiling, by verbal expressions such as saying "I like this" or "This is fun" or by more indirect vocalizing such as singing as an accompaniment of the activity, e.g., "choo, choo, train go along." Other behavioral indicators would be repetition of activity or resumption of activity with clear evidence of enjoyment.

3. *How often does the child show a sense of humor during play?* By

SOURCE. Excerpted from "The Role of Play in Cognitive Development," *Young Children*, 1967, **6**, pp. 364–369.

"sense of humor" is meant rhyming and gentle teasing ("glint-in-the-eye" behavior), as well as an ability to see a situation as funny as it pertains to himself or others.

4. *While playing, how often does the child show flexibility in his inter-action with the surrounding group structure?* This may be judged by the child joining different groups at any one play period and becoming part of them and their play activity, and by being able to move in and out of these groups by his own choice or by suggestion from the group members without aggressive intent on their part.

A factor analysis of the results led Lieberman to conclude that these scales tapped a single factor of playfulness in these children. But the finding to which we wish to call attention in the present case is the significant relation which was found between playfulness and ability on several creative tasks. That is, children who were rated as more playful were also better at such tasks as: a) suggesting novel ideas about how a toy dog and a toy doll could be changed to make them more fun to play with; b) giving novel plot titles for two illustrated stories that were read and shown to the children; and c) giving novel lists of animals, things to eat, and toys. Unfortunately, the problem with Lieberman's work, as well as with much other work involving creativity measures, is that intelligence loads more heavily on the separate variables of playfulness and creativity than these latter variables relate to each other. Consequently, we cannot be sure whether the findings reflect a distinctive relation between playfulness and creativity or whether these variables are two separate manifestations of intelligence as measured by conventional intelligence tests.

And yet it seems to make sense that the variations in response which constitute playful exercise should be similar to the required variations in response on creativity tests. In other words, these two variables appear to be structurally similar. Our confidence that this may indeed be the case is bolstered by some recent work of Wallach & Kogan (1965) who found that if they gave their creativity tests in a situation in which the subjects were free from usual test pressures, they did indeed obtain creativity scores which were in the main statistically distinct from conventional intelligence test scores. Their conditions for producing these results were individual testing, a complete freedom from time pressures, and a *game-like approach* to the task. The experimenters were introduced to the subject as visitors interested in children's games, and for several weeks prior to testing, spent time with the children in an endeavor to heighten this impression. From this work, Wallach & Kogan concluded that creativity is indeed something different from conventional intelligence and that its manifestation is facilitated in a playful atmosphere. In consequence it may be concluded that if playfulness and creativity co-vary as Lieberman discovered, it is not a function of their separate relations to intelligence.

Play and Novel Repertoires

What then is the functional relation between the two? While there are various possibilities, only one will be presented here as the concern is more with research than it is with theory. The viewpoint taken is that when a child plays with particular objects, varying his responses with them playfully, he increases the range of his associations for those particular objects. In addition, he discovers many more uses for those objects than he would otherwise. Some of these usages may be unique to himself and many will be "imaginative," "fantastic," "absurd," and perhaps "serendipitous." Presumably, almost anything in the child's repertoire of responses or cognitions can thus be combined with anything else for a novel result, though we would naturally expect recent and intense experiences to play a salient role. While it is probable that most of this associative and combinatorial activity is of no utility except as a self-expressive, self-rewarding exercise, it is also probable that this activity increases the child's repertoire of responses and cognitions so that if he is asked a "creativity" question involving similar objects and associations, he is more likely to be able to make a unique (that is, creative) response. This is to say that play increases the child's repertoire of responses, an increase which has potential value (though no inevitable utility) for subsequent adaptive responses.

In order to test this relation, the writer hypothesized that children would show a greater repertoire of responses for those toys with which they had played a great deal than for those with which they had played less. More specifically, it was hypothesized that both boys and girls would have a greater repertoire of responses with objects for their own sex than for opposite sex objects. In order to control for differences in familiarity, like and opposite sex toys were chosen that were familiar to all subjects. Four toys were selected that had been favorites during the children's year in kindergarten. The girls' toys were dolls and dishes; the boys' were trucks and blocks. It was expected that as they had all known and seen a great deal of all of these toys throughout the year, they would not differ in their familiarity with the toys, as measured by their descriptions of them, but that they would differ in their response variations with these toys as measured by their accounts of the usages to which the toys could be put. Nine boys and nine girls of kindergarten age were individually interviewed, and the investigator played the "blind" game with them. That is, of each toy, he asked, pretending that he was blind: "What is it like?" (description), and "What can you do with it?" (usage). Each child responded to each toy. The interviews were conducted in a leisurely manner, the longest taking 45 minutes and the most usages given for one object being 72 items. The results were that the sexes did not differ from each other in their descriptions of the four objects. Both sexes did differ, however, in the total number of usages given for each toy and the number of unique usages. Boys were able to give more usages and more unique usages for trucks and blocks than they could give for dolls and dishes, although they had not differed between the two sets in their descriptions. Similarly, the girls displayed a larger repertoire for the objects with which they had most often played, dolls and dishes, than for trucks and blocks which had also been in the kindergarten all year, but with which they had not played extensively (Sutton-Smith, 1967).

As the number of responses was not related to intelligence, and as the children showed equal familiarity with all objects (as judged by their descriptions), it seemed reasonable to interpret their response to this adaptive situation (asking them questions) as an example of the way in which responses developed in play may be put to adaptive use when there is a demand. This principle may apply to games as well as play. While most of the activities that players exercise in games have an expressive value in and for themselves, occasionally such activities turn out to have adaptive value, as when the subject, a healthy sportsman, is required in an emergency to run for help, or when the baseball pitcher is required to throw a stone at an attacking dog, or when the footballer is required to indulge in physical combat in war, or when the poker player is required to consider the possibility that a business opponent is merely bluffing. In these cases, we need not postulate any very direct causal connection between the sphere of play and the sphere of adaptive behavior, only the general evolutionary requirement that organisms or individuals with wider ranges of expressive characteristics, of which play is but one example, are equipped with larger response repertoires for use in times of adaptive requirement or crisis. This appears to be true phylogenetically (Welker, 1961). The finding that the variety of games (Roberts & Sutton-Smith, 1961) and the complexity of art (Barry, 1957) have increased with cultural evolution is consonant with such a point of view on the cultural level.

Play and the Representational Set

But there is perhaps an even more essential way in which play might be related to cognition. Beginning with the representational play of two-year-olds, there develops a deliberate adoption of an "as if" attitude towards play objects and events. The child having such an attitude continues to "conserve" imaginative identities throughout the play in spite of contraindicative stimuli. This cognitive competence is observable both in solitary play, social games, and in the children's appreciation of imaginative stories. Yet it is not until five to seven years of age that children can conserve the class identities of such phenomena as number, quantity, space, and the like, despite contraindicative stimuli. Paradoxically the factor which prevents children from conservation of class identities appears to be the very stimulus bondedness which they are able to ignore in their play. The question can be raised, therefore, as to whether the ability to adopt an "as if" or representational set in play has anything to do with the ability to adopt representative categories on a conceptual level. The only available data are correlational in nature, but again they show a correspondence between the status of the play and the status of the cognition. In Sigel's studies of cognitive activity, lower-class children who exhibited an inability to categorize in representational terms were also impoverished in their play, showing a high frequency of motoric activity, minimal role playing, and block play of low elaboration (Sigel & McBane, 1966). The evidence suggests the possibility that play may not only increase the repertoire of available responses, but that, where encouraged, it may also heighten the ease with which representational sets can be adopted towards diverse materials.

The difficulty with the studies so far cited, however, is that we cannot be sure whether play merely expresses a pre-existing cognitive status of the subjects or whether it contributes actively to the character of that status. That is, is the play constitutive of thought or merely expressive of thought? More simply, does the player learn anything by playing?

Play as Learning

The view that something is learned by play and games has long been a staple assumption in the "play way" theory of education and has been revived amongst modern educators under the rubric of game simulation (Bruner, 1965; Meier & Duke, 1966). Evidence for effects of particular games on particular learnings are few, although where research has been carried out, it seems to be of confirming import. Research with games involving verbal and number cues seems to show that games result in greater improvement than occurs when control groups receive the same training from more orthodox workbook procedures (Humphrey, 1965, 1966). Similarly, research with games requiring the exercise of a variety of self-controls seems to indicate social improvements in the players

(Gump & Sutton-Smith, 1955; Sutton-Smith, 1955; Redl, 1958; Minuchin, Chamberlain, & Graubard, 1966). As an example of this type of field research, the present investigator used a number game to induce number conservation in young children between the ages of 5-0 and 5-7 years. The game known traditionally as "How many eggs in my bush?" is a guessing game in which the players each hide a number of counters within their fist, and the other player must guess the number obscured. If he guesses correctly, the counters are his. The players take turns and the winner is the player who finishes up with all the counters. Each player begins with about 10 counters. Children in the experimental group showed a significant improvement from a pre- to post-test on number conservation as compared with children in the control group. The game apparently forced the players to pay attention to the cues for number identity or they would lose, be cheated against, be laughed at, and would certainly not win (Sutton-Smith, 1967).

Given these demonstrations that learning can result as a consequence of game playing, we are perhaps in a better position to interpret those other studies of games which show that continued involvement in games is correlated with important individual differences in player personality and cognitive style. For example, a series of studies has been carried out with the game of Tick Tack Toe (Sutton-Smith, Roberts, et al., 1967). Tick Tack Toe is the most widespread elementary game of strategy and is a game in which players compete to see who can get three crosses or circles in a row on a grid-shaped diagram. A series of studies with this game has shown that children who are better players are indeed very different from those who are losers. More importantly, distinctions have been established between those who tend to win on this game and those who tend to draw. Although these children do not differ in intelligence, they do differ in a number of other ways. Boys who are winners are also perceived as "strategists" by their peers on a sociometric instrument. They are better at arithmetic; they persevere at intellectual tasks; they are rapid at making decisions. Boys who are drawers, on the other hand, are less independent, more dependent on parents and teachers for approval, and more conventional in their intellectual aspirations. Girls who are winners are aggressive and tomboyish, whereas girls who are drawers are withdrawing and ladylike. These results support the view that there are functional interrelations between the skills learned in games and other aspects of player personality and cognitive style.

Similarly, cross-cultural work with games seems to show that games are tied in a functionally enculturative manner to the cultures of which they are a part. Thus, games of physical skill have been shown to occur in cultures where there is spear-throwing and hunting. The older tribal members introduce and sustain these games which have a clearcut training value.

Games of chance occur in cultures where there is punishment for personal achievement and an emphasis upon reliance on divinatory approaches to decision-making (Roberts & Sutton-Smith, 1966); games of strategy occur in cultures where the emphasis is on obedience and diplomacy as required in class and intergroup relations and warfare (Roberts, Sutton-Smith, & Kendon, 1963).

Still, all this research, though it implies functional relations between games and culture patterns, and between games and cognitive styles is like the pedagogic research mentioned above. The latter clearly demonstrates that one can gain a pedagogic and cognitive advantage by use of games for training purposes, but the research is weak insofar as it does not allow us to draw conclusions concerning the particular facets of the games that have the observed influence. The multi-dimensional character of play and of games makes it difficult to specify the key variables which are effective in bringing about the cognitive changes. We do not know yet what interaction between player desire to win and attention to the correct cues brings about the demonstrated learning. This is a subject for future research.

In conclusion, the intent of the present account has been to indicate that there is evidence to suggest that play, games, and cognitive development are functionally related. But the relation, it has been stressed, is a loose one. Play, like other expressive characteristics (laughter, humor, and art), does not appear to be adaptive in any strictly utilitarian sense. Rather, it seems possible that such expressive phenomena produce a superabundance of cognitions as well as a readiness for the adoption of an "as if" set, both of which are potentially available if called upon for adaptive or creative requirements. Given the meagreness of research in this area, however, it is necessary to stress that these are conclusions of a most tentative nature.

References

Aldrich, N. T. Children's level of curiosity and natural child-rearing attitudes. Paper presented at Midwestern Psychol. Assn., Chicago, May 1965.

Beach, F. A. Concepts of play in animals. *Amer. Natur.*, 1945, **79**, 523–541.

Berlyne, D. C. *Conflict, Arousal and Curiosity.* New York: McGraw-Hill, 1960.

———. Laughter, humor, and play. In G. Lindzey & E. Aronson (Eds.). *Handbook of Social Psychology*, (2nd Ed.), in press.

Bruner, J. S. Man: a course of study. *Educational Services Inc. Quarterly Report,* 1965, **3**, 85–95.

de Grazia, S. *Of Time, Work, and Leisure*. New York: Twentieth Century Fund, 1962.

Erikson, E. H. *Childhood and Society*. New York: Norton, 1963.

Gilmore, J. B. Play: a special behavior. In R. N. Haber (Ed.), *Current Research in Motivation*. New York: Holt, Rinehart & Winston, 1965.

Goffman, I. *Encounters*. Indianapolis: Bobbs-Merrill, 1961.

Gump, P. V. & Sutton-Smith, B. The "it" role in children's games. *The Group*, 1955, **17**, 3–8.

Humphrey, J. H. Comparison of the use of active games and language workbook exercises as learning media in the development of language understandings with third grade children. *Percept. mot. Skills*, 1965, **21**, 23–26.

———. An exploratory study of active games in learning of number concepts by first grade boys and girls. *Percept. mot. Skills*, 1966, **23**, 341–342.

Hurlock, E. B. Experimental investigations of childhood play. *Psychol. Bull.*, 1934, **31**, 47–66.

Levin, H. & Wardwell, Eleanor. The research uses of doll play. *Psychol. Bull.*, 1962, **59**, 27–56.

Lieberman, J. N. Playfulness and divergent thinking: an investigation of their relationship at the kindergarten level. *J. genet. Psychol.*, 1965, **107**, 219–224.

Marshall, H. Children's plays, games, and amusements. In C. Murchison (Ed.), *Handbook of Child Psychology*. Worcester: Clark Univ. Press, 1931, 515–526.

Marshall, Helen R. & Shwu, C. H. Experimental modification of dramatic play. Paper presented at the Amer. Psychol. Assn., New York, Sept. 1966.

Maw, W. H. & Maw, E. W. Personal and social variables differentiating children with high and low curiosity. *Cooperative Research Project* No. 1511, Wilmington: Univ. of Del., 1965, 1–181.

Mead, George H. *Mind, Self, and Society*. Chicago: Univ. of Chicago Press, 1934.

Meier, R. L. & Duke, R. D. Game simulation for urban planning. *J. Amer. Institute of Planners*, 1966, **32**, 3–18.

Minuchin, Patricia, Chamberlain, P., & Graubard, P. A. A project to teach learning skills to disturbed delinquent children. Paper presented at the 43rd Annual Meeting of the Amer. Orthopsych. Assn., San Francisco, April 1966.

Piaget, J. *Play, Dreams, and Imitation in Childhood*. London: Heinmann, 1951.

Redl, F. The impact of game ingredients on children's play behavior. *Fourth Conference on Group Processes*. New York: Josiah Macy, Grant Foundation, 1958, 33–81.

Rheingold, Harriet L. *Maternal Behavior in Mammals*. New York: John Wiley, 1933.

Roberts, J. M. & Sutton-Smith, B. Child training and game involvement. *Ethnology*, 1962, **1**, 166–185.

————. Cross cultural correlates of games of chance. *Behav. Sci. Notes,* 1966, **3**, 131–144.

Roberts, J. M., Sutton-Smith, B., & Kendon, A. Strategy in folk-tales and games. *J. soc. Psychol.,* 1963, **61**, 185–199.

Sigel, I. E. & McBane, B. Cognitive competence and level of symbolization among five year old children. Paper read at Amer. Psychol. Assn., New York, Sept. 1966.

Sutton-Smith, B. A game of number conservation. Unpublished manuscript, Bowling Green State Univ., 1967.

————. *The Games of New Zealand children.* Berkeley: Univ. of Calif. Press, 1959.

————. Novel signifiers in play. *Merrill-Palmer Quarterly,* 1968, **14**, 159–160.

————. The psychology of games. *National Education,* 1955, Pt. 1, 228–229 & Pt. 2, 261–263 (Journal of New Zealand Educational Inst.).

Sutton-Smith, B., Roberts, J. M., *et al.* Studies in an elementary game of strategy. *Genet. psychol. Monogr.,* 1967, **75**, 3–42.

Sutton-Smith, B., Rosenberg, B. G., and Morgan, E. The development of sex differences in play choices during preadolescence. *Child Developm.,* 1963, **34**, 119–126.

Wallach, M. A. & Kogan, N. *Modes of Thinking in Young Children.* New York: Holt, Rinehart & Winston, 1965.

Welker, W. I. An analysis of exploratory and play behavior in animals. In D. W. Fiske & S. R. Maddi (Eds.), *Functions of Varied Experience.* Homewood, Ill.: Dorsey, 1961.

17

The Message "This Is Play"

Gregory Bateson

When people talk about play, they tend to say what it is not—"it is not real" or "it is not serious"—and then the rest of the sentence gets rather vague when the speaker realizes that play is serious.

The word "not" is somehow very important in this, and I want to invite you first of all to consider that word before we get on to the subject of play at all. I am going to approach the matter experimentally. Let me put it to you like this: We live in a universe of namables (Figure 1). Within that universe we make classes. Let me make here the class of chairs. I now want you quickly, without thinking too much about it, to name for me some of the "not chairs." . . .

You have just suggested "tables," "dogs," "people," "autos." Let me suggest one now: "tomorrow." Does it make you a little uncomfortable when I say tomorrow is not a chair?

A Voice: Schizophrenic!

Bateson: Thank you! It would seem that there are two senses in which the word "not" is used. There are these things, which for lack of a better term I will call the proper ground for the class of chairs—the class of chairs being a figure as against that ground—and a second sense, in which the "not" indicates what I will call the improper non-chairs. Among these in the outer zone we have "tomorrow," and—amongst other things

SOURCE. Republished from *Group Processes*, B. Schaffner (Ed.), New York: Josiah Macy Foundation, 1956, pp. 145–151, with permission of the author and the publisher.

—*the class of chairs* which evidently is not a chair. This namable—the class of chairs—demarcated by this inner line, is clearly not here where I have shown it, but out there among the "improper not-chairs."

We also have in the outer zone the class of non-chairs which evidently is one of the "not chairs," and the moment we use the "not" in this improper sense, we are forced thereby into making a class a member of itself. The "class of non-chairs" is now one of its own members.

Fremont-Smith: Making a class a member of itself.

Bateson: The class of non-chairs is not a chair, is it?

Fremont-Smith: That is right.

Bateson: Then, it is one of the things that is certainly outside of this inner group and evidently outside of the proper ground for the inner group.

Fremont-Smith: Therefore, it becomes a chair.

Bateson: No; it becomes an "improper non-chair." The class of improper non-chairs is an improper non-chair. Now, this is a matter which has bothered philosophers since 600 B.C. and which was seriously considered by Whitehead and Russell (1). Russell resolved the matter by saying that whenever we define a class, we must never include in the ground for that class anything of different "logical type" from the members of the class. That was excellent, and is a nice rule for scientific exposition. The definition of a class is a subjective process.

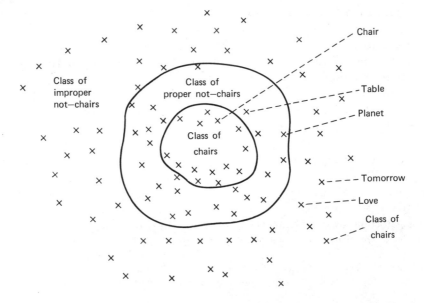

Fig. 1   Diagram for discussion purposes referred to as "onionskin."

Frank: When you define a class of chairs, you are still not prevented from having improper non-chairs, although you have defined the class in terms of its background.

Bateson: That is what Whitehead pointed out, that Russell, in laying down the rule, is in fact drawing a line which will delimit the background by excluding from it the "improper" items. But this sort of line is what Russell forbids by the rule which he himself lays down.

Peck: Where you draw the line depends partly on how you define your classification initially, doesn't it?

Bateson: Yes. I took chairs, which are fairly simple things.

Peck: Yes, but it depends on how you define your class of chairs; that is going to determine where you draw your next line, the "not" chairs.

Bateson: Yes.

Peck: Where you draw the line for the boundary of "not" chairs determines the boundary of the background.

Bateson: Yes. The choice of the class of chairs sets up a logical typing of a certain kind. It determines the typing of the ground and so determines the contents of the outermost area. The last is a very open group. I have deliberately not put a line outside it.

Peck: I mean that the size of the area of the "not" chairs, not the improper non-chairs, is determined by the way you define your class of chairs.

Schaffner: Would the point be that you cannot define anything by saying it isn't this, but you can define something by saying it is this, and then define another class of things by saying it is this, but different from the first class?

Bateson: No. The point I wanted to get across to you is not a point in logic and philosophy, but a point in psychology, a very important one; namely, that we all, in so far as we are not schizophrenic, have a preference for stopping at the boundary of the "proper" non-chairs. That is, when I ask you for a list of the not-chairs, you give me names which can appropriately be included here.

Erikson: Other objects in space.

Bateson: Concrete things in space.

Erikson: Determined in time.

Bateson: I have maltreated your habits of thought by mentioning "tomorrow"—a temporal concept. Suppose I say "love" or any abstract concept, or any relational concept. Suppose I had said the relationship "greater than."

Wheeler: Which is abstract.

Bateson: Suppose I had said "play."

Birdwhistell: Suppose you had said "gas."

Bateson: "Gas" would have been a strange one. If I had mentioned a molecule, you would not have worried too much; but now, suppose I say "congeries of molecules"? Chairs are congeries of molecules.

This discussion of "not chairs" is my way of examining the statement that there is somehow a "not" implicit in the word play, e.g., play is "not" serious. To approach it in another way, there is this peculiarity about play, that with the word "not" also goes the word "really," apparently used with the same sort of ambiguity as the word "not." For example, a child is playing at being an archbishop. There are then two verbal forms which we can use: we may say, "he is not really an archbishop," or we may say, "he is really an archbishop." In psychoanalytic parlance, we say, "he is really a child," or, "he is really an archbishop," or, "he is really being his father," but if there were a real archbishop in the room, we would say, "the child is not an archbishop."

These are the questions which I hope we will dissect in this discussion. I am trying to steer you away from what is ordinarily called interpretation. If we see an Australian tribe ritually eating kangaroos and saying that these kangaroos are ancestors, many analysts of this Australian culture will say that they are not really ancestors; it is really only their fathers that the Australians are eating. But I am proposing that we steer away from asking, "for what do these kangaroos stand?" Rather, let us ask, "what is the relationship between the eating of the kangaroo and that other for which it stands?" And that other may often, as far as we are concerned, be unidentified.

One of the most conspicuous things is that the relationship between symbol and referent tends to be multiple. It is a kangaroo, it is an ancestor, it is papa, it is self, and so on. The moment you encounter these play and ritual phenomena, you encounter multiple coding so that the answer to the question "for what does this activity stand?" tends for very basic reasons, to be a blank. We may offer one interpretation, and the imagination of the playing child may be willing to accept that interpretation, but it would also have been willing to accept a dozen others.

Someone has said that we know that play is important to children because it is in play that they learn role behavior. What I would like to say is that there is an element of truth in that, no doubt, but there seems to be a much more important truth in that it is by play than an individual learns that there are sorts and categories of behavior.

Birdwhistell: It is exploratory.

Bateson: No; that is not what I am trying to say. The child is playing at being an archbishop. I am not interested in the fact that he learns how to be an archbishop from playing the role; but that he learns that there is such a thing as a role. He learns or acquires a new view, partly flexible and partly rigid, which is introduced into life when he realizes that behavior can, in a sense, be set to a logical type or to a style. It is not the learning of the particular style that you are playing at, but the fact of stylistic flexibility and the fact that the choice of style or role is related to the frame and context of behavior. And play itself is a category of behavior, classified by context in some way. First of all, do I make myself clear in a general way to what it is I hope we will talk about?

Frank: Would you elaborate the second point about style being in terms of context? I am not sure about that.

Bateson: Yes. Let me take the case of a schizophrenic patient to whom I shall be referring again during the discussion. This is a man of thirty-five whose utterance, at the time I am speaking of, was virtually unintelligible to the uninstructed ear; it was what is called schizophrenic word salad. He could accept a cigarette; he could refuse a cigarette. He could produce a certain number of usually nonverbalized affirmatives and negatives and certain sorts of actions that indicated what he might want but, at that time, he was not able to make any connected speech of more than two or three words that made any sense at a nonschizophrenic level.

I took him out to the hospital golf course. He was obviously frightened. He wanted me to hit my ball first, which I did. I didn't dare pull my stroke deliberately because I was sure he would be aware if I did, but I was fortunate and only cut a hole in the grass. He then took his shot and drove very nicely to the first hole; he played golf in a perfectly acceptable manner for the first four holes, during which time he said those things which one golfer ordinarily says to another while playing. From a verbal transcript of what took place, you would have concluded, "These are ordinary people, neither of whom is schizophrenic, playing golf."

At the fourth hole, he fluffed a shot and shifted into schizophrenic style again. I am concerned now to illustrate how play sets a frame for behavior. There was a frame set for a certain style of action, and within this frame he could function. But when the frame was modified by competition and when he started to fail it became a little harder.

Birdwhistell: In these situations in which you feel that the child is playing in order to learn that there are roles, could we say that the child is learning that this is a way of escaping (or living beyond) the immediately sensible punctiform present? That is, is this one way in which he learns about other space-times and how to relate and to predict in terms of them?

Bateson: I think many people would object to your calling them space-times. But I have deliberately used the vocabulary loosely. I started with the word "role"; I discarded "role," because I was not satisfied with it. I substituted "style." I then substituted the "framing context."

If you wish to call the categories "space-times," I am willing to stretch a point; I want to get across the idea of what I am talking about, that there are frames or categories.

Peck: To return to my earlier question, as it now seems increasingly relevant, what I tried to say before when I was talking about the defining of chairs was, that I could conceive of someone who would start to feel uncomfortable before you mentioned "tomorrow" and also after you left "tables" and started on "dogs." Now when you talk about your schizophrenic patient, the way he conceives of golf, this very much determines where next lines are drawn.

Bateson: That is, if we call the inner area (Figure 20) the class of chairs, you want me to draw around it then a sort of onionskin structure. So that "tables" will be among the immediate not-chairs and "dogs" are going to be located further out and, let us say, planets will be still further from the central area.

Hasler: Are you talking about stratified categories?

Bateson: Yes, something like that. And I will agree that a culture, a shared understanding between people of how they are going to talk or communicate, is a system of stratification of categories like that. Within a culture, we have a consensus about what sort of things are going to be the "not" objects of the subject that we are talking about. But what I have just said about a culture is also true of the frames and contexts within that culture. These too, though in lesser degree, modify the individual's expectations as to what are to be the "not" objects.

I would throw out to you in passing, because I think it is relevant to the question, the idea that play is one of the ways in which we learn what the "not" objects are and what the system of stratification of the "not" object is. That was what I meant when I said we do not learn specific roles when playing at being an archbishop. We learn something about the whole structuring of the frame of "not" objects.

Fremont-Smith: Would you say that the young child, then, cuts across all these lines because he is unaware of any of them? It isn't that he learns each one separately but rather that he learns to discriminate within a mass of objects the non-objects, the non-objects for mother first and then for other people. His discovers within a totality that there are these discriminations rather than learning each one separately. Do I make myself clear?

Bateson: Yes; the child is certainly not learning the things separately. We are not concerned with learning separately. We are concerned, I believe, with the learning of a conceptual structuring of the universe.

Chapter VII

Developmental Approaches

Play is not only a behavioral phenomenon, it is also a developmental one with its own distinctive sequences. Erikson has described these sequences as follows:

The child's play begins with and centers on his own body. This we shall call autocosmic play. It begins before we notice it as play, and consists at first in the exploration by repetition of sensual perceptions, of kinesthetic sensations, of vocalizations, etc. [Next he plays with people or things.] The microsphere, i.e., the small world of manageable toys, is a harbour which the child establishes, to return to when he needs to overhaul his ego. But the thing-world has its own laws: it may resist reconstruction, or it may simply break to pieces; it may prove to belong to someone else and be subject to confiscation by superiors. Often the microsphere seduces the child into an unguarded expression of dangerous themes and attitudes which arouse anxiety and lead to sudden play disruption. This is the counterpart in waking life of the anxiety dream. It can keep children from trying to play just as the fear of night terror can keep them from going to sleep. If thus frightened or disappointed in the microsphere, the child may regress into the autosphere, day dreaming, thumb sucking, masturbating. On the other hand if their first use of the thing world is successful and is guided properly, the pleasure of mastering toy things becomes associated with the mastery of the traumata which were projected on them, and with the prestige gained through such mastery (1950, p. 194).

Finally, at nursery school age playfulness reaches into the macrosphere, the world shared with others. First these others are treated as things, are inspected, run into, or forced to "be horsie." Learning is necessary in order to discover what potential play content can be admitted only to fantasy or only to autocosmic play; what content can be successfully represented only in the microcosmic world of toys and things; and what content can be shared with others and forced upon them. . . . As this is learned each sphere is endowed with its own sense of reality and mastery. For quite a while, then, solitary play remains an indispensable harbor for the overhauling of shattered emotions after periods of rough going in the social seas (1950, p. 194).

Erikson's sequence of autocosmic, microcosmic and macrocosmic levels of play has a parallel, though not a counterpart, in Piaget's sequence of sensory-motor play, symbolic play and rule games. Something of the substance of these various sequences is hinted at in earlier articles by Hurlock, Parten, Peller, and Erikson; and their broad lines are once again restated in the introduction to the chapter on animal play. Unfortunately, there is no parallel in recent work to the interest in developmental changes demonstrated by the normative studies of the 1920s.

The chapter includes a preliminary indication of what a modern structural approach to play might look like and indicates one of the directions that might be taken by future descriptive approaches to developments in play ("A Syntax for Play and Games"). In addition there is an article by Rivka Eifermann reporting on her extensive investigations in Israel and her tests of various aspects of the play-and-game theories of Piaget, Roberts and Sutton-Smith, and Smilansky. Eifermann's data is sufficiently important that a few comments are in order.

First, Eifermann's data confirms the critique of Piaget in the following chapter, namely, that his developmental description of games beyond the age of five years is incorrect, or at least, it is incorrect for Israel and New Zealand, though it might possibly have been correct for Geneva.

Second, Eifermann's explanatory notion of "challenge" as a key in games is consistent with our emphasis later in this chapter on the production of disequilibrial outcomes in both play and games. It is also consistent with the earlier studies of Redl and associates (1959), in which game "challenges" were a key concept.

Third, Eifermann's test of the Roberts and Sutton-Smith conflict-enculturation hypothesis, while interesting, lacks the ethnographic materials that would be necessary for an adequate test. They would claim that the games would exist where there was conflict about the functions modeled by the games. Whether or not rural children are less interested in competitive games depends, according to their thesis, on whether these children are more conflicted about competition in physical or intellectual terms. They might be expected to be more in conflict about physical competition than urban children and, therefore, play more games of physical skill but Eifermann's presentation unfortunately combines all types of competition into the one category.

Still, the general effect of Eifermann's work is to move the developmental study of games to an entirely new empirical level. The field has been practically at a standstill since the work of Lehmann and Witty in 1927.

18

Social Play in Childhood*

Rivka R. Eifermann

Introduction

In my contribution to this volume, I intend to discuss certain developmental and sociocultural trends in the play activities of children, mainly of the ages between six to fourteen. Some of these trends are of a general, perhaps even universal nature; others are culture-dependent. I shall present a few of our research findings (Eifermann, 1970a, 1970b, 1971) on freely formed play groups engaged in unstructured informal play as well as in structured rule-governed games. In the light of these findings, I shall criticize certain claims made by various authors, often without any serious observational basis, and attempt to offer interpretations that will refine some of these claims, and serve as alternative or complementary conceptions to others occurring in the literature.

Before embarking on this task, however, I shall briefly describe the methods by which our data was obtained.[1] It seems to me that while theories of play have been available in abundance, and will doubtless be

* A large portion of the author's research described in this chapter was supported by the PL 480 Education Research Program, U.S. Department of Health, Education and Welfare, Office of Education, Bureau of Research, under Contract No. OE-6-21-010. This chapter will also appear in a forthcoming book of readings on games by Eli M. Bower and Loyda M. Shens.

[1] A more detailed description appears in Rivka R. Eifermann, *School Children's Games*, U.S. Office of Education, Bureau of Research. June, 1968. (Mimeographed report)

discussed in other chapters of this volume, systematic large-scale observations necessary for testing many of the hypotheses offered have been remarkably scarce. Observations, to the degree that they were conducted at all, were either made on a small selected, unrepresentative population, mainly in therapeutic sessions (e.g., Erikson, 1963 and Peller, 1954) or on very limited samples of children, mainly of preschool age (e.g., Parten, 1943 and Piaget, 1951). The other rather widely used method of play inventories (e.g., Lehman and Witty, 1927, Boyton and Wang, 1944, and Rosenberg and Sutton-Smith, 1960), has reliability problems (Sutton-Smith, 1965) and lacks quantified information in depth, while analysis of available ethnographic records (e.g., Roberts and Sutton-Smith, 1962) suffers from obvious sampling biases, from mostly sketchy and incomplete descriptions of the games played, and from insufficient information on their relative prevalence in the culture.

Methods of Observation

During the years from 1964 to 1966, we, a group of some 150 observers, conducted observations on play activities of close to fourteen thousand children in Israel. Our observations were conducted in two stages, a preparatory one lasting some six weeks (three times per week) in 1964, and the main one lasting between fourteen and eighteen months (once per week) in 1965-66. The interval between the two stages was used to select our main stage sample of schools, to plan the observations in detail, and to design a record sheet which, in the light of preliminary findings, would be convenient to use, would allow a reliable recording to be made of the observations, would be as detailed as is compatible with the time at the disposal of the observers, and would be economical for further processing by computer.

THE CHILDREN OBSERVED

The two stages of the observations were each conducted in fourteen schools, with one school overlapping during both stages. There were also additional observations in the neighborhood of two of the schools.

All of the schools selected for the main stage were coeducational state schools and included the standard eight grades of primary school (ages 6 to 14), with 200 to almost 800 pupils in attendance. Since the observations took place during the ten-minute main recess period, only such schools were selected in which this period occurred at the same time for all grades and in which the school playground was then open to all children. Moreover, schools in which certain play activities were prohibited during recess (e.g., soccer or other ball games, or free wrestling), were excluded from our sample. In addition to these precautions, particular care was taken to avoid, as far as possible, systematic differences in the size of different parts of our subsamples of schools, as well as in the general facilities available in the school grounds and buildings.

Seven of the schools were of an upper-middle ("high") and seven of a low ("low") socioeconomic level. The mean socioeconomic level of each school was calculated on the basis of a random sample of pupils from each grade in every school, totaling 200 children in every case. The five variables included in the rating were father's occupation, parents' educational level and, where relevant, size of the family and number of rooms occupied by it, and parents' country of origin and their year of immigration. The socioeconomic level for the "high" schools ranged, on a 0 to 8 point scale, from 6.11 to 4.53 points and for the "low" schools from 2.83 to 0.47 points. In addition, the level of school achievement for each school was computed on the basis of the mean scores of all eighth-grade pupils, obtained on a state school examination during the two years of our investigation. This level, on a 40 to 100 point scale, ranged from 83.0 to 73.5 for the "high" schools and from 66.0 to 61.0 for the "low" schools.

The sample of schools was selected so as to constitute, as far as possible, a balanced design of the following variables in addition to the two already mentioned: Community structure (town, new immigrant small-town, village, and kibbutz), geographic location (North, Center, and South) and culture (Jewish and Arab). The five "low" Jewish schools are officially recognized as culturally deprived and are included in the Israeli version of the Head-Start Program. The distribution of the schools is presented in Diagram 1.

OBSERVERS, COORDINATOR AND CONTACT

The team of observers consisted of an average of nine observers per school—the exact number for each school was determined on the basis of its size and layout. The same team of psychology students served as observers in one "high" and one "low" town school, while in all other schools the observers were local teachers, all selected and trained for their research task. On the basis of our experience in the first stage, we selected from the team of each school a suitable coordinator and, finally, assigned to every school a contact man from our Center in Jerusalem, who attended every one of the observations, thereby strengthening the direct contact between the Center and the school.

SOME DETAILS

The method of observation stipulated that the area be subdivided so that each observer covered, on the average, five play groups. The observers

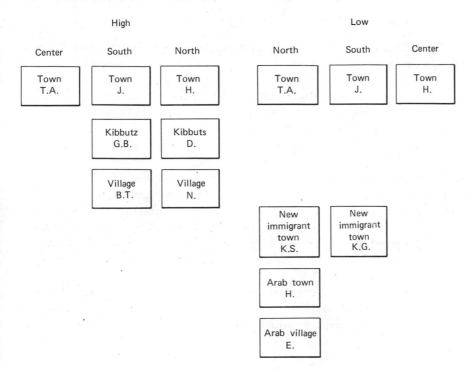

Diagram 1 Distribution of main stage sample by socioeconomic level, geographic location, community structure, and culture.

positioned themselves at the beginning of each observation period in the assigned sections (in playgrounds and school buildings) and recorded, on the record sheets specially designed for this purpose, the relevant items of information about each play group in their section. The coordinators and contact men were engaged in preventing multiple recording of groups moving, during their play, from section to section and in dealing with other emergencies such as the unusual crowding of a particular section.

During the first observations, the presence of the observers caused considerable disturbance to the normal activity in the playfield. Children asked questions, became secretive, and even began performing for our benefit. They were freely shown the record sheet and told that "we want to write a book about all your games." Surprisingly quickly, they then returned to their normal activities, paying no particular attention to the observers on the play scene. The children readily answered our questions (concerning their grade and the game they were up to), often before we finished asking them, "so as not to be disturbed."

Methods of Recording

The record sheet (Diagram 2) contained items of information (upper frame) as well as specific information about each play group (lower frame). As can be seen, most items were presented in multiple-choice form.

Interobserver reliability tests between pairs of observers were conducted by placing two observers in a section normally covered by one of them. Both recorded independently all groups they observed in the complete section. There were four such test observations altogether, so that each of a pair of observers conducted two observations in their own section and two in an unfamiliar section (which probably reduced reliability to some extent). In addition, during these test observations, the coordinator and the contact man were ordered to supervise them and were freed from their normal duties, whose aim was, among others, to increase reliability. The mean percentage agreement on all items of observation thus obtained ranged, in the different schools, from 82.5 to 92.2.

A central item in the record sheet was the *name of the game*. The information recorded in this item was in itself obviously insufficient for purposes of identification, since some play activities that go by the same name are in fact completely different, while the same such activity will sometimes be called different names in different playgrounds. Play activities that had no accepted names were named by the observers; some of these *unstructured* play activities, were named, for example, "catching bees" (kibbutz), "army training" (village), "Snow White" (town), "Mom, Dad, and Daughter" (immigrant town) and "the pyramids (Arab village). They were briefly described by the observers immediately following the observation. Descriptions of *structured,* rule-governed games were independently obtained in special interviews and demonstrations, conducted by the coordinator and the contact-man. Thus an encyclopedia of over 2000 games was compiled, which includes, in addition to such well-known games as soccer, tag, marbles, hopscotch, chess, and cards—each in a sometimes bewildering number of variants—other much less known and less widespread games, such as guessing and fortune-telling games, again often in a large number of variants. Examples of game descriptions appear in Eifermann, 1971.

Observations of play activities in streets and improvised playgrounds, after school hours, were conducted on similar lines, but there were some differences, the most important of which were the following: The observation time was increased to at least two and up to four hours (with two shifts of observers, when required), allowing for a much more detailed description of the dynamics of the play activities during such a long period; the

Name of observer
Amira Giora

Frame 1

Number of observer	Date			School sign	Grades missing		Wind	Weather		Lack of information	
	Day	Month	Year					Precipitation	Temperature		
1–4	5–6	7–8	9–10	11–15	16–20	24	25	26	27	28	29
						If all X	(1) none	(1) none	(1) cold	1 observer late	
					1 2 3 4 5 6 7 8		2 windy	2 drizzle	2 warm	2 observer missing	X
								3 rain	3 hot	3 other reason	1
								4 snow	4 humid		
0 1 2 4	0 7	1 1	6 5	1 1 2 0 1							

Frame 2

	Group no.	Surface	Ethnic group	Game termination	Length of game	Manner of play	Name of game	Number of participants by grade								
	11–13	16	17	18	19	20	21–25	1	2	3	4	5	6	7	8	
		1 paved	1 oriental	1 ball	1 long	(1) play		32-33	34-35	36-37	38-39	40-41	42-43	44-45	45-46	—
		(2) sand/soil	2 achkenazi	(2) internal quarrel	(2) short	2 quarrel	Hospital tag							6	1	B O Y s
dup 0 0 3		3 indoors	(3) both	3 external quarrel		3 both										80
		4 stony		4 new game				64-65	66-67	68-69	70-71	72-73	74-75	76-77	78-79	—
		5 lawn		5 weather										4		G i r l s
		6 mud		6 teacher												X
		9 other		7 faded												2
				8 out/ended												
				9 other												

Diagram 2 Main stage record sheet (Frame 1: general information; Frame 2: recordings for one play group). Adapted from Rivka R. Eifermann, *Determinants of children's game styles*, 1971, by Permission of the Israel Academy of Sciences and Humanities, Jerusalem.

children at play included also pre- and post-grade-school ages. In order to meet these conditions, the record sheet had to be adapted and, more specifically, expanded.

Critique of Piaget's Conception in the Light of Systematic Observations

We can now turn to the critical discussion of certain claims as to the universality and culture dependency of children's play activities.

INCREASE WITH AGE IN PARTICIPATION IN GAMES WITH RULES

It is probably appropriate to start with the contributions of the grand master, Jean Piaget. On p. 146 of his book, *Play, Dreams and Imitation in Childhood* (1951), Piaget states that, in contradistinction to other forms of play, "games with rules . . . *increase* in number, both *absolutely* and *relatively* [our italics], with age. They are almost the only ones that persist at the adult stage." These claims are definitely disconfirmed by our findings. The analyses conducted thus far, separately on each of eight of our schools (two kibbutz schools, one Jewish and one Arab village school, two Jewish and one Arab town schools, and one new-immigrant town school), quite definitely show that the percentage of play participants in rule-governed games out of all children in each grade declines, without exception, in the upper school grades. This decline is both absolute and relative. It sets in as early as the second grade in some "high" schools and as late as the sixth grade in one "low" school. (The exact relationship between school level and age at which play participation reaches its peak has been discussed elsewhere [see the report mentioned in footnote 1].) Figure 1 presents the percentage of play participants in rule-governed games by grade, out of all children in each grade, in all eight schools taken together. Table 1 presents the corresponding numerical data.

At this point, it is, however, necessary to take a closer look at Piaget's usage of the term "games with rules." Piaget confines his term "games with rules," which does not coincide with our (and we believe, the customary) usage of the term "rule-governed games," to "games with sensory-motor combinations (races, marbles, ball games, etc.) or intellectual combinations (cards, chess, etc.) *in which there is competition between individuals (otherwise rules would be useless)* [our italics]" (*ibid.,* p. 144), implying that rules and competition necessarily go together. But this implication seems to be a rash one. First, in addition to competitive

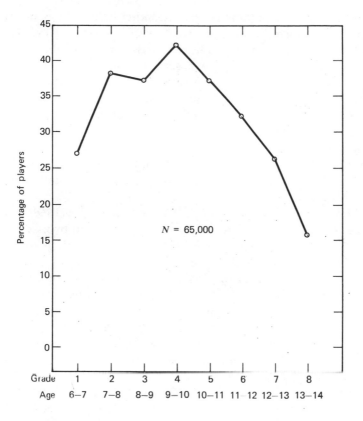

Fig. 1 Percentage of play participants in rule-governed games by grade, out of all children in each grade.

Table 1[a]

Number of Play Participants in Rule-Governed Games by Grade, and Their Percentage Out of All Children in Each Grade

	Grade							
	1	2	3	4	5	6	7	8
N	6498	9615	9669	10646	9480	8208	6842	4042
Percentage	27.1	38.5	37.5	42.3	37.4	32.8	26.6	16.1

[a] Because of the large size of the samples, no statistical tests of significance were deemed necessary.

games, whether the competition is between individuals or between groups, there are also cooperative rule-governed games (such as hand-clapping games, cat's cradle games, and ritualistic games). True enough, in competitive games violations of some of the rules by which they are governed carry sanctions, while this is not the case in cooperative games, nor, as a matter of fact, universally true for all rules even in competitive games. But this only shows that the connection between rules and sanctions is not a necessary one. It is even far from obvious that sanctionless rules should be regarded as in some way derived from sanction-carrying rules, though statements to this effect are often found in the literature and occur also in Piaget's writings. It would, however, carry us too far to go into further details here.

Second, there definitely are also individual games governed by rules, and such rules are by no means "useless." Breaking them by inadvertence may even, on occasion, carry a conventional sanction such as to *have* to start all over again, and children feel this obligation very strongly, even when playing unobserved. Breaking a rule of such a game through cheating will, of course, not be overtly self-punished in this way, but some players will sometimes at least have a bad conscience about it. The facts are that there are just various types of rules; it would therefore be useful to classify rule-governed games according to which and how many of these types are effective in them. Confining our attention to just one such type will only arbitrarily restrict our vision. True enough, as has already been shown elsewhere (see the report mentioned in footnote 1), few school children engage in individual play altogether, and still fewer in playing individual rule-governed games, but the number and variety of such games is by no means negligible and their treatment should certainly not be omitted from an adequate theory of children's play.

However, in order to examine Piaget's claims on his own ground also, we conducted a further analysis of participation in competitive rule-governed games, Piaget's "games with rules." Table 2 and Figure 2

Table 2[a]

Number of Play Participants in Competitive Rule-Governed Games by Grade, and Their Percentage Out of All Children in Each Grade

	Grade							
	1	2	3	4	5	6	7	8
N	5471	8030	8517	9266	8235	7351	6087	3603
Percentage	22.9	32.1	33.0	36.8	32.5	29.4	23.6	14.3

[a] Because of the large size of the samples, no statistical tests of significance were deemed necessary.

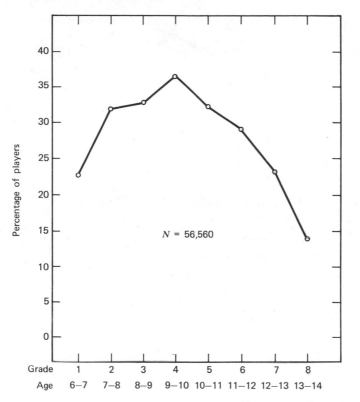

Fig. 2   Percentage of play participants in competitive rule-governed games by grade, out of all children in each grade.

present the data for competitive rule-governed games, corresponding to Table 1 and Figure 1, respectively, for all rule-governed games. The close resemblance between the two figures may explain, in part, how Piaget could have so easily overlooked the existence of noncompetitive rule-governed games and claimed, more or less, that "there just ain't no such animal."

We have seen that, in addition to making the claim about the absolute increase in playing rule-governed games with age, Piaget also makes a corresponding claim for its *relative* increase. Figure 3 and the corresponding Table 3 show the percentage of players in grades 1 to 8 who participated (a) in all rule-governed games and (b) in competitive rule-governed games, out of all players in the eight schools analyzed. It may be seen that, contrary to Piaget's explicit statement quoted above and, indeed, to what is probably a rather general assumption, there is a significant

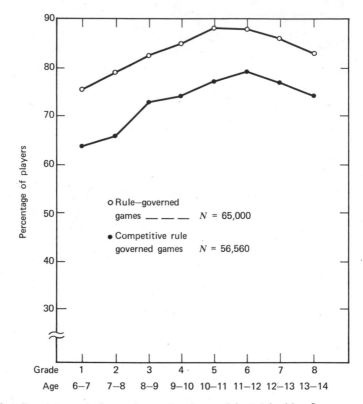

Fig. 3   Percentage of players by grade who participated in (a) rule-governed games and (b) competitive rule-governed games, out of all players in each grade.

relative *decline* in participation in such games in the upper school grades, which sets in as early as in the sixth grade for all structured games, and the seventh grade, for competitive games.

This decline is by no means confined to children playing at school. It holds equally for children observed at play *out of school,* in streets and improvised play fields situated in the neighborhood of one of our "low" schools, as is strikingly exhibited in Table 4 and Figure 4. Moreover, out of school, the decline in participation in rule-governed games and in competitive such games went on *beyond school age.*

"PRACTICE" PLAY AND "SYMBOLIC" PLAY

Piaget's claims about the constant increase in participation in rule-governed games are anchored in theoretical considerations. According to Piaget, "assimilation" is "the principle of all play" (e.g., Piaget, *ibid.,*

Table 3[a, b]

Percentage of Players who Participated in (a) Rule-Governed Games and (b) Competitive Rule-Governed Games, Out of All Players in Each Grade

	Grade							
	1	2	3	4	5	6	7	8
(a) Rule-governed games	75.5	79.1	82.7	85.1	88.7	88.5	86.5	83.1
(b) Competitive rule-governed games	63.6	66.0	72.9	74.1	77.1	79.2	76.9	74.1

[a] Because of the large size of the samples, no statistical tests of significance were deemed necessary.

[b] The numbers of players are those presented in Table 1 for (a), and in Table 2 for (b).

p. 168) and unstructured play is "the primacy of assimilation over accommodation" (e.g., Piaget, *ibid.*, p. 87). To put it briefly, the child only gradually learns to accommodate himself to "reality" and, does so only as a result of the pressure of internal and external forces (both physical and social) and because of a need to expand his acquaintance with the environment. In the young child there is thus, of necessity, a lack of equilibrium between his "egocentric" tendency to mold the environment so as to make it comply with his own needs (and it is this molding process that Piaget calls "assimilation") and his readiness to accommodate himself to the environment ("accommodation").

Play is the expression of this disequilibrium and is, in its pure form, wholly assimilative. Both in the early stage of (motor or mental) "practice" play and in the later stage of "symbolic" play, the child performs with skills he has recently acquired (through accommodation) and re-enacts experiences he has had in his recent past. By playing them out in his own time and place and in his own way, the child assimilates both skills and experiences, in the sense that they are now performed purely "for the pleasure of being the cause" or "for the feeling of mastery" (and thus also, in symbolic play, for liquidation, compensation, or in anticipation of particularly pleasant or unpleasant experiences), without the constraints of constant collision with reality. Thus, in "practice" play the child will, for example, run, jump, throw, and even talk—or combine such activities—for no extrinsic purpose. In "symbolic" play he will,

Table 4[a]

Percentage of Players Who Participated Out of School, in (a) Rule-Governed Games and (b) Competitive Rule-Governed Games, Out of All Players in Each Grade and Age Group

					Grade					
	Pre-school	1	2	3	4	5	6	7	8	Post-school
(a) Rule-governed games										
N	471	294	509	493	463	475	449	272	196	57
Percentage	34.3	50.1	54.3	59.3	59.8	66.4	66.4	66.7	65.8	54.8
(b) Competitive rule-governed games										
N	379	258	442	426	419	435	413	252	175	49
Percentage	27.6	44.0	47.1	51.2	54.1	60.8	61.1	61.8	58.7	47.1

[a] The differences between the following pairs of grades are significant both for rule-governed games (a), and for competitive rule-governed games (b): preschool and grade 1: $p < 0.01$, for both (a) and (b); grades 2 and 3: $p < 0.01$, for (a) and $p < 0.05$ for (b); grades 4 and 5: $p < 0.01$, for both (a) and (b); and grades 8 and post-school: $p < 0.05$, for both (a) and (b).

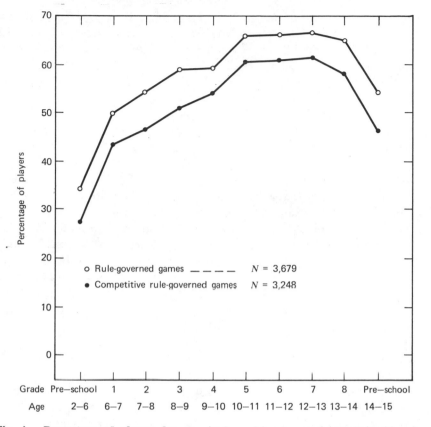

Fig. 4   Percentage of players by age (and grade) who participated in (a) rule-governed games and (b) competitive rule-governed games, out of all players in each age group.

likewise, separately or in combination, substitute real objects with make-believe objects or even sheer declarations, and play roles and perform dramatic scenes alone or with companions, real or imaginary.

"Practice" games, which are the earlier to appear, last "far beyond childhood. This does not mean, of course, that practice games are as numerous, either absolutely or relatively, at all ages. On the contrary, as new acquisitions become fewer and fewer and other types of games appear, with symbols and rules, the frequency of practice games diminishes as time goes on after the appearance of language" (*ibid.,* p. 114). As for symbolic play, it should be noted that Piaget does "not make an essential distinction between individual symbolic games and those involving more than one person" (*ibid.*, p. 112). Nevertheless, "collective symbolism" gradually replaces the earlier "egocentric" symbolism. As with the earlier practice games, so also the decline in collective symbolism comes about because such games evolve into games with rules. Furthermore, both these types of play gradually lose their ludic quality as they become increasingly adaptive or "constructional" in character and thus occupy "a position half-way between play and intelligent work [in the case of 'practice' games], or between play and imitation [in the case of symbolic play]" (*ibid.*, p. 113).

"Only games with rules are not subject to this law of involution" (*ibid.*, p. 146). Yet we have seen, in spite of this and contrary to Piaget's claims, that play participation in such games declines in the upper school grades. Let us now examine some of our data in order to determine how the two types of *unstructured* play, that of "collective symbolic" play and that of "practice" play (which includes such activities as just jumping, or jumping into, out of, from, etc.; just running, throwing or kicking an object at, into, etc.; and walking on, around, while keeping balance, etc.), in fact fare at various age levels. Though this examination is yet incomplete, it may contain some hints as to further work worth doing, both in data gathering and in theorizing.

Table 5 gives the number and relative percentages of play participants in these two unstructured play activities, separately for one "high" and one "low" school. A test of significance of differences between proportions of independent samples was conducted on each of successive pairs of grades, separately for the "high" and the "low" school, and for the two play categories. No significant differences in extent of participation in symbolic play were found between successive pairs of grades within the "high" school, whereas in the "low" school the decline in participation in such play from the first to the second pair of grades was significant at the $p < .01$ level; and from the third to the fourth pair of grades at the $p < 0.05$ level. In order to test for the significance of the differences between proportions of the same pairs of grades in the "high" and the "low" school, the same statistical analysis was applied.

It was found that the proportion of participants in collective symbolic play in grades 1 and 2 in the "low" school was significantly greater than in the "high" school ($p < .01$), and that the reverse was the case in grades 7 and 8. The fact that no significant differences were found between pairs of successive grades within the "high" school indicates, in support of Piaget's claims, that by age 6 and above, symbolic play has declined in that school to a more or less relatively stable level. On the other hand, the sharp decline in the proportion of participation in col-

Table 5

Number of Play Participants in (a) Collective Symbolic Play and (b) Practice Play in One "High" and One "Low" School, in Successive Pairs of Grades, and Their Percentage Out of All Players of Unstructured Games

	"Low" Grades				"High" Grades			
	1–2	3–4	5–6	7–8	1–2	3–4	5–6	7–8
Collective-symbolic play								
N	225	82	61	5	51	89	29	14
Percentage	26.0	9.7	9.7	2.0	5.4	11.1	9.5	6.7
Practice play								
N	73	69	38	25	47	36	19	25
Percentage	9.9	8.3	6.1	10.4	5.0	4.5	6.2	12.0

lective symbolic play from grades 1 and 2 to 3 and 4 in the "low" school, and the significant difference in the extent of participation in such play in grades 1 and 2 of that school as against the "high" school, suggests that "low" children reach the peak of symbolic play at a later age than do "high" children. Other corresponding differences have been discussed elsewhere (see the report mentioned in footnote 1, as well as Eifermann, 1970a-1971).

While our analysis of collective symbolic play tends to support Piaget's statements, it may be seen from Table 4 that there is a rise in the percentage of participation in "practice" play from grades 5 and 6 to 7 and 8, in both the "high" and the "low" school. A test of significance of difference between proportions showed this difference to be significant in both schools ($p < .01$, and $p < 0.05$, in the "high" and in the "low" school, respectively).

This finding is of particular importance for our discussion, since it contradicts Piaget's claims about a necessary decline in "practice" play with age. Though our analysis is still incomplete, it already appears that participation in at least some forms of "practice" play increases again in the upper school grades. This could explain, to a large extent, the discrepancy between Piaget's statements and our findings (discussed earlier in this chapter) concerning play participation in games with rules at various ages. I shall now discuss this point in some more detail.

I tend to believe that Piaget's conclusions derive from a mistaken notion that

in games with rules there is an absolute equilibrium between assimilation to the ego—the principle of all play—and social life. There is still sensory-motor and intellectual satisfaction, and there is also the chance of individual victory over others, but these satisfactions are as it were made "legitimate" by the rules of the game, through which competition is controlled by a collective discipline, with a code of honour and fair play. This third and last type of play [the first two types were "practice" and "symbolic" play] is therefore not inconsistent with the idea of assimilation of reality to the ego, while at the same time it reconciles this ludic assimilation with the demands of social reciprocity (*ibid.,* p. 168).

In other words and put roughly, games with rules are wholly explicable in terms of assimilation and social accommodation. It seems to me a definite exaggeration to see in assimilation the principle of all play and to delegate, in rule-governed games, everything else to "social life." It appears that there is at least one additional factor that plays a decisive role in playing games, which is by no means clearly reducible to either assimilation or social accommodation, namely, the *challenge* that the game offers the player.

Challenge—The Neglected Factor

The meaningfulness of a challenge presented by a game to a player is a function of both the individual's relevant capacities and his cultural surroundings. Thus, a game will present a meaningful challenge to the child only if the degree of skill and understanding required for playing it, or for fulfilling a certain role in it, is both within the child's capacities, and is at the same time such as not to predetermine completely the outcome of a particular round of this game. A child of ten will not often engage in just piling a number of toy bricks one on top of the other (an act of pure assimilation), nor will he readily participate in a competitive game such as hopscotch or tag with a child much younger or much older than himself (unless the rules of the game are flexible enough to allow for more or less equalization, of their chances of victory through handicapping, either by appropriate alterations of the standard rules on the basis of "meta-rules" or by suitable assignments of values to relevant parameters).

VARIETY OF CHALLENGES

The challenge provided by culturally approved games ("forbidden games," again, offer their own special challenges and rewards, but will not be discussed here), will be of a variety of kinds. All structured rule-governed games pose the intellectual challenge of having to master the rules of the game, which need not always be a trivial affair, and of having to act consistently in conformance with them, again not necessarily a trivial affair since, after all, the child knows very well that the rules are in a certain important sense self-imposed, and has, therefore, to fight the constant temptation to break them.

Challenge in Competitive Games. In addition, competitive rule-governed games (such as marbles or hopscotch) pose the vital challenge of attaining inter-subjectively recognized distinction, both the good feeling of being able to excel and the prestige, admiration and envy from the fellow players; in some such games, a formal notion of winning is defined, putting before the player a well determined aim, and in a further subclass of these games, winning will be accompanied by material gain, thereby increasing the challenge still further or, rather, producing a new kind of challenge.

Challenge in Group Games. Competitive rule-governed group games (such as soccer or cops and robbers), pose the additional challenge of a still different kind, *viz.* that of having to act in effective coordination with other participants in one's own group. On the other hand, some of the challenges inherent in individual competitive games might recede.

Challenge in Cooperative Games. The particular type of challenge of having to act in coordination with others is still more characteristic of cooperative, noncompetitive, rule-governed games such as coordinated hand-clapping, certain ritualistic guessing or rhyming games, and perhaps also dancing games. Though in such games there is, of course, no place for winning and material gain, the challenge of achieving excellence might still be very much noticeable and effective.

Practice Play as Preparation for Challenge. Let us not forget that many games offer not an all-or-none challenge, but rather a gradable challenge of improving one's skills, physical or mental, sometimes with no obvious maximum to such self-improvement. The attraction of the rather widespread activity of practice play, which is often not strictly regulated by the rules of the full-fledged "real" game, may thus be understood, at least partly, as lying in its serving as a preparation for meeting the real challenge yet to come with a better chance for success.

Challenge in Unstructured Play. Even completely unstructured, informal playing, whether in isolation or within a social setting, often presents obvious challenges to the player. These may involve the exertion of physical or mental effort, such as in building, with great care and attention, a tunnel in the sand, or it may involve drawing on considerable social resourcefulness, as demonstrated by young children playing peek-a-boo with an adult and contriving to keep him at it sometimes to the point of exasperation. On the other hand, a game that presents a meaningful challenge to children of a certain age, being appropriate to their skills and understanding, might fail to do so for older children, or even for children of the same age but different sex, in spite of remaining equally attractive in these respects, for the simple reason that "it isn't done" in a particular cultural surrounding. I shall not enter here into an analysis of the genesis of this phenomenon[3], but the phenomenon as such cannot be doubted. Let me perhaps just mention that Ariès, in his book, *Centuries of Childhood* (1960), states that some games nowadays considered as exclusively a children's privilege have in the past been regarded as equally suitable for adults, and that Stendhal, in a letter to his sister written in 1800 (when he was seventeen years old), mentions playing hide-and-seek with his buddies. (See *Selected Letters*, 1952.)

ROLE DISTANCE

A girl of twelve will, in many cultures, no longer engage in playing tag as a formal game, though she may fool around in chasing another girl and put no less effort into this informal activity than she did five years

---

[3] Such a discussion is found, for instance, in Sutton-Smith and Rosenberg (1961).

earlier trying to tag her. The sheer fact that everybody around knows that this is not a formal game of tag is sufficient to demonstrate *role distance* (Goffman, 1961, Blau, 1967), allowing her to have her cake and eat it, too. She will enjoy the exertion of trying to meet a self-imposed challenge without having to take upon herself the stigma of playing a "childish" game. An older child may, similarly, not lose face when he (or she) "just" jumps rope or hopscotch, "just" throws or kicks objects at, or into, not too seriously, and not according to the rules of a particular game. Such, indeed, are the "practice" games presented in Table 4, and the relative rise in participation in them in the upper school grades, lends support to our interpretation. Goffman (1961) describes how the seven-to-eight year old child demonstrates "distance" from the role of a conforming merry-go-round horse-rider (which he was, a few years earlier), by testing the limits of what can be done on the horse (riding no-hands, etc.), often to the dismay of the merry-go-round operator. When still older, the rider will display role distance by making a big joke of the whole situation. The challenge involved in successfully pulling off such a display is, I would like to suggest, a major attraction of an otherwise absurd situation.

Another rather obvious but nevertheless insufficiently discussed mechanism for obviating the "it's no longer done at my age" syndrome, is to turn games of skill into sports or athletics, thus enabling the adolescent to continue with play activities of enduring challenge without the stigma of a childish form of realization.[4]

Sociocultural Factors

SYMBOLIC PLAY AND CULTURAL BACKGROUND

First, let me comment briefly on Smilansky's reported findings to the effect that in Israel "culturally deprived children, aged from three to seven years, in spite of their development in the language learning process,[5] do not develop the ability to engage in symbolic play" (1968, p. 58); they do, nevertheless, graduate to the next stage of competitive games with rules.

---

[4] On another occasion, in the report mentioned in footnote 1, I called attention to a further interesting phenomenon, *viz.* the fact that as the child grows older, there is an increase in other forms of social interaction, most noticeably in conversation and discussion, which then replace play to some extent.

[5] That is, in spite of the fact that culturally deprived children of seven have certainly reached the level of three-to-four-year-old "advantaged" children, in development of linguistic skills.

We have not yet processed our observations of kindergartners conducted after school hours to a degree that would have enabled us to carry out a direct comparison between Smilansky's and our own findings, along all corresponding age groups. Nevertheless, the data on the symbolic play of children aged 6 to 14, presented in Table 5, is pertinent to the present issue. The "low" school presented in that table is populated by "disadvantaged" children (the school is included in the local version of the Head Start Program). Rows 1 and 2 of columns 1 and 5 of this table, dealing with children aged 6 to 8, indicate that at this age, "culturally deprived" children not only do develop the ability to engage in symbolic play but that they also engage in such play at a significantly higher rate than do their "advantaged" peers. I would tend to interpret this finding as suggesting that disadvantaged children reach the peak of their symbolic play activity at a later age than do other children. Smilansky, however, having herself given brief consideration to this possibility, strongly argues against it and claims that the difference between the two populations in regard to symbolic play is not due to different rates of development, but is rather of a qualitative nature, based on different cultural background and socialization processes. Indeed, she presents her findings as contradicting Piaget's statement that the stage of symbolic play is a universal phenomenon and suggests that the very existence of this stage of play is culture-dependent. This is definitely the way in which Smilansky is interpreted by Sutton-Smith (1969).

It is, therefore, particularly interesting to note that, as Smilansky herself says, most disadvantaged children in Israel were born to immigrants from Middle Eastern and North African countries. The cultural background of most of them is, therefore, close to that of the predominantly Arabic-speaking population of these countries. Yet an analysis of symbolic play among the pupils of our two Arab schools flatly contradicts the presumption that Arab culture provides a poor ground for the growth of symbolic play. As an example, let me state that in the Arab village of our sample, over 35 percent of all players engage in playing variants of sociodramatic games such as "bus," "taxi," and "plane", whereas in our "high" and "low" Jewish schools, presented in Table 5, the players engaged in all forms of symbolic play account for no more than about 3 percent of all players! Indeed, in the Jewish schools, all forms of unstructured play taken together account, on the average, for approximately 25 percent of all players. It seems, therefore, that a comparison of Israeli cultures and subcultures cannot by itself lead to a rejection of Piaget's hypothesis concerning the universality of symbolic play, though there are obvious cultural differences in the amount of engagement in such play.

THE CONFLICT-ENCULTURATION HYPOTHESIS

Above, I examined Piaget's hypothesis concerning the extent of participation in rule-governed competitive games from the point of view of its distribution over different age groups. I shall now briefly consider the extent of participation in such games in different subcultures, with reference to the "conflict-enculturation hypothesis" of Roberts and Sutton-Smith (1962). This hypothesis is mainly concerned with cultural differences in the style of games and assumes that "children, seriously limited in size, skill and power, yet motivated to achieve and anxious about being able to do so, can seldom find in full scale cultural participation sufficient behavioral opportunities to match adequately both their desire and their anxious incompetence" (1963). The resulting fear of failure enhances children's "curiosity" and involvement in expressive models (and specifically in games) that offer opportunities for rivalry or competition in which the child has a fair chance of winning, and in which he can overcome a previous failure by playing another round of the game, and moreover, in which the consequences of losing are drastically reduced in comparison with real-life situations. Thus, on the one hand the game serves as a mechanism of personality adjustment by assuaging conflicts, and on the other hand, it has enculturative value for the competences required in the culture, since it provides opportunities for buffered learning of activities requiring competitive styles characteristic to the culture, *viz.*, of strategy, physical skill, or chance.

The Conflict Hypothesis Tested. As already pointed out by Millar (1968), the investigators' own findings on the relative predominance of various game styles in different cultures do not necessitate an assumption on the relief from inner conflict as the basis of involvement in a game. Nevertheless, the dual "conflict-enculturation" hypothesis deals, in exhibition of a synthesis rather unusual for functional explanations in the social sciences, with possible psychogenic antecedents as well as with sociogenic consequences of game involvement. Roberts, Sutton-Smith, and their associates did not themselves put the conflict hypothesis to test, since their data, based primarily on ethnographic records and questionnaire responses, did not lend itself to such an analysis. Their hypothesis leads to the prediction that rural children, who have more opportunities than do urban children for real participation in the adult world (e.g., helping at work), should develop fewer or less intensive conflicts and, hence, a more restricted interest in competitive game styles. This hypothesis has been tested in six of our schools, three urban and three rural. The results are presented in Table 6.

Table 6 presents the total number of play participants in competitive

Table 6[a]

Number of Play Participants in Competitive Rule-Governed Games, in Each of Three Urban and Three Rural Schools, and Their Percentage Out of All Children in Each School, Respectively

	Urban			Rural		
	Jewish Town/ High	Jewish Town/ Low	Arab Town	Arab Village	Jewish Village	Kib-butz
N	7553	6817	5400	3456	8668	2876
Percentage	24.0	32.7	26.3	14.0	36.6	33.4

a Because of the large size of the samples, no statistical tests of significance were deemed necessary.

games, and their percentage out of all children present on successive days of observation in each of the following six schools, four of them Jewish—"high" town, "low" town, village and kibbutz—and two of them Arab—town and village. It can be seen from the table that the data contradicts the conflict interpretation of game involvement, except for that of the Arab village school. The fact that significantly more Jewish rural children participate in competitive games as compared with their urban peers and, moreover, that the difference established is clearly not just a cultural one (compare the Arab town school with the village school) excludes the possibility of interpreting the results simply in terms of relative cultural differences. To this should be added the fact that a large proportion of fathers in the Arab village are employed as construction workers outside their village and are, as a result, often absent from home. The conflict interpretation would lead to the prediction that such conditions should be conducive to greater game involvement than conditions in the more stable Jewish village, which is almost totally agricultural.

THE ENCULTURATIVE FUNCTION OF AGE-HOMOGENEOUS PLAY GROUPS

While the conflict interpretation of game involvement probably needs revision, the sociological hypothesis that competitive interaction with peers—on a lowered scale and with a fair chance of winning—may have enculturative functions, must still be considered separately. Indeed, the theory of emergence of homogeneous age groups developed by Eisenstadt (1956), which predates the "conflict-enculturation" hypothesis, runs on somewhat similar lines. In essence, Eisenstadt argues that "age-homogeneous groups . . . tend to arise in those societies in which the family or kinship unit cannot ensure, or even impedes, the attainment of full social status by its [adult] members" (*ibid.*, p. 54). Now in urban communities, the transition from childhood to adulthood is, in general, less smooth than in rural communities. The roles and modes of interaction acquired in the particularistic family setting will be even less relevant to those required for appropriate social behavior in urban surroundings. Preparation for adult life in achievement-oriented societies can be better obtained during childhood and particularly during adolescence by interaction in age-homogeneous groups in which the processes of status acquisition and of achievement evaluation are more like those going on in adult life than those in the family setting.

Age-Homogeneity in Play Groups Tested. In accordance with this theory (of which I have, of course, presented only one aspect, which appears to be particularly relevant), one should expect that a higher percentage of children will play in age-homogeneous groups in urban than in rural schools. This expectation has indeed been verified in our findings: 66 percent of all players in rural schools ($N = 30,476$) played in age-homogeneous groups versus 79 percent in town schools ($N = 67,528$). No part of this difference is caused by differences in socioeconomic level: the percentage of age-homogeneous play in all "high" schools was 74.8, versus 74.6 in all "low" schools.

Since Eisenstadt stresses the importance of age groups during adolescence, it seemed pertinent to conduct a more detailed analysis comparing the extent of age-homogeneous play in grades 5 and 6 (ages 11 and 12) with grades 7 and 8 (ages 13 and 14). This analysis was carried out for three urban and three rural schools, and care was taken to have as great a variety as possible with regard to socioeconomic level ("high" or "low") and culture (Jewish or Arab, village or kibbutz), as well as to keep the populations constant (at approximately 500, with the exception of the kibbutz, where we had to make do with 200).

Table 7 shows that in two out of the three town schools, there was a definite increase in the percentage of age-homogeneous play participation, while in the third school there was a slight but still significant decrease. On the other hand, there was a very noticeable decrease in all three rural schools including, and even more pronouncedly so, the kibbutz school.

This, too, is in general agreement with Eisenstadt's theory. However, according to his views, "age groups . . . attain their fullest formalization and importance in the kibbutz" (*ibid.*, p. 178). This fact expresses itself, for instance, in the much greater extent of adherence to organized youth movements. The major cause for this divergence lies in the educational policy that requires children to be brought up within their own communities in the kibbutz.

One might then, perhaps, have expected that the percentage of age

Table 7[a]

Number of Play Participants in Age-Homogeneous Groups in Grades 5-6 and 7-8 in Each of Three Urban and Three Rural Schools, and Their Percentage Out of All Players in Each Pair of Grades, Separately for Each School

	Urban						Rural					
	Jewish Town/High		Jewish Town/Low		Arab Town		Arab Village		Jewish Village		Kibbutz	
Grades	5-6	7-8	5-6	7-8	5-6	7-8	5-6	7-8	5-6	7-8	5-6	7-8
N	1867	953	2885	1181	1244	1211	1721	518	2133	1067	810	519
Percentage	82.8	87.4	84.3	81.2	71.9	79.5	74.9	61.8	75.9	65.8	70.4	49.8

[a] The differences between proportions between the two pairs of grades in each school are all significant at $p < .001$ level.

group play would increase among adolescent kibbutz children at least as much as, if not more than, among urban children. Table 7, column 12 shows that the exact opposite is the case. This, however, is probably due to the fact that at exactly that time, at the transition from the 6th to the 7th grade, children are required to take a much larger part in the general kibbutz work than before, so that play within age groups then loses much of its previous function.

Summary

Many theories of play proposed so far have suffered from the lack of a sound basis of systematic, large-scale observations by which they could be seriously tested. As a matter of fact, so far there was not even a methodology available by which such observations could be conducted and encoded for computer processing. Indeed, some theories of play did not fare too well when tested against our large samples of systematic observations. It is my conjecture that these shortcomings in theorizing are in some measure due to the neglect of one major factor, that of *challenge*, which, so it seems, cannot be easily reduced to the other factors taken into consideration in extant theories.

More in detail, I think I was able to demonstrate, on the basis of systematic large-scale observations on the play behavior of Israeli children, the following points:

1. Piaget's claim to the effect that games with rules increase in number, both relatively and absolutely, with age, replacing the earlier "practice" and "symbolic" play, has to a considerable extent been disconfirmed by our findings. We have found that: (a) on the contrary, an absolute *decline* in participation in games with rules sets in at a certain age, around 11 on the average; (b) at a somewhat later age, a relative *decline* in participation in games with rules sets in; this was confirmed by observations conducted at school as well as in streets and improvised playfields; and (c) the corresponding rise in participation in unstructured play is due, at least in part, to a return to some forms of practice play.

On the other hand, we have verified, in accord with Piaget's general statements (though he is not concerned here with differences due to socioeconomic level), that symbolic play, in the one "high" school that was tested for this purpose, is already rare at the age of 6 to 8—and remains steadily so throughout school—while in the corresponding "low" school, there was still some noticeable symbolic play in the two first grades, with a significant decline thereafter.

Piaget's explicit assumption that all rule-governed games are competitive has been found lacking, both in theory and in observation. There *is* a point in playing multiperson rule-governed but noncompetitive games, e.g., of the cooperative type, and there is a definite sense in which a single person can play a game with rules. Children have been observed to play such games.

My own suggestion is that the general decline in participation in rule-governed games is partly due to the decline in the amount of objective challenge posed by the games, and partly to the fact that even such games whose objective challenge does not diminish may turn, because of sociocultural pressures, into formal sports and athletics or, when such a functional change is inappropriate, may degenerate into unstructured play, thereby enabling the player to display *role distance* and thus to continue the enjoyment of playing, without losing face.

2. Smilansky's claims that Israeli "culturally deprived" children (mainly born to immigrants from Middle Eastern and North African countries) do not develop the ability to engage in symbolic play have been disconfirmed by our findings. Indeed, we have found that such children, between the ages of 6 and 8, engage in social symbolic play to a greater extent than do the other children and, moreover, that Arab children (presumably culturally related to the Jewish Middle Eastern and North African group) engage in such play to a far greater extent than do any of their Jewish peers.

3. Roberts and Sutton-Smith's "conflict" interpretation of game involvement, which leads to the prediction that rural children should engage in competitive play to a greater extent than do urban children, was not confirmed by our findings.

4. On the other hand, their complementary "enculturation" hypothesis found indirect confirmation when formulated in terms of Eisenstadt's theory of the perpetuation of homogeneous age groups. The prediction, derived from this theory, that a higher percentage of children will play in age-homogeneous groups in urban than in rural schools, was fully confirmed by our findings. The seeming exception in the case of kibbutz children aged 12 to 14 is probably due to the change in their status within the kibbutz society, created by taking upon themselves, at the transition from the 6th to the 7th grade, much greater responsibilities in the general kibbutz work.

References

Ariès, P. *Centuries of childhood.* New York: Vintage Books, 1965. (First French ed., 1960)

Blau, Peter M. *Exchange and power in social life.* New York: Wiley, 1967.

Boyton, Paul L. and Wang, James D. Relation of the play interests of children to their socio-economic status. *J. genet. Psychol.,* 1944, **64**, 129–138.

Eifermann, Rivka R. Level of children's play as expressed in group size. *Brit. J. ed. Psychol.,* 1970a, *40*,2,161-170.

Eifermann, Rivka R. Cooperativeness and egalitarianism in kibbutz children's games. *Human Relat.,* 1970b, *23*,6, in press.

Eifermann, Rivka R. *Determinants of children's game styles.* Jerusalem: The Israel Academy of Sciences and Humanities, 1971, in press.

Eisenstadt, S. N. *From generation to generation.* New York: Free Press, 1956.

Erikson, E. H. *Childhood and society.* (2nd ed.) New York: Norton, 1963.

Goffman, E. *Encounters.* Indiana: Bobbs-Merrill, 1961.

Lehman, H. C. and Witty, P. A. *The psychology of play activities.* New York: A. S. Barnes, 1927.

Millar, Susanna. *The psychology of play.* London: Pelican, 1968.

Parten, M., and Newhall, S. M. Social behavior of preschool children. In Barker, R. G., Kounin, J. S., and Wright, H. F. (Eds.), *Child behavior and development.* New York: McGraw-Hill, 1943, 505–525.

Peller, Lilli. Libidinal phases, ego development and play. *Psychoanal. Study of the Child,* 1954, **IX**, 178–198.

Piaget, J. *Play, dreams and imitation in childhood.* London: Routledge and Kegan Paul, 1962. (First French ed., 1951).

Roesnberg, B. G. and Sutton-Smith, B. A revised conception of masculine-feminine differences in play activities. *J. genet. Psychol.,* 1960, **96**, 165–170.

Roberts, J. M., and Sutton-Smith, B. Child training and game involvement. *Ethnology,* 1962, **I**, 166–185.

Smilansky, Sara. *The effect of sociodramatic play on disadvantaged pre-school children.* New York: Wiley, 1968.

Stendhal. *Selected letters.* (Introduced by E. Boudot-Lamotte.) New York: Grove Press, 1952.

Sutton-Smith, B. Play preference and play behavior: A validity study. *Psychol. Rep.,* 1965, **16**, 65–66.

Sutton-Smith, B. The two cultures of games. In G. S. Kenyon (Ed.), *Aspect of Contemporary Sport Sociology.* Chicago: Athletic Institute, 1969, pp. 135–147.

Sutton-Smith, B., and Rosenberg, B. G. Game involvement in adults. *J. soc. Psychol.,* 1963, **60**, 15–30.

Sutton-Smith, B., and Rosenberg, B. G. Sixty years of historical change in the game preference of American children. *J. Amer. Folklore,* 1961, **74**, 17–46.

19

A Syntax for Play and Games

Brian Sutton-Smith

The present paper takes its cue from Piaget, who indicated that the only adequate description of play is in terms germane to play's own structures. Piaget however, sought to use the structures of intelligence as a model for the structures of play, this being consistent with his own belief that structurally speaking, affective, cognitive or ludic structures would be essentially the same at a particular age level. The present point of view, however, is that the use of a structural descriptive system appropriate for one class of functions to describe another class of functions, can result in oversight as to the peculiarities of that latter class. For this reason the arbitrary choice has been made here to use one ludic system as a model for another. It seems reasonable that if descriptive concepts drawn from games are used to describe play, the disservice to the latter will be less serious than when the descriptive concepts are derived from ego-functions, cognitions, etc., as has traditionally been the case.

 In the companion volume, *The Study of Games*, a formal game is defined as "an exercise of voluntary control systems, in which there is a contest between powers, confined by rules in order to produce a disequilibrial outcome." This definition has its roots in studies conducted much earlier by Fritz Redl and Paul Gump, and more recently by John M. Roberts. The confinement by rules means that the games prescribes the roles, the interaction patterns, the performances, and the procedures for action as well as the spatiotemporal contexts. Granting the tentative nature of this particular systematic game account it does provide leads for looking at play activities. Using Piaget's paradigm, and making the assumption that play is the precursor of games, we can look at the play for the ludic infrastructures that lead to the game elements as defined above.

The game elements contain a statement of purpose, a statement of actor-counteractor relationships, a statement of performances, a statement of the spatiotemporal context, and finally a statement of outcome determinants. Taking first the question of *purpose*, it is important to stress that we are discussing ludic purposes and not the players' psychological or sociologically derived motives, which are relevant to the understanding of play, but not relevant to the description of structure. If games are a contest of powers, then it may follow that play is a *test* of powers, a test of cognitive, affective, and conative powers. Such a view would certainly fit the oft-repeated statement that the pleasure in play is the pleasure of function, or the pleasure of mastery. It would also suggest that a first step in the analysis of play purpose might be to catalogue the powers being tested. The powers tested in infancy are largely motor and sensory, while throughout early childhood symbolic elements play an increasing part. It would be interesting to know whether all novel adaptive capacities are tested in play, or whether only certain of these are introduced. At the other end, in late childhood and adulthood, the focus in game contests is on the testing of physical, strategic, and fortunistic powers. What lies between the motor play of infants and these contests of adults is less clear in the literature, though we have a lead on some of the important elements in the article by Peller (Chapter IV), and in the works of such writers as Isaacs (1933), Lowenfeld (1935), and Hartley et al. (1952). Isaacs, for example, documents play involving possession, power, rivalry, inferiority, strangers, scapegoats, sexual curiosity, etc. When we arrive at childhood proper, games themselves can be categorized in terms of the motives, race, chase, attack, capture, harassment, hunt, rescue, and seduction, which were developed by Redl, Gump, and their coworkers and are stated in detail later. What these ludic purposes suggest is that whatever the classes of testing in preschool play, by childhood these have been narrowed down to a more limited array and these in turn are further narrowed down to physical skill, strategy and luck and their combinations by adulthood, though skill and strategy, may be themselves considered hierarchic organizations of chase, attack, and capture.

Although this statement of ludic purposes derives directly from Roberts and Sutton-Smith's definition of games as a contest of powers, it does injustice to various other elements of game purpose already mentioned in previous chapters. For example, are we now to speak of play as a *test* of voluntary controls or as an *exercise* of voluntary controls? Is it the testing or the voluntary-control exercise that is most critical? Are they two aspects of the same phenomena, or should we regard exploration, the testing of powers, and the exercise of voluntary controls as three different classes of behavior, reserving the term play for the latter of these? Our preference would be for the view that either exploration or testing only become play when voluntarily undertaken.

In order to crystallize the matter, however, some attention must be paid to the *outcome of play*. In games the outcome is disequilibrial. Someone ends up being a winner. One could argue likewise that the intentionality of play is to do things differently; to make a unique response to customary circumstances; and to move events away from their cognitive and affective equilibria. Whereas much of life is given over to removing disequilibria and reacquiring some physical and psychological homeostasis, the intention of play may be, by contrast, to test what occurs when one upsets these customary balances. If such an intention could be granted, then the emergence of the novel responses, playfulness, and transformations discussed in previous chapters would be explicable. Admittedly, it is not easy to discuss play or any other behavioral phenomena in this way. Language and logical systems are structured to make sense, whereas it may well be that play and games are structured to make nonsense out of ordinary expectations. Like Mardi Gras and cocktail parties, they may require some paleologic for their comprehension, and the problem with our systematic descriptions may lie in our own inability to develop this illogic of nonsense. It seems likely that it is only by focusing on the unique transformations that occur in play that we will begin to accumulate the empirical data that such a theory of play as a disequilibrial phenomenon would require.

Another game element in terms of which play can be analyzed structurally is the reciprocal relationships between the *actors and counteractors*. Children's infant play does not, on the surface, contain such "social" elements. On the other hand, considering that the infant does not really differentiate himself from the "socius," we can perhaps find the intraludic counterpart to his later role-playing action and counteraction, in his own ludic reversing of the direction of action. Freud's stress on the shift from passivity to activity may be a key here. When Piaget demonstrates the child repeating an action previously carried out with adaptive intent, but now with ludic intent, he is demonstrating such counteraction. For example, at two months he observed that the baby "adopted the habit of throwing his head back to look at familiar things from this new position . . . he seemed to repeat this movement with ever increasing enjoyment and ever decreasing interest in the external result; he bought his head back to the upright position and then threw it back again time after time laughing loudly" (1951, p. 91). Piaget was impressed mainly with the repetitive quality of this play. But perhaps this is largely a matter of what adults can recognize. Play is repetitive of previous adaption if that is what one is looking for. What would an observer see if he were focusing on change? Relative to his earlier actions, the infant's innovation may have been quite considerable. Precisely in what way did the infant flinging back his head alter the character of his earlier responses so that his own response incongruity caused him amusement?

By the second year of life, these "passive-active" reversals give way to subject-object reversals. There are object-object reversals (a block becomes a cup) and self-other reversals (the player is mother). One object stands for another, and one action stands for another. Apparently, if Piaget's descriptions are reliable, such piecemeal counteractions or "imitations" precede larger-scale identifications with other persons and other objects that tend to emerge in the third year. Whatever the details, however, it looks as though these reversals are reversals in terms of prior adaptations, imitations, or models. The reversal is not within the play; it is between the play and the prior adaptive behavior. At least, this is what has been emphasized in most accounts, though it could be incorrect. The tension within the play might actually consist of an alternation between a mimicked adaptive act (or image) and its incongruous counterpart. At this point, therefore, we should leave open the question of whether play disequilibria exist primordially in an internal or external relationship. Judging by later developments, *both* of these relationships are always involved. Players do things in games that are internally disequilibrial, and that are out of character with their other nongame behaviors.

By the third year, the reversals are clearly a part of the play itself. Now the child incorporates into his solitary play conversations between different voices that act and counteract. These dyadic interactions within the play include behavior and words between the player and her doll (self-other dyads), and between the mother and her child—that is, the player and her doll (other-other dyads). The third year of life features these miniature social systems within the child's play. In approximately the fourth year, other characters are added so that a plurality of relationships can be represented. The subject may impersonate one or several people, and imaginary characters are added. Some have said that the transformational character of the play now reaches a peak of "imaginativeness" or "unreality." Klinger and others have argued that after this point children's play becomes more realistic. This may be true or it maybe an adultcentric mistake. Is the "reality" of chess or football more real than the reality of "bogeyman"? Or is it simply that as adults we are more familiar with our own ludic forms? If one takes a more anthropological attitude to our adult cultural forms, and classifies our sports, games, entertainments, carnivals, television operas, etc. as a part of the prevailing mythological system (they redundantly reconcile, rehearse, and restate the themes of cultural life), then questions have to be raised about the notion that there is increasing "reality" in children's play after the age of four years.

But this is an aside. Continuing the present focus on action and counteraction of roles as a structural feature of play, the years between four and seven are characterized by multiple forms of orderly collective play (houses, trucks, shops, schools, etc). Now the action and counteraction is social rather than solitary. Furthermore, there is often a powerful orderliness and control by implicit rules in these childhood groups (Ferenc, 1949). From the work of Isaacs on scapegoating, (1933), and the work of Caillois on mask societies and shamans (1961), it is clear that the action and counteraction often revolve around one dominant player and a group of less powerful players. The usual accounts of childhood leadership in terms of status, popularity, and intelligence seem too impotent to account for the imaginative seizures of young children either in the face of bogeymen, or in accord with their own shamans. The Lord of the Flies might be a more useful social model.

Another source of information on the role relationships of this age period can be derived from the pastimes that were once traditional fare for the 4-to-7-year age group. These were the organized round and singing diversions that don't quite fit the classification of games, songs, dramas, or dances, but share some of the characteristics of all of these and that have usually been termed "pastimes" by folklorists. Some of these involve unison pantomime behaviors (Ring a Ring a Roses, Luby Loo), usually in circle formation. Others require the differentiation of a central player acting out a song of marriage (Farmer in the Dell, In and out the Windows) or death (Poor Sally). Sixty years ago in the days of the play party, a child would graduate from these forms to the line forms during middle school years (Three Dukes, Nuts in May), and couple forms in adolescence in which the central player was now the fool left over without a partner (Jolly Miller). This transformation is still in part paralleled in the sequence of children's kissing games where these exist (Sutton-Smith, 1959[c]).

In addition to these singing games for the four-to-seven-year age group, there were also dialogue dramas featuring two central actors and a group —usually a witch, a mother, and her children, with traditional dialogue spoken by the various characters. In general, the children were naughty, the witch stole them, and the mother retrieved them. The role organization of the singing games was collaborative and ritualistic. Thus Punchinello goes through a sequence of actions in the middle of the ring and is imitated by the chorus circling around him. The Punchinello is actor and the others are counter-actors, but the outcome is not open-ended. Actor and counteractor are part of a dyadic ritual. In the dialogue game, the pattern is more like that of a game. There is a formal contest between the mother and the witch. It is only prevented from being a genuine game by the fact that the outcome is *not* uncertain. It is always the same, which makes the play more of a drama than a game.

Nevertheless, the role alternations of these pastimes do presage those that will become important in games proper.

In the Farmer in the Dell, for example, some of the players will alternatively choose and then be chosen, and while their behavior is ritually prescribed, this role alternation is similar to that required in games proper. One of the questions in Piagetian cognitive theory has to do with the acquisition of such reversible operations. How do children move from a stage in which they think only in terms of obvious covariances, to one in which they develop a logical notion of the operation of which the stimulus covariances are only the outward manifestation? The answer from traditional games is that they get a ritual introduction into reversibility prior to having to handle it by themselves. But we should be quite clear that this is not real role reversal (in the sense that "to hide" you must understand "to seek" and vice versa). In the Farmer in the Dell, we have role alternation, taking turns. The actions are complementary but in a more static way. The chorus is not the reverse of the farmer in the same way that hiding reverses seeking. In Punchinello, for example, the chorus imitates the central player. It is an example of what some psychologists have termed *matched dependency*. Furthermore, various games exist that mix together these ritual elements and genuine games— for example, London Bridge, which begins with a choral game but ends with a tug-o-war, and a Tisket a Tasket, which ends with a game of tag. Though noticeably in these transition game forms, it is possible all the time for some players, or some of the time for all players, to continue the simple choral roles, while some of the players take the game roles.

In sum, there is abundant evidence, in these pastimes of the four-to-seven year olds, of social actions and counteractions, paving the way for the true role reversibility of games proper.

The first group of true games are the central-person games of midchildhood (seven through ten years). Here the action takes place between a central player and a group of relatively undifferentiated others. These protogames do not have fixed sides or ultimate winners. Sides are transitory and winning is episodic. The following list of motives, actors, and counteractors combines the two structural elements that have been discussed up to this point. The list is derived from the work of Gump, Redl, and Sutton-Smith.

Role of Actor	Motive of Play	Role of Counteractor
To overtake	Race	To stay ahead
To catch, tackle, tag	Chase	To outdistance, dodge, elude
To overcome barrier, enter a guarded area, overpower a defense; to injure psychologically or otherwise	Attack	To defend an area or a person, to ward off, to be on guard
To take, person, symbol	Capture	To avoid being taken
To tease, taunt, lure; to mistake or unsuccessful attack	Harassment	To see through, to move suddenly and punish an attacker, to bide time
To find by chance or clue (object, person)	Search	To hide, to cover or mislead, to feign
To spring prisoner; to be savior	Rescue	To be jailer, to guard against escape
To tempt another to forbidden action	Seduction	To resist, to have self-control

In developmental terms, the actions and counteractions characteristic of five to seven years are those of hiding and seeking (as in Hide and Seek) and chasing and eluding (as in Tag). From seven to eight years we add capture and rescue (as in Relievo or Frozen Tag); and by nine and ten years, attack and defense (Dodge Ball; King of the Mountain).

These are not all the elements, but they give some idea of the purposes and reciprocal relationships between the actors and counteractors in the central-person games of childhood. If this sequence, which is derived from large-scale normative studies both in New Zealand and in the United States, has developmental validity, then these role systems should appear in the given chronological sequence everywhere. In order to see whether there is such an implicit developmental ordering of role systems, in this investigator's current research, children are being asked to invent games. They are provided with the game's purposes and some of the properties and rules. For example, they are given a checker board or a parcheesi board and asked to use those properties to make a game of *chase* or a game of *attack*. Although these data have not yet been fully analyzed, young children, when given the cue to attack, often convert it into one to chase; this is also a more frequent feminine response. The younger boys have problems with the symbolic confines of the task and will sometimes roll the checkers around as if they were stones and thus develop physical pursuit or attack games, rolling the checkers after each other. When attack is developed by a younger child, it may not include any concept of defense. This is particularly interesting because exactly the same sort of thing occurs cognitively when children are making physical judgments. They notice some alien perceptual characteristic of an operation but ignore the rest. As these studies proceed, a more precise idea should be developed of the various steps taken by children in internalizing the rules that underlie the ludic systems. These studies are of a preliminary character; what they aim at is the psychic structures that underlie games and sports.

In syntactical terms, what one might hope for would be the development of motif trees. For example the games of Tag and Relievo, which include respectively, the reciprocations of chase and elude and capture and rescue, are the games that seem to be prerequisites for Prisoner's Base, which involves all these elements. Similarly, Football is, in these terms, a combination of dodge ball and tag (See Diagram 1). In syntactic

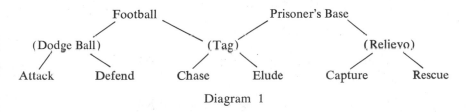

Diagram 1

terms, the motives of chase or elude are like morpheme elements (the performances within chase would be phonemic), and the games themselves with the reciprocal arrangements would then become the syntax. Instead of subject and predicate, we have actor and counteractor. A game like football is, in these terms, a paragraph.

Actually, while the diagram does some justice to Prisoner's Base, which is a relatively simple game that used to be played by twelve-year-olds in the days prior to football, it does not do justice to the latter, which contains many other dimensions not reflected in this motif tree.

Beyond the statement of the structural elements of the powers to be tested, the disequilibria to be realized and the actors and counteractors to be described, all games contain additional statements about the performances and the spatiotemporal controls. A summary list of some of these matters requiring consideration for an analysis of play follows, although we will not expatiate on its implications at this time. They will be treated more fully in *The Developmental Psychology of Children's Games* (in press).

Game Required Performances
    A. Body Contact
    B. Body Movement
    C. Type of Motor Performance
    D. Type of Language Performance
    E. Type of Intellectual Performance
    F. Type of Emotive Performance

Game Required Spatial Controls
    A. Performance Reversal
    B. Rule Complexity
    C. Spatial Obstacles
    D. Territorial Imagery
    E. Ecological Territory
    F. Immunity Symbols
    G. Prop Imagery
    H. Types of Props
    I. Spatial Deployment of Players

Game Required Temporal Controls
    A. Ecological
    B. Structural
    C. Outcomes

Finally we come to the symbolic outcome, which has to do with winning and the way in which the players resolve their conflict. One can talk here of the types of approach to the opponent:

1. Indirect and neutral (Darts)
2. Direct and neutral (Football)
3. Indirect and symbolic (Chess)
4. Direct and symbolic (Marbles)
5. Indirect and actual (Ball Tag)
6. Direct and actual (Boxing)

and of the intensity of winning.

1. Winning is merely episodic and passes from player to player.
2. A single player wins but others may share his victory by taking second or third place, or a smaller share of the possessions.
3. A single player takes all, or eliminates all others as players.
4. A team wins.

5. Those who fail lose property (or have it damaged).
6. Those who fail suffer penalties within or after the game.
7. Those who fail are physically punished.

In general, the age trend is for approaches to the other actor to become more direct and actual with age (with boxing the acme); and with the intensity of winning reaching its peak at older-age levels. These are modified in a variety of ways at earlier age levels.

The intention of the present account, however, is only to give sufficient details to justify the view that it is possible to make a structural and developmental approach to play and games in ludic terms alone. Given such a structural analysis, the more customary psychological questions as to the antecedents and consequents of play become both better informed and more profitable.

Chapter VIII

Theoretical Overviews

This field has been noted more for its theoretical or speculative essays than for its scientific accumulations of data. Again and again there have been reviews of "theories" that have contributed practically nothing to science, though they have contributed a great deal to undergraduate essays. Play has been said to result from "surplus energy," "recreation," "racial and cultural recapitulation," or "biologically preparatory activity." The present work includes a review by Gilmore that has the virtue both of being recent and of having led to several empirical studies. For a more generalized account of the earlier studies as well as more recent ones, *The Psychology of Play* by Susanna Millar (1968) is a useful contemporary source.

There follows a critique of Piaget by Sutton-Smith and a reply by Piaget. Piaget's paper and the response, when compared with D. El'Konin's in the previous chapter, present us with useful contrasts. In D. El'Konin's view, symbolic play begins essentially with the adult's example. The child uses, as play objects, those things that the adult has suggested he use this way. The child plays because the adult provides the model. To readers who are familiar with Piaget's works and Piaget's emphasis on the active role of the child in creating his own play symbols, D. El'Konin's descriptions come as a considerable surprise. We have mentioned that the importance of adults becomes clearer when we look at the disadvantaged children discussed by Smilansky (1968). These children did not evidence the usual variety of imaginative activities. Their play activities consisted of a fairly redundant and realistic replication of the activities of powerful adults. They played with their toys only in repetitive and realistic ways. Is the difference between D. El'Konin and Piaget, then, a difference in the children they were observing? Is it that D. El'Konin is dealing with disadvantaged children in Russian nursery schools, while Piaget deals with the upper-status progeny of his own home and other professionals in Geneva? Or is the difference, rather, one of focus? D. El'Konin, with a socially determinist and rather traditional viewpoint, seeks to derive play from the activity of others (thus play is an epiphenomenal activity), while Piaget, characteristically concerned with the inherent qualities of organisms, places more stress on the formal role of play in the organism's activity. There is another and perhaps even more important contrast between the two theorists. For Piaget, play is a form of thought, which he says is especially necessary during early childhood, when realistic forms of thought are not available. Play as a hypostatized form of assimilative activity becomes less necessary when the maturing individual is able to maintain a more adequate balance between his assimilative activity (fantasy) and his accommodation (realistic adjustment). D. El'Konin, following Vygotsky, argues rather that play is not an infant substitute for mature thought, but a step towards the development of internal activity. Because in play the child separates the meaning of things from their original objects, to that extent he develops the beginnings of internalized meanings. Play does not cease with school age; it is internalized.

The point of view of Sutton-Smith, in contrast to that of Piaget, is that play continues throughout life, and in sympathy with the views of Vygotsky, is that it becomes increasingly internalized. Unlike Vygotsky, however, Sutton-Smith's viewpoint is that it is play that is internalized. Play does not disappear into "directed internalized thought," but continues as games on the one hand and as an internalized expressive system (fantasy) on the other. Adult counterparts to child's play are the daydreams and ruminations that occupy so much of waking time. It is usually said that play decreases with age. What decreases is the overt expressions (except for game players). We do not know whether these internal forms of adult ruminative play occupy more or less time than the overt forms of early childhood.

The most important recent contribution to this literature is *Daydreaming: An Introduction to the Experimental Study of Inner Experience* by Jerome L. Singer. In a sense, his book marks the end of a period in which the major interest in play and fantasy has been in their cathartic properties. It heralds a renewed interest once again in the preparatory or rehearsive functions of play and fantasy, an interest already documented in the studies of animal play and cognitive development in the previous chapters.

20

Play: A Special Behavior

J. Barnard Gilmore

Certainly everyone knows what play is not, even if everyone can't agree on just what play is. Play seems to represent that definitionally impossible "wastebasket" category of behavior, the unmotivated act. Consider these traditional definitions of play (they are actually miniature theories of play) as drawn from Mitchell and Mason (1934):

Spencer: Activity performed for the immediate gratification derived, without regard for ulterior benefits; Lazarus: Play is activity which is in itself free, aimless, amusing or diverting; Seashore: *Free self expression* for the pleasure of expression; Dewey: Activities not consciously performed for the sake of any result beyond themselves; Stern: Play is voluntary, self-sufficient activity; Patrick: Those human activities which are free and spontaneous and which are pursued for their own sake alone, interest in them is self-sustaining, and they are not continued under any internal or external compulsion; Allin: Play refers to those activities which are accompanied by a state of comparative pleasure, exhilaration, power, and the feeling of self-initiative; Curti: Highly motivated activity which, as free from conflicts is usually, though not always, pleasurable (pp. 86–87).

It is clear that the person who wishes to understand play behavior has set himself a difficult task if he uses either his intuitive sense of the term or the above comments as a beginning point of reference, since the definition of play will determine both the theorizing about and the research

SOURCE. Republished from R. N. Haber, (Ed.), *Current Research in Motivation*, Holt-Rinehart, 1966, with the permission of author and publisher.

done with play. To be scientifically workable, any definition must be precise; but "play" is an abstract and global sort of behavior, one that eludes precision. In the past, play has been a thing to be inferred, not the sort of behavior that elicits clear agreement with respect to its presence or absence.

It will be the purpose of this paper to explore the possible causes and effects of play in children, as suggested both by theorists of play and by research on play behavior. Play will be defined arbitrarily by the following behavioral example: a young child takes a piece of cloth and, as if the cloth were human, makes it "go to sleep." While behaviors as divergent as the dancing-like movements of apes and the sober assembly of model airplanes by adolescents have been considered to be play, we will knowingly restrict ourselves to this narrow (and not necessarily "pure") case. Perhaps in thinking about this one small play episode, concepts and distinctions will emerge that could lead to a clearer and more extensive definition of play.

Theories dealing with the causes and the effects of play fall into two general categories. First are those theories concerned only with the antecedents of play and with the inferred purposes of play; these theories regard the specific content of play behaviors as irrelevant. These theories will be termed *classical theories* of play since they spring from the psychological *zeitgeist* prior to World War I. A second general category of play theories, more recent in origin, views the specific form that play takes as being crucial for specifying the causes and effects of play. The play theories of Piaget and of psychoanalysis represent this type of theory.

The Classical Theories of Play

One of the oldest theoretical statements concerning the significance of play is attributed to both Schiller (1875) and to Spencer (1873), although it appears likely that its germ was to be found in educational literature long before their time. Briefly stated, this theory holds that play is the result of a surplus of energy, a surplus that exists because the young are freed from the business of self-preservation through the actions of their parents. The energy surplus finds its release in the aimless exuberant activities that we term play. This theory is usually referred to as the *surplus energy theory* of play. It postulates, first, a quantity of energy available to the organism and, second, a tendency to expend this energy, even though it is not necessary for the maintenance of a life balance, through goal-less activity (play). In the terms of the surplus energy theory, then, the play behavior represented by the young child's making a cloth toy "go to sleep" would be seen as essentially unpredictable and meaningless behavior, pushed into being by the automatic production of unneeded energies. The going-to-sleep-play could just as well have been any other sort of play-like behavior with no consequences for the surplus energy theory of play. The surplus energy theory of play is an appealing one, and it has been put forward in a variety of forms, most notably by Tolman (1932), Tinklepaugh (1942), and Alexander (1958).

A second classical theory of play sees this activity not as the product of a surplus of energy, but rather as the product of a deficit of energy. Play is here seen as a method by which spent energy can be replenished. This theory, the *relaxation theory* of play, is associated primarily with Lazarus (1883) and with Patrick (1916). Essentially, play is seen by these men as a mode of dissipating the inhibition built up from fatigue due to tasks that are relatively new to the organism. Thus, play is found most often in childhood. Play not only replenishes energy for the as-yet-unfamiliar cognitive activities of the child, but, because it also reflects "deeprooted race habits" (by which is meant phylogenically acquired behaviors that are *not* therefore new to the organism), play is the one activity that shows very little build-up of inhibition over time. This theory of play would view the "making-the-toy-sleep" episode as a simple restful activity caused by the fact that the child was psychically too fatigued to do anything else.

A great many of the general theorists who have considered the meaning of play have seen it as a form of instinctive behavior. The number of theorists who have seen play in this light approaches two dozen, as cited by Britt and Janus (1941) and by Beach (1945). Perhaps the most eloquent of these theorists is Karl Groos (1898, 1908a) whose theory has come to be known as the *preexercise theory* of play. Play for Groos is seen as the product of emerging instincts, something that fixes these instincts and exercises them in preparation for their maturation time. The episode of play we have taken for our working definition would be explained by the preexercise theory as possibly for the first stirrings of a parental instinct.

At about the time Karl Groos' preexercise theory was becoming known, G. Stanley Hall (1906) put forward his *recapitulation theory*, which saw play not as an activity that developed future instinctual skills, but rather one that served to rid the organism of primitive and unnecessary instinctual skills carried over by heredity. Hall was the first to conceive of stages of play; he postulated that each child passes through a series of play stages corresponding to, and recapitulating, the cultural stages in the development of races. Wundt (1913) was another well-known proponent of the recapitulation theory of play. The recapitulation theory would seem to place the episode of "making-the-cloth-toy-sleep" in the category of a vestigial primitive behavior, perhaps magicoreligious in original intent.

Another theory-like approach to play came from the work of Appleton (1910). She studied play in primitive cultures and in children, and she concluded that play is a response to a generalized drive for growth in the organism; it is not instinctual preexercise as conceived by Groos. Appleton saw as the basis for play a hunger in the organism for growth to a stage at which the instinct can operate. Thus, play serves to facilitate the mastery of skills necessary to the function of adult instincts. The child plays because he wants this mastery and he "knows" that play is the method by which he may achieve it. There are other theories of play, mostly in the educational literature, which are akin to this one in their stress of a self-actualizing basis for play, but they will not be traced here. Theories of play such as Appleton's we will term *growth theories*.

Similar to the growth theories are the *ego-expanding theories* of play put forward first by K. Lange (1901), and later by Claparède (1911, 1934). "Ego" here means the reality-meeting and reality-mapping aspects of cognitive life. Thus, Lange sees play as being nature's way of completing the ego and Claparède sees play as an expressive exercising of the ego and the rest of the personality, an exercising that strengthens developing cognitive skills and aids the emergence of additional cognitive skills.

These, then, are the purely classical theories of play. They are classical insofar as all of them view the specific content of play behaviors as being more or less incidental to the causes of play generally. Surprisingly, there are essentially no research data relevant to these theories of play, so that if one wishes to evaluate their worth he must rely on observations and personal impressions (see Hurlock, 1934). This is not to imply that the classical theories of play are untestable. On the contrary. A direct consequence of the surplus energy theory of play, for instance, is that children should play more when rested than when they are fatigued. Speaking generally, this seems to be the case, yet the limits of this "truth" need empirical testing. A direct consequence of the relaxation theory of play would be that any person should do better on a new task following a period of play than after having done some different new task. Perhaps there is more reason to question this hypothesis than was the case with the hypothesis drawn from the surplus energy theory of play.

The preexercise theory of play is only as impressive as the concept of human instincts. If one grants the existence of a parental instinct, then it should be possible to design an experiment that denies the opportunity for parent-role play and evaluates the influence of this restriction on later parental behavior. The recapitulation theory predicts that children's play should mirror the development of cultures, so that we should never see a child play at a "higher" function before he first plays at a "lower" one. Of those we have called classical theories of play, only the growth theories and the ego-expanding theories of play admit of no ready, testable derivatives. From the standpoint of the person who wishes to understand the causes and the effects of play, the classical theories have only two major drawbacks. First, they do not undertake to explain the wide individual differences found in human play behavior, and second, they have produced no important research data to support their various positions.

The newer theories of play differ from the classical play theories primarily in that they invoke explanations of play behavior based on dynamic factors of individual personality, and they are geared to explaining individual shifts in play behavior. These newer theories of play will be called the *infantile dynamics theories* of play, after Piaget. The most elaborated of the infantile dynamics theories are those of Piaget and psychoanalysis; but two early theories belonging in this category are those of Lewin (1933) and Buytendijk (1934).

For Lewin, play occurs because the cognitive life-space of the child is still unstructured, resulting in a failure to discriminate between the real and the unreal. It is easy then, for the child to pass into the region of playful unreality where things are changeable and arbitrary. Lewin does not elucidate this thesis further, except to state that in childhood a force or tendency arises to leave the region of reality, especially when this region is dominated by an "overstrong pressure."

Like Lewin, Buytendijk holds that a child plays because he is a child, because his cognitive "dynamics" do not allow any other way of behaving. The four main characteristics of the child's dynamics that determine this fact for Buytendijk are: a lack of motor and mental coherence or coordination, an inability to delay or detour, a need to achieve sympathetic understanding (what he has called a "pathic" attitude) as opposed to objective knowledge, and an ambivalence toward all objects, especially strange ones. Thus, play is an expression of the child's uncoordinated approach to the environment; it allows a pathic understanding of the environment and achieves immediate ends. But play is also ambivalent and reflects only a temporarily prepotent approach tendency to objects. Play for Buytendijk is rhythmic, reflecting the relaxation phase of a tension-relaxation cycle. Finally, Buytendijk's infantile dynamics theory asserts that children (as well as animals) *"play"* only with images, which constitute the actual expression of the child's pathic understanding. Within the framework of the infantile dynamics theory, play is the child's way of thinking. In these last theories of play the explanation of our definitional example of play would be that it represents a straightforward working outcome of the "forces" identified in the theories. Thus, the play of "making-the-cloth-sleep" is the symbolic way children come to comprehend the act of going to sleep, when they try to think about such a thing. Piaget's theory would offer a generally similar explanation for such play behavior.

Piaget's Theory of Play

Piaget's theory of play goes a good deal beyond that of Buytendijk. While Piaget sees play as the inevitable result of the child's cognitive structure, he has formulated the problem more precisely. "Play is but a part of the whole infantile dynamics, and although we agree that it derives from them, the question to be answered is in what conditions it does so, and why it does not always do so" (1945, p. 160).[1]

Speaking generally, Piaget sees play as the product of a stage of thinking, through which the child must pass in developing from an original egocentric and phenomenalistic viewpoint to an adult's objective and rationalistic outlook. More specifically, in situations in which the person has any basis for behaving, every human encounter with the environment has two discriminable aspects that are central to Piaget's general theory of behavior. On the one hand, a person recognizes, categorizes, and utilizes events in terms of previous habits, conventions, and preferences. He bends reality to fit what he "knows." On the other hand, a person notes unique aspects of a new encounter and takes account of these in an effort to change, modify, or in some way adjust himself to better fit the new reality. These two aspects of behavior are always fused and always present. One aspect can *predominate* over the other, however, and distinguishing them at the theoretical level is crucial for Piaget's theory of behavior and play. Piaget implies that these two aspects of behavior spring from different sources, appear at different times, and develop at different rates. It is this fact of cognitive dynamics that is said to lead us to see so much play in children.

[1] Piaget's entire discussion of his theory of play is contained in his book *Play, Dreams and Imitation in Childhood*. This book is quite difficult to read or to interpret without prior grounding in Piaget's more general theory of behavior, as put forward in his many other works. Since these other works are not directly relevant to Piaget's theory of play, however, only the 1945 work has been cited in this paper. For the interested reader, an excellent introduction to Piaget has been written by J. H. Flavell and published by Van Nostrand: *The Developmental Psychology of Jean Piaget* (1962).

Play, for Piaget, is all behavior in which the aspect of adjustment to fit reality (that is, the aspect of mental accommodation to things as they really are) is deemphasized. Play occurs insofar as behavior is purely one of "taking in," of bending reality to fit one's existing forms of thought. Since this is an aspect of all behavior, every behavior has at least some play-like aspects. One can't speak of play versus non-play in the Piagetian schema of things; behaviors are only less or more playful insofar as they do or do not make some attempt to cope with reality.

Piaget has distinguished three broad categories of play. Early in a child's life any newly mastered motor ability will be performed over and over in different contexts. All objects that the infant encounters are bent to fit this new behavior pattern regardless of their suitability. No new learning takes place during such behavior, and there is every evidence of pleasure from the child. This is an example of what Piaget has distinguished as practice play. The definitional play example of making the rag "go to sleep," which was taken as the model for this paper, is an example of what Piaget has distinguished as symbolic play. The rag is treated as if it were alive, and it is played with so as to symbolize what is salient for the child in the concept of going to sleep. Piaget distinguishes a third major category of play that he has termed "games with rules." This type of play develops latest in children, and is exactly what its title suggests.

3 types

① Practice Play

② Symbolic Play

③ games c̄ rules

Piaget has said that play is seen insofar as thoughts and objects are bent to fit existing concepts or thought patterns while some obvious and logical aspects of things are ignored, or deemphasized. This is precisely what occurs in dreaming, and Piaget sees a close link between the play of children and the dreaming process. Just why we revert to a play-like mode of thought in sleep is not a matter that Piaget's theory has undertaken to explain. Instead, *the process is accepted as a given,* and Piaget is content to describe and label the important aspects of this process.

In the same way, Piaget has described how the traditional play of childhood comes about. As a newborn, a human has only the most rudimentary reflex abilities to recognize and incorporate his experiences, or to make allowances for any unique aspects of his experiences. (And these, remember, are the two functions with which Piaget's theory always deals.) Piaget postulates, however, a tendency in all living organisms to make repeated contact with any slightly novel event; and in the newborn, this tendency "forces" new awareness, new habits, new expectations, and new distinctions regarding the environment as a whole. There is, then, an increase in the modes of response to the environment, and the two functions with which piaget deals become more discriminable, each from the other. The infant gradually becomes able to act by habit and to ignore the now reduced number of unique components to a given experience.

Thus, as the infant becomes able to behave in a play-like fashion, that is, without regard to any but the familiar and habitual aspects of the situation, this very potential for play begins to be immediately realized. The play potential is realized for the same sorts of reasons that a coin tossed many times will realize its potential for showing some "heads." It is the nature of the child that his cognitive structure will lead to play.

Why then does play drop out as the child grows up? Piaget suggests there are two answers. First, as we have noted, adults can and do show some play-like behavior, as for instance in dream life. But they also do so, to varying degrees, in many other areas. Doodling is an example of one of the *most* play-like adult behaviors. Thus, one answer is that play doesn't drop out, it remains in certain new areas of adult experience and in "unconscious" behaviors. A second answer as to why play drops out seems to be that as the child has more experiences, he can more easily respond to things as they are, rather than to things only insofar as he has known them. Put another way, the child acquires new possibilities for inventing improved, more rational, modes of handling encounters with the unfamiliar environment. With the development of this ability, then, the tendency to resort to actions that are only partially appropriate to a situation (play behavior) is reduced. Eventually, with adult mastery of the environment, the person has a greatly reduced "need" to resort to bending reality to fit his state of the moment.

To summarize Piaget's position so far, play is the behavior seen whenever there is a preponderance of that aspect of all behavior that involves taking in, molding, and using things, all in terms of one's current inclination and habit, without deference to any aspects of so behaving that might not "fit" in some sense. Play *can* occur only insofar as behaviors are sophisticated enough to show differentiation between (a) the taking-in aspect of behavior that bends reality to fit the self and (b) the self-modifying aspects of behavior that bend the self to fit reality. Play *can* occur only insofar as there are many different modes of thought and action into which reality may be bent. Thus it is that the newborn shows no play, and that until middle childhood more and more play is seen. Finally, play *will not* occur insofar as more adaptive responses become familiar and can be easily invented when needed. Thus it is that play is reduced in prominence in late childhood.

Piaget's theory calls for a sharp distinction between the causes of play and its effects. It is to the latter that we next turn. There are two important by-products of play behavior according to the Piagetian formulation. The first such by-product is joy, pleasure, or some closely related affective state. This is clearest in the earliest "practice play" behavior of children. The infant of eight months will repeat a movement that shakes a rattle over and over again, while showing the most obvious signs of delight. For Piaget, play brings with it "the functional pleasure of use." At older ages the pleasure seen in play is primarily one of efficacy (see White, 1959); that is, it is the less visible pleasure of self-assertion. Yet as the child grows older and his play becomes more symbolic, the pleasure attendant on play becomes less obvious. Even so, pleasure is one of Piaget's implicit criteria of play behavior, and the absence of pleasure from what might otherwise be considered play behavior suggests that a reality-based attempt to learn may be prominent in such behavior.

The second by-product of play, within the framework of Piaget's theory, is an adaptive one. Play is seen as functioning in such a way that it prevents new abilities, both physical and mental, from being lost due to disuse. Play fixes and retains the new abilities since it is just such abilities that are likely to be getting the most attention when "reality" is getting very little. Thus, on the basis of Piaget's theory, if play behavior were to be prevented somehow—a difficult thing since the sources of play are presumed to be internal—then many fewer abilities and concepts would remain available to the child. (As it stands, however, Piaget's theory would not preclude the possibility of reforming all abilities that were once available.) It can be seen that an understanding of play behavior may well have important implications for the education of all young children.

On the basis of his theory of play and his more general theory of cognitive development, Piaget has developed a system for categorizing various types of play behavior. We shall not explore this system here, except to note that Piaget has set aside two categories to identify play that, in addition to the typical by-products already noted, serves to reduce an unpleasantness for the child. The first such category of play has been termed *compensatory combinations,* and it refers to behavior that "improves" reality by distorting it to fit more agreeable and desired thoughts. For example, Piaget's daughter pretended to be carrying her newborn cousin after being told that she must not touch the baby. The second such category of play Piaget has termed *liquidating combinations,* and it refers to behavior that has been freed from a need to allow for the presence of strong affect that, originally, came connected with the play-provoking situation. For example, having been frightened by the sight of a dead duck, Piaget's daughter later played at imitating the motionless bird and made her dolls "see" a dead duck without fear. In setting aside these two special categories of play, Piaget has recognized a possible source of play that is taken as the core for what we shall term the *cathartic theory* of play, of which the *psychoanalytic theory* of play is the most recent and most lucid variant.

The Cathartic and Psychoanalytic Theories of Play

The cathartic theory of play has roots that extend as far back as the writings of Aristotle (see Mitchel & Mason, 1934). Briefly, the cathartic theory sees play as reflecting the child's attempt to master situations that at first were too much for him. Carr (1902) was among the earliest to put forward this theory of play. Groos (1908b) extended his preexercise theory of play somewhat to include a cathartic aspect. Reaney (1916), Robinson (1920), and Curti (1930), all have elaborated variations on the cathartic theory of play.

The *psychoanalytic theory* of play is a special case of the more general cathartic theory. The psychoanalytic play theory was first introduced by Freud (1908, 1920, 1926) incidental to considerations of phantasy and repetition behaviors. Freud thought of play as being closely related to phantasy behavior; in fact he defined play as phantasy woven around real objects (toys), as contrasted with pure phantasy, which is daydreaming. Play, for Freud, shares many of the unconscious determinants that shape dream life, and in his respect Freud's theory of play is similar to that of Piaget.

Freud distinguished two classes of wishes, either of which he considered to be a necessary source of play. First, there are the wishes a child has to be big, grownup, or in the shoes of someone more fortunate. Thus, in accordance with an inherited tendency to seek immediate pleasure, even if this pleasure must be in part hallucinated, the child phantasies some situation he would like to see exist. Second, the child can be driven into play by his wishes to take the active role in all painful encounters that have been passively suffered. Play arising from this source does so in accordance with an inherited tendency to repeat, over and over, any experience that has been too much for the child. Thus, Erikson has observed:

[Individual child play] often proves to be the infantile way of thinking over difficult experiences and of *restoring a sense of mastery,* comparable to the way in which we repeat, in ruminations and in endless talk, in daydreams and in dreams during sleep, experiences which have been too much for us (1959, p. 85).

In the psychoanalytic theory of play "a sense of mastery" is the most typically cited *effect* of play. It is important to note, however, that this mastery feeling is necessarily restricted to play that serves to reverse a previous painful experience. Play that is purely wish fulfillment will have as its effect the feeling of "pleasure" that is presumed to be inherent in all reductions of psychic tension according to psychoanalytic theory. Play that springs from wishes can have the effect not only of a circumvention of reality, but, as Waelder (1932) has pointed out, play can also circumvent the action of the superego. In play one can presumably achieve the physically or the morally impossible.

More recently there have been some important refinements of, and additions to, the more general psychoanalytic theory of play described so far. Anna Freud (1936) has pointed out that one effect of imitative play, in those cases where the imitated object is feared, is a lessening and binding of the fear either of the object or of what the object may represent for the child. Thus, play may serve not only to lower anxiety around a given context through promotion of active coping devices, but it may serve a *defensive* purpose as well by denying any grounds for anxiety. The exact formula under which imitative play may accomplish any defensive ends has not been suggested. One could speculate, however, that it does so under the magic formula: "Since the object and I are so alike, it will fear me just as I fear it; it will also love me just as I love me, and it will not surprise me by anything it may do, for I would be likely to do similar things myself."

Erikson (1937, 1940, 1950, 1951, 1959) is well known for his recent contributions to a psychoanalytic theory of play. While agreeing with Freud regarding the major sources of play, Erikson has emphasized the coping effects of play. He has said: "I propose the theory that the child's play is the infantile form of the human ability to deal with experience by creating model situations and to master reality by experiment and planning" (1950, p. 195). Perhaps more important has been Erikson's contribution of the concept of play disruption. Not only does anxiety lead to play of a relevant nature, suggests Erikson, but play can get out of hand, as it were, thus mobilizing the very anxiety with which it is trying to deal. The result is an abrupt stop in play behavior. Says Erikson: "The human animal not only plays most and longest, it also remains ready to become deadly serious in the most irrational contexts" (1940, p. 562). In addition to Erikson, a number of psychoanalytic theorists have put forward their own elaborations of the theory of play introduced by Freud. Among the most notable are Klein (1929), Peller (1954), and Alexander (1958).

With this background on the cathartic theories of play, consider how they would account for the making-the-rag-go-to-sleep play of our working example: There is a certain degree of psychic pain caused the young child when he is told to go to sleep, for the child wishes both to comply and to remain awake. Further, the child does not want to feel he must submit to adult demands. Thus, the sleep play of our example occurs as a cathartic, wish-impelled response to this lingering psychic pain. It is regrettable that the precise manner in which psychic conflict produces play behavior is not spelled out in any of the cathartic theories. While the implication that play occurs as a response instrumental to the reduction of psychic pain is always strong, the cathartic theories of play have never quite made the full distinction that pain reduction as an *effect* of play does not demonstrate that pain is necessarily a *cause* of play behavior.

On Evaluating the Infantile Dynamics Theories of Play

The psychoanalytic theory of play and Piaget's theory of play are well developed and explicit, but, curiously enough, these theories, too, have led to little, if any, research. Both theories are based on close and careful observation, yet neither has led to an experimental assessment. A search of the play literature reveals that the two great areas in which play has been studied are those of (a) cataloguing the leisure activity of children according to their location along many different dimensions, and (b) observing the doll "play" of different children for components of various behaviors, especially aggression.

A comprehensive summary of all but the recent studies of play preferences can be found in Britt and Janus (1941). This research is of tangential relevance to the theories under consideration, however, and much of it suffers from a variety of limiting problems in design. More relevant is the research with doll play, a literature that has been summarized by Levin and Wardwell (1962). Doll play assessment derives from psychoanalytic theory; it proceeds on the assumption of the validity of psychoanalytic hypotheses. Thus, while doll play research has provided certain observational data that generally can be interpreted as supporting the psychoanalytic theory of play, such research is not free from its own assumptions and is not directed specifically toward testing the psychoanalytic theory of play. There is nothing unscientific about the study of play or about the testing of play theories, yet to date only the author (Gilmore, 1964) seems to have a relevant test of the infantile dynamics play theories of Piaget and psychoanalysis.

On the basis of Piaget's general theory of play, especially on the basis of his comments regarding the role of novelty in predisposing play and regarding pleasure as an accompaniment (albeit a presumed effect) of play, Gilmore hypothesized that children would prefer to play with toys that were somewhat novel for them, as opposed to simple toys. It was further hypothesized that anxious children would prefer to play with novel toys over simple toys less than would non-anxious children, but would prefer to play with toys relevant to the source of their anxiety (as opposed to irrelevant toys) more than would non-anxious children. Three studies were conducted to check these hypotheses.

The first study, observational in design, employed children hospital-ized for tonsillectomy as "anxious" subjects. Matched control subjects, ranging in age from five years through eight years, were seen in their school. All subjects were presented with toys representing dimensions of (a) novelty (or complexity) and (b) relevance and irrelevance to hospital-ization. The primary measure of play was the time each subject spent touching the toys. The results of this study strongly supported the hypothesis that anxious children prefer anxiety-relevant toys more than do non-anxious children. All children preferred novel toys, however, and there was no evidence to support the hypothesis that nonanxious children would prefer novel toys more than would anxious children. The first study admitted to two important possibilities, however. Children who came for tonsillectomy may still have been different than their matched control counterparts, thus determining their preference for hospital-relevant toys. And it may have been the *interest* of the hospital routine that led to hospital play, without the children's obvious anxiety having been in any way causal. A second, experimental study was done to con-trol these possibilities.

In the second study, then, children were randomly assigned to an anxious or non-anxious condition. Subjects volunteered to join a club and expected some sort of initiation, possibly painful, involving the eyes or the ears. Anxious subjects were further divided, on a random basis, into two groups, those expecting auditory and those expecting visual pain. The remaining group, of nonanxious subjects, was told there would be no painful initiation. Play materials were presented twice to every sub-ject, before and after "the initiation." The toys represented both (a) novel or simple and (b) auditory- or visual-relevant dimensions. Thus, toys which were anxiety-relevant for half the anxious subjects were the anxiety-irrelevant toys for the remaining half of the anxious subjects, and vice versa. Time spent with the toys again served as the measure of play. The "initiation" assessed the fear level of each subject, and results from this measure gave excellent evidence that the anxiety manipulations were effective as intended.

In this experimental, second study, results for the auditory fear group gave further support to the hypothesis that anxious children prefer anxiety-relevant toys over anxiety-irrelevant toys. It was suggested that a ceiling effect may have prevented similar results from appearing in the visual fear group since even when not anxious, all subjects preferred the visual toys. Again, no evidence was found to support the hypothesis that anxious children will prefer novel toys less than will nonanxious chil-dren. Novel toys were heavily preferred to simple toys by all subjects.

A third study was done to check on the stability of the auditory fear data in view of the absence of similar findings in the visual fear condition.

In this third study, an auditory fear group and a nonanxious control group were created exactly as in the previous study. Further, a new, non-anxious "auditory control" group was set up in which subjects expected an enjoyable auditory "initiation." This new group served to control completely for any possibility that the *salience* of the forthcoming auditory experience might be producing the auditory-toy play instead of the anxiety generated by the expectation. As in the second study, results showed that the anxiety manipulations worked as intended. Further, both the standard control subjects and the new auditory control subjects showed play preferences mirroring those of the previous control group. Thus, the salience of the expected auditory initiation does not seem to account for the findings of these studies. However, the new auditory fear subjects showed a significant *avoidance* of anxiety-relevant toys when they were anxious.

The findings of this third study were just opposite to the findings of the previous study, and they did not support the hypothesis derived from the psychoanalytic theory of play. There was no noticeable difference between the schools or subjects in these last two studies on the basis of which to explain the dramatic shift in observed play under conditions of anxiety. There was, however, a suggestion that the anxious subjects in this third study were more afraid than were the previous anxious subjects. Recalling Erikson's description of play disruption when anxiety becomes too great, it might be postulated that unusually anxious subjects in this third study found the anxiety-relevant toys too frightening to play with.

Two conclusions seem warranted from these three studies viewed as a whole. First, toy novelty or simplicity does not interact appreciably with a child's anxious state to produce changes in toy preferences. All children seem to prefer novel (or complex) toys over "simple" toys. Thus, the data from these studies fit the Piagetian theory of play without, at the same time, providing great support for it. Secondly, one can conclude that the presence of anxiety changes a child's preferences for toys relevant to his anxiety, but this change can be an increased or decreased preference, depending upon as yet unspecified additional factors. Thus, the psychoanalytic theory of play received some tentative support from the data of these studies, especially if that play theory is expanded to include play-avoiding behavior under conditions of heightened anxiety.

The studies just described constitute only the beginning of what will certainly have to be a great many experiments probing the causes and effects of play. Play is a special behavior, one that will be difficult to explore for many initially unsuspected reasons. The very ambiguity of the term "play," the uncertainty as to just how different behaviors may be to still qualify as "play," will constantly work to divide and confuse all who do not first consider and communicate their personal definitions of the term. And if research on theories of play is to be carried out, a satisfactory dependent measure of play will have to be devised. Gilmore (1964) used as his play criterion the touching of toys, but this measure has obvious limits. These are only the first of the problems that research in play will meet.

If research on play is scarce and difficult to do, it cannot also be said that theories of play are either scarce or untestable. A great deal of theoretical attention has been paid to play behavior. A great many hypotheses stand ready to be investigated on the basis of the theories of play. The question remains: Why will a young child take a piece of cloth and "make it go to sleep?"

21

Piaget on Play: A Critique

Brian Sutton-Smith[1]

It is contended that Piaget's attempt to reduce play to a function of thought is vitiated by his concern with a restricted class of intellectual operations and by his copyist epistemology. By resting the origin of representation on a copyist notion of imitation and by permitting play only the function of replicating concepts, Piaget deprives play of any genuinely constitutive role within thought. The contradictory consequences both in terms of the evidence about play's ontogenesis and Piaget's ultimate resort to more characteristic affective and conative explanations are discussed.

Piaget's (1951) *Play, Dreams and Imitation in Childhood* is the most recent of many attempts to make sense out of the theoretically anomalous subject matter of play. With the possible exception of psychoanalytic play theory, it is the most conceptually elaborate account of play yet to be presented and, in addition, includes the best available examples of the sequence of play activities in the first years of life. It is intention of this paper to argue that Piaget's thesis, to the effect that play may be interpreted functionally as an activity subordinated to adaptive intelligence,

SOURCE. Republished from the *Psychological Review*, 1966, Vol. 73, No. 1, 104–110, with permission of the American Psychological Association.

[1] This paper owes much to the stimulation of a visiting associate professorship in the Psychology Department and the Heinz Werner Institute of Developmental Psychology at Clark University, 1963–64. I am particularly indebted to Joseph Glick of Yale University and Bernard Kaplan of Clark University for their comments and suggestions.

leads to contradictions within his own system. The present analysis will maintain that Piaget's epistemological assumptions and his concern with directed thought lie at the base of his misconstrual of play.

Piaget's Epistemological Assumptions

Piaget's treatment of play is inseparable from his theorizing on intelligence. His root metaphor for the origins of intelligence in human beings is the process of biological adaptation in lower organisms. He is said to have been impressed in his earlier studies of mollusks by the way in which these lower organisms, while accommodating to the environment, also actively assimilated it in accord with their own schemas of action.

An image of an active organism which both selects and incorporates stimuli in a manner determined by its structure, while at the same time adapting its structure to the stimuli, emerged from these early studies as a ready made model for cognitive development [Flavell, 1963, p. 36].

The concepts of assimilation and accommodation which were said to be applicable to lower organisms were also claimed to have applicability to the "intelligent" activities of higher organisms. These two became the indissociable functional invariants in Piaget's conceptual system for the description of intelligence:

Accommodation of mental structure to reality implies the existence of assimilatory schemata apart from which any structures would be impossible. Inversely, the formation of schemata through assimilation entails the utilization of external realities to which the former must accommodate . . . [1954, pp. 352–353].

Having made assimilation and accomodation ultimate categories of adaptive intelligence, Piaget sought to express other (related) functions in these same terms. Imitation and play came to be formulated as particular types of relationships between accomodation and assimilation. When accommodation to external reality dominated over assimilation, there existed the state which Piaget termed imitation. Alternatively, if assimilation of external reality to preexisting concepts occurred, then there was the state to which the term play was given. Imitation and play were said to be polarized examples of the activity of intelligence: "Intelligent adaptation, imitation and play are thus three possibilities and they result according as there is a stable equilibrium between assimilation and accommodation or primacy of one of these two tendencies over the other [1951, p. 86]." From this description it follows that imitation and play should be explicable in terms of the same processes that determine adaptive or intellective functioning. Leaving aside whether Piaget has shown

that imitation is explicable in terms of his categories of adaptive functioning, it will be argued that his attempt to treat play within these categories
is inadequate.

The Asymmetry of Imitation and Play

There are Hegelian overtones in Piaget's view that imitation and play are
dialectical opposites which are gradually reconciled in a higher synthesis
as the adaptive intellectual structures of logic progressively succeed them.
But closer examination of the respective roles of these two functions
within his system suggests that imitation and play are not related as
equipotent thesis and antithesis. Piaget verges, it is true, on the suggestion
that in the origin of representative thought, imitation supplies the images
and play supplies the symbols, But this antiphonal relationship is alluded
to ambiguously [1951, p. 3; 1960, p. 126], and, for the greater part, only
imitation is given a key role in the origin of concepts. Imitation is said
to be a source of representation, but play is used largely as an *illustration*
of what representation is like.

Piaget has criticized some of his predecessors, among other things, for
their copy theory of knowledge or their naïve realism. He has insisted that
representative thinking is not merely a copy of external reality, but is
rather the outcome of a long process of interaction between the organism
and the environment with each modifying the other over time. As indicated above, he has stated this interaction in terms of the concepts of
assimilation and accommodation. It is very clear from the corpus of his
writings that he does not favor a copyist epistemology. Paradoxically
enough, however, when the relationships between imitation and play are
examined closely, the view emerges that Piaget has implicitly imported
just such a copy theory into his own explanation of the processes of imitation, and that it is this implicit copyist notion of imitation which
ultimately leaves play intellectually functionless within his system. To
illustrate: The process of accommodation is portrayed as establishing for
the subject a photographic-like negative of external reality. Imitation is
said to be an extension of such negatives into positive action. "The function of imitation seems to be to produce this set of 'positives,' which cor-
respond to the 'negatives' of accommodation and which, at each new
'printing,' make new reconstitutions and anticipations possible [1951,
p. 84]." In due course, it is said, these imitations become interiorized as
images, and then, later, when these images become attached to, and differentiated from, external symbols during intelligent activity or during

play, they are transformed into concepts. It follows that sustaining and initiating this whole process of representative activity are the encapsulated photographic negatives which occur during accommodation. It may be true to say, as Piaget does, that this accommodation is "an *active* copy and not a trace or a sensory residue of perceived objects [1960, p. 126; italics mine]," but accommodation is nonetheless conceived as a *copy* and given the initiating and sustaining role in his formulation of representative activity.

Now it is conceivable that Piaget intends to say that, when the interiorized images become attached to symbols in adaptive intelligent activity, this process of attachment changes the interiorized images. But whether or not this is the case, and this is not relevant here, it is certainly true that in Piaget's systematic accounts of play such an attachment of symbols is not said to bring about any such change in images. Piaget's definition of play as predomination of assimilation over accommodation specifically precludes any such change. Instead the encapsulated images derived from accommodation determine the character of the activity. Play merely diversifies the symbols. As "reproductive assimilation," or "assimilation of reality to the ego," play can merely repeat; it can never originate. We thus have a situation in which the symbols of play are merely the reproductions of images preestablished through the copyist activity of imitation following accommodation. On this interpretation then, imitation is an essential factor in the constitution of representative activity, whereas play is not. It has no essential role in the structure of intellect as conceived by Piaget. Intelligence cannot proceed without imitation. It can proceed without play. It is hardly necessary to emphasize that there are alternative points of view which grant to the processes of symbol formation a more active role in the constitution of thought than this copyist theory of Piaget's seems to imply (Werner & Kaplan, 1963). Greater internal cogency is given to the present critique, however, by showing that this implicit copyist notion of the origin of concepts leads to peculiarities within the system itself which are neither selfconsistent nor consistent with the known data concerning play.

The Disjunction of Cognitive and Affective Functions

Having deprived play of an active, intellective role in the constitution of new concepts, Piaget is forced into a series of substitute explanations. Unlike imitation which has the one definition, play is provided with a variety of definitions. At times it is referred to as "reproductive assimilation" (1951, p. 87), as "generalizing assimilation" (1951, p. 100), but also as "pure assimilation" (1951, p. 87), "mere assimilation" (1951, p. 89), and "distorting assimilation" (1951, p. 102). The latter three terms do not occupy any systematic status within Piaget's theory of intelligence as do the first two. They are never defined, and it is not entirely clear just what they can mean. It is this lack of a functional role for play within the structure of intelligence which apparently forces Piaget to find alternative nonintellective functional explanations for play, which he does not have to provide for imitation. It is said, for example, that play exists in childhood because thought is not adequate to its tasks:

The prevalence of play among children is therefore to be explained not by specific causes peculiar to the realm of play, but by the fact that the characteristics of all behaviors and all thought are less in equilibrium in the early stages of mental development than in the adult stage [1951, p. 147].

But why is there assimilation of reality to the ego instead of immediate assimilation of the universe to experience and logical thought? It is simply because in early childhood this thought has not yet been constructed, and during its development it is inadequate to supply the needs of daily life [1951, p. 166].

These quotations make it clear that play is not considered as making any intrinsic contribution to thought, but is instead some sort of compensation for thought's inadequacy. This interpretation is made explicit when Piaget says that the function of play is to serve ego continuity. "It follows that for the child assimilation of reality to the ego is a vital condition for continuity and development precisely because of the lack of equilibrium of this thought, and symbolic play satisfies this condition both as regard to signifier and signified [1951, p. 166]." But, surely, it is difficult to maintain that play is merely a polarity of thought, that the "prevalence of play . . . is therefore to be explained not by . . . causes peculiar to the realm of play," and then to invoke this concept of ego continuity which is not a concept intrinsic to Piaget's account of the nature of intelligence. This invocation of "ego continuity" does, in fact, suggest that play has some other function to serve which is quite distinct from thought. The notion of ego continuity as the function of play bears close resemblance to the concept of ego mastery as presented in psychoanalytic accounts, particularly that of Erikson (1950). But to rest play's positive contribution on such grounds is to lead to a disjunction of cognitive and affective functions, quite inconsistent with Piaget's own repeated stress that the two are not separable. If play has a constitutive affective function of this sort (ensuring ego continuity), Piaget's general position of affective-cognitive relations requires that it should also have a constitutive intellective function.

The Disjunction of Directed and Undirected Thinking

It would be wrong to imply that Piaget's particular treatment of play stems perhaps from an accident in his epistemology. The approach is more deepseated than that for there is a consistency between his account of infant thought and his account of adult thought. It has been shown that in his treatment of infant thought he gives an initiating role to images which derive from accommodation to external reality. In adult thought also he is concerned with those coherent formal structures of intellect that have to do with accommodation to and control over the external world. In particular he is concerned with the correspondence between "the structures described by logic and the actual thought processes studied by psychology [1957, p. xvii]." He is not concerned with those less directed aspects of adult thought usually referred to by such terms as reverie, creative imagination, or divergent thinking. Yet in the opinion of some, the latter have a great deal to do with novel forms of adaptation. It would not be farfetched to speculate, in fact, that if there is an intrinsic relationship between play and thought, it is more likely to be with these latter forms of divergent intellectual operations than with the directed forms which concern Piaget.

Piaget's formulation of adult thought has a number of consequences which are consistent with the epistemological orientation already outlined. For example, his view that the thinking of the young child is relatively disequilibrial is again similar to the empirical view which says that since thought copies reality, young children who are inexperienced will have more imperfect copies than older persons. Of course, stated in Piaget's terms, the young organism plays a more active role in acquiring its copies than was the case in the traditional empirical view, and unlike that view there is a telic quality to Piaget's formulation of the young child's operations. They appear to be "successive approximations to a kind of ideal equilibrium or end state never completely achieved [Flavell, 1963, p. 47]." The difficulty with this approach for Piaget's own point of view is that it is not consistent with his stage theory which says that each stage of thinking has a characteristic organization and completeness of its own. It is difficult to see how there can be both "equilibration" of early stages and the view that these early stages are relatively less in equilibrium than later stages. The problem can be located in the different usages of the term "equilibrium" which Piaget employs both to refer to characteristics of intellectual organization at one time or stage and to refer to the ontogenetic status of the organism in general. Apart from the semantic confusion in having such entities as "disequilibrial equilibriums," either stage or ontogenetic usage leads to difficulties with respect to the definition of play as a polarity of thought.

If it is said that when an intellectual structure is disrupted by intractable data the lack of intellectual resources in childhood (the disequilibrial ontogenetic state) leads to the use of play as an affective holding action, this is again to give play no genuine cognitive function. Yet, if it said that play is a true polarity of thought in the sense of reestablishing equilibrium through genuinely cognitive means at any one stage (the implied stage theory), this is equally unfortunate for the theory as it stands. If, for example, some divergent thinking function is attributed to the "distorting assimilations" of play, this requires a reconsideration of the role of divergent thinking not only in children's thinking but also in the development of adult thinking. If play does not simply "distort" old concepts, whatever such a phrase can mean, but also originates new concepts, then the whole account of the genesis of intellectual structures from childhood through adulthood has to be changed.

Piaget appears to have chosen rather to make a disjunction between the operations of thought in adulthood and the operations of thought in childhood, in addition to the formal differences between sensory-motor, concrete, and abstract operations which are already a part of his theory. Thus it is said that childhood thinking is bolstered by the affective operations of play, but the thinking of adults is not. From Piaget's viewpoint as undirected thinking, fantasy, play, etc., are specifically childlike and mainly compensatory, that is, having nothing to do with the development of particular kinds of intellectual operations, they may be confined to the infantile stage and regarded as irrelevant to the nature of adult intellectual operations.

The Ontogenesis of Play

It is legitimate to ask whether the evidence on play supports Piaget's point of view. His view that play is merely a buttress to an inadequate intelligence leads to the corollary that as that intelligence increases in efficiency and adequacy, play will cease to be important in the development of the mind. In Piaget's unilinear account of the ontogenesis of intellectual structures, play has such a transient position. Thus it is said that from about the age of 4 years onwards symbolic games decline because the child becomes capable of greater adaptive activity and is more realistic: ". . . progress in socialization instead of leading to an increase in symbolism transforms it more or less rapidly into an objective imitation of reality [1951, p. 139]." "Rule games . . . mark the decline of children's games and the transition to adult play, which ceases to be a vital function of the mind when the individual is socialized [1951, p. 168]." On the basis of the evidence about play several objections can be raised to the view that the symbolic games of childhood are simply replaced by more realism with age, and that play which is "vital" in childhood ceases to be vital in adulthood. In general it can be maintained with equal cogency that, rather than a decrease in the symbolic play function with age, what we actually find is a shift in the applications and the differentiation of this function. First, the early rule games of children continue to be heavily loaded with symbolic elements which play a part in determining outcomes equal in importance to skill. In the host of singing games of young girls, for example, it is the one who is arbitrarily chosen as Punchinello or as Farmer-in-the-Dell who determines the outcome. Similarly, in the great group of central-person games of early childhood which model the family drama, it is the player chosen by the arbitrary counting-out processes or the player with the role vestments of Caesar or Red Rover who decides by fiat when the game will start, when the players will run, etc. (Sutton-Smith, 1959). Here the play symbolism has been collectivized, but it has hardly been decreased, or given way to greater realism. In Piaget's (1932) treatment of games he was concerned with a game (marbles) in which the symbolism was much less pronounced, marbles being more age appropriate at the end of early childhood, around 9–10 years, whereas these other games just mentioned tend to flourish from 7 through 9 years. Furthermore, in that treatise, play at games was used to illustrate moral and social development rather than to provide the basis for an understanding of the play function. In a sense, Piaget (1932) first uses games to illustrate the development of morality, while he later (1951) uses play to illustrate the development of thought. Neither time does he deal systematically with the peculiar functions of games or play in human development. Perhaps it is this tendentiousness of approach that leads Piaget to discount the continuing influence of play in psychological development. Even when children's games are mainly matters of physical or intellectual skill, as from 10 years onwards, however, it is difficult to accept Piaget's view that this is simply a matter of play being converted from a symbolic to a realistic application. The total game performance still remains basically a symbolic procedure. There is, after all, little that is precisely rational about a game of football or a game of basketball. In fact, there is support for the point of view that such sports are best conceived as modern ritualized dramas of success and failure (Sutton-Smith, Roberts, & Kozelka, 1963) and as such have little that is either rational or real about them. Furthermore, it is the thesis of Huizinga (1949) that play (if not sport) does continue to be a vital function of mind even in socialized adults and that it permeates all their vital activities including those of a cultural sort and those of an economic and political nature. Recent cross-cultural work showing the full implication of games in culture would appear to substantiate this view (Roberts, Arth, & Bush, 1959; Roberts & Sutton-Smith, 1962; Sutton-Smith & Roberts, 1964). Though preschool egocentric symbolic play may decrease with age, play nevertheless finds expression in the midst of a variety of other cultural and social forms. It is thus not displaced by realism or by greater rationality, nor does it cease to be a vital function with age. Instead it becomes more differentiated and more representative in its contents of the other forms of human development. Without such a point of view it is difficult to understand the verbal play of adults, their social and sexual play, their rituals and their carnivals, their festivals and fairs, and their widespread and diversified playfulness.

This present criticism of Piaget's view of play as a transient, infantile stage in the emergence of thought parallels Vygotsky's (1962) criticism of Piaget's notion of egocentric speech as a transient, infantile stage in the emergence of socialized speech. Vygotsky maintained that in the course of ontogeny egocentric speech does not give way to socialized speech, but becomes transformed into inner speech which may itself be differentiated according to autistic or logical ends. Similarly, it has been maintained here that children's play does not give way to intelligent adaptation, but becomes differentiated in a variety of ways. The difference between Vygotsky's criticism and the present one, however, hinges on the fact that both Piaget and Vygotsky are talking about the ontogenesis of the same function—speech—whereas here two functions are involved, intelligence and play, which Piaget attempts to amalgamate into a single function (intelligence) and an aborted variant (play). It should be noted in conclusion that Piaget's various earlier treatments of undirected thinking in children, their animism, artificialism, etc., as transient, infantile stages in development are susceptible to similar criticism (Piaget, 1928, 1929, 1930).

Conclusion

It has been contended that Piaget's major concern with directed rather than undirected intellectual operations together with his implicit copyist epistemology have made it impossible for him to deal consistently with play. He has attempted to make it a function of thought without giving it any intellective function within thought. And he has been unable to give it such a function within thought because in his epistemology concepts are ultimately copies derived from an appropriate to an external reality. As play does not copy but "distorts" reality, it can have no intrinsic place in such an epistemology. As a result, Piaget is forced finally to explain play in terms of the type of affective and conative functions that are familiar in other play theories. (This is not to imply that there are not parallels between cognitive operations and play contents at given ages. It is the virtue of Piaget's observations that in this respect they complement those of psychoanalysts and sociologists which tend to be highly selective in terms of play content reflecting their own characteristic theoretical orientations. But the existence of such parallels between the operations of thought and the structures of play conveys nothing in itself about the function of play.)

While it has not been the purpose of this paper to propose any alternative theoretical approach to play or to criticize Piaget's play theory from alternative points of view, a brief mention of an alternative epistemology and the quite different approach to play which it entails may serve to highlight the legitimacy of the present criticism in epistemological terms. Ernst Cassirer (1953) explicitly opposes the view that concepts are copies of external reality. They are rather modes through which reality is constructed on a level transcending the simple sign functioning of lower organisms. From an epistemologically constructivist viewpoint of this sort play might well be taken as a very positive illustration of the thinking process because it involves the construction of symbols to create new conceptual domains. Though from Cassirer's point of view, play would have to be just one of many such symbolic modes with its own characteristic properties, others being art, myth, science, etc., for Cassirer's point of view with respect to symbolic development is not only constructionist, it is also multilinear. Piaget with his contrasting copyist assumption and his unilinear notion of thought is forced to reduce all forms of symbolic activity to the single copyist form of adaptive thought. And on the evidence of the internal inconsistencies to which this leads, his approach does not appear to have been fruitful for the explanation of play.

The present criticism of Piaget's theoretical system which focuses on the inadequacy of his epistemology when applied to play probably has relevance for the interpretation of divergent-thinking activities in general, such as creativity, originality, expressiveness, etc. At the same time this criticism probably has less relevance to such convergent-thinking operations as the understanding of physical causality, spatial relations, etc., with which Piaget is mainly concerned and for which his copyist assumption may be more intrinsically relevant. For whatever may be said here about Piaget's theory of play, there is no intention to detract from the conceptual flexibility of his system when applied to the child's understanding of the operations of the physical world. In that area man and mollusk share a common concern, and Piaget's epistemology appears to be revealing.

References

Cassirer, E. *The philosophy of symbolic forms.* Vol. 1. New Haven: Yale Univer. Press, 1953.

Erikson, E. H. *Childhood and society.* New York: Norton, 1950.

Flavell, J. H. *The developmental psychology of Jean Piaget.* New York: Van Nostrand, 1963.

Huizinga, J. *Homo ludens: The play element in culture.* London: Routledge & Kegan Paul, 1949.

Piaget, J. *The language and thought of the child.* New York: Harcourt, Brace, 1926.

Piaget, J. *Judgment and reasoning in the child.* New York: Harcourt, Brace, 1928.

Piaget, J. *The child's conception of the world.* New York: Harcourt, Brace, 1929.

Piaget, J. *The child's conception of physical causality.* London: Kegan Paul, 1930.

Piaget, J. *The moral judgment of the child.* London: Kegan Paul, 1932.

Piaget, J. *Play, dreams and imitation in childhood.* London: Hienemann, 1951.

Piaget, J. *The construction of reality in the child.* New York: Basic Books, 1954.

Piaget, J. *Logic and psychology.* New York: Basic Books, 1957.

Piaget, J. *The psychology of intelligence.* Paterson, N.J.: Littlefield & Adams, 1960.

Roberts, J. M., Arth, M. J., & Bush, R. R. Games in culture. *American Anthropologist,* 1959, **61**, 597–605.

Roberts, J. M., & Sutton-Smith, B. Child training and game involvement. *Ethnology,* 1962, **1**, 166–185.

Sutton-Smith, B. *The games of New Zealand children.* Berkeley: Univer. California Press, 1959.

Sutton-Smith, B., & Roberts, J. M. Rubrics of competitive behavior. *Journal of Genetic Psychology,* 1964, **105**, 13–37.

Sutton-Smith, B., Roberts, J. M., & Kozelka, R. M. Game involvement in adults. *Journal of Social Psychology,* 1963, **60**, 15–30.

Vygotsky, L. S. *Thought and language.* Cambridge: Massachusetts Institute of Technology Press, 1962.

Werner, H., & Kaplan, B. *Symbol formation.* New York: Wiley, 1963.

22

Response to Brian Sutton-Smith

Jean Piaget

The interesting criticism that Sutton-Smith has made of my play theory calls, I feel, for a brief reply. I must confess that I have some difficulty in recognizing the opinions that this author attributes to me, and I think that his formulations of them derive from the fact that he has only been able to assess that portion of my work that has been translated into English.

I have never, either implicitly or explicitly, expressed the view that knowledge is a copy of reality because such a view is contrary to my position with respect to the nature of intelligence. My whole conception of intellectual operations is based on the premise that to know or to understand is to transform reality and to assimilate it to schemes of transformation. In particular, I have never said that representative or symbolic thought, including concept formation, is derived from imitation (in the form of an accommodative copy). On the contrary, in my view, all concepts are derived first from the action and then from the operation, which is another way of saying that concepts are the expression of an assimilation by schemes of transformation.

In fact, the reality that intelligence tries to grasp consists of a series of states (A, B, C, etc.) and transformations which modify these states (A into B, B into C, etc.). One can, therefore, distinguish two components of cognitive functions:

SOURCE. Republished from the *Psychological Review*, 1966, Vol. 73, No. 1, 111–112, with the author's and publisher's permission.

There is first of all a figural component that does not itself constitute a copy but rather a more or less approximate description of reality states and their configurations. The figurative component is derived from perception, imitation, and imagery (graphic or mental) or from interiorized imitations.

There is secondly a cognitive component which takes account of transformations and which builds upon sensorimotor actions, interiorized actions, and finally, thought operations which are derived from actions and not at all from imitation.

In other words, when studying perception, mental imagery, etc. (research not yet published in English), I have tried to show that the figural aspects of cognitive functions are never sufficient to explain representative or conceptual knowledge. Indeed, the figurative components only play a useful role to the extent that they are subordinated to the cognitive component. It seems clear to me that knowledge of a "state" cannot be reduced to a copy of this state, but necessarily consists in an assimilation of this state to a preoperational scheme or a postoperational concept. In fact, to understand a state one must understand the transformations from which the state results which, let us repeat, excludes all types of copy knowledge.

The role of play in this system seems clear. Play is an exercise of action schemes and therefore part of the cognitive component of conception. At the same time, however, play manifests the peculiarity of a primacy of assimilation over accomodation which permits it to transform reality in its own manner without submitting that transformation to the criterion of objective fact. Regardless of what Sutton-Smith says, play fits into this system without becoming subordinated to accomodative imitation. Imitation only plays the role of a symbolic instrument from the moment that sensorimotor play becomes symbolic. This last point leads us to an examination of the symbolic function.

The sensorimotor functions (including sensorimotor play and perception) are not symbolic inasmuch as they only use undifferentiated signifiers (indexes or signals). The symbolic function begins around 1–1/2–2 years of age with the appearance of differentiated signifiers (signs and symbols) and consists in representing various figurative and cognitive schemes by means of these signifiers. In other words, the symbolic signifiers are derived from imitation, which, before becoming interiorized, is already a kind of symbolization in action. This fact, however, in no way implies that symbolic instruments should be confused with figural aspects of thought. Perception is figurative, but not symbolic, while language is symbolic (in the broad sense), but not figurative. Interiorized imitation and images are, on the contrary, at the same time figurative and symbolic.

Mental imagery in particular is the product of interiorized imitation and not the simple residue of perception as it was previously believed.

If symbolic play uses imitation, it is exclusively as a symbolic instrument. This follows because there are only two ways that an absent situation can be represented; it can either be described by language or evoked by imitative gestures or images. This in no way means, however, that symbolic play can be reduced to imitation since play is exclusively an assimilation of reality to the self. Nonetheless, since it is symbolic it needs signifiers, and it borrows them either from language or from the only other source of symbols, that is to say, gestural or interiorized imitation.

It seems clear now that the criticisms that Sutton-Smith has made of our theory are unfortunately the result of a series of misunderstandings and that the opinions that he attributed to us, which indeed deserve to be criticized, are fortunately not our views. There remains, however, one other point that must be clarified. The author defends the idea that symbolic play does not diminish but rather differentiates during the course of development. This is certainly true in one sense of the word. In becoming differentiated, however, it at the same time becomes more and more adequately adapted to reality (construction games, etc.). This is the sense in which I speak of play as diminishing with age. And it does diminish if one takes, as I do, the essential property of play to be the deformation and subordination of reality to the desires of the self.

Finally, Sutton-Smith makes an allusion to Vygotsky's conception of egocentric language. I have already replied in length to Vygotsky's insightful remarks. However, if we are to take up the problem of egocentrism again, which goes hand in hand with the deforming processes of assimilation, we must also situate language and play in the overall context of the individual and social actions of the child. In studying the collaboration of children in collective actions, R. F. Nielsen has found an evolutionary law which resembles to a great extent what I used to call the passage from egocentrism to cooperation.

23

A Reply to Piaget: A Play Theory of Copy

Brian Sutton-Smith

Summary of First Article

It was asserted that without so intending, Piaget had developed a copy theory of play; that in accounting for play's cognitive components, he had derived them from copies of earlier accommodative behavior. In defense of this assertion, it was pointed out that Piaget's descriptions of play itself as "confusions" and "distorting assimilations"; his suggestion that play was a phenomenon relevant only to the intellectual disequilibrations of childhood, and his attribution of predominantly affective rather than cognitive functions to such childhood play were themselves features of a theory of play that gave it a derivative, compensatory, or infantile status, rather than a constitutive role in thought. It was stated that Piaget had attempted to make play a function of thought without imparting to it any truly intellectual function within thought itself. It was suggested that if play be considered an intellectual function, perhaps it would be nearer to divergent thought processes than to convergent ones, or again, that perhaps play was best thought of as an entirely different type of process rather than as simply a form of thought.

Summary of Piaget's Reply

Piaget responded that since he considered play a transformational cognitive activity, he could not possibly have a copy theory of play. Any

internalization of prior activity could only be an instrument of this transformational activity.

Reply

Consider first *function*. The question that still has to be put to Piaget is
the one originally directed. If play is such a "vital" cognitive function
in early childhood, what does it do cognitively? The generalization that
play is a transformational activity, that it involves the primacy of assimilation over accommodation without submitting that transformation
to the criterion of objective facts, is not matched either in Piaget's present
response or in the early book by any systematic accounting of the function of these transformations. After all, is it necessary for this type of
ludic assimilation to occur? Is subsequent thought in some way based on
it? Can adaptive thought proceed without it? Is it an accident or an essential to thought? Piaget gives no clear answers to these functional questions. The anomaly therefore remains that Piaget posits play as a
function of cognition, but does not explicate the nature of that function.

My own prejudice is in favor of a broader view of human adaptation
than that which has been typically followed by psychologists or in the
present case by Piaget. From this point of view, play is not solely a cognitive function (nor solely affective or conative), but an expressive form
sui generis with its own unique purpose on the human scene. It does not
subserve "adaptive" thought as Piaget defines it (though of course it can
do that); it serves to express personal meanings. It is therefore remarkable
in cognitive terms for its uniqueness, in affective terms for its personal
expression of feeling, and in conative terms for its autonomy. From this
point of view, there is a cognitive "reductionism" about Piaget's approach,
and a denial of the multiqualitative nature of expressive forms, of which
play is only one, others of which are art, drama, poetry, etc., all of which
have functions over and beyond any service that they may give to constructive intelligence.

Second, with respect to *structure*, Piaget does not concentrate on the
structural uniqueness of each play transformation, but instead focuses
on the way in which the play parallels the adaptive cognitive structure
of a given age level. Despite his declared interest in play as a transforming
activity, the character of that transformation is not studied. Rather he is
interested in play as a copy of the serious intelligence. My own view is
that Piaget has not proceeded to such a study of the intricacies of these
transformations because he has been concerned primarily with intelligence (as he defines it) and not with play. Like most "idealistic" philos-

ophers (for example, Furth, 1969), he subordinates imagination to reason, and has, therefore, nothing very fruitful to say about imagination. One must go to Corinne Hutt's study or the animal observations of Eible-Eibesfeldt to gain some notions of what these transformations look like structurally. Again, it is my own prejudice that one of the difficulties that play poses to any theory of convergent intelligence or equilibrating adaptation, is that it has a relatively high component of disjunctive intent. That is, it is disequilibrial on purpose—not by mistake, by cognitive deficit, or by affective deficiency. Like festivals and Mardi Gras, like mountaineering and tight-rope walking, it is tension-enhancing. Equilibrial theorists often reduce this phenomenon to some higher-order adaptation. But that is like reducing the game to its outcome. The players are inclined to insist instead that their intent is not the ultimate resolution but the momentary imbalance. In short, to study play structurally is to study the character of disequilibrum or novelty. Presumably there are characteristic types of transformations (risks, disequilibrations) that children test in their play at different age levels. The threat of Piaget's reductive account is that it focuses observation away from these intrinsic matters, rather than furthers their illumination. From this point of view, if play contributes anything of worth to constructive intelligence, it is most probably novel responses or novel signifiers; this is, if you like, a play theory of copy.

Chapter IX

Conclusion

In the first article, Gregory Stone observed that the meaning and significance of play and games has changed with historical changes in culture. Stone might similarly argue that the difference between D. El'Konin's emphasis on the social determination of play, Piaget's emphasis on play as a polarity of thought inwardly structured, and Sutton-Smith's emphasis on play as an expressive and self-representative behavior, neatly parallels the differences between Riesman's broad cultural categories of tradition-directed, inner-directed and other- (or consumption-) directed societies (1950). Whatever one thinks of the historical validity of Riesman's categories, it gives one pause to realize that these three approaches may themselves be culturally determined formulations in one way or another. The implication follows that some clarity with respect to cultural and philosophical assumptions is necessary even in a psychology of play. There is no speaking with a universal and objective voice. In fact, the attempt to provide such universality leads to uncertainty as to the mutual relations between diverse ideas and diverse data. It is like trying to fit together pieces from separate jigsaw puzzles. What is possible, at least in ideal terms, is a declaration of the assumptions, or more fittingly, in the present context, of the ground rules for the particular theoretical games.

The readings in this book have tended to exemplify a tension between at least two types of theoretical frame. There has been on the one hand a concern with the formal structures of play as expressive systems and on the other, a more conventional psychologist's concern with the antecedents

343

and consequences of play—or in philosophical terms, on the one hand a concern with forms and on the other with causes. These are two different ways of looking at the same phenomena; each has long philosophical traditions, and each has different consequences.

Form is usually emphasized when the investigator believes that his subject matter is of primary and not derivative importance. The approach to the study of form can be mathematical (as in games theory), logical (as in the example from Bateson), or descriptive, as in the following example from Huizinga. Play is:

a free activity standing quite consciously outside "ordinary" life as being "not serious," but at the same time as absorbing the player intensely and utterly. It is an activity connected with no material interest, and no profit can be gained by it. It proceeds within its own fixed boundaries of time and space and according to fixed rules and in an orderly manner. It promotes the formation of social groupings which tend to surround themselves with secrecy and to stress their difference from the common world by disguise or other means (1949, p. 13).

Actually, Huizinga's descriptions vary between those that could be made by observation and those that would have to derive from the player's reports. When he says, for example, that the fun of playing resists all analysis and all logical interpretation (1949, p. 3), he is reporting from a phenomenological stance—though there is no reason why such self-reports could not be made systematic and thus quantified. In recording children's play, however, we are confined to descriptive observations. One of the arguments presented throughout this work has been that because of play's treatment as a derivative response-system for expressing affects, cognitions, or whatever, the task of systematic description has not been seriously undertaken. Though the view might also be presented that, as all expressive systems are so unique and vagarious, description has been particularly difficult. Still, even within a causal framework, adequate description is an essential. The approach tentatively advocated in the reading "A Syntax for Play and Games" is that we should borrow the dimensions for play description from conceptual models that have proven useful in describing games. In that reading, play was described in terms of power testing, disequilibrial outcomes, voluntary controls, actors and counteractors, and spatial and temporal contexts. Tentatively, play was *described as an exercise of voluntary control systems with disequilibrial outcomes.* Whether the disequilibria were to be regarded as internal to the play, as consisting of the relationship between play and other behaviors or as both of these, was left for future research. Whether this or some other definition is found to be most useful, the important point to be reiterated is that play should be described primarily in terms of "behaviors," of "responses" that make sense in terms of play and games, rather than in terms of some other behavior systems.

It is the causes or more appropriately, the functional relationships of play, that have been the major focus of most investigators however. Any concern to understand how play can be used most appropriately in schools or with children of different backgrounds necessitates such a causal approach. We have traced the earlier and more recent ecological approaches to causation. There are chapters given to the analysis or play in terms of functional notions that center on anxiety, mastery, compensation, novel responses, "as if" sets, logical categories, instigating stimuli and agents, motive states, phylogenetic and ontogenetic sequences, response transformations, and the testing of powers. All of these functions are relevant to the understanding of play, even if no one of them provides a sufficient explanation by itself. Through play as "a projective system" they may be illuminated, even if they cannot subsume the forms of play to their own function.

We conclude, then, as we began with the assertion that the psychology of child's play, must involve at least the two major "games" that have been discussed above. The functional understanding of play is of great practical and contemporary importance. Its formal or expressive meaning may be of even greater long-term significance for understanding the commitment of children and adults to the existence within which they find themselves.

Bibliography on Play

The emphasis in this bibliography is on children's play. The related topics of leisure, games, and sports are dealt with in the companion work, *The Study of Games.*

Abadi, M. Psicoanalisis del jugar (Psychoanalysis of playing). *Revista de Psicoanalisis,* 1964, **21** (4), 366–373.

Abely, P., & Melman, C. Le jeu, le ludisme, la parade, en pathologie mentale. Etude clinique et approche psychoanalytique. La jocotherapie. (Games, play and the parade in mental pathology: Clinical study and psychoanalytic approach. Play therapy). *Annales Medico-psychologiques,* 1963, **121** (1), 353–390.

Ackerman, N. W. Constructive and destructive tendencies in children. *Amer. J. Orthopsychiat.,* 1937, **7**, 301–319.

Albino, R. C. Defenses against aggression in the play of young children. *British Journal of Medical Psychology,* 1954, **27**, 61–71.

Alexander, F. A contribution to the theory of play. *Psychoanalytic Quarterly,* 1958, **27**, 175–193.

Almy, M. Spontaneous play: An avenue for intellectual development. *Child Study Center Bulletin,* 1966, **28** (2), 2–15.

Ames, L. B. Postural and placement orientations in writing and block behavior: Developmental trends from infancy to age ten. *Journal of Genetic Psychology,* 1948, **73**, 45–52.

Ames, L. B. Free drawing and completion drawing: A comparative study of pre-school children. *Journal of Genetic Psychology*, 1945, **66**, 161--165.

Ames, L. B. & Learned, J. Imaginary companions and related phenomena. *Journal of Genetic Psychology*, 1946, **69**, 147–167.

Amen, E., & Renison, Nancy. A study of the relationship between play patterns and anxiety in young children. *Genetic Psychology Monographs*, 1954, **50**, (11), 3–41.

Ammons, C. H., & Ammons, R. B. Research and clinical applications of the doll-play interview. *Journal of Personality*, 1952, **21**, 85–90.

Ammons, C. H., & Ammons, R. B. Aggression in doll-play: Interviews of two to six-year-old white males. *Journal of Genetic Psychology*. 1953, **82**, 205–213.

Ammons, R. B. Reactions in a projective doll-play interview of white males two to six years of age to differences in skin color and facial features. *Journal of Genetic Psychology*, 1950, **76**, 323–341.

Ammons, R. B., & Ammons, H. S. Parent preferences in young children's doll-play interviews. *Journal of Abnormal and Social Psychology*, 1949, **44**, 490–505.

Anderson, H. H. Domination and integration in the social behavior of young children in an experimental play situation. *Genetic Psychological Monographs*, 1937, **19**, 341–408.

Angell, E. D. *Play*. Boston: Little, Brown and Company, 1910.

Angrilli, A., Liebman, O. B., & Gross, C. Observations of semi-structured play in teacher education. *Journal of Teacher Education*, 1964, **15**, 415–419.

Appleton, L. E. *A comparative study of the play activities of adult savages and civilized children*. Chicago: University of Chicago Press, 1910.

Aries, P. *Centuries of childhood*. New York: Knopf, 1962, 62–99.

Atkinson, J. W. (Ed.) *Motives in fantasy, action, and society*. Princeton, N.J.: Van Nostrand, 1958.

Axline, V. M. *Play therapy: The inner dynamics of childhood*. Boston: Houghton Mifflin Company, 1947.

Axline, V. M. Entering the child's world via play experiences. *Progress of Education*, 1950, **27**, 68–75.

Axline, V. M. Observing children at play. *Teachers College Record*, 1951, **52**, 358, 363.

Axline, V. M. Play therapy procedures and results. *American Journal of Orthopsychiatry*, 1955, **25**, 618–626.

Bach, G. R. Young children's play fantasies. *Psychological Monographs*, 1945, **59** (2), 3–69.

Bach, G. R. Father-fantasies and father-typing in father-separated children. *Child Development*, 1946, **17**, 63–80.

Baggally, W. A note on a child's game. *International Journal of Psychoanalysis,* 1947, **28**, 198–201.

Bailey, M. W. A scale of block constructions for young children. *Child Development,* 1933, 4, 121–139.

Baker, R. Having fun is work nowadays. *New York Times News Service,* July 29, 1964.

Baldwin, J. M. *Mental development in the child and the race.* New York: Macmillan, 1895.

Balint, M. Love for the mother and mother-love. *International Journal of Psychoanalysis,* 1949, **30**, 251–9.

Barker, R. G., Kounin, J. S., & Wright, H. F. *Child Behavior and Development,* New York: McGraw-Hill, 1943, 441–458.

Barker, R. G., Dembo, L., & Lewin, K. Frustration and regression: an experiment with young children. *University of Iowa Studies in Child Welfare,* 1941, **18**, No. 386.

Barnett, S. A. Exploratory behavior. *British Journal of Psychology,* 1958, **49**, 289–310.

Barton, P. H. Play as a tool of nursing. *Nursing Outlook,* 1962, **10**, 162–164.

Baruch, D. W. Aggression during doll-play in a pre-school. *American Journal of Orthopsychiatry,* 1941, **11**, 252–260.

Bateson, G. A theory of play and fantasy. *Psychiatric Research Report,* 1955, **2**, 39–51.

Bateson, G. The message "This is play." In B. Schaffner (Ed.), *Group Processes: Transactions of the Second Conference.* New York: Josiah Macy Foundation, 1956. Pp. 145–246.

Beach, F. A. Current concepts of play in animals. *American Naturalist,* 1945, **79** (785), 523–541.

Beiser, H. R. Play equipment for diagnosis and therapy. *American Journal of Orthopsychiatry,* 1955, **25** (4), 761–770.

Bell, J. E. Perceptual Development and the drawings of children. *American Journal of Orthopsychiatry,* 1952, **22**, 386–393.

Bender, L. 10. Discussion. Therapeutic play techniques symposium, 1954. *American Journal of Orthopsychiatry,* 1955, **25** (4), 784–787.

Bender, L., & Schilder, P. Form as a principle of the play of children. *Journal of Genetic Psychology,* 1936, **49**, 254–261.

Bender, L., & Woltmann, A. G. The use of puppet shows as a psychotherapeutic method. *American Journal of Orthopsychiatry,* 1936, **6**, 341–354.

Bender, L., & Woltmann, A. G. Play and psychotherapy. *Nervous Child,* 1941, **1**, 17–42.

Benjamin, H. Age and sex differences in the toy preferences of young children. *Journal of Genetic Psychology,* 1932, **41**, 417–429.

Benoit, E. P. The play problem of retarded children. *American Journal of Mental Deficiency,* 1955, **60,** 41–55.

Bernhart, E. N. Developmental stages in compositional construction of children's drawings. *Journal of Experimental Education,* 1942, **11,** 156–184.

Berlyne, D. E. Exploratory and epistemic behavior. In S. Koch (Ed.) *Psychology as a science,* Vol. V. New York: McGraw-Hill, 1963, pp. 284–364.

Berlyne, D. C. Laughter, humor, and play. In G. Lindzey and E. Aronson (Eds.), *Handbook of social psychology,* N.Y. Addison-Wesley, (2nd Ed.), 1970, pp. 795–852.

Berlyne, D. C. *Conflict, arousal and curiosity.* New York: McGraw Hill, 1960.

Berlyne, D. E. Novelty and curiosity as determinants of exploratory behavior. *British Journal of Psychology,* 1950, **41,** 68–80.

Berlyne, D. E. The present status of research on exploratory and related behavior. *Journal of Individual Psychology,* 1958, **14,** 121–126.

Berne, E. *Games people play.* New York: Grove Press, 1964.

Bertoye, P. M. Les jeux du Nourrisson (The games of infants). *Lyon Medical,* 1963, **210,** 861–874.

Biber, B. Premature structuring as a deterrent to creativity. *American Journal of Orthopsychiatry,* 1959, **29,** 2.

Bills, R. E. Nondirective play therapy with retarded readers. *Journal of Consulting Psychology,* 1950, **14,** 140–149.

Bingham, H. C. Parental play of chimpanzees. *Journal of Mammals,* 1927, **8,** 77–89.

Bixler, R. "Nondirective play therapy." Unpublished master's thesis, Ohio State University, 1942.

Bladergroen, W. J. *Speel goed met speelgoed* (Good playing with playthings). The Hague: W. P. Van Stockum & Zoon, 1957.

Bladergroen, W. J. *Waarmee spelen onze kleuters?* (What do our little ones play with?). Ijmuiden: Vernande Zonen, 1961.

Blazer, J. Fantasy and its effects. *Journal of Genetic Psychology,* 1946, **70,** 163–182.

Blow, S. E. *Symbolic education: A commentary on Froebel's "mother play",* International Education Series, Vol. 26. New York: D. Appleton, 1897.

Boehm, E. L. Choosing playthings. *Child Study Center Bulletin,* 1927, **5,** 7–9, 16.

Boll, E. S. The role of pre-school playmates: A situational approach. *Child Development,* 1957, **28,** 327–342.

Bond, M. H. Play on a higher level. *Journal of Health, Physical Education and Recreation,* 1965, **36,** 33–34.

Boon, A. A. Aspekte des Kinderspiels (Aspects of children's play). *Praxis der Kinderpsychologie und Kinderpsychiatrie,* 1952, **1,** 217–227.

Bossard, J. H. S., & Boll, E. S. Peer groups: Pre-school and later age. In *The sociology of child development.* New York: Harper & Row, 1966, pp. 386–403.

Bott, H. Observation of play activities in a nursery school. *Genetic Psychological Monographs*, 1928, 4, 44–88.

Bowen, W. P., & Mitchell, E. D. *The theory of organized play*. New York: A. S. Barnes & Company, 1923.

Bowen, W. P. The influence of play activities on racial physique and morals. *National Education Association of the United States: Journal of Proceedings and Addresses*, 1912, 50, 1142–1146.

Boynton, P. L., & Ford, Z. A. The relationship between play and intelligence. *Journal of Applied Psychology*, 1933, 17, 294–301.

Boynton, P. L., & Wang, L. L. Relationship between children's play interest and their emotional stability. *Journal of Genetic Psychology*, 1944, 64, 119–127.

Boynton, P. L., & Wang, L. L. Relation of the play interests of children to their economic status. *Journal of Genetic Psychology*, 1944, 64, 129–138.

Bremer, G. "The effect of two fantasy environments on children's doll-play responses." Unpublished master's thesis, State University of Iowa, 1947.

Brewster, P. G. *American non-singing games*. Norman: Univ. of Oklahoma Press, 1953.

Bridges, K. M. Banham. Occupational interests of three-year-old children. Ped. Sem. and *J. Genet. Psychol.*, 1927, 34, 415–423.

Bridges, K. M. Banham. The occupational interests and attention of four-year-old children, *Journal of Genetic Psychology*, 1929, 36, 551–570.

Britt, S. H., & Balcom, M. M. Jumping rope rhymes and the social psychology of play. *Journal of Genetic Psychology*, 1941, 58, 289–306.

Britt, S. H., & Janus, S. Q. Toward a social psychology of human play. *Journal of Social Psychology*, 1941, 13, 351–384.

Brownman, M. T., & M. C. Templin. Stories for younger children in 1927–1929 and 1952–1955. *Elementary School Journal*, 1959, 59, 324–327.

Brubaker, M. The child in his play group. *National Education Association of the United States: Addresses and Proceedings*, 1928, 66, 429–432.

Bühler, C. The child and its activity with practical material. *British Journal of Educational Psychology*, 1933, 3, 27–41.

Bühler, K. The imagination of the child at play. In *The Mental Development of the Child*. New York: Harcourt, Brace & Co., 1930. Pp. 9–10 and 91–96.

Burch, W. R. The play world of camping: Research into the social meaning of outdoor recreation. *American Journal of Sociology*, 1965, 70, 604–612.

Burgers, J. M. Curiosity and play: Basic factors in the development of life. *Science*, 1966, 154, 1680–1681.

Burton, M. S. Play: Effects of leisure time on personality and the Christian life. *Adult Leader*, 1930, 5, 492.

Bush, R. B., & Rigby, M. The play hour. *Psychology Clinic*, 1929–1930, 18, 44–51.

Butler, Incentive conditions which influence visual exploration. *Journal of Experimental Psychology*, 1954, 48, 19–23.

Buytendijk, F. J. J. *Wesen und sinn des spiels. Das spielen des menschen und der tiere als erscheinungsform der lebenstriebe.* (Essence and sense of play. The play of humans and of animals as the outward appearance of vitality.) Berlin: Wolff, Neue Geist Verl., 1934.

Cahn, P. The role of play in the development of fraternal relationships of an older brother. *Sauvegarde,* 1949, 4, 40–52.

Caillois, R. *Man, play and games.* New York: Free Press of Glencoe, 1961.

Cain, A. C. On the meaning of playing crazy in borderline children. *Psychiatry,* 1964, **27**, 278–289.

California Recreational Inquiry Committee. *Report of the State Recreational Inquiry Committee.* Sacramento, 1914.

Call, Justin D., & Marschak, Marianne. Styles and games in infancy. *Journal of the American Academy of Child Psychiatry,* 5(2), 1966, 193–210.

Cameron, N. *The psychology of behavior disorders.* Cambidge: Houghton Mifflin, 1947.

Cappell, M. D. Games and the mastery of helplessness. In Slovenko, R., & Knight, J. A. (Eds.), *Motivations in play, games and sports.* Springfield, Ill.: Chas. C Thomas, 1967, pp. 39-55.

Card Playing. *Encyclopaedia Britannica,* Vol. 4, Chicago: Benton, 1959.

Carlson, B., & Ginglend, D. *Play activities for the retarded child.* Nashville: Abingdon Press, 1961.

Carlson, E. Games in the classroom. *Saturday Review,* April 15, 1967, 62–64 and 82–83.

Carr, H. A. The survival values of play. *Investigations of a department of psychology and education. University of Colorado.* 1902, 1 (1), 1–47.

Carroll, R., & Abshier, M. To play is the thing. *Journal of Health, Physical Education, Recreation,* 1966, **37**, 33–34.

Carter, T. M. Play problems of gifted children. *School and Society,* 1958, **86**, 224–225.

Cassirer, E. *Essay on man.* New Haven, Conn: Yale University Press, 1944.

Chalmers, T. Value of play in nursing severely subnormal children. *Nursing Mirror,* 1966, **122** (25), 12–16.

Chastaing, M. Jouer n'est pas jouer (To play is not to play). *Journal de Psychologie et Normale Pathologie,* 1959, **65**, (3), 303–326.

Chateau, J. *L'enfant et le jeu* (The child and play). University of Strasbourg, Paris: Editions de Scarbee, 1954.

Children's Games. *Encyclopaedia Britannica,* Vol. 5, Chicago: Banton, 1959.

Claparede, E. Sur la nature et la fonction de jeu (Concerning the nature and function of play). *Archives de Psychologie,* Geneve, 1934, 24, 350–369.

Cleverdon, D. A work-play program for the trainable mental deficient. *American Journal of Mental Deficiency,* 1955, **60**, 56–70.

Cockrell, D. L. A study of the play of children of pre-school age by an unobserved observer. *Genetic Psychological Monographs,* 1935, **17**, 377–469.

Coe, G. A. Philosophy of play. *Religious Education*, 1956, 1, 220–222.

Cohen, J. The ideas of work and play. *British Journal of Sociology*, 1953, 4, 312–322.

Cohn, Fay. Fantasy Aggression in children as studied by the doll-play technique. *Child Development*, 1962, 33, 235–250.

Collard, Roberta R. Fear of strangers and play behavior in kittens with varied social experience. *Child Development*, 38 (3), 877–891.

Collard, Roberta R. Social and Play Responses of First-Born and Later-Born Infants in an Unfamiliar Situation. *Child Development*, 1968, 39, No. 1, 325–333.

Conn, J. H. The play interview as an investigation and therapeutic procedure. *Nervous Child*, 1948, 7, 257–286.

Conn, J. H. The child reveals himself through play: The method of the play interview. *Mental Hygiene*, 1939, 23, 49–70.

Conn, J. H. Children's awareness of sex differences. II. Play attitudes and game preferences. *Journal of Child Psychiatry*, 1951, 2, 82–99.

Conn, J. H. Play interview therapy of castration fear. *American Journal of Orthopsychiatry*, 1955, 25 (4), 747–754.

Cook, H. C. *The play way: An essay in educational methods.* New York: Fred Stokes, 1928.

Coriat, I. The unconscious motives of interest in chess. *Psychoanalytic Review*, 1941, 28, 30.

Corn, F. S. Fantasy aggression in children as studied by the doll-play technique. *Child Development*, 33, 235–250.

Cornelius, R. Games minus competition. *Childhood Education*, 1949, 26, 77–79.

Cousinet, R. Enquête sur ce que pensent les écoliers du jeu et du travail (Investigation of what students think of play and work). *Journal of Psychology and Normal Pathology*, 1951, 44, 556–568.

Cramer, M. W. Leisure time activities of economically privileged children. *Social Science Research*, 1950, 34, 444–450.

Cratty, B. J. Motivation, motives and movement. In *Movement behavior and motor learning.* Philadelphia: Lea and Febiger, 1964. Pp. 161–165.

Croswell, T. R. Amusements of Worcester school children. *Pedagogical Seminary*, 1899, 6, 314–371.

Curry, N. E. Factors influencing a child's readiness to play with other children. *Journal of Nursery Education*, 1961, 16 (3–4), 97–103, 60–61.

Curtis, H. S. *Education through play.* New York: The Macmillan Company, 1915.

Daniels, C. R. Play group therapy with children. *ACTA Psychotherapeutica* (Basel), 1964, 12, 45–52.

Davis, D. C. Play: A state of childhood. *Childhood Education*, 1965, 42, 242–244.

Davis, J. E. *Play and mental health: Principles and practices for teachers.* New York: Barnes, 1938.

Davis, J. E. A theoretical formulation of play as life exercise. *Mental Hygiene,* 1954, **38,** 570–575.

Davis, John M. A reinterpretation of the Baker, Dembo and Lewis study of frustration and regressions. *Child Development,* 1958, **29,** 503–506.

Dearden, R. F. The concept of play. In Peters, R. S. (Ed.), *The concept of education* New York: Humanities Press, 1967.

de Grazia, S. *Of time, work, and leisure.* New York: Twentieth Century Fund, 1962.

Delucia, L. A. The toy preference test: A measure of sex-role identification. *Child Development,* 1963, **34,** 107–117.

Dember and Earl. Analysis of exploratory, manipulatory and curiosity behaviors. *Psychological Review,* 1957, **64,** 91–96.

deMille, R. *Put your mother on the ceiling: Children's imagination games.* New York: Walker & Co. 1967.

De Nevi, D. Fantasy and creativity. *Child & Family,* 1967, **6** (2), 23–27.

Despert, J. L. A method for the study of personality reactions in pre-school children by means of analysis of their play. *Journal of Psychology,* 1940, **9,** 17–29.

Despert, J. L. Play analysis in research and therapy. In N. D. Lewis, & B. L. Pacelli, *Modern trends in child psychiatry.* New York: International University Press, 1945. Pp. 219–255.

Dewey, J. *Democracy and education: An introduction to the philosophy of education.* New York: The Macmillan Company, 1916.

Dewey, J. Play. In P. Monroe (Ed.), *A cyclopedia of education,* Volume 4. New York: The Macmillan Company, 1913. Pp. 725–727.

Dow, M. L. Playground behavior differentiating artistic from nonartistic children. *Proceedings of Iowa Academy of Science,* 1933, 40, 197. *Psychological Monographs,* 1933, **45,** 82–94.

Drake, E. Play, a time of discovery. *Instructor,* 1966, **75,** 32.

Dulles, F. R. *America learns to play.* New York: D. Appleton-Century Company, 1940.

Dundee, A. On game morphology: A study of the structure of nonverbal folklore. *New York Folklore Quarterly,* 1964, 276–288.

Eble, K. E. The art of learning? It's child play. *The National Observer,* January 23, 1967, p. 22.

Eibl-Eibesfeldt, I. Concepts of ethology and their significance in the study of human behavior. In H. W. Stevenson, E. H. Hess, & H. L. Rheingold (Eds.), *Early Behavior,* New York: Wiley, 1967, 127–146.

Ekstein, R. Puppet play of a psychotic adolescent girl in the psychotherapeutic process. In *The psychoanalytic study of the child,* Volume 20. New York: International University Press, Inc., 1965. Pp. 441–480.

Ekstein, R. Pleasure and reality, play and work, thought and action. *Journal of Humanistic Psychology,* Fall, 1963, 20–31.

Ekstein, R. *Children of time and space, of action and impulse*. New York: Appleton, 1966, p. 207.

Ekstein, R. Lili E. Peller's psychoanalytic contributions to teaching. *Reiss-Davis Clin. Bull.*, 4, 1967, p. 6.

Elkish, P. Significant relationships between the human figure and the machine in the drawing of boys. *American Journal of Orthopsychiatry*, 1952, **22**, 79-85.

El'Konin, D. Symbolics and its function in the play of children. *Soviet Education*, 1966, **8**, 35–41.

Ellis, A. C., & Hall, G. S. A study of dolls. *Pedagogical Seminary*, 1896, 4, 129–175.

Erikson, E. H. *Childhood and society*. New York: Norton, 1963.

Erikson, E. H. Studies in the interpretation of play; Part I. Clinical observations of play disruption in young children. *Genetic Psychology Monographs*, 1940, **22**, 557–671.

Erikson, E. H. Further exploration in play construction: Three spatial variables in their relation to sex and anxiety. *Psychological Bulletin*, 1941, **38**, 748.

Erikson, E. II. Clinical studies in childhood play. In R. G. Barker et al. (Eds.), *Child behavior and development*. New York: McGraw-Hill, 1943. Pp. 411–428.

Erikson, E. H. Toys and reasons. In *Childhood and society*. New York: Norton, 1950. Pp. 182–218.

Erikson, E. H. Sex differences in play configurations of pre-adolescents. *American Journal of Orthopsychiatry*, 1951, 21 (4), 667–692.

Erikson, E. H. Sex differences in the play configurations of American pre-adolescents. In M. Mead & M. Folfenstein (Eds.), *Childhood in contemporary cultures*. (Phoenix ed.). Chicago: The University of Chicago Press, 1963. Pp. 324–341. *American Journal of Orthopsychiatry*, 1951, 21, 667–692.

Erikson, F. H. Play interview of 4 year old hospitalized children. Purdue, Indiana. *Monographs of the Society for Research in Child Development*, 1958, **23** (3), Whole No. 69, 1–77.

Escalona, S. Play and substitute satisfaction. In Barker, R. G., Kounin, J. S. & Wright, H. F. (Eds.), *Child behavior and development*, New York: McGraw-Hill, 1943, 363–378.

Etkes, A. B. Challenge a child at play: A learning experience. *American School Board Journal*, 1966, **153**, 26–28.

Fales, E. A rating scale of the vigorousness of play activities of pre-school children *Child Development*, 1937, **8**, 15–46.

Fales, E. A comparison of the vigorousness of play activities of pre-school boys and girls. *Child Development*, 1937, **8**, 144–158.

Farwell, L. Reactions to kindergarten, first and second grade children to constructive play materials. *Genetic Psychological Monographs*, 1930, **8**, 431–562.

Fauna, A. J. A study of the relationship between personality factors and patterns of free time behavior. *Dissertation Abstracts,* 1966, **26** (8), 4795–4796.

Ferenc, M. Group leadership and institutionalization. *Human Relations,* 1949, **2**, 23–43.

Feshbach, S. The drive-reducing function of fantasy behavior. *Journal of Abnormal and Social Psychology,* 1955.

Fielder, A. E. Assumed similarity measures as predictors of team effectiveness. *Journal of Abnormal and Social Psychology,* 1954, **49**, 381–388.

Fineman, J. Observations on the development of imaginative play in early childhood. *Journal of American Academy of Child Psychiatry,* 1962, **1**, 167–187.

Forbush, W. B. Manual of play. Philadelphia: George W. Jacobs & Company, 1914.

Foster, J. C. Play activities of children in the first six grades. *Child Development,* 1930, **1**, 248–254.

Fraleigh, W. P. Influence of play upon social and emotional adjustment with implications for physical education. *College Physical Education Association Proceedings,* 1956, 268–273. *Dissertation Abstracts,* 1956, **16**, 495–496.

Frank, L. K. Play in personality development. *American Journal of Orthopsychiatry,* 1955, **25**, 576–590.

Frank, L. K. Role of play in child development. *Childhood Education,* 1964, **41**, 70–73.

Frank L. K. and Hartley, R. E. Play and personality formation in pre-school group. *Personality,* 1951, **1**, 149–161.

Frank, R. W. Protestantism and play. *Social progress,* 1935, **26**, 24, 26.

Freud, Anna. The concept of developmental lines. *Psychoanalytical Study Child,* 1963, **18**, 245, 261.

Freud, S. A. *A general selection.* In Rickman, J. (Ed.), London: Hogarth Press, 1937.

Freud, S. *Beyond the pleasure principle,* Standard Edition, Vol. 18. London: Hogarth, 1955.

Freud, S. *Psychopathic characters on the stage* (1905), Standard Edition, Vol. 7. London: Hogarth Press, 1953, p. 303.

Freud, S. The relation of the poet to daydreaming. Trans. by Grant Duff. I. F. *Delusion and dream and other essays,* Rieff, P. (Ed.). Boston: Beacon, 1956, 122–133.

Freud, S. Creative writers and daydreaming. In J. Strachey (Ed.), *The standard edition of the complete psychological works of Sigmund Freud.* London: Hogarth, 1962, Vol. IX, p. 142–153.

Freud, S. *The interpretation of dreams.* (Trans. A. A. Brill). New York: Modern Library, 1950, (Chap. 7).

Freud, S. *Jokes and their relation to the unconscious* (1905). Standard Edition, Vol. 8, London: Hogarth Press, 1955, pp. 14, 121, 128, 169–170, 225, 227.

Freud, S. *A phobia in a five year old boy* (1909). Vol. 10, Standard Edition. London: Hogarth, 1955, p. 52, 85.

Frey, B. G. Free play period develops motor skills and personality attitudes. *Illinois Education*, 1950, **38**, 292–293.

Friedlander, B. Z. Three manipulanda for the study of human infants' operant play. *Journal of Experimental Analysis of Behavior*, 1966, **9**, 47–49.

Friedlander, B. Z. Effects of stimulus variation rates contingency and intermittent extinction of a child's incidental play for perceptual reinforcement. *Journal of Experimental Child Psychology*, 1966, **4** (3), 257–265.

Fries, M. E. The value of play for a child development study. *Understanding the Child*, 1938, **7**, 15–18.

Froebel, F. Pedagogics of the kindergarten. London: Appleton, 1895. (Translated by J. Jarvis).

Fuchs, N. R. Play therapy at home. *Merrill-Palmer Quarterly*, 1957, **3**, 89–95.

Furfey, P. H. Pubescence and play behavior. *American Journal of Psychology*, 1929, **41**, 109–111.

Fuxloch, K. Das soziologische im spiel des kindes (The siciology in the play of children). *Zeitschrift für Angewandte Psychologie und Psychologishe Forschung Beirheft*, 1930, **53**, 1–6.

Gaier, E. K. & Collier, M. J. The latency stage story preferences of American and Finnish children. *Child Development*, 1961, **31**, 431–451.

Galluser, U. M. Leik–teoriar (Theories of play). *Norsk Pedagogisk Tidsskrift*, 1961, **45** (9–10), 349–358.

Gandy, G. The play activities of children: A comparative study. *Wing*, 1963, **1**, 11–12. (Physical Education Society, St. Mary's College, Strawberry Hill, England).

Garrison, Charlotte. *Permanent play materials for young children*. New York: Scribner, 1926.

Gattegno, C. Etude sur le jeu (Study on play). *Bulletin de l'Institute de'Egypte* (Cairo), 1945.

Gesell, A. *The child from five to ten*. New York: Harper, 1946.

Gesell, A., & Lord, E. E. A psychological comparison of nursery school children from homes of low and high economic status. *Pedagogical Seminary*, 1927, **34**, 339–356.

Getzels, J. W., & Jackson, P. W. *Creativity and intelligence*, New York: Wiley, 1962.

Gewirtz, J. L. An investigation of aggressive behavior in the doll play of young Sac and Fox Indian children, and a comparison to the aggression of Midwestern white pre-school children. *American Psychologist*, 1950, **5**, 294–295.

Ghosh, S. Play instinct. *Indian Journal of Psychology*, 1935, **10**, 159–162.

Giddens, A. Notes on the concepts of play and leisure. *Sociology Review*, 1964, **12**, 73–89.

Gillin, J. L. The sociology of play. *American Journal of Sociology,* 1914, **19,** 825–834.

Gilmore, J. B. Play: A special behavior. In R. N. Haber (Ed.), *Current research in motivation.* New York: Holt, Rinehart, & Winston, 1966, Pp. 343–355.

Gilmore, J. B. The role of anxiety and cognitive factors in children's play behavior. *Child Development,* 1966, **37** (2), 397–416.

Ginott, H. G. Play therapy: The initial session. *American Journal of Psychotherapy,* 1961, **15,** 73–88.

Ginott, H. G. Play group therapy: A theoretical framework. *International Journal of Group Psychotherapy,* 1958, **8** (4), 410–418.

Ginott, Haim G., Lebo, Dell. Play therapy limits and theoretical orientation. *Journal of Consulting Psychology,* 1961, **25,** 337–340.

Gitelson, M. Clinical experience with play therapy. *American Journal of Orthopsychiatry,* 1938, **8,** 466–478.

Gitelson, M. (Chairman), Ross, H., Homberger, E., Allen, F., Blanchard, P., Lippmann, H. S. Gerard, M., & Lowery, L. Section on play therapy. *American Journal of Orthopsychiatry,* 1938, **8,** 499–524.

Gitelson, M., & Erikson, E. H. Play therapy. *American Journal of Orthopsychiatry,* 1937, **8** (3), 499–524.

Gladden, W. *Amusements: Their uses and abuses.* North Adams, Jas. T. Robinson, 1866, pp. 7, 9–10, 20–21

Glynn, D M. Freedom of playworld. *Times Educational Supplement.* February 26, 1965, **2597,** 586.

Goffman, I. *Encounters.* Indianapolis: Bobbs-Merrill, 1961.

Golberg, S., Godfrey, L., & Lewis, M. Play behavior in the year old infant: Early sex differences. Paper presented at meeting of Society for Research in Child Development, New York, 1967.

Graffiti—indoors and out—said to mirror society. *Medical Tribune,* April 22–23, 1967, p. 14.

Graham, M. Crowds and the like in vertebrates. *Human Relations,* 1964, **17** (4), 377–390.

Graham, M. Doll-play phantasies of Negro and white primary-school children. *Journal of Clinical Psychology,* 1955, **11,** 29–33.

Green, E. H. Group play and quarreling among pre-school children. *Child Development,* 1933, **4,** 302–307.

Greenacre, P. Play in relation to creative imagination. *Psychoanalytic Study of the Child,* 1959, **14,** 61–80.

Greenberg, P. Competition in children: An experimental study. *American Journal of Psychology,* 1932, **44,** 221–248.

Greenson, R. R. On gambling. *American Imago,* 1947, **4,** 61.

Greenwood, E. Dancing. *Bulletin of the Menninger Clinic,* 1942, **6,** 78.

Griffith, W. J., & Stringer, W. F. "The Effects of Intense Stimulation Experienced During Infancy on Adult Behavior in the Rat." *J. Compar. & Physiol. Psychol.*, 1952, **45**, 301–306.

Griffiths, R. *A study of imagination in early childhood.* London: Kegan Paul, 1935.

Groos, K. *The play of animals.* New York: D. Appleton, 1898. (Translated by .E. L. Baldwin).

Groos, K. Das Spiel als katharsis (Play as a catharsis). *Zeitschrift für Paediatrie Psychologie*, 1911, **12**, 353–367.

Groos, K. *The play of man.* New York: D. Appleton, 1901. (Translated by E. L. Baldwin, 1913).

Groos, K. *Das spiel, zwei vortrage* (Play, two lectures). Jena: Fischer, 1922.

Groos, K. Wesen und Sinn des Spiels. Bemerkungen im anschluss an die von F. J. Buytendijk unter obigem titel veroffentlichte schrift (Essence and sense of play. Observations concerned with the book published by F. J. Buytendijk under the above title). *Zeitschrift für Psychologie*, 1934, **133**, 358–363.

Guanella, F. M. Block building activities of young children. *Archives of Psychology*, 1934, **174**, 1–92.

Guerney, B., Jr. Use of adult responses to codify children's behavior in a play situation. *Perceptual and Motor Skills*, 1965, **20**, 614–616.

Gulick, L. H. Psychological, pedagogical and religious aspects of group games. *Pedagogical Seminary*, 1899, **6**, 135–150.

Gulick, L. H. *Philosophy of play.* New York: Charles Scribner's Sons, 1920.

Gump, P., & Yueng-Hung, M. Active games for physically handicapped children. *Physical Therapy Review*, 1954, **34**, 171.

Gump, P., & Sutton–Smith, B. Activity-setting and social interaction: A field study. *American Journal of Orthopsychiatry.* 1955, **25** (4), 755–760.

Gump, P. V., & Sutton–Smith, B. The "it" role in children's games. *The Group*, 1955, **17** (3), 3–8.

Gump, P. V., Schoggen, P., & Redl, F. The behavior of the same child in different milieus. In R. G. Barker (Ed.), *The stream of behavior.* New York: Appleton-Century Crofts & Meredith Publishing Company, 1963, Pp. 169–202.

Gump, P. V., & Sutton–Smith, B. Therapeutic play techniques. In N. J. Long, W. W. Morse, & R. G. Newman (Eds.), *Conflict in the classroom: The education of emotionally disturbed children.* Belmont: Wadsworth Publishing Company, 1965. Pp. 414–418.

Gump, P. V., Sutton-Smith, B., & Redl, F. *Influence of camp activities on camper behavior.* Wayne State University Library, 1955.

Haiding, K. Proeve van overeenkomst tussen enkele Javaanse en Europese Kinderspelen (Essay on similarity between simple Javanese and European children's games). *Volkskunde*, 1954, **55** (2), 60–71.

Haldane, J. B. S. Discussion on plays and vacuum activities. In *L'Instinct dans le comportement des animaux et de l'homme.* Paris: Masson, 1956.

Hall, G. S. *Youth: Its education, regimen and hygiene.* New York: Appleton, 1907.

Hall, G. S. *Adolescence: Its psychology and its relation to physiology, anthropology, sociology, sex crime, religion and education.* New York: Appleton, 1916, pp. 202–236.

Hall, G. S. *Aspects of child life and education.* New York: D. Appleton & Company, 1921.

Hall, T. W. Some effects of anxiety on the fantasy play of preschool children. *Dissertation Abstracts,* 1966, **27** (1–B), 302–303.

Halnan, H. H. "A study of father-child relationships using a doll play technique." Unpublished master's thesis, Stanford University, 1950.

Hambridge, G., Jr. Structured play therapy. *American Journal of Orthopsychiatry,* 1955, **25** (3), 601–617.

Hamilton, S. The educational value of play. *National Education Association of the United States: Addresses & Proceedings,* 1919, **57**, 637–642.

Hammer, L. F. *The Gary Public Schools: Physical training and play.* New York: General Education Board, 1918.

Harlow, H., & Harlow, M. Social deprivation in monkeys. *Scientific American* Nov., 1962, p. 10.

Harlow, H. F., Harlow, M. K., & Meyer, R. "Learning motivated by a manipulatory drive." *Journal of Experimental Psychology,* 1950, **40**, 228–234.

Harms, E. Children's play and abnormal behavior. *Nervous Child,* 1948, **7**, 229–232.

Harms, E. Play diagnosis: Preliminary considerations in a sound approach. *Nervous Child,* 1948, **7**, 233–240.

Hartley, E. L., & Swartz, S. A pictorial doll-play approach for the study of children's intergroup attitudes. *International Journal of Opinion Attitude Research,* 1951, 5, 261–270.

Hartley, R. E. *New play experiences for children: Planned play groups, miniature life toys and puppets.* New York: Columbia University Press, 1952.

Hartley, R. E. *Growing through play: Experiences of Teddy and Bud.* New York: Columbia University Press, 1952.

Hartley, R. E., Frank, L. K., & Goldenson, R. *Understanding children's play.* New York: Columbia University Press, 1952.

Hartley, R. E., & Goldenson, R. M. *The complete book of children' play.* New York: Crowell, 1957.

Hartmann, K. Spielaspekte des jugendkrawalls (Aspects of play in juvenile rioting). *Zeitschrift für Psychotherapie und Medizin Psychologie,* 1958, **8**, 159–170.

Hartmann, K. Spielaspekte des jugendkrawalls: Objective spielmerkmale (Aspects of play in juvenile rioting: Objective characteristics of play). *Zeitschrift für Psychotherapie und Medizin Psychologie*, 1959, **9**, 108–121.

Hartmann, K. On the functions of play. *Journal of Psychotherapy and Medical Psychology*, 1960, **10**, 205–214.

Harvey, O. J. An experimental approach to the study of status relations in informal groups. *American Sociological Review*, 1953, **18**, 357–367.

Haun, P. Re-creation. In *Recreation: A medical viewpoint*. New York: Teachers College, Columbia University Bureau of Publications, 1965. Pp. 18–48.

Hauser, I. Das kind und sein spiel (Child and his play). *Heilpädgogische Werkblatter*, 1953, **22**, 47–50.

Hawley, J. M. The twentieth century Protestant outlook. *Methodist Review*, 1900, **49**, 317.

Haworth, J. The relationship between the play of a group of school children and their personality traits. *Bulletin of the British Psychological Society*, 1957, **32**, 19.

Haworth, M. R., & Menolascino, F. J. Video-tape observations of disturbed young children. *Journal of Clinical Psychology*, 1967, **23** (2), 135–140

Hayes, J. R. The maintenance of play in young children. *Journal of Comparative and Physiological Psychology*, 1958, **51**, 788–794.

Heathers, G. Emotional dependence and independence in nursery school play. *Journal of Genetic Psychology*, 1955, **87**, 37–57.

Heckhausen, H. Entwurf einer psychologie des speilens (Sketch for a psychology of playing). *Psychologische Forschung*, 1964, **27** (3), 225–243.

Heinig, C. Play and play material. *Recreation*, 1931, **25**, 18–19, 50.

Hendrick, I. Work and the pleasure principle, *Psychoanalytic Quarterly*, 1943, **12**, 311.

Henry, J., & Henry, Z. Doll play of Pilaga Indian children. In H. A. Murray & Kluckholn (Eds.), *Personality in native society & culture*. New York: Knopf, 1948.

Herron, R. E., & Frobish, M. J. Computer analysis and display of movement patterns. *Journal of Experimental Child Psychology*, 1969, **8**, 40–44.

Hetzer, H. *Das volkstumliche kinderspiel* (Popular child's play). Wein: Deutscher Verlag für Jugen und Volksund, 1927.

Higgins, J. M. Social behavior of four year old children during outdoor play in day care centers. *Dissertation Abstract*, 1966, **27** (4A), 993–994.

Hilgard, Ernest. Impulsive versus realistic thinking. In Ralph N. Haber (Ed.), *Current research in motivation*. New York: Holt, Rinehart, and Winston, 1966.

Hils, K. *The toy: Its value, construction and use*. (Trans. by E. Fitzgerald.) Chester Springs, Pa.: Dufour Editions, 1961.

Symposium on Hobbies. In *Bulletin Menninger Clinic*, 1942, **6**, 65–102.

Holbrook, D. *Children's games*. Bedford, England: Gordon Fraser, 1957.

Hollenberg, E. A study of some effects of child-training practices on doll play behavior. Unpublished master's thesis, State University of Iowa, 1949.

Hollenberg, E., & Sperry, M. Some antecedents of aggression and effects of frustration in doll play. *Personality*, 1951, 1, 32–43.

Holway, A. R. Early self-regulation of infants and later behavior in play interviews. *American Journal of Orthopsychiatry*, 1949, 19, 612–623.

Homburger, E. Configurations in play: Clinical notes. *Psychoanalytical Quarterly*, 1937, 6, 139–214.

Homburger, E. Traumatische Konfigurationen im spiel (Traumatic configuration in play). *Imago*, 1937, 23, 447–156. *Zeitschrift Psychoanalytical Padagogical*, 1937, 11, 262–292.

Honzik, M. P. Sex differences in the occurrence of materials in the play constructions of pre-adolescents. *Child Development*, 1951, 22, 15–35.

Horne, B. M., & Philleo, C. C. A comparative study of the spontaneous play activities of normal and mentally defective children. *Journal of Genetic Psychology*, 1942, 61, 33–46.

Howard, D. Ball bouncing customs and rhymes in Australia. *Midwest Folklore*, 1959, 9 (2), 77–87.

Howard, D. The "Toodlembuck-Australian" children's gambling device and game. *Journal of American Folklore*, 1960, 73 (287), 53–54.

Hubsch, L., & Reininger, K. Zur psychologie des kinderspiels und der geschlechtsunterschiede im kindergartenalter (Contribution to the psychology of children's play and differences of sex at kindergarten-age). *Zeitschrift für Angewandte Psychologie*, 1931, 40, 97–176.

Huizinga, J. *Homo-Ludens: A study of the play element in culture*. London: Routledge & Kegan Paul, Ltd., 1949. (Translated by R.F.C. Hull.)

Hulson, E. L. An analysis of the free play of ten four-year-old children through consecutive observations. *Journal of Juvenile Research*, 1930, 14, 188–208.

Hulson, Eva. Block constructions of four-year-old children. *Journal of Juvenile Research*, 1930, 14, 209–222.

Humphrey, J. H. Comparison of the use of active games and language workbook exercises as learning media for the development of language understanding with third grade children. *Perceptual and Motor Skills*, 1965, 21, (1), 23–26.

Humphrey, J. H. An exploratory study of active games in learning of number concepts by first grade boys and girls. *Perceptual and Motor Skills*, 1966, 23 (2), 341–342.

Hurlock, E. B. Experimental investigations of childhood play. *Psychological Bulletin*, 1934, 31, 47–66.

Hurlock, E. B. Play. In *Child Development*. New York: McGraw Hill, 1956. Pp. 321–365.

Hurlock, E. B., & Burstein, M. The imaginary playmate: A questionnaire study. *Journal of Genetic Psychology*, 1932, **41**, 380–392.

Hutchinson, W. Play as an education. *Contemporary Review*, 1903, **84**, 375–394.

Hutt, C. Exploration and play in children. *Symposium of the Zoological Society of London*, 1966, **18**, 61–81.

Hutt, C. Exploration of novelty in children with and without upper CNS lesions, and some effects of auditory and visual incentives. *ACTA Psychologica*. In press.

Ilg, F. L., & Ames, L. B. *The first five years of life*. New York: Harper Brothers, 1940. Pp. 251–253.

Inhelder, E. Zur psychologies eininger Ver Haltensweisen-Besonders des Spiels-von Zootieren (On the psychology of some behavior patterns especially of play—in zoo animals). *Zeitschrift für Tierpsychologie*, 1955, **12**, 88–144.

International Council for Children's Play. Groningen, September 14–17, 1961. *Spel en speelgoed in onze tijd* (Play and playthings in our time). Ijmuiden: Vermande Zonen, 1964.

Ireland, R. R. Significance of recreational maturation in the educational process: The six ages of play. *Journal of Educational Sociology*, 1959, **32**, 356–360.

Issacs, S. The nature and function of fantasy. *International Journal of Psycho-analysis*, 1948, **29**, 73–97.

Isaacs, Susan. *Social development in young children*, N.Y.: Harcourt, Brace, 1933.

Isch, Maria J. Fantasied mother-child interaction in doll play. *Journal of Genetic Psychology*, 1952, **81**, 233–258.

Jackson, L., & Todd, K. M. *Child treatment and the therapy of play*. (2nd ed.). New York: Ronald Press, 1950.

Jacquin, G. *L'education par le jeu* (Education by play). Paris: Editions Fleurus, 1921.

Janus, S. Q. An investigation of the relationship between children's language and their play. *Journal of Genetic Psychology*, 1943, **62**, 3–61.

Jary, P. Mother-infant relations in langurs. In H. L. Rheingold (Ed.), *Maternal behavior in mammals*. New York: Wiley, 1963, 282–304.

Jeffre, I. M. Fantasied mother-child interaction in doll play. *Journal of Genetic Psychology*, 1952, **81**, 233–258.

Jersild, A., Markey, Frances, & Jersild, Catherine T. Children's fears, dreams, wishes, daydreams, likes, dislikes, pleasant and unpleasant memories. *Child Developments Monographs*, 1933, No. 12.

Jersild, A. T., & Meigs, Margaret, F. Direct observation as a research method. *Review of Educational Research*, December, 1939, 1–14.

Jewell, P. A., & Loizis, C. (Eds.). *Play, exploration and territory in mammals*. Proceedings of a symposium, Zoological Society of London, November, 1965. New York: Academic Press, 1966.

Johnson, Buford, & Courtney, Dorthy M. Tower building. *Child Development*, 1931, **2**, 161.

Johnson, E. Z. Attitudes of children toward authority as projected in their doll play at two age levels. Unpublished doctoral dissertation, Harvard University, 1951.

Johnson, G. E. Education by play and games. *Pedagogical Seminary*, 1894, **3**, 97–135.

Johnson, G. E. *Education by play and games*. Boston: Ginn & Company 1907.

Johnson, H. M. *The art of block building*. New York: Day, 1933.

Johnson, L. C. The effect of father absence during infancy on later father-child relationship using a doll-play technique. Unpublished master's thesis, Stanford University, 1952.

Johnson, M. W. The effect on behavior of variations in the amount of play equipment. *Child Development*, 1935, **6**, 56–68.

Johnston, M. K., Kelley, C. S., Harris, F. R., & Wolf, M. An application of reinforcement principles to development of motor skills of a young child. *Child Development Monographs*, 1966, **37** (2), 379–387.

Jones, E. The problem of Paul Morphy: A contribution to the psychoanalysis of chess. *International Journal of Psychoanalysis*, 1931, **12**, 1.

Jones, H. E. *Development in adolescence*. New York: Appleton-Century, 1943.

Jones, T. D. The development of certain motor skills and play activities on young children. *Child Development Monographs*, 1939, **26**, 1–180.

Kanner, L. Play investigations and play treatments of children's behavior disorders. *Journal of Pediatrics*, 1940, **17**, 533–546.

Kardos, E., & Peto, A. Contributions to the theory of play. *British Journal of Medical Psychology*, 1956, **29**, 100–112.

Kaufman, H., & Becker, G. M. The empirical determination of game-theoretical strategies. *Journal of Experimental Psychology*, 1961, **61**, 462–468.

Kawin, Ethel. *The wise choice of toys*. Chicago: Univ. of Chicago Press, 1934.

Keene, F. W. *Fun around the world*. New York: McGraw, 1955, p. 50.

Keesing, F. M. Recreative behavior and culture change. In A. F. C. Wallace (Ed.), *Men and culture*. Philadelphia: University of Pennsylvania, 1960. Pp. 130–133.

Kepler, H. *The child and his play*. New York: Funk & Wagnalls, 1932.

Keri, H. Ancient games and popular games: Psychological essay. *American Image*, 1958, **15**, 41–89.

Klein, Melanie. *The psychoanalysis of children*. London: Hogarth Press, 1932.

Klein, M. Personification in the play of children. In *Contributions to psychoanalysis, 1921–1945*. London: Hogarth Press, 1948. Pp. 215–226.

Klein, M. The psychoanalytic play technique. *American Journal of Orthopsychiatry*, 1955, **25**, 223–237.

Klein, M. Die psychoanalytische spieltechnik: Ihre geschichte und bedeutung (The history and significance of psychoanalytic play technique). *Psyche*, 1959, **12**, 687–705.

Klinger, E. The development of imaginative behavior-implications of play for a theory of fantasy. *Psychological Bulletin,* in press.

Knight, R. P. Contract bridge. *Bulletin of the Menninger Clinic,* 1942, **6**, 68.

Koch, H. L. The relation in young children between characteristics of their playmates and certain attributes of their siblings. *Child Development,* 1957, **28**, 175–202.

Koestler, Arthur. *The Act of creation.* New York: Macmillan, 1964.

Kraus, R. G. *Play activities for boys and girls.* New York: McGraw-Hill, 1957.

Kubie, L. S. Competitive sports and the awkward child. *Child Study Center Bulletin,* 1954, **31**, 10–15.

Kulla, M. A therapeutic doll-play program with an emotionally disturbed child. *Dissertation Abstracts,* 1966, **27** (4B), 1291.

Lambert, H. E. A note on children's pastimes. *Swahili,* 1959, **30**, 74–78.

Langer, Susanne. *Mind: An essay on human feeling.* Vol. I. Baltimore: Johns Hopkins, 1967.

Larkin, S. D. Study of leisure time activities of children. *Child Welfare,* 1930, **24**, 472–475.

Layman, A. E. Block play—an essential. *Elementary School Journal,* 1940, **40**, 607–613.

Lazarus, M. *Über die reize des spiels* (Concerning the fascination of play). Berlin: Dummler, 1883.

Lebedinskaya, Y. I., & Polyakova, A. G. Certain age modifications of the inter-action of the first and second signal systems in children two to seven years of age. *The central nervous system and behavior.* U. S. Department of Health, Education and Welfare, Public Health Service. December 1, 1959, 488–499.

Lebo, D. Theoretical framework for non-directive play therapy: Concepts from psychoanalysis and learning theory. *Journal of Consulting Psychology,* 1958, **22**, 275–279.

Lee, D., & Hutt, C. A playroom designed for filming children: A note. *Journal of Child Psychology and Psychiatry,* 1964, **5** (3–4), 263–265.

Lee, J. *Play in education.* New York: The Macmillan Company, 1922.

Lee, J. The child's leisure. *Playground,* 1931, **24**, 13–14.

Lehman, H. C. Growth stages in play behavior. *Pedagogical Seminary,* 1926, **33**, 273–288.

Lehman, H. C. Community differences in play behavior. *Pedagogical Seminary,* 1926, **33**, 477–490.

Lehman, H. C., & Michie, O. C. Extreme versatility versus paucity of play interests. *Pedagogical Seminary,* 1927, **34**, 200–208.

Lehman, H. C., & Wilkerson, D. A. The influence of chronological age versus mental age on play behavior. *Journal of Genetic Psychology.* 1928, **35**, 312–324.

Lehman, H. C., & Witty, P. A. Playing school—A compensatory mechanism. *Psychological Review,* 1926, **33**, 480–485.

Lehman, H. C., & Witty, P. A. *The psychology of play activities.* New York: A. S. Barnes & Company, 1927.

Lehman, H. C., & Witty, P. A. The play behavior of 50 gifted children. *Journal of Educational Psychology,* 1927, **18**, 259–265.

Lehman, H. C., & Witty, P. A. Periodicity and play behavior. *Journal of Educational Psychology,* 1927, **18**, 115–118.

Lehman, H. C., & Witty, P. A. Play activity and school progress. *Journal of Educational Psychology,* 1927, **18**, 318–326.

Lehman, H. C., & Witty, P. A. A study of play in relation to intelligence. *Journal of Applied Psychology,* 1928, **12**, 369–397.

Lehman, H. C., & Witty, P. A. A study of play in relation to pubescence. *Journal of Social Psychology,* 1930, **1**, 510–523.

Leland, H., Walker, J., & Toboada, A. N. Group play therapy with a group of post-nursery male retardates. *American Journal of Mental Deficiency,* 1959, **63**, 848–851.

Leland, H., & Smith, D. Unstructured material in play therapy for emotionally disturbed brain damaged, mentally retarded children. *American Journal of Mental Deficiency,* 1962, **66**, 621–628.

Leland, H., & Smith, D. *Play therapy with mentally subnormal children.* New York: Grune & Stratton, 1965.

Leonard, A. Toys for toddlers. *Today's Health,* Dec. 1952, **60**, 42–43.

Lerner, E., & Murphy, L. B. Methods for the study of personality in young children. *Monograph of the Society for Research in Child Development,* 1941, **6** (4), 159–252.

Leton, D. A. The factor structure of diagnostic scores from school play sessions. *Psychology in the Schools,* 1966, **3** (2), 148–153.

Levenstein, P., & Sunley, R. An effect of stimulating verbal interaction between mothers and children around play materials. *American Journal of Orthopsychiatry,* 1967, **37** (2), 334–335.

Levin, H., & Sears, R. R. Identification with parents as a determinant of doll-play aggression. *Child Development,* 1956, **27**, 135–153.

Levin, H., & Turgeon, V. F. The influence of the mother's presence on children's doll-play aggression. *Journal of Abnormal Social Psychology,* 1957, **55**, 301–308.

Levin, H., & Wardwell, E. The research uses of doll play. *Psychological Bulletin,* 1962, **59** (1), 27–56.

Levine, J. Humor in play and sports. In Slovenko, R., & Knight, J. A. (Eds.), *Motivations in play, games and sports.* Springfield, Ill.: Chas. C Thomas, 1967, 55–63.

Levinson, B. M. The inner life of the extremely gifted child, as seen from the clinical setting. *Journal of Genetic Psychology,* 1961, **99**, 83–88.

Levy, D. M. Hostility patterns in sibling rivalry experiments. *American Journal of Orthopsychiatry*, 1936, **6**, 183–257.

Levy, D. M. Use of play technique as experimental procedure. *American Journal of Orthopsychiatry*, 1933, **3**, 266–277.

Lewis, E. The function of group play during middle childhood in developing the ego complex. *British Journal of Medical Psychology*, 1954, **27** (1), 15–29.

Lieberman, J. N. Playfulness and divergent thinking: An investigation of their relationship at the kindergarten level. *Journal of Genetic Psychology*, 1965, **107**, 219–224. *Dissertation Abstracts*, 1964, **15** (6), 36–77.

Lieberman, J. N. Construction of a measuring instrument for playfulness and nonplayfulness as a personality trait in adolescents. Paper presented at the meeting of the Eastern Psychological Association, Boston, April, 1967.

Lieberman, J. N. Playfulness: An attempt to conceptualize a quality of play and of the player. *Psychological Reports*, 1966, **19**, 1278.

Lieberman, J. N. Playfulness and divergent thinking: An investigation of their relationship at the kindergarten level. *Journal of Genetic Psychology*, 1965, **107**, 219–224.

Lewin, Kurt. *Field theory in social science.* Dorwin Cartwright, Ed. N. Y.: Harper, 1951.

Liss, E. Play techniques in child analysis. *American Journal of Orthopsychiatry*, 1936, **6**, 17–22.

Long, N. J., Morse, W. C., & Newman, R. G. Adjunctive therapies. In *Conflict in the classroom: The education of emotionally disturbed children.* Belmont: Wadsworth Publishing Company, 1965.

Loomis, E. A., Jr. Play patterns in schizophrenic and mentally defective children. United States Public Health Service Research Grant Application M-824 (R), February 25, 1955.

Loomis, E. A., Hilgeman, L. M., & Meyer, L. R. Childhood psychosis. II. Play patterns as nonverbal indices of ego functions: A preliminary report. *American Journal of Orthopsychiatry*, 1957, **27**, 691–700.

Lorenz, K. Plays and vacuum activities. In *L'instinct dans le comportement des animaux et de l'homme.* Paris: Masson, 1956.

Lorenz, K. *Instinctive behavior,* 1st Ed. (Trans. and ed. by C. Schiller). New York: Int. Univs., 1957, p. 99.

Lovass, O. I., Freitag, G., Gold, V. J., & Kossorla, I. C. Recording apparatus and procedure for observation of behavior of children in free play settings. *Journal of Experimental Psychology*, 1965, **2**, 108–112.

Low, H. R. How children learn to play at different levels. *Understanding the child*, 1938, **7** (4), 11–14.

Lowenfeld, M. *Play in childhood.* London: Gollancz, 1935.

Lowenfeld, M. The theory and use of play in the psychotherapy of children. *Journal of Mental Science*, 1938, **84**, 1057–1058.

Lowenfeld, V. *Your child and his art.* New York: Macmillan, 1954.

Lowrey, L. G. Introduction: Therapeutic play techniques symposium, 1954. *American Journal of Orthopsychiatry,* 1955, **25** (3), 574–575.

Lunzer, E. A. Intellectual development in the play of young children. *Educational Review,* 1959, 11, 205–223.

Luria, A. R., & Yudovich, F. I. *Speech and the development of mental processes in the child.* London: Staples, 1959.

Lynn, D. B. Development and validation of a structured doll play test for children. *Quarterly Bulletin of Indiana University Medical Center,* 1955.

Lynn, D. B., & Lynn, R. The structured doll-play test as a projective technique for use with children. *Journal of Projective Techniques,* 1959, **23,** 335–344.

Lynn, R. A study of the responses of four and six-year-olds to a structured doll-play test. Unpublished master's thesis, Purdue University, 1955.

Maccoby, Eleanor E. The taking of adult roles in middle childhood. *Journal of Abnormal and Social Psychology,* 1961, **63** (3), 493–503.

Maccoby, M., Modiano, N., & Lander, P. Games and social character in a Mexican village. *Psychiatry,* 1964, **27,** 150–162.

MacDonald, M., McGuire, C. and Havighurst, R. J. Leisure activities and socioeconomic status of children. *American Journal of Sociology,* 1949, **54,** 505–519.

Machotka, P. The development of aesthetic criteria in childhood: I. Justification of preference. *Child Development,* 1966, **37,** 877–885.

Maddi, S. Exploratory behavior and variation seeking in man. In Fiske, D. W., & Maddi, S., (Eds.), *Functions of varied experience.* Homewood, Ill.: Dorsey, 1961, p. 253–277.

Manwell, E. M., & Mengert, A. G. A study of the development of two and three-year-old children with respect to play activities. *University of Iowa Studies on Child Welfare,* 1934, **9,** 67–111.

Margolin, E. B., & Leton, D. A. Interest of kindergarten pupils in block play. *Journal of Educational Research,* 1961, **55,** 13–18.

Markey, Frances. Imaginative behavior in preschool children. *Child Development Monograph,* 1935, No. 18.

Marshall, H. R. Relations between home experiences and children's use of language in play interactions with peers. *Psychological Monographs,* 1961, **75,** No. 5.

Marshall, Helen, & Doshi, Rohini. Aspects of experience revealed through doll play of preschool children. *Journal of Psychology,* 1965, **61,** 47–57.

Marshall, H. Children's plays, games and amusements. In C. Murchison (Ed.), *A handbook of child psychology.* Worcester, Massachusetts: Clark University Press, 1931. Pp. 515–526.

Marshall, H. R. Relations between home experiences and children's use of language in play interactions with peers. *Psychological Monographs General and Applied,* 1961, **75,** 1–77.

Marshall, Helen R., & Shwu, C. H. Experimental modification of dramatic play. Paper presented at the American Psychological Association, New York, Sept. 1966.

Mason, W. A. Determinants of social behavior in young chimpanzees. In A. M. Schrier, H. F. Harlow, & F. Stollnitz (Eds.), *Behavior of nonhuman primates.* Vol. 2. New York: Academic Press. 1965, 335–364.

Mason, W. A., Harlow, H. F. and Ruepig, R. R. The development of manipulatory responses in the infant rhesus monkey. *J. Comparative Physiological Psychology,* 1959, **52,** 555–558.

Mason, W. A. Motivational aspects of social responsiveness in young chimpanzees. In H. W. Stevenson, E. H. Hess, & H. L. Rheingold (Eds.), *Early behavior: comparative and developmental approaches.* New York: Wiley, 1967, 103–126.

Mason, W. A., Saxon, S. V., & Sharpe, L. G. Preferential responses of young chimpanzees to food and social rewards. *Psychological Record,* 1963, **13,** 341–345.

Matterson, Elizabeth M. *Play and playthings for the preschool child.* Baltimore, Md. Penguin Books, 1967.

Maw, W. H., & Maw, E. W. Personal & social variables differentiating children with high and low curiosity. *Cooperative research project,* No. 1511, Wilmington: University of Delaware, 1965, 1–181.

May, H. L. *Leisure and its use: Some international observations.* New York: Barnes Company, 1928.

McCandles, B. R., & Hoyt, J. M. Sex, ethnicity and play preferences of pre-school children. *Journal of Abnormal and Social Psychology,* 1961, **62,** 683–685.

McCulloch, C. M. A log of children's out-of-school activities. *Elementary School Journal,* 1957, **58,** 157–165.

McDowell, M. S. Frequency of choice of play materials by pre-school children. *Child Development,* 1937, **8,** 305–310.

McElvaney, M. E. Four types of fantasy aggression in the responses of "rebellious" and "submissive" children to the Driscoll Playkit, structured by parental-demand and neural studious stress. Unpublished doctor of philosophy dissertation, Teachers College, Columbia University, 1958.

McGhee, Z. A study in the play life of some South Carolina children. *Pedagogical Seminary,* 1900, **7,** 459–491.

McIntosh, P. C. *Sport in society.* London: C. A. Watts, 1963.

McPherson, C. A. The value of play in meeting the emotional needs of young children in the hospital. *Bibliotheca Paediatrica,* 1965, **84,** 181–182.

Mead, George H. *Mind, self, and society.* Chicago: Univ. of Chicago Press, 1934.

Meer, L. H. Play things for children. *The delineator,* 1931, 118, **25,** 73–74.

Mehlman, B. Group play therapy with mentally retarded children. *Journal of Abnormal and Social Psychology,* 1953, **48,** 53–60.

Meister, D. Adjustment of children as reflected in play performance. *Journal of Genetic Psychology,* 1948, **73,** 141–155.

Meister, R. Spiel und arbeit als gegensatzliche verhaltungsweisen menschlicher tatigkeit (Play and work as opposite movements showing the suppression of human activity). *Vierteljahrschrift für Jegendk,* 1932, **2,** 145–154.

Menninger, K. Chess. *Bulletin of the Menninger Clinic,* 1942, **6,** 80.

Menninger, K. *Love against hate.* New York: Harcourt, 1942, pp. 167–188.

Menninger, K., & Menninger, J. Recreation and morale—some tentative conclusions. *Bulletin of the Menninger Clinic,* 1942, **6,** 100.

Menninger, W. C. Psychological aspects of hobbies: A contribution to civilian morale. *American Journal of Psychiatry,* 1942, **99,** 122.

Menninger, W. C. Recreation and Mental Health, *Recreation,* Nov., 1948.

Meyer, H. M. On the readiness for play and instinctive behavior. *Zeitschrift für Tierpsychologie,* 1956, **13,** 442–462.

Millar, S. *The Psychology of Play.* London: Pelican, 1968.

Millichamp, D. A. Another look at play. *Institute of Child Study Bulletin* Toronto, 1953, **15** (4), 1–13.

Mishra, D. Recreation of Baiga children. *Vanyajati (India),* 1958, **6** (2), 70–73.

Mistry, D. K. The Indian child and his play. *Sociology Bulletin,* 1959, **8** (1), 86–96.

Mitchell, E. D., & Mason, B. S. *The theory of play.* New York: Barnes, 1948.

Monroe, W. S. Play interests of children. *Addresses and Proceedings of the National Education Association,* 1899, **38,** 1084–1090. *American Educational Review,* 1899, 4, 358–365.

Montgomery, K. C., & Monkman, J. A. The relation between fear and exploratory behavior. *Journal of Comparative & Physiological Psychology,* 1955, **48,** 132–136.

Montgomery, K. C., & Segall, M. Discrimination learning based upon the exploratory drive. *Journa lof Comparative & Physiological Psychology,* 1955, **48,** 225–228.

Moore, T. Realism and fantasy in children's play. *Journal of Child Psychology and Psychiatry,* 1964, **5,** 15–36.

Moore, T., & Ucko, L. E. Four to six: Constructiveness and conflict in meeting doll play problems. *Journal of Child Psychology and Psychiatry,* 1961, **2,** 21–47.

Moore, O. K., & Anderson, A. R. Some Puzzling Aspects of Social Interaction. *Review of metaphysics,* XV (1962), 409–433.

Morris, D. J. Discussion on plays and vacuum activities. In *L'Instinct dans le comportement des animaux et de l'homme.* Paris: Masson, 1956.

Moustakas, C. E. Emotional adjustment and the play therapy process. *Journal of Genetic Psychology,* 1955, **86,** 79–99.

Moustakas, C. E. The frequency and intensity of negative attitudes expressed in play therapy: A comparison of well-adjusted and disturbed young children. *Journal of Genetic Psychology*, 1955, **86**, 309–325.

Moustakas, C. E., & Schalock, H. D. An analysis of therapist-child interaction in play therapy. *Child Development*, 1955, **26**, 143–147.

Moustakas, C. E. *Children in play therapy*. New York: McGraw-Hill, 1953.

Moyer, K. E., & Gilmer, B. von H. Attention spans of children for experimentally designed toys. *Journal of Genetic Psychology*, 1955, **87**, 187–201.

Moyer, K. E., & Gilmer, B. von H. Experimental study of children's preferences and use of blocks in play. *Journal of Genetic Psychology*, 1956, **89**, 3–10.

Murphy, L. B. *Personality in young children*. New York: Basic Books, Inc. 1957.

Murphy, Lois. *Social behavior and child personality*. New York: Columbia Univ. Press, 1937.

Murphy, L. B. Experiments in free play. In E. Lerner, & L. B. Murphy (Eds.), Vol. I. Methods for the study of personality in young children. *Monograph of the Society for Research on Child Development*, 1941, **6** (4), 159–252.

Mussen, P. H., & Rutherford, E. Effects of aggressive cartoons on children's aggressive play. *Journal of Abnormal and Social Psychology*, 1961, **62**, 461–464.

National Association for Retarded Children. *A bibliography for parents and professionals in the area of recreation for the mentally retarded*. New York: National Association for Retarded Children.

Neale, R. E. Religion and play. *Crossroads*, 1967, **17** (4), 67–95.

Neugebauer, H. Spiel und phantasie in der fruhen kindheit meines sohnes (Play and fantasy in the early childhood of my sons). *Zeitschrift fur Angewandte Psychologie*, 1932, **42**, 220–258.

Neumeyer, M. H. *Leisure and recreation: A study of leisure and recreation in their sociological aspects*. New York: Ronald Press Company, 1958.

Newell, H. W. Play therapy in child psychiatry. *American Journal of Orthopsychiatry*, 1941, **11**, 245–251.

Nice, M. M. A child's imagination. *Pedagogical Seminary*, 1919, **26**, 171–201.

Nissen, H. W., Chow, H. L., & Semmes, J. Effect of restricted opportunity for tactual, kinaesthetic, and manipulative experience on the behavior of the chimpanzee. *American Journal of Psychology*, 1951, **64**, 485–507.

Ottson, L. G. Play therapy as a preliminary exercise to prothesis training in abnormalities of the extremities. *Svensk Lakartidn*, 1964, **61**, 1678–1691.

Palmer, L. A. *Play life in the first eight years*. Boston: Ginn and Company, 1916.

Papst, M. Z. Das verhalten von kindern in einfachen trategischen spielen (Behavior of children in simple strategic games). *Zeitschrift für Psychologie*, 1966, **172**, 17–39.

Parker, F. Sport, play and physical education in cultural perspective. *Journal of Health, Physical Education and Recreation*, 1965, **36**, 29–30.

Parten, M. B. Social participation among pre-school children. *Journal of Abnormal and Social Psychology,* 1932, **27**, 243–269.

Parten, M. B. Social play among pre-school children. *Journal of Abnormal and Social Psychology,* 1933, **28**, 136–147.

Paschal, B. J. Work or play? *Peabody Journal of Education,* 1965, **43**, 175–178.

atrick, G. T. W. The psychology of play. *Pedagogical Seminary,* 1914, **21**, 469–484.

Patrick, G. T. W. The play of a nation. *Science Monthly,* 1921, **13**, 350–362.

Patrick, G. T. W. *The psychology of relaxation.* Boston & N.Y.: Houghton-Mifflin, 1916.

Payne, W. Acquisition of strategies in gaming situations. *Perceptual and Motor Skills,* 1965, **20**, 473–479.

Peller, L. E. Models of children's play. *Mental Hygiene,* 1952, **36**, 66–83.

Peller, L. E. Libidinal phases, ego development and play. *Psychoanalytical Study of the Child,* 1954, **9**, 178–198.

Peller, L. E. Libidinal development as reflected in play. *Psychoanalysis,* 1955, **3** (3), 3–12.

Peller, L. E. Daydreams and children's favorite books. *Psychoanalytical Study of the Child,* 1959, **14**, 414–433.

Pepitone, Albert; McCauley, Clark & Hammond, Peirce. Change in attractiveness of forbidden toys as a function of severity of threat. *Journal of Experimental Social Psychology,* **3** (3), 1967.

Perryman, L. C. Dramatic play and cognitive development. *Journal of Nursery Education,* 1962, **17**, 183–188.

Pfeifer, S. Ausserungen infantilerotisaken triebe im spiele. *Imago,* 1919, **5**, 243–283.

Phenix, P. H. Play element in education. *The Educational Forum,* 1965, **29**, 297–306.

Phillips, R. H. The nature and function of children's formal games. *Psychoanalytical Quarterly,* 1960, **29**, 200–207.

Phillips, R. H. Children's games. In Slovenko, R., & Knight, J. A. (Eds.), *Motivations in play, games and sports.* Springfield, Ill.: Chas. C Thomas, 1967, 63–73.

Phillips, R. H. Doll play as a function of the realism of the materials and the length of the experimental session. *Child Development,* 1945, **16**, 123–143.

Piaget, J. El juego simbolico (Symbolic play). *Archives of Neurobiologie,* 1934, **14**, 357–362.

Piaget, J. *Play, dreams and imitation in childhood.* New York: W. W. Norton and Company, 1962.

Piaget, J. Response to Brian Sutton-Smith. *Psychological Review,* 1966, **73**, 111–112.

Piaget, J. *The moral judgment of the child.* Glencoe, Illinois: Free Press, 1948.

Pickard, P. M. The seriousness of play. In *The activity of children*. London: Longmans, Green and Company, Ltd., 1965, pp. 65–83.

Piers, M. Play and mastery. *Reiss-Davis Clinical Bulletin*, 1967, 4, p. 51.

Pintler, M. H. Doll play as a function of experimenter-child interaction and initial organization of materials. *Child Development*, 1945, 16, 145–166.

Pintler, M. H., Phillips, R., & Sears, R. R. Sex differences in the projective doll play of pre-school children. *Journal of Psychology*, 1946, 21, 73–80.

Pope, C. H. Texas rope-jumping rhymes (Accompanying children's play). *Western Folklore*, 1956, 15 (1), 46–48.

Potter, S. *The Theory and practice of gamesmanship*. New York: Holt, Rinehart and Winston.

Proudfoot, B. F. An Edinburgh street game. *Ulster Folklife*, 1957, 3 (1), 74–75.

Rabin, A. I. *Growing up in the kibbutz*. New York: Springer, 1965.

Radler, D. H., & Kephart, N. C. *Success through play*. New York: Harper, 1960.

Rafferty, J. E., Tyler, B. B., & Tyler, F. B. Personality assessment from free play observations. *Child Development*, 1960, 31, 691–702.

Rainwater, C. E. *The meaning of play*. Chicago: University of Chicago Press, 1915.

Rainwater, C. E. The origin of the play movement. In *The play movement*. Chicago: University of Chicago Press, 1922, pp. 13–44.

Rainwater, C. E. *The play movement in the United States*. Chicago: University of Chicago Press, 1922.

Rainwater, C. E. Play as collective behavior. *Journal of Applied Sociology*, 1924, 8, 217–222.

Rank, B. T. The therapeutic value of play. *Understanding the child*, 1938, 7, 19–23.

Ravenhill, A. Some results of an inquiry into the play interests of English elementary school children. *Child Study*, 1911, 3, 121–142.

Reaney, M. J. The correlation between general intelligence and play ability as shown in organized group games. *British Journal of Psychology*, 1916, 7 (2), 226–250.

Redl, F. The impact of game ingredients on children's play behavior. In B. Schaffner (Ed.), *Group processes,* Transactions of the fourth conference. New York: Josiah Macy, Jr., Foundation, 1959, pp. 33–81.

Redl, F., & Wineman, D. *Children who hate*. Glencoe: Free Press, 1951.

Reece, L. H. The play needs of children aged 6 to 12. *Marriage and Family Living*, 1954, 16, 131–134.

Reeves, W. Report of the committee on street play. *Journal of Educational Sociology*, 1931, 4, 607–613.

Reider, N. Board Games in General. In Slovenko, R., & Knight, J. A. (Eds.), *Motivations in play, games and sports*. Springfield, Ill.: Chas. C Thomas, 1967, 266–273.

Reider, N. Chess. Oedipus, and the Mater Dolorosa. *International Journal of Psychoanalysis*, 1959, **40**, 320–333.

Reider, N. Preanalytic and psychoanalytic theories of play and games. In Slovenko, R., & Knight, J. A. (Eds.), *Motivations in play, games and sports*. Springfield, Ill.: Chas. C Thomas, 1967, 13–39.

Rheingold, H. Controlling the infant's exploratory behavior. In E. M. Foss (Ed.), *Determinants of Behavior II*. New York: Wiley, 1963, 67–104.

Rheingold, H. L. *Maternal behavior in mammals*. New York: Wiley, 1963.

Riedman, S. R. *The physiology of work and play: A textbook of muscle activity*. New York: Dryden Press, 1950.

Riggs, A. F. *Play: Recreation in a balanced life*. Garden City, New York: Doubleday, 1935.

Robbins, F. G. *The sociology of play, recreation and leisure time*. Dubuque, Iowa: University Press, 1955.

Roberts, J. M., Arth, M. J., & Bush, R. R. Games in culture. *American Anthropologist*, 1959, **61**, 597–605.

Roberts, J. M., & Sutton-Smith, B. Child training and game involvement. *Ethnology*, 1962, **1**, 166–185.

Roberts, J. M., Sutton-Smith, B., & Kendon, A. Strategy in games and folk tales. *Journal of Social Psychology*, 1963, **61**, 185–199.

Roberts, J. M., & Sutton-Smith, B. Cross cultural correlates of games of chance. *Behavior Science Notes*, 1966, **3**, 131–144.

Roberts, M. P. A study of children's play in the home environment. *University of Iowa Studies on Child Welfare*, 1934, **8**, 33–98.

Robinson, Eleanor Louise. The form and the imaginative content of children's block buildings. Dissertation abstract. 1959, **19**, 2651.

Robinson, E. F. Doll play as a function of the doll family constellation. *Child Development*, 1946, **17**, 99–119.

Robinson, E. S. The compensatory function of make believe play. *Psychological Review*, 1920, **27**, 429–439.

Robinson, E. S. Play. In *Encyclopedia of social science*. New York: Macmillan, 1934, pp. 160–161.

Rogerson, C. H. *Play therapy in childhood*. London: Oxford University Press, 1939.

Romero, E. Juegos infantiles tradicionales en el Peru (Traditional children's games in Peru). *Folklore in America*, 1955, **3** (3), 94–120.

Romswinckel, C. Het Kleuterspel en het creatieve in de mens (Infant play and the creative in man). *Psychologische Achtergroden*, 1953, **5**, 138–142.

Rose, A. W. Toward understanding the concept and functions of play. *Educational Theory*, 1956, **6**, 20–25.

Rosenberg, B. G., & Sutton-Smith, B. Revised conception of masculine-feminine differences in play activities. *Journal of Genetic Psychology*, 1960, **96**, 165–170.

Rosenberg, B. G., & Sutton-Smith, B. The measurement of masculinity and femininity in children: An extension and revalidation. *Journal of Genetic Psychology*, 1964, **104**, 259–264.

Rosenzweig, S., & Shakow, D. Play technique in schizophrenia and other psychoses. I. Rationale. II. An experimental study of schizophrenic constructions with play materials. *American Journal of Orthopsychiatry*, 1937, **7**, 32–47.

Ross, H. The teacher game. In R. S. Eissler *et al.* (Eds.), *The psychoanalytic study of the child*. New York: International University Press, Inc., 1965. Pp. 228–297.

Roubiczek, L. E. The most important theories of play. *Ztschr f Psychoanal Paedagogik*, Vienna, 1932, **6**, 248.

Rubinowitz, G. Childhood play program. *School Activities*, 1957, **29**, 87–88.

Russell, E. S. Playing with a dog. *Quarterly Review of Biology*, 1936, **11**, 1–15.

Ryder, J. M. Aggression with balloons, blocking, and doll play. In L. M. Stolz (Ed.), *Father relations of warborn children*. Stanford: Stanford University Press, 1954, pp. 212–243.

Salisbury, E. C., & Ivey, H. Block building in a reading readiness program. *Childhood Education*, 1940, **16**, 221–225.

Sapora, A. V., & Mitchell, E. D. *The theory of play and recreation*. New York: Ronald Press, 1961.

Sargent, H. Spontaneous doll play of a nine year old boy. *Journal of Consulting Psychology*, 1943, **7**, 216–222.

Sartre, J. P. *Existential Psychoanalysis*. N. Y. Philosophical Library, 1953, 117–118.

Sato, M. Jido chusin yugiryoho no shoki ni okeru chiryo kankei no ginmi (A study of the therapeutic relationships in child-centered play therapy). *Bunka*, 1957, **21** (1), 160–171, 267–268.

Scarr, S. Genetic factors in activity motivation. *Child Development*, 1966, **37**, 663–673.

Schachtel, Ernest G. *Metamorphosis*. New York: Basic Books, 1959.

Scharfe, N. V. Play in education. *Childhood Education*, 1962, **39**, 117–121.

Schiffer, A. L. The effectiveness of group play therapy as assessed by specific changes in a child's peer relations. *American Journal of Orthopsychiatry*, 1967, **37** (2), 219–220.

Schiffer, M. The use of the seminar in training teachers and counselors as leaders of therapeutic play groups for maladjusted children. *American Journal of Orthopsychiatry*, 1960, **30**, 154–165.

Schiller, F. *Essays, aesthetical and philosophical. London*, George Bell, 1875.

Schimel, J. L. Sports, games and love. In Slovenko, R., & Knight, J. A. (Eds.),

Motivations in play, games and sports. Springfield, Ill.: Chas. C Thomas, 1967, 204–219.

Schlosberg, H. The concept of play. *Psychological Review,* 1947, **54,** 229–231.

Schorsch, R. S. *The Psychology of Play.* Notre Dame: Univ. of Notre Dame, 1942.

Schrut, A. The importance to children of the communication aspects of play. Unpublished manuscript, Beverly Hills, California, 1965.

Schrut, A. Fantasy games aid child's emotional growth. *Science News,* 1966, **90,** 83.

Schwender, N. Game preferences of 10,000 fourth grade children. Unpublished doctoral dissertation, Columbia University, 1932.

Scott, J. P. *Animal behavior.* New York: Doubleday, 1963.

Seagoe, M. V. Children's play as an indicator of cross cultural and intra-cultural differences. *Journal of Educational Sociology,* 1962, **35,** 278–283.

Seagoe, M. V., & Murakami, K. A comparative study of children's play in America and Japan. *California Journal of Educational Research,* 1961, **12,** 124–130.

Searl, M. N. Play, reality and aggression. International Journal of Psycho-analysis, 1933, **14,** 310–320.

Sears, Pauline S., & Pintler, Margaret H. Sex differences in doll-play aggression. *American Psychologist,* 1947, **2,** 420. (Abstract)

Sears, R. R. Influence of methodological factors on doll-play performance. *Child Development,* 1947, **18,** 190–197.

Sears, P. S. Doll-play aggression in normal young children: Influence of sex, age, sibling status, father's absence. *Psychological Monographs,* 1951, **65** (Whole No. 323).

Sears, R. R. Influence of methodological factors on doll-play performance. *Child Development,* 1947, **18,** 190–197.

Sears, R. R., Pintler, M., & Sears, P. S. Effect of father separation on preschool children's doll-play aggression. *Child Development,* 1946, **17** (4), 219–243.

Sears, R., & Lewin, H. Identification with parents as a determinant of doll-play aggression. *Child Development,* 1956, **27,** 135–153.

Shallit, R. The dramatic play of ten nursery school children. *Child Development,* 1932, **3,** 359–362.

Shesh, D. E. Measurements of aesthetic sense of children. *Psychologia,* 1966, **9,** 236–238.

Shoemaker, R. *All in play: Adventures in learning.* New York: Play Schools Association, 1958.

Shugart, G. The play history: Its application and significance. *Journal of Psychiatric Social Work,* 1955, **24,** 204–209.

Shure, M. B. Psychological ecology of a nursery school. *Child Development,* 1963, **34,** 979–992.

Siegel, A. E., & Kohn, L. Permissiveness, permission and aggression: The effect of adult presence or absence on aggression in children's play. *Child Development*, 1959, **30**, 131–141.

Siegel, A. W. Adult verbal behavior in play therapy sessions with retarded children. *Journal of Speech and Hearing Disorders*, 1963, Monograph Supplement 10, 34–38.

Simmel, E. The "Doctor Game," illness and the profession of medicine. International Journal of Psychoanalysis, 1926, **7**, 470–483.

Simon, H. A. A comparison of game theory and learning theory. *Psychometrika*, 1956, **21**, 267–272.

Simpson, G. Diagnostic play interviews. *Understanding the Child*, 1938, **7** (4), 6–10.

Singer, J. L., & Streiner, B. F. Imaginative content in the dreams and fantasy play of blind and sighted children. *Perceptual and Motor Skills*, 1966, **22** (2), 475–482.

Singer, J. L. Imagination and waiting ability in young children. *Journal of Personality*, 1961, **29**, 396–413.

Singer, J. L. *Daydreaming: An introduction to the experimental study of inner experience*. New York: Random House, 1966, Chap. 6.

Singer, J. L. & McCraven, V. Patterns of daydreaming in American sub-cultural groups. *International Journal of Social Psychiatry*, 1962, **8**, 272–282.

Sisson, G. Children's plays. In E. Barnes (Ed.), *Studies in education*. (Stanford University), 1896, **1**, 171–174.

Slawik, A. Schnecke und spirale in japanischen kinderspichen (The snail and the spiral in Japanese children's games). *Beitrage Japanologie*, 1955, **1** (2), 42–43.

Slovenko, R., & Knight, J. A. (Eds.), *Motivations in play, games and sports*. Springfield, Ill.: Chas. C Thomas, 1967.

Smilansky, S. The effects of sociodramatic play on disadvantaged children. New York: John Wiley & Sons, 1968.

Smith, O. W. Spatial perception and play activities of nursery school children. *Perceptual and Motor Skills*, 1965, **21**, 265.

Smith, P. A. Some phases of the play of Japanese boys and men. *Pedagogical Seminary*, 1909, **16**, 256–267.

Solomon, J. C. Active play therapy. *American Journal of Orthopsychiatry*, 1938, **8**, 479–498.

Solomon, J. C. Play technique and the integrative process. *American Journal of Orthopsychiatry*, 1955, **25** (3), 591–600.

Spence, L. *Myth and ritual in dance, game and rhyme*. London: Watts & Co., 1947.

Spencer, H. *Principles of Psychology*. New York: Appleton, 1873.

Sperry, M. An experimental study of the effects of disapproval of aggression on doll play. Unpublished master's thesis, State University of Iowa, 1949.

Sperry, Margaret. An experimental study of the effects of disapproval of aggression on doll play. Unpublished master's thesis, State Univ. of Iowa, 1949.

Stamp, I. M. An evaluation of the Driscoll Playkit used with incomplete stories as an instrument for the diagnosis of personality. Unpublished Ed.D. dissertation, Teachers College, Columbia Univ., 1954.

Stanley, H. M. Professor Groos and theories of play. *Psychological Review*, 1899, **6**, 86–92.

Stier, T. J. B. Spontaneous activity of mice. *Journal of Genetic Psychology*, 1930, **4**, 67–101.

Stokes, A. The Development of Ball Games. In Slovenko, R., & Knight, J. A. (Eds.), *Motivations in play, games and sports*. Springfield, Ill.: Chas. C Thomas, 1967, 387–399.

Stone, G. P. American sports: Play and display. In Larrabee, E., & Meyersohn, R. (Eds.), *Mass Leisure*. New York: Free Press of Glencoe, 1958, pp. 253–264.

Stone, G. P. The play of little children. *Quest*, 1965, Monograph IV, 23–31.

Stone, L. J. Group play techniques. *Monographs of the Society for Research in Child Development*, 1941, **6**, 105.

Stone, L. J. Experiments in group play and readiness for destruction. Part II in E. Lerner & L. B. Murphy (Eds.), Methods for the study of personality in young children. *Monographs of the Society for Research in Child Development*, 1941, **6** (4), 101–150.

Strachan, J. *What is play?* Edinburgh: David Douglas, 1877.

Strang, R., Harris, E., & Harris, D. Let's bring back children's play with study discussion program by Strang. *PTA Magazine*, 1965, **60**, 28–30.

Subotrik, L., & Callahan, R. J. A pilot study in short term play therapy with institutionalized educable mentally retarded boys. *American Journal of Mental Deficiency*, 1959, **63**, 730–735.

Sullenger, T. E., Parke, L. H., & Wallin, W. K. The leisure time activities of elementary school children. *Journal of Educational Research*, 1953, **46**, 551–554.

Sullivan, H. S. *Conceptions of Modern Psychiatry*. New York: Norton, 1953, 223–4.

Sutton-Smith, B. The Meeting of Maori and European cultures and its effects upon the unorganized games of Maori children. *J. Polynesian Society*, 1951, **60**, 93–107.

Sutton-Smith, B. What is a junk playground? *National Education*, 1952, **35**, 8–9. (Journal of the New Zealand Educational Institute.)

Sutton-Smith, B. A postscript on junk playgrounds. *National Education*, 1952, **34**, 398–399.

Sutton-Smith, B. New Zealand variants of the game Buck Buck. *Folklore*, 1952, **63**, 329–333.

Sutton-Smith, B. The fate of English traditional games in New Zealand. *Western Folklore*, 1952, 11, 250–253.

Sutton-Smith, B. The traditional games of New Zealand children. *Folklore*, 1953, 12, 411–423.

Sutton-Smith, B. The game rhymes of New Zealand children. *Western Folklore*, 1953, 12, 411–423.

Sutton-Smith, B. Seasonal games. *Western Folklore*, 1953, 12, 186–193.

Sutton-Smith, B., and Gump, P. V. Games and status experience. Recreation, 1955, 48, 142–174.

Sutton-Smith, B. The Psychology of games. *National Education*, 1955, Pts. 1 and 2, 228–229, 261–263. (Journal of New Zealand Educational Institute.)

Sutton-Smith, B. Play settings and social interaction. *National Education*, 1956, Pts. 1 and 2, 13–15, 59–61.

Sutton-Smith, B. The games of New Zealand children. Berkeley: University of California Press, 1959(a).

Sutton-Smith, B. A formal analysis of game meaning. *Western Folklore*, 1959, 18, 13–24(b).

Sutton-Smith, B. The kissing games of adolescents in Ohio. *Midwestern Folklore*, 1959, 9, 189–211(c).

Sutton-Smith, B. Some comments on the class diffusion of children's lore. *Midwestern Folklore*, 1959, 9, 225–228(d).

Sutton-Smith, B. The cruel joke series. *Midwestern Folklore*, 1960, 10, 11–22.

Sutton-Smith, B. Play preference and play behavior: A validity study. *Psychological Reports*, 1965, 16, 65–66.

Sutton-Smith, B. Piaget on play: A critique. *Psychological Review*, 1966, 73 (1), 104–110.

Sutton-Smith, B. Role replication and reversal in play. *Merrill-Palmer Quarterly*, 1966, 12, 285–298.

Sutton-Smith, B. The role of play in cognitive development. *Young Children*, 1967, 22, 361–370.

Sutton-Smith, B. Novel responses to toys. *Merrill-Palmer Quarterly*, 1968, 14, 159–160.

Sutton-Smith, B. Games, play and daydreams. *Quest*, 1968, 10, 47–58.

Sutton-Smith, B. The folkgames of the children. In Tristram Coffin (Ed.) *Our Living Traditions*. New York: Basic Books, 1968, 179–191.

Sutton-Smith, B. The Two Cultures of Games. In G. S. Kenyon (Ed.) *Aspects of Contemporary Sport Sociology*. Chicago: Athletic Institute, 1969.

Sutton-Smith, B. The Psychology of Childlore: The Triviality Barrier, *Western Folklore*, 1970, 29, 1–8.

Sutton-Smith, B. Review of Smilansky, S. (op. cit.). *The Record*, 1970, 71, 529–532(a).

Sutton-Smith, B. Games, play and controls. In J. P. Scott (Ed.) *Social Control.* Univ. of Chicago Press, in press.

Sutton-Smith, B. *The developmental psychology of children's games.* Penguin Books, in press.

Sutton-Smith, B., Roberts, J. M., & Kozelka, R. M. Game involvement in adults. *Journal of Social Psychology,* 1963, **34,** 119–126.

Sutton-Smith, B., & Roberts J. M. Rubrics of competitive behavior. *Journal of Genetic Psychology,* 1964, **105,** 13–37.

Sutton-Smith, B., & Roberts, J. M. An elementary game of strategy. *Genetic Psychological Monographs,* 1967, **75,** 3–42.

Sutton-Smith, B., & Roberts, J. M. The cross-cultural and psychological study of games. In Gunther Luschen (Ed.) *The cross-cultural analysis of games.* Champaigne, Ill.: Stipes, 1970, pp. 100–108.

Sutton-Smith, B., & Rosenberg, B. G. Sixty years of historical change in the games of American children. *Journal of American Folklore,* 1961, **74,** 17–46.

Sutton-Smith, B., Rosenberg, B. G., & Morgan, E. Jr. The development of sex differences in play choice during preadolescence. *Child Development,* 1963, **34,** 119–126.

Tarrants, K. In favor of blocks. *California Journal of Elementary Education,* 1950, **18,** 169–193.

Terman, L. M., & Burks, B. S. The gifted child. In C. Murchison (Ed.), *A handbook of child psychology.* Worcester: Clark University Press, 1933. Pp. 773–801.

Thomas, G., Coates, S., & Abbott, P. Children at play. *Times Educational Supplement,* 1963, **2508,** 1297–1301.

Thompson, H. Spontaneous play activities of 5-year-old children. *Psychological Bulletin,* 1936, **33,** 751.

Thompson, W. R., & Heron, W. The effects of restricting early experience on the problem-solving capacity of dogs. *Canad. J. Psychol.,* 1954, **8,** 17–31.

Tilton, J. R., & Ottinger, D. R. Comparison of the toy play behavior of artistic, retarded and normal children. *Psychological Reports,* 1964, **15,** 967–975.

Tyler, L. E. The relationship of interests to abilities and reputation among first grade children. *Educ. Psychol. Measmt.,* 1951, **11,** 255–264.

Ulman, E. Art therapy. In N. J. Long, W. W. Morse, & R. G. Newman (Eds.), *Education of emotionally disturbed children.* Belmont, California: Wadsworth, 1965, pp. 196–199.

Umanskii, L. I. Nekotorye tipologicheskie razlichiia v igrovykh deistuiiakh detei (Some typological differences in children's play activities). *Doklady Akademiya Pedagagicheskikk Nauk RSFSR,* 1961, **3,** 61–64.

Umanskii, L. I. An experimental study of typological characteristics of the nervous system in children from play material. In *The central nervous system and behavior*. Washington: U. S. Department of Health, Education and Welfare Public Health Services, December, 1959, pp. 973–988.

Updegraff, R., & Herbst, E. K. An experimental study of the social behavior stimulated in young children by certain play materials. *Journal of Genetic Psychology*, 1933, **42**, 372–391.

Valentine, C. W. A study of the beginnings and significance of play in infancy. *British Journal of Educational Psychology*, 1938, **8**, 285–306.

Van Alstyne, D. *Play behavior and choice of play materials of pre-school children.* Chicago: University of Chicago Press, 1932.

Vance, T. F., & McCall, L. T. Children's preferences among play materials as determined by the method of paired comparison of pictures. *Child Development*, 1934, **5**, 267–277.

Van Dalen, D. B. A study of certain factors in their relation to the play of children. *Research Quarterly*, 1947, **18**, 279–290.

Van Dalen, D. B. A differential analysis of the play of adolescent boys. *Journal of Educational Research*, 1947, **41**, 204–213.

Vermeer, E. A. Le jeu sa signification et son importance pour l'enfant (Play its significance and its importance for the child). *International Review of Education*, 1956, **2** (2), 189–199.

Verry, E. E. A study of mental and social attitudes in the free play of pre-school children. Master's thesis, State University of Iowa, 1923.

Verry, E. E. A study of personality in preschool play groups. *Journal of Social Forces.* 1925. **3.** 645–648.

Vernon, M. D. The development of imaginative construction in children. *British Journal of Psychology*, 1948, **39**, 102–111.

Volberding, E. Out-of-school behavior of eleven-year-olds. *Elementary School Journal*, 1948, **48**, 432–441.

Von Schiller, J. C. F. Letters upon the aesthetic education of man. *Literary and Philosophical Essays, The Harvard Classics,* Vol. 32. Elliot, G. W. (Ed.), New York: P. F. Collier & Son, 1910, 221–313.

Waelder, R. The psychoanalytic theory of play. *Psychoanal. Quart.*, 1933, **2**, 208–224.

Wallace, E. H. Selected out-of-school factors that affect Negro elementary school children. *J. Educ. Res.*, 1960, 137–140.

Wallach, M. A., & Kogan, N. *Modes of thinking in young children: A study of the creativity-intelligence distinction.* New York: Holt, Rinehart & Winston Inc., 1965.

Walters, R. H., & Parke, R. D. Exploratory behavior and play patterns. In Lippsitt, L. P. and Spiker, C. C. (Eds.), *Advances in child devel.* Vol. 2. New York: Academic Press, 1956, 74–78.

Waltmann, A. G. The use of puppetry in therapy. In N. Long, W. Morse, & R. Newman (Eds.), *Conflict in the classroom: The education of emotionally disturbed children.* Belmont, California: Wadsworth, 1965, pp. 202–208.

Wang, J. D. The relationship between children's play interests and their mental ability. *Journal of Genetic Psychology*, 1958, **93**, 119–131.

Wang, J. D. A study of certain factors associated with children's play interests. Unpublished doctoral thesis, George Peabody College for Teachers, 1941.

Wang, J. D. The relationship between children's play interests and their mental ability. *J. Genet. Psychol.*, 1958. **93**, 119–131.

Washburn, R. W., & Hilgard, J. R. A quantitative clinical method of recording social behavior of young children. *Journal of Genetic Psychology*, 1934, **45**, 290–405.

Waters, P. S. The value of play as a means of social education for the feeble-minded. *Proceedings and Adresses of the American Study on the Feeble-Minded*, 1932, **37**, 359–376.

Weiss-Frankl, A. B. Diagnostic and remedial play. *Understanding the Child*, 1938, **7** (4), 3–5.

Weiner, B. Play and recreation activities for young mentally retarded boys in a residential pre-academic program. *American Journal of Mental Deficiency*, 1953, **57**, 594–600.

Welker, W. I. Variability of play and exploratory behavior in chimpanzees. *Journal of Comparative and Physiological Psychology*, 1956, **49**, 84–89.

Welker, W. I. Effects of age and experience on play and exploration of young chimpanzees. *Journal of Comparative and Physiological Psychology*, 1956, **49**, 223–226.

Welker, W. I. Some determinants of play and exploration in chimpanzees. *Journal of Comparative and Physiological Psychology*, 1957, **50**, 181–185.

Welker, W. I. Genesis of exploratory and play behavior in infant racoons. *Psychological Reports*, 1959, **5**, 764.

Welker, W. I. An analysis of exploratory and play behavior in animals. In Fiske, D. W., & Maddi, S. R. (Eds.), *Functions of varied experience*. Homewood, Illinois: The Dorsey Press, Inc., 1961.

Werner, H., & Kaplan, B. *Symbol Formation*, 1964, New York: Wiley.

Werner, J. Das Spiel der Kinder (Play of children). Abstract in *Kolner Vierteljahshefte für Soziologie*, 1926, **5**, 411–444.

White, R. W. Motivation reconsidered: The concept of competence. *Psychological Review*, 1959, **66**, 297–333.

Whitted, B. A., & Scott, R. B. Significance of a play program in the care of children in a general hospital. *Journal of the National Medical Association*, 1962, **54**, 488–491.

Williams, F. N. Value of play. *School and Community*, 1966, **52**, 17.

Wilson, L. A. The influence of a child purpose on the perseverance of young children. *J. Exp. Educ.*, 1955, **23**, 353–358.

Winnicott, D. W. Why children play. In *The child, the family and the outside world*. Middlesex, England: Penguin Books, Ltd., 1964, Pp. 143–146.

Winstel, B. The use of a controlled play situation in determining certain effects of maternal attitudes in children. *Child Development*, 1951, **22**, 299–311.

Witty, P. A. A study of deviates in versatility and sociability of play interests. *New York Teachers College Contributions to Education*, 1931, **470**, 1–57.

Witty, P. A., & Beaman, V. The play of mental deviates. *Mental Hygiene*, 1933, **17**, 618–634.

Wolf, A. W. M., & Boehm, E. L. *Play and playthings*. New York: Child Study Association of America, 1930, pp. 1–7.

Wolff, P. H. Developmental and motivational concepts in Piaget's sensorimotor theory of intelligence. *American Academy of Child Psychiatry*, 1963, **2**, 224–243.

Woltmann, A. G. Concepts of play therapy techniques. *American Journal of Orthopsychiatry*, 1955, **25** (4), 771–783.

Yarrow, L. J. The effect of antecedent frustration on projective play. *Psychological Monographs*, 1948, **62** (6), 42.

Index